SONG INTERPRETATION
21ST-CENTURY POP MUS

Song Interpretation in 21st-Century Pop Music

Edited by

RALF VON APPEN
University of Gießen, Germany

ANDRÉ DOEHRING
University of Gießen, Germany

DIETRICH HELMS
University of Osnabrück, Germany

ALLAN F. MOORE
University of Surrey, UK

LONDON AND NEW YORK

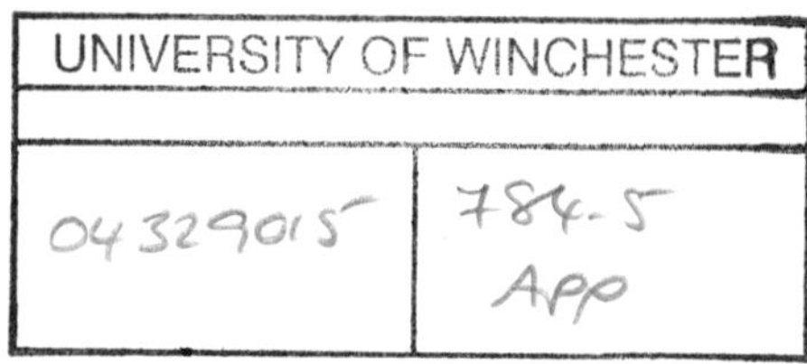

First published 2015 by Ashgate Publishing

Published 2016 by Routledge
2 Park Square, Milton Park, Abingdon, Oxfordshire OX14 4RN
711 Third Avenue, New York, NY 10017, USA

First issued in paperback 2016

Routledge is an imprint of the Taylor & Francis Group, an informa business

British Library Cataloguing in Publication Data
A catalogue record for this book is available from the British Library.

The Library of Congress has cataloged the printed edition as follows:
Song interpretation in 21st-century pop music/edited by Ralf von Appen, André Doehring, Dietrich Helms, and Allan F. Moore.
pages cm. -- (Ashgate popular and folk music series)
Includes index.
ISBN 978-1-4724-2800-4 (hardcover)
1. Popular music--Analysis, appreciation. 2. Popular music--2001-2010--History and criticism. 3. Popular music--2011-2020--History and criticism. I. Appen, Ralf von, 1975- II. Doehring, André. III. Helms, Dietrich. IV. Moore, Allan F.
MT146.S66 2015
782.42164'117--dc23

2014035200

ISBN 13: 978-1-138-63050-5 (pbk)
ISBN 13: 978-1-4724-2800-4 (hbk)

Bach musicological font developed by © Yo Tomita

Contents

List of Figures *vii*
List of Music Examples *ix*
List of Tables *xi*
Notes on Contributors *xiii*
General Editors' Preface *xxi*

Introduction 1
Ralf von Appen, André Doehring, Dietrich Helms and Allan F. Moore

PART I LISTENING ALONE

1 Death Cab for Cutie's 'I Will Follow You Into The Dark' as Exemplar of Conventional Tonal Behaviour in Recent Rock Music 9
Walter Everett

2 Ear Candy: What Makes Ke$ha's 'Tik Tok' Tick? 29
Ralf von Appen

3 Metrical Ambiguity or Microrhythmic Flexibility? Analysing Groove in 'Nasty Girl' by Destiny's Child 53
Anne Danielsen

4 Pragmatic 'Poker Face': Lady Gaga's Song and Roman Jakobson's Six Functions of Communication 73
Dietrich Helms

5 Can't Get Laid in Germany – Rammstein's 'Pussy' (2009) 97
Dietmar Elflein

6 An Analysis of Space, Gesture and Interaction in Kings of Leon's 'Sex On Fire' 115
Simon Zagorski-Thomas

7 Andrés's 'New For U': New for Us. On Analysing Electronic Dance Music 133
André Doehring

8 So Just What Kind of Life Is This? Amy Macdonald's 'This Is The Life' 157
Allan F. Moore

PART II LISTENING TOGETHER

9 An Ambiguous Murder: Questions of Intertextuality in PJ Harvey's 'The Words That Maketh Murder' 175
Cláudia Azevedo, Chris Fuller, Juliana Guerrero, Michael Kaler and Brad Osborn

10 Interpreting Meaning in/of Janelle Monáe's 'Tightrope': Style, Groove and Production Considered 197
Frederike Arns, Mark Chilla, Mikko Karjalainen, Esa Lilja, Theresa Maierhofer-Lischka and Matthew Valnes

11 'Can't Keep it to Myself': Exploring the Theme of Struggle in the Fleet Foxes' 'Helplessness Blues' 213
Paul Carter, Samantha Englander, Alberto Munarriz, Jadey O'Regan and Eileen Simonow

12 How to Make a Global Dance Hit: Balancing the Exotic with the Familiar in 'Danza Kuduro' by Lucenzo featuring Don Omar 231
Félix Eid, María Emilia Greco, Jakub Kasperski, Andrew Martin and Edin Mujkanović

13 Analytical Approaches to Björk's 'Crystalline': A Convergence of Nature and Technology 253
Phil Allcock, Natalia Bieletto, Maxime Cottin, Katharine Nelligan and Yvonne Thieré

Index *277*

List of Figures

3.1	Waveform (amplitude/time) and sonogram (frequency/time) of bars 1–2 of the chorus (A) of 'Nasty Girl' (extract from first chorus)	60
3.2	Waveform (amplitude/time) and sonogram (frequency/time) of last vocal line in the chorus (A) of 'Nasty Girl' (bars 7–8 in the first chorus)	61
3.3	Waveform (amplitude/time) and sonogram (frequency/time) of transition from duple to triple feel in vocals in the chorus of 'Nasty Girl' (bars 6–8 in the first chorus)	62
3.4	Waveform (amplitude/time) and sonogram (frequency/time) of bar 1 of the first chorus (A) of 'Nasty Girl'	63
3.5	Waveform (amplitude/time) and sonogram (frequency/time) of bar 1 of the verse (B) of 'Nasty Girl' (extract from first verse)	65
4.1	Functions of language and what they refer to (Jakobson, 1960, p. 353 and p. 357)	75
6.1	'Sex On Fire', spectrograph of the transition from verse 1 to chorus 1 (about 0:45 to 0:54) produced in the Sonic Visualiser software package	129
7.1	Proportion of literature on EDM published 1976–2013 (n = 328)	136
7.2	Type of literature on EDM published 1976–2013 (n = 328)	136
9.1	'The Words That Maketh Murder', instrumentation schema	177

List of Music Examples

1.1 Voice-leading sketch of Bruce Springsteen, 'If I Should Fall Behind' (*Lucky Town*, 1992) 11
1.2 Voice-leading sketch of Death Cab for Cutie, 'I Will Follow You Into The Dark' (*Plans*, 2005) 15
1.3 Voice-leading sketch of Nirvana, 'In Bloom' (*Nevermind*, 1991), chorus 21
1.4 Voice-leading sketch of The Strokes, 'Evening Sun' (*First Impressions of Earth*, 2006), bridge 24

2.1 'Tik Tok', (fictitious) initial idea 30
2.2 'Tik Tok', verse 1, 0:00–0:08 31
2.3 'Tik Tok', bars 1–8, 0:00–0:16 33
2.4 'Tik Tok', bars 9–14, 0:16–0:28 35
2.5 'Tik Tok', bars 41–6, 1:20–1:32 35
2.6 'Tik Tok', bars 17–32, 0:32–1:04 36
2.7 'Tik Tok', bars 17–32, 0:32–1:04 37
2.8 'Tik Tok', bars 25–32, 0:48–1:04 37
2.9 'Tik Tok', rhythmical structure of bars 25–6, 0:48–0:52 38
2.10 'Tik Tok', bars 65–80, 2:09–2:40 38
2.11 'Tik Tok', bars 9–11, 0:16–0:22 40
2.12 'Tik Tok', bars 17–24, 0:32–0:48 42
2.13 'Tik Tok', bars 65–8, 2:09–2:16 43

3.1 Timeline structured according to a basic pulse in three and four 56
3.2 Virtual figure implied by synth bass and vocals in the chorus section A in 'Nasty Girl' 64
3.3 Virtual figure implied by synth bass and vocals in section B in 'Nasty Girl' 65

4.1 Bass line of 'Poker Face' (not in chorus) 77
4.2 'Poker Face', melodic line 1 (intro, verse, pre- and post-chorus) 77
4.3 'Poker Face', melodic line 2 (bridge) 77

7.1 'New For U', one bar of the beat 142
7.2 Outline of the outer voices of 'Time Is The Teacher' beginning at 0:25 147

7.3a Andrés's edited sample of 'Time Is The Teacher' 147
7.3b Andrés's edited sample as heard in the hypermetre of 'New For U' 147

8.1 Opening guitar and vocal motifs of Amy Macdonald's 'This Is The Life' 161

9.1 'The Words That Maketh Murder', opening autoharp pattern 180
9.2 'The Words That Maketh Murder', transcription of percussion and autoharp 181
9.3 'The Words That Maketh Murder', middleground and background voice-leading graphs 182

10.1 'Tightrope', the bass pattern as it appears in (a) the verses and (b) the choruses 199
10.2 'Tightrope', the first two measures of the verse 202
10.3 'Tightrope', the first four measures of the chorus 203
10.4 Harmonic outline of Janelle Monáe's 'Tightrope' (2010), featuring Big Boi 204

11.1 'Helplessness Blues', transition from Section A into B 218
11.2a 'Helplessness Blues', verse 1 of Section B (3:05) 221
11.2b 'Helplessness Blues', verse 2 of Section B (3:39) 221
11.3 'Helplessness Blues', triplets in Section A (0:38) 222
11.4 'Helplessness Blues', voice leading and harmonic support for Section A 224
11.5 'Helplessness Blues', harmonic functions of Section B 225

12.1 Harmonic voice leading of 'Danza Kuduro' 246

13.1 Unordered pitch-class collection used in 'Crystalline' 257
13.2 'Crystalline', gameleste pattern of verse 1 (0:00–0:14) 258
13.3 'Crystalline', vocal melody, first line 259
13.4a 'Crystalline', chorus, vocal melody (first appearance at 0:44) 259
13.4b 'Crystalline', chorus, bass line (first appearance at 1:07) 260
13.5 'Crystalline', $^{17}_{8}$ drum pattern at 1:31 262

List of Tables

3.1 Schematic outline of sections in 'Nasty Girl' 58

4.1 Form of 'Poker Face' 78
4.2 Phatic signs in 'Poker Face' 87

5.1 'Pussy', formal structure 104
5.2 'Pussy', chorus 105
5.3 'Pussy', chorus, formal structure 106
5.4 'Pussy', verse 106
5.5 'Pussy', drum rhythms 107
5.6 'Pussy', pre-chorus 107

7.1 Form of 'New For U' 145

8.1 Formal/textural scheme of Amy Macdonald's 'This Is The life' 159
8.2 Syllable count in the first verse and chorus of Amy Macdonald's 'This Is The Life' 164

9.1 'The Words That Maketh Murder', formal structure 178

11.1 'Helplessness Blues', phrase structure of Section B 220
11.2 'Helplessness Blues', beats per strophe in Section B 225

12.1 2–3 Son clave 237
12.2 Reggaeton dembow groove 238
12.3 'Danza Kuduro', groove 238
12.4 Rhythmic breakdown of ancillary parts for 'Danza Kuduro' 240
12.5 'Danza Kuduro', form 243

13.1 'Crystalline', form sections 261
13.2 'Crystalline', original lyrics and our spelling of the sounding words as recorded by Björk 268

Notes on Contributors

Phil Allcock completed his BMus and MA degrees at Lancaster University. His MA research explored the ways in which glam rock artists of the early 1970s articulated gender and identity. Phil completed his PhD in Popular Musicology at the University of Huddersfield. His thesis took an interdisciplinary approach to analysing the musical style of Sir Elton John, exploring issues such as stardom, celebrity, gender, and identity. Other research interests include how computer software can be used in conjunction with traditional analytical methods in order to benefit our understanding of the music, and the way in which technology has impacted upon how we interact with music.

Dr **Ralf von Appen** holds a PhD in musicology from the University of Gießen (Germany), where he has been working as a teaching and research assistant since 2004. He has been a board member of the German GfPM (German Society for Popular Music Studies) since 2008, and is a co-editor of the academic online journal *Samples* (www.gfpm-samples.de). Von Appen has published a book on the aesthetics of popular music (*Der Wert der Musik. Zur* Ästhetik *des Populären*, 2007), co-edited a book on researching sound in popular music (*Pop Sounds*, 2003), and has published several papers dealing with the history, psychology, analysis and aesthetics of popular music. In 2009/2010 he was a visiting professor at the University of Vienna, Austria.

Frederike Arns has a Master's degree in 'Media and Music' from Hochschule für Musik, Theater und Medien, Hannover, and wrote her thesis about political hip-hop and Public Enemy. She wrote her Bachelor's thesis about staging strategies of punk and the Sex Pistols, and works as a music journalist for the oldest German hip-hop magazine *Backspin*.

Cláudia Azevedo has been postdoctoral researcher and lecturer in Popular Music Analysis at the Program of Post-Graduation in Music (PPGM) at Universidade Federal do Estado do Rio de Janeiro (UNIRIO) since September 2010. She holds a PhD and an MA in Music and a degree in Communication Studies/Journalism. She is co-editor of the book *Made in Brazil* (forthcoming) and is a member of the editorial board and reviewer for the Brazilian academic journal *Música Popular em Revista*. She was a visiting researcher at the Department of Musicology at the University of Oslo (February to August 2008) and served as assistant editor and reviewer for *IASPM Journal* (2010–11).

Natalia Bieletto obtained her BA degree in flute performance and her Master's in Musicology at the Universidad Nacional Autónoma de México. She is a PhD candidate in Musicology at the University of California, Los Angeles. Her field of research concerns the elaboration of difference through music-making, with a special focus on the music of Latin America. Her dissertation addresses the role of the *carpas* shows – a Mexican version of vaudeville – in the elaboration of social class in Mexico in the early twentieth century. Her work has been presented in Mexico, Spain, North America, Latin America and the Caribbean. She has teaching experience in Mexico and at UCLA and was a visiting lecturer for the MA programme of Musicology at the Universidad de Chile.

Paul Carter is an Assistant Professor at State University of New York College at Oneonta. It is a 5,000-undergraduate college that is home to a 500-student programme in the music industry. There he teaches Music Theory and Musicianship of Contemporary Popular Music and also directs an a cappella group Hooked on Tonics. He is interested in the theory of music and its pedagogy as it relates to pop, rock and hip-hop music. He has presented at conferences on the music of Steely Dan, on transcription as a pedagogical device and the use of GarageBand as a musicianship instructional aid. His dissertation (2005) (http://rave.ohiolink.edu/etdc/view?acc_num=ucin1116202928) is about harmonic root motion patterns as they affect the structure of pop songs. Carter continually plays and sings in pop music performances and recordings.

Mark Chilla is a PhD student in Music Theory at the Indiana University Jacobs School of Music. His research interests include aspects of musical style in rock and blues music from the 1960s, as well as current hip-hop music. He has taught music theory courses at Indiana University and Butler University, and is currently a radio announcer at WFIU, a local NPR affiliate, where he also hosts a music show.

Maxime Cottin holds a PhD in musicology from the University of Nice Sophia Antipolis (France), where he is currently teaching popular music history and analysis. His dissertation explores the notion of maximalism in progressive rock music. He presented several papers about the music of King Crimson at different international conferences and published an article in *Revue de Musicologie*. His researches also investigate the musical language of early twentieth-century composers, such as Bartók, Scriabin and Szymanowski.

Anne Danielsen is Professor and head of research at the Department of Musicology University of Oslo, Norway. Her recent research deals with in-depth studies of the rhythm of popular music. She has published *Presence and Pleasure: The Funk Grooves of James Brown and Parliament* (2006) and *Musical Rhythm in the Age of Digital Reproduction* (2010).

Dr **André Doehring** studied musicology and sociology and is working as a musicologist at the University of Gießen (Germany). He is a member of the advisory board of the German GfPM. His current research topics focus on jazz, electronic dance music and the sociology of music. He has written a book on popular music journalism, *Musikkommunikatoren. Berufsrollen Organisationsstrukturen und Handlungsspielräume im Popmusikjournalismus* (2011), and papers on the methodology of popular music analysis.

Félix Eid is a Bolivian/Brazilian guitarist, ethnomusicologist and music educator, is currently a Professor at UFMS (Universidade Federal de Mato Grosso do Sul), Brazil. Félix Eid studied guitar in Bolivia and later in Spain, with a scholarship by 'Fundación Carolina' for young Latin American musicians. He then moved to Brazil, where he studied Music Education at the 'Instituto de Artes – UNESP', and later on received an MA in Ethnomusicology, also at UNESP, under the supervision of Dr Alberto T. Ikeda. Félix Eid's main area of interest and expertise, both in performance and research, is Latin America's music and culture.

Dr **Dietmar Elflein** is a Lecturer in Music at the University of Braunschweig and at the Hochschule der populären Künste, Berlin. He has worked as composer and producer of popular music. His book, *Schwermetallanalysen. Die musikalische Sprache des Heavy Metal* (2010), is about the analysis of heavy metal.

Samantha Englander lives in Seattle, Washington, USA. She received her Bachelor of Music from the University of North Carolina at Chapel Hill and her MA in Music Theory from the University of Washington. Her research interests include formal function in contemporary popular music and Second Viennese School serialism.

Walter Everett is Professor of Music in Music Theory at the University of Michigan. He is the author of the two-volume book *The Beatles as Musicians* (1999) and of *The Foundations of Rock* (2008), and has also edited *Expression in Pop-Rock Music* (2000). Everett's writings on rock music, Schenkerian theory, and nineteenth-century Lieder have appeared in many academic music theory and musicology journals and book collections, and he has spoken at numerous universities and conferences.

Chris Fuller's PhD research was focused on the composers Harrison Birtwistle and Steve Reich, following an MA thesis that explored various issues of musical style and interpretation in popular music analysis. Using the work of Jacques Derrida as an example, he attempted to address certain issues that arise when combining the disparate value-systems of traditional music analysis and poststructuralism. Disillusioned, he has since abandoned his research following the closure of the music department at Lancaster University, UK, where he was studying.

María Emilia Greco is a Professor of Musical Analysis and Counterpoint in the Arts and Design School at National University of Cuyo (Mendoza, Argentina). She is a PhD candidate in Social Sciences at the University of Buenos Aires, Argentina. Her research interests include traditional and regional music and their role in the social construction of identity, and also the links between new technologies and current music practices.

Juliana Guerrero obtained her BA in Arts and her PhD in Arts History and Theory at the University of Buenos Aires, Argentina, with a doctoral dissertation 'Music and humour in Les Luthiers' work (1967–2012)'. She holds a teaching assistant position at the University of Buenos Aires and is currently participating in the research project 'Argentinean Popular Music'. Her fields of interest include theories of humour and research methodologies for Argentinean popular music in the twentieth century. Since 2012 she has been the editor of the Argentinean musicological journal *El oído pensante*.

Dietrich Helms is Professor of Music History at the School of Educational and Cultural Studies at the University of Osnabrück, Germany. He studied musicology, English and sociology at the universities of Münster (Germany), East Anglia and Oxford (UK). He has been one of three chairpersons of GfPM (German Society for Popular Music Studies) since 2005. Since 2002 he has been co-editor of 'Beiträge zur Popularmusikforschung', a yearbook published by GfPM. He was co-founder of *Samples* (www.gfpm-samples.de), an online journal he helped to edit from 2002 to 2011. He has published widely on music at the court of Henry VIII, popular music, music of early modern times and musical theatre for children.

Michael Kaler is a musician and scholar who is deeply engaged in exploring the intersections between esoteric religion, extraordinary experiences, music, transcendence, and improvisation. He has published widely on such diverse topics as early Egyptian Christianity, Gnosticism, the Grateful Dead, and the religious implications of musical improvisation. He received a doctorate in religious studies from Laval University in 2006 under the supervision of Louis Painchaud, did postdoctoral studies at McMaster University working with Annette Yoshiko Reed, and completed his doctoral work in ethnomusicology at York University, Canada, in 2014, working with Rob Bowman. Kaler has taught at the University of Toronto, York University, and McMaster University, and, in addition to his academic work, performs regularly in and around Toronto, playing rock, folk, rebetiko and experimental music.

Mikko Karjalainen studied jazz double bass at the Conservatory of Amsterdam (BA) and musicology at the University of Amsterdam. He wrote his Master's thesis on music as knowledge (MA Musicology) and New Orleans brass band tradition (Research MA Art Studies). Music, and especially performance, as cultural practice is at the heart of Karjalainen's academic interest. He is currently working on a PhD research plan on music and technology in performance.

Jakub Kasperski works in the Musicology Department of Adam Mickiewicz University in Poznań, Poland. His doctoral thesis (2012) was one of the first works in Poland on popular music. His research interests include the history and methodology of popular music research (dominant writings, theories, schools and methodological approaches), and institutional processes of incorporation of popular music into the academic canon. Recent work deals with gender in heavy metal, vocal expression in nu metal, Polish rock, the influence of technology on the dissemination and aesthetics of music, the 'song family' concept in cover version studies, 'ubiquitous music', and Fryderyk Chopin's reception in popular music circles.

Esa Lilja, PhD, is a composer, musician, music teacher and postdoctoral researcher at the University of Helsinki, and the author of the book *Theory and Analysis of Classic Heavy Metal Harmony*. Lilja's research interests include music theory and analysis (especially Schenkerian and Riemannian), musical perception, acoustics, and music education.

Theresa Maierhofer-Lischka had a doctoral scholarship from 2009 until 2011. She works as a high school teacher and as a lecturer in the didactics of French at the University of Osnabrück, Germany. Besides reviews of various books and conferences, she has published several essays on French rap music (amongst others 'La colère en tant qu'outil d'analyse pour le processus de communication dans le rap', 2012). Her doctoral thesis about the issue of violence in French rap music was published in 2013.

Andrew Martin, PhD, is Professor of Music at Inver Hills College, Inver Grove Heights, Minnesota, USA, where he teaches courses in music history, music analysis, and directs the African music ensemble and steel drum band. A champion of new music and living composers, Martin has performed widely as a percussionist throughout the United States and Europe and shared the stage with such ensembles as the St Paul Chamber Orchestra, Prague Academy Orchestra, Slovak Radio Orchestra, and the Indianapolis Chamber Orchestra. Martin's research areas focus on intersections between American and Caribbean music as well as popular and folk music and musicians during the Cold War. Martin has published widely on the above topics and presented numerous lectures and conference papers throughout the United States, Canada, Caribbean, Europe and China. His first book *Military Might, Melodious Music: The US Navy Steel Band 1957–1999* is forthcoming in 2015.

Allan F. Moore is Professor of Popular Music at the University of Surrey, UK. His chief research interests lie in the domain of the interaction of music and lyrics in recorded song in the service of potential readings. He is on the editorial board of

Popular Music and on the advisory boards of other journals and book series. He is series editor of Ashgate's 'Library of Essays in Popular Music', editor of the *Cambridge Companion to Blues & Gospel Music* and *Analysing Popular Music* (2009), and author to date of five monographs including *Rock: The Primary Text* and *Song Means*.

Edin Mujkanović works as a composer, musician and research fellow at the Institute of Musicology and Music Pedagogy of the University of Osnabrück, Germany. His PhD project deals with the aesthetics and performance practice of the different forms of contemporary flamenco guitar. It is his aim to mediate between music theory and music practice. His research interests include various fields of popular music, music aesthetics as well as music and politics. In particular he focuses on issues like identity, continuity and change in Latin American and Mediterranean music cultures and on ideas of hybridity and authenticity.

Alberto Munarriz, originally from Buenos Aires, began his post-secondary music studies at McGill University. After receiving a BMus in Jazz Performance in 2004, Alberto moved to New York in order to begin his graduate studies in musicology at CUNY's Aaron Copeland School of Music. In 2007 he moved to Toronto and is currently finishing a doctorate in ethnomusicology at York University. Alberto has studied double bass with Ed Tait, Jim Vivian (Toronto), Alec Walkington (Montreal) and Juan Pablo Navarro (Buenos Aires) and has had the opportunity to play with Joseph Macerollo, Patrick Boyle, and Guillermo Fernandez, among many others. Alberto's doctoral research has been funded in part by the Social Sciences and Humanities Research Council of Canada and the Ontario Government. In 2011 Alberto spent seven months travelling across Western Europe studying the numerous dialogues informing the evolution of contemporary tango. He is a founding member of Toronto's premier tango ensemble Payadora.

Kath Nelligan completed a PhD in musicology at the Conservatorium of Music, University of Melbourne, Australia. Kath's research interests include popular music studies, feminism and sociology. Her current research focuses specifically on female singer-songwriters and concepts of empowerment and has presented this work at a number of national and international conferences. She is the recipient of two research scholarships, an Honours Scholarship awarded to her by the University of Western Sydney and an Australian Postgraduate Award which she received whilst completing her PhD at the University of Melbourne. She is a recipient of a Dean's Medal for Outstanding Scholarship and appeared on the Dean's Merit List for academic excellence in 2005, 2006, and 2007. Kath is also a performer and composer of acoustic pop and electronic music.

Jadey O'Regan received her PhD in musicology at Griffith University (Queensland Conservatorium). Her thesis was a musicological exploration of the Beach Boys' early 'surf, cars and girls' music in the 1960s. In the last year she has lectured and tutored across three universities, teaching music analysis, popular music history, production analysis and performance at Macquarie University, The Sydney Conservatorium of Music and the University of Western Sydney. Prior to this, Jadey completed a Bachelor's degree in Popular Music (with Honours) majoring in music production. Jadey is also a performing musician and songwriter.

Brad Osborn is Assistant Professor of Music Theory at the University of Kansas and Chair of the Society for Music Theory Popular Music Interest Group. His published research addresses the compositional intricacies of post-millennial rock music, and his current work is aimed at questions of meaning and perception in the music of the British rock group Radiohead. As the recording artist BradleyHeartVampire, Brad composes and releases experimental rock music, all of which is freely available on Bandcamp.

Eileen Simonow is a doctoral researcher in Media and Culture Studies in the Research Training Group 'Materiality and Production' at Heinrich-Heine University in Düsseldorf, Germany, where she also is a lecturer at the department of Media and Culture Studies. She holds an MA in Musicology from Robert Schumann School of Music and Media and an MA in German Language and Literature. Her scholarly interests include music videos, the intersections of music and literature, opera production, hip-hop culture, and music in TV series. She has written on jazz in German-language literature and the use of music in the TV series 'True Blood'. She currently works as an editor and analyst at a media agency and regularly gives introductory lectures on operas and their respective productions at the Deutsche Oper am Rhein, Düsseldorf.

Yvonne Thieré studied musicology and (music) pedagogy at the University of Gießen (Germany), where she is now working as a research and teaching assistant and writing her PhD thesis. Her main research interests lie in the field of the analysis and interpretation of the singing voice in popular music, focussing on basic physiological processes and resultant acoustic characteristics of means of vocal expression as well as on interpretive approaches to their (combined) occurrences in various singing styles.

Matthew Valnes earned a PhD in Music Theory from the University of Pennsylvania. His main areas of research are improvisation and live performance in African American popular music, focusing specifically on funk.

Simon Zagorski-Thomas is a Reader in Music at the London College of Music, University of West London. He is co-director of the annual Art of Record Production Conference, author of *The Musicology of Record Production* (Cambridge University Press) and co-editor of *The Art of Record Production* (Ashgate). Before entering academia he worked as a producer with artists such as Phil Collins, Bill Bruford, The Mock Turtles and Courtney Pine.

General Editors' Preface

Popular musicology embraces the field of musicological study that engages with popular forms of music, especially music associated with commerce, entertainment and leisure activities. The *Ashgate Popular and Folk Music Series* aims to present the best research in this field. Authors are concerned with criticism and analysis of the music itself, as well as locating musical practices, values and meanings in cultural context. The focus of the series is on popular music of the twentieth and twenty-first centuries, with a remit to encompass the entirety of the world's popular music.

Critical and analytical tools employed in the study of popular music are being continually developed and refined in the twenty-first century. Perspectives on the transcultural and intercultural uses of popular music have enriched understanding of social context, reception and subject position. Popular genres as distinct as reggae, township, bhangra, and flamenco are features of a shrinking, transnational world. The series recognises and addresses the emergence of mixed genres and new global fusions, and utilises a wide range of theoretical models drawn from anthropology, sociology, psychoanalysis, media studies, semiotics, postcolonial studies, feminism, gender studies and queer studies.

Stan Hawkins, Professor of Popular Musicology, University of Oslo &
Derek B. Scott, Professor of Critical Musicology, University of Leeds

Introduction

Ralf von Appen, André Doehring, Dietrich Helms and Allan F. Moore

See that mirror ball on the front cover? Ever wondered what it looks like from the other side? It's not too hard to guess but we will never know for sure. There is no position from which one person will be able to observe the whole thing at once. If we walk across the room, who knows whether the side we have just examined does not change? It surely will as it keeps moving and as the lights change its appearance.

In a way, the same goes for the music we are listening to: we can make some sense of our own experience of listening to some particular music, but we cannot assert that from a different perspective the experience of listening will be the same. So far, published analyses of music (be it classical, jazz, folk or popular) have always been written by individual scholars. But listening to and making sense of music is a very subjective business. No two listeners will have the same impressions, associations and emotions – although, due to cultural conditions, their reactions might resemble each other or, at times, partly overlap. An individual researcher can only ever speak for herself. Thus, there is no God-like perspective to interpret from, no one *true* interpretation since each interpretation is based on the personal (listening) experience of the author. This important aspect has not been adequately considered in the existing literature. In his recent *Song Means*, though, Allan F. Moore makes this case: 'it is now widely (and rightly) accepted that we cannot presume an objective position from which to write hermeneutically' (Moore, 2012, p. 330). He closes his book advocating subjectivity and mistrusting objectivity:

> I urge you, if you encounter claims purporting to identify "the meaning" of a particular song, or claims as to "the way to hear" something, with the implication "the only way ..." or "the right way ...", *disbelieve them.* I, and any other writer, can only write from my/our own individual perspective. (ibid.)

Song Interpretation in 21st-Century Pop Music is the attempt to take this advice seriously and to take the next step: it brings together researchers from different spatial and cultural backgrounds and encourages them to compare their individual hearings and to discuss the ways they make sense of specific songs.

A propos songs: existing books on the analysis of popular music usually focus on theory and methodology, and discuss parts of songs only briefly as examples. One often gets the impression that songs are being chosen mainly to illuminate and exemplify the theoretical position. In this book the obverse is the aim: it is the songs that take centre stage and that are given priority. The editors are convinced that there cannot be just one universal method of music analysis, but that every subject and every issue demands a different set of tools, depending on the subject of research, the issue to be answered and the individuality of the researcher: the tools must be appropriate to the task. Consequently, the authors of the following chapters utilise a broad range of different approaches. As a result, the book will supply readers with a whole range of methods and an awareness that not every method may be effective in answering every question. Methods and theories will have to prove their use value in the face of a specific song, chosen from a heterogeneous, contemporary repertoire.

And talking about repertoire: from the beginning of popular musicology, classically trained musicologists were inclined to turn towards 'progressive' styles and more complex compositions. Because these songs seemed to respond better to their methods of analysis, which focused on their 'artfulness', most of the early analyses deal with songs by the Beatles or British progressive rock from the 1960s or 1970s. Even today, most songs and styles that are mentioned in books on popular music analysis originate from these canonised decades and styles, whereas analyses of top 40 pop, hip-hop or electronic dance music are only considered in publications dedicated exclusively to one of those styles – and are still hard to find. As a further consequence of this musicological focus on classic and experimental rock, there are many books and papers that are particularly interested in harmony and voice-leading, while methods of analysing sound and record production, or rhythm and groove are still underdeveloped. For this reason, this book confines itself to a repertoire that has not yet been thoroughly studied. All songs analysed here are from the new millennium. Because the most widely popular styles are too often ignored by academics, this collection aims to shed light on how popular tunes that many listen and dance to work musically. Therefore, it encompasses a broad palette, highlighting mainstream pop (Lady Gaga, Ke$ha, Lucenzo, Amy Macdonald), but also accounting for critically acclaimed 'indie' styles (Fleet Foxes, Death Cab for Cutie, PJ Harvey), R&B (Destiny's Child, Janelle Monáe), popular hard rock (Kings of Leon, Rammstein) and current electronic music (Andrés, Björk).

A subsidiary intention of the book is to show that musicological analysis is not necessarily an aim in itself, but a toolbox that can be used to address many different issues of broader relevance. Unpacking the music, or exploding the mirror ball, is one thing. What is to be gained from doing so, is another. Thus, the authors have been encouraged not to confine their interest to how these songs function as works of art, not narrowing their view to understand merely how the compositions work structurally. Instead, their research also embraces social contexts. The chapters on Rammstein and Janelle Monáe, for instance, link analytical findings with issues of national and black female identity respectively. The analysis of the global dance hit 'Danza Kuduro' shows how languages and features of different musical cultures are utilised to achieve success in as many markets as possible. Other chapters use analytical methods to create compelling semantic interpretations. The piece on Fleet Foxes' 'Helplessness Blues' for example shows how this song manages to vividly express a young man's worldview and the quest for an own identity. In this way, the book advocates the use of musicological analysis for other, more relevant purposes, and not to 'prove' how some structurally complex songs are 'great' as works of art. Like a mirror ball, songs reflect their surroundings and that is part of what makes them attractive. If we want to make sense of them we should try to observe them in action, in their natural habitat and not on the examination table of our laboratory. And if we look hard enough we might even see ourselves reflected.

All in all, the book you are holding in your hands is the product of our fundamental belief that analysis is an appropriate and very powerful, yet still too often underestimated, tool for researching popular music. It is the product of several attempts undertaken over the years to change the problematic situation outlined above. In 2009 co-editors Ralf von Appen and André Doehring organised a two-day workshop with about 15 German-speaking participants at the University of Gießen to discuss desiderata for future research in this field. Building on this, in 2010 the German ASPM (which changed its name to GfPM – Gesellschaft für Popularmusikforschung/German Society for Popular Music Studies in 2014) dedicated their annual conference to popular music analysis and invited Walter Everett, Allan F. Moore and Simon Zagorski-Thomas for keynote presentations.[1] In September 2011 finally, Appen, Doehring and Dietrich Helms organised a five-day summer school at the University of Osnabrück, Germany, on the subject of 'Methods of Popular Music Analysis', funded by the German Volkswagen Foundation. Twenty-six young, mostly postgraduate researchers from 12 countries in three continents were invited to discuss, apply and bring forward current research in this field. In the mornings internationally acclaimed scholars gave keynote presentations: Allan F. Moore (on interpretation), Walter Everett (on harmony and voice-leading), Anne Danielsen (on rhythm) and Simon Zagorski-Thomas (on sound and record production). In the afternoons the postgraduates formed five groups to collaboratively analyse and interpret a current pop song over the course of this week and to present their results on the final day. The keynote speakers provided theoretical writings for the groups' preparation and joined their discussions of the songs.

Group Analysis as Method

The concept of the summer school was to offer a structure that, on the one hand, incorporated seminars given by the invited lecturers, thus giving the opportunity for the top-down knowledge transfer known from most school and university teaching. On the other hand, we intended to activate the participants in what is by all accounts from the field of pedagogy a good way of achieving sustainable

[1] The proceedings have been published (Helms and Phleps, 2012).

learning progress. So the participants were given the task of analysing a song in the course of the week and to present their results on the final day.

But why did we not assign everybody an individual song, choosing instead the format of group work, where five to six individuals had to work on one song together? We have learned from our own academic teaching that working in groups is a complicated and challenging way of collaborating with other people. But according to our experience, group work can also produce excellent results, bringing with it positive effects considering social learning: the realisation that only by taking other members of the group as equal partners in achieving a now no longer individual, but common goal, is a valuable and often forgotten experience in a society where self-reliance is the key marker of success. Additionally, the positive motivational effect of group work known from social psychology becomes apparent: group members with lower levels of experience make special efforts to join the group (the 'indispensability effect') and get help from members with higher experience ('social compensation').

Usually, the results of group work vary considerably from results each member of the group would have achieved alone. As with the mirror ball, the whole might be more than the sum of its parts. And in the case of analysis, it is this very fact that is particularly appealing to us. As we consider the (analytical) understanding of music an individual act of interpretation that cannot be avoided, analysing music in groups teaches us to communicate this individual experience to others. In addition, we have to learn to listen to their understandings of the music, which are of equal weight and importance, no matter how contradictory they may seem at first. When every member of a group is arguing for his or her own interpretation by connecting it to the sounding structure of the music that may have provoked this meaning, then group work will put forth on a small-scale what musical analysis is all about in the first place: the communication of your individual interpretation of a piece of music to enhance our common understanding of it.

So much for theory.

In practice, we were confronted with several issues that we had not foreseen. Working in groups was not familiar to all the participants. This may be explained by their different cultural backgrounds and by the overall impression that in academia it is individualism and not cooperation that is highly appreciated. So basic skills of working in groups, such as jointly agreeing rules and issues of discussion, had to be established while the groups were already working. Along with the different cultural backgrounds came different theoretical paradigms that in effect led to further debates about suitable methods of analysing and interpreting the music. And then there was also the fact that English was the chosen language at the summer school. Consequently, the native speakers had a larger share in the discussions and almost all of a sudden Schenkerian voice-leading charts that are a common tool in North American music theory but much less so in Europe, Australia and Latin America, were being used to demonstrate harmonic/melodic relationships. From an epistemological point of view, the processes that could be observed in the work of these groups are highly revealing. The members from Latin American countries questioned what they felt to be the hegemony of Anglophone popular music studies. Heavy metal fans wondered how one could seriously work on mainstream hits. Followers of Schenker were confronted by adherents of cultural studies, fanciful hermeneuticists by sober formalists. More serious, still, has been the challenge for the groups to finish their papers by sending emails around the globe where keeping up a discussion with no face-to-face setting turned out to be a tricky business – especially, when you have to deal with many different time zones.

All this may sound discouraging at first and seems to argue against the format of group analysis. But we still believe its benefits are worth pursuing since it is here, where the problems of the musicological community (if there is one) engaged in analytical activities can not only be found, but can be solved in miniature. All around the world scholars of different race/class/gender, theoretical background and educational status engage themselves in the research of popular music. And for most of them, English is not their first language. What we can learn from the results of the group works gathered herein, is how we might come to a closer collaboration in networks or groups in general.

In studies jointly written by groups the contents are tested and discussed thoroughly before publication whereas the ideas in papers by single authors have to be proven convincing or wrong *after* publication – when the damage is done, so to speak. Few scholars are fortunate enough to have the experience that their papers arouse an intensive discussion among their colleagues. Few will ever know whether their readers accept their ideas or not. Group work, however, produces the inter-subjectively shared knowledge of a group of scholars. In our case it is the approved inter-subjective knowledge of scholars from all over the world. The findings may not be as detailed as studies by single authors, but the details presented are more likely to be credible, as they already had to convince more individuals than just the single author himself. By all means, it always has to be kept in mind that the aim of this process is not simply to find a common denominator or a compromise, as this would ignore the valuable effects of diversity and subjective hearing mentioned above – it is process as process which is perhaps most valuable. In this regard, there are issues which, as a community, we might do well to consider. What, for instance, might be the future for the sort of negotiated analyses we trial here? The practice of responding to others' analyses and interpretations presented as conference papers is well tested (at least with established musics), but the aim of such responses is still to refine an individual perspective rather than negotiate a shared one. What happens in the real world? To what extent are listeners' understandings changed by the journalism they read, the conversations they have, the shared experience at the gig, and to what extent do we know? Indeed, if such negotiation does indeed take place, is it worth asking whether we actually want to model what happens in the 'real world'? Are there ways of convincingly mapping the process of coming to an understanding? Or, alternatively, might we not, as academics, perhaps have some responsibility to do something different (and stick with our singular papers)? After-session pub musings these may be, but our focus on methodology normally stops short of pondering them. Perhaps it shouldn't.

All in all, the participants as well as the organisers and lecturers considered this experiment a success and decided to transform the results – not only concerning the specific songs, but also their experiences about academic working in intercultural groups – into a book. To this end, the groups reworked and finished their drafts via email. The lecturers agreed to contribute original song analyses, each approaching their song by reflecting on their own theoretical and methodological background. So first, in Part I, be prepared to become familiar with the methods of leading scholars by witnessing how they apply them to a specific song. In Part II then, you will see how the groups combined and interlocked these and other approaches to make sense of their own listening experience. Enjoy!

We have to thank the Volkswagen foundation and Ashgate for making the summer school and this resulting book possible. We thank all of the participants for a great week in Osnabrück and for struggling so hard to get the results fixed. Cheers for Thomas Phleps for his support and especially for Yvonne Thieré for working day and night to turn 13 drafts into a perfectly formatted book. Danke!

References

Helms, D. and Phleps, T. (eds), 2012. *Black Box Pop. Analysen populärer Musik.* Bielefeld: Transcript.

Moore, A.F., 2012. *Song Means: Analysing and Interpreting Recorded Popular Song*. Farnham: Ashgate.

PART I
Listening Alone

Chapter 1

Death Cab for Cutie's 'I Will Follow You Into The Dark' as Exemplar of Conventional Tonal Behaviour in Recent Rock Music

Walter Everett

Nearly all rock music depends upon the tonal system to which listeners constantly, if unconsciously, compare each example in order to maintain their tonal bearings.[1] Some songs, artists and styles adhere more closely to the norms of that system than do others; some are compliant, others adventurous. Frequently, affects tied to a song's poetic text can be meaningfully found in the shapes and dynamics of particular tonal events. This chapter will aim at relating aspects of voice leading and harmony in Death Cab for Cutie's tonally conventional yet beautiful and inspiring 2005 song, 'I Will Follow You Into The Dark', to tonal norms so as to provide an understanding of the manifold aspects of its musical structure and to suggest how the song's poetic concerns are thereby supported and enhanced. If it might seem disappointing at first to scrutinise a conventional structure rather than one more elaborate and potentially more 'interesting', I hope that this chapter will prove useful in countering the assertion made by many critics of tonal analysis that rock music does not behave in the same ways as did the much earlier styles that explored and developed the same system underlying tonal relations.[2] Despite the subject's relative simplicity, matters of interest and subtlety will hopefully appear here nonetheless, especially in efforts to suggest how this song and others linked to it may take advantage of many facets of the underlying tonal system in the expression of ideas central to their poetic texts.

---

[1] I have outlined many aspects of rock's interaction with the tonal system in my essays 'Making Sense of Rock's Tonal Systems' (Everett, 2004a) and 'Pitch Down the Middle' (Everett, 2007), and in the book, *The Foundations of Rock* (Everett, 2009), particularly its chapters 7–11, which illustrate principles of melodic and harmonic construction through examples of rock and pop music drawn from the years 1955–69. The same principles apply in later rock music.

[2] The reader who wishes to move to a far more complex analysis might wish to consult my essays on the music of Steely Dan (Everett, 2004b) or Paul Simon (Everett, 1997), which are based on the same principles exercised in this chapter. Indeed, PJ Harvey's 'The Words That Maketh Murder', the subject of a later chapter of this book, contains a wildly rich tonal structure based on twistings of age-old norms.

'I Will Follow You Into The Dark' has been selected for its intriguing subject matter (the singer's first-person character represents one member of a couple as he looks ahead to their deaths), its sonic clarity (a single vocal line accompanied by acoustic guitar constitutes the entire texture), its popularity (as a single from the *Billboard* Top-Five album, *Plans*, as a song featured in many top-rated television programmes and major motion pictures, and as the subject of several cover versions), its critical acclaim (thumbs up from Christgau n.d. and *Pitchfork*) and the comprehensibility of its relationship to the underlying tonal system.[3] The song's poetic theme, its sparse texture, its generally diatonic setting and many aspects of its voice leading and harmonic scheme recall all of these aspects of Bruce Springsteen's contemplative prior 'If I Should Fall Behind', and this similarity leads me to begin my project with an investigation of the earlier song. But many details of the musical structure of 'I Will Follow You Into The Dark' correspond closely with patterns basic to songs produced throughout rock's history because they are endemic to the tonal system itself. The strength of these basic events will be demonstrated by showing how most of the characteristic tonal ideas in 'I Will Follow You Into The Dark' are also heard in other rock songs of many diverse styles appearing in the two decades surrounding the turn of the millennium.

An Antecessor from Springsteen

An examination of the Springsteen ballad will precede the study of the Death Cab song. 'If I Should Fall Behind' was introduced in the 1992 album, *Lucky Town*, but is perhaps better known as the E Street Band's quiet closer on their 1999–2000 'Reunion' tour through its appearance on the *Live In New York City* CD and DVD (both 2001). 'If I Should Fall Behind' is a tender, touching and haunting ballad given an acoustic accompaniment (featuring in its studio version a strummed guitar, sustained organ and mandolin) of slow-moving chord changes, sung by its author as a solo except for a few brief double-tracked descant lines that bring prominence to selected phrase endings. Making a pledge of eternal devotion, the singer declares that come what may, he will never leave his beloved. Even though the two may occasionally lose their stride, causing one's hand to 'slip free' of the other's in the 'twilight' (verse 1) and 'the shadows of the evening trees' (verse 3), these separations will be only momentary, and the listener infers that death would have no more power over the couple's inseparability than would the most minor terrestrial intrusions.

Example 1.1a sketches the voice leading of Springsteen's vocal parts and the harmonic role of the accompaniment for both the verse and the bridge, the latter of which is performed just once, after the second of three verses (= a classic AABA

[3] 'I Will Follow You Into The Dark' was featured in both *Scrubs* and *Grey's Anatomy* in 2009. Robert Christgau (n.d.) praised the track as the album's only 'Choice Cut'. Tangari (2005) calls this song 'the album's quiet centerpiece'.

Example 1.1a Voice-leading sketch of Bruce Springsteen, 'If I Should Fall Behind' (*Lucky Town*, 1992)

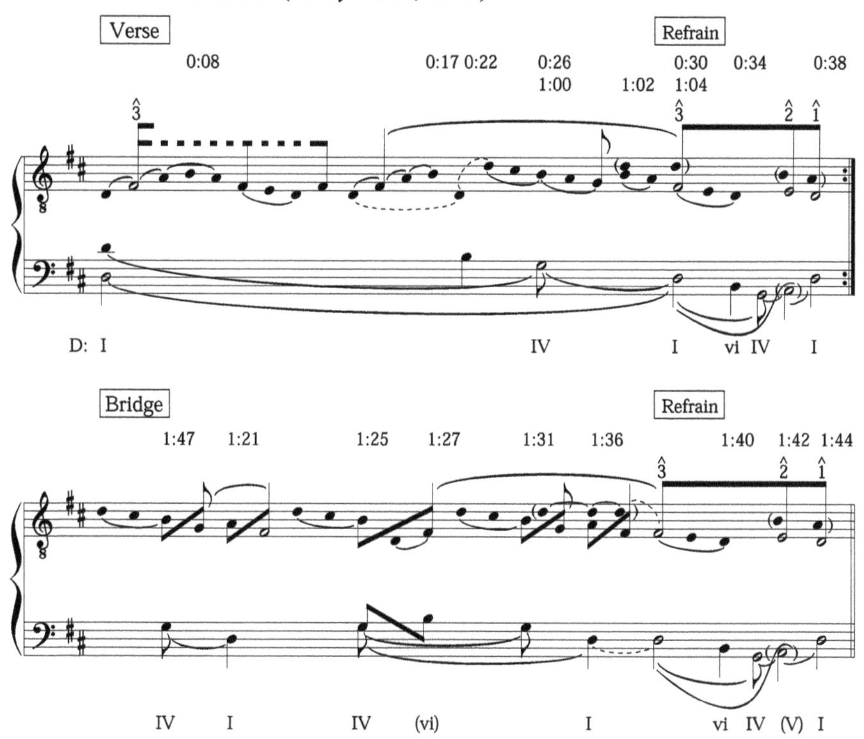

Example 1.1b

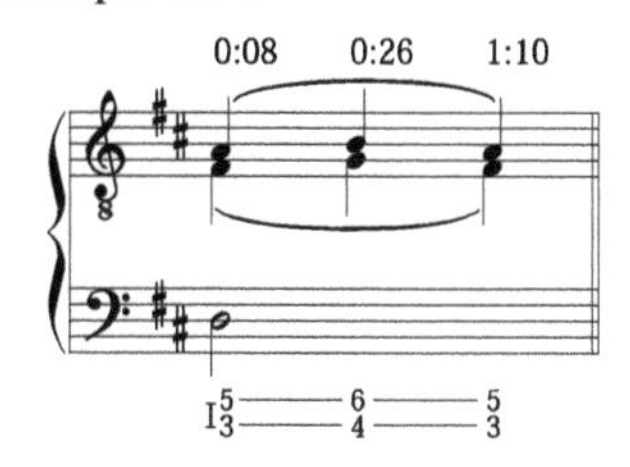

form). Both sections include the refrain, 'I'll wait for you; should I fall behind, wait for me', allowing for casual variation of the conditional clause as captured in the title. Parenthesised in the treble staff of the graph are the scattered moments of descant harmony; all other pitches shown there belong to the lead vocal. The descant deviations from the lead line suggest both the separation of singer and beloved when their steps fall 'so differently' at 1:02–1:04 (the upper voice maintaining the upper first scale degree in oblique motion against the $\hat{6} - \hat{5} - \hat{3}$ fall in the lead vocal) and the unification of the pair with solid fifth doublings (B – A above E – D) of the structural $\hat{2} - \hat{1}$ descents in the refrains of the second verse and bridge, replaced by even more unanimous octave doublings on E – D in the coda. At 1:34–1:37 in the bridge's refrain, the final appearance of a descant part repeats the first scale degree as if a beacon 'that the other may see' the couple's unchanging ultimate goal.

Rhythmic events are not my focus, but I am taken aback by a 'missing' measure in the bridge, whose irregular 7 + 8 phrase rhythm is produced by the hypothetical elimination of a single bar of IV, which had begun at 1:25. The expected second bar of this chord is arrestingly elided at 1:27 by an unwelcome minor vi chord at 1:27, portraying the sinister reality of 'what this world can do'. In the graph a lone unfolding symbol in the tenor range suggests that the B-minor rupture prolongs IV without adding any harmonic value, as if there only for its evocative colour contrast, in recognition of a poetic potential difficulty within the third of the IV chord. Had the parallel unfolded vocal thirds continued throughout the bridge without this disruption below, we might have attained the ideal expressed in the opening line of this section as supported by the IV – I neighbour resolution at 1:17–1:22, by which 'everyone dreams of a love lasting and true'.

The singer emphasises the fifth scale degree, A, but this is not to be understood as the primary tone for a five-line descent through the G of 0:27 to the F♯ of 0:30 and beyond. The vocal part instead represents a three-line from primary tone F♯, made clear by the parallel thirds, A/F♯ (0:08–0:24) – B/G (0:26–0:29) – A/F♯ (0:30), that prolong the opening tonic with a neighbouring $^6_4$, as clarified in Example 1.1b. The bridge makes this construction even less ambiguous; the same parallel thirds given the unfolding symbols there are interrupted with the stumble of a fourth on the ominous vi chord discussed above. The unfolding of parallel thirds, that is to say the unification of two (mostly) parallel voices in a single vocal part, seems the perfect musical emblem for the lyric's comforting side-by-side theme.

The verse is based on a descending I – vi – IV arpeggiation (heard twice, as it is repeated in the refrain). This progression introduces the minor vi chord, later to be heard more ominously, as a shadow that first falls over the singer and companion at 0:22 when he acknowledges that the two may 'lose our way'. The dark root of the vi chord, B, is foreshadowed in the vocal line, in which this sixth scale degree behaves first as a complete neighbour to the fifth of tonic (at 0:08) but then is given autonomy as a non-resolving escape tone from A at the appearance of 'twilight' (0:17–0:18). This B at 0:18 truly does exist in twilight: it is a newly emancipated neighbour still consonant above its supporting I chord (and suggestive thus far of nothing darker than the major-pentatonic scale), but in retrospect its value quickly emerges as the germ of the troubling vi to come.

The goal of the descending arpeggiation, IV, does not act as a dominant preparation, but rather as support for the same neighbour resolution to I shown in Example 1.1b. Tension-bearing dominant harmony makes no appearance in this song; it's gentle plagal cadences everywhere. In the refrain, however, the strength of the vocal line's second scale degree at the point of cadence implies where a V might have been expected to appear, and so the graph's parentheses in the bass line indicate the missing structural element, as the guitar's IV accompanies what the singer prefers to render as a ii $^{6}_{5}$ chord, altogether realised as IV with added sixth (and elided V).[4]

'I Will Follow You Into The Dark': The Song and Its Verse Structure

It is unknown whether members of Death Cab for Cutie knew 'If I Should Fall Behind' when Ben Gibbard wrote and recorded 'I Will Follow You Into The Dark' as a solo contribution to the group's 2005 album, *Plans*, or whether Gibbard has since become aware of any correspondences between the two songs. Regardless of the composer's intent, there are some relationships that link the songs' tonal qualities that are of interest given the poetic themes shared by these songs but by no others that come to mind. Death Cab for Cutie (an act named for a song performed by the Bonzo Dog Doo Dah Band in the Beatles' 1967 television special, *Magical Mystery Tour*) is a Bellingham, Washington-born quartet whose first four albums were released on an indie label, Barsuk Records. The last of these, *Transatlanticism* (2003), was a major hit. The band has had an emo reputation, partly because of their grim name and partly because a melancholy air enfolds some of their thoughtful lyrics; it is also known for its focus on melodic invention. *Plans* – recorded over the course of a month on a farm outside North Brookfield, Massachusetts – was the group's first album released after signing with the major label, Atlantic. Debuting at #4 on the *Billboard* 'Hot 200' album chart in August, 2005, and remaining there for 50 weeks, *Plans* was certified gold by the RIAA in 2006 and platinum two years later. At the time of the album's recording (following a few changes of drummer), the band was comprised of Ben Gibbard (vocals, guitars), Chris Walla (guitar, keyboards and production), Nick Harmer (bass) and Jason McGerr (drums).

Of *Plans*, bassist Nick Harmer says, 'This is a pretty introspective record … There are a lot [more] questions about growing older, responsibility and doubt than there are declarations and answers' (Hammer, cited in Clark, 2006). Gibbard himself, on the album's title and theme:

> I don't think there's necessarily a story, but there's definitely a theme here. One of my favorite kind of dark jokes is, "How do you make God laugh? You make a plan." Nobody ever makes a plan that they're gonna go out and get hit by a car.

[4] In the very subdued version of this song performed on the 1999–2000 tour, Springsteen, Steven Van Zandt, Nils Lofgren, Patti Scialfa and Clarence Clemons take turns singing solo lines (Clemons's vocal is prefaced by his tenor sax solo), and then in the coda all come together for five-part a cappella gospel harmony. Here, all tonal elements of the studio recording discussed above are preserved, but this is not the case in the song's strongly recomposed setting as a traditional Irish folk waltz sung by Springsteen and Scialfa with the Sessions Band in Dublin, 2007. In this version, the V chord absent in other settings imposes itself strongly, half and authentic cadences replacing all of the model's plagal motions.

> A plan almost always has a happy ending. Essentially, every plan is a tiny prayer to Father Time. I really like the idea of a plan not being seen as having definite outcomes, but more like little wishes. (Gibbard, cited in Clark, 2006)

Note that this concern over a fateful disruption of planned-for gratification is the same idea phrased at the point of rupture in phrase rhythm and voice leading in Springsteen's bridge: 'Now everyone dreams of love lasting and true, oh, but you and I know what this world can *do*.' The 'Death Cab' in the referential Bonzo song was taking Cutie to her planned destination before she was made to pay the ultimate 'fare'. The notion of death as fateful interruption that joins the band's name to the linked demise of both members of a romantic couple in 'I Will Follow You Into The Dark' also plays out elsewhere on *Plans*: the song 'Soul Meets Body', in which a bus station is seen as the emblem of a portal to 'far-off destinations', includes the line, 'If the silence takes you, then I hope it takes me too'.

The recording of the understated 'I Will Follow You Into The Dark' with a small acoustic six-string was an impromptu affair. Producer Chris Walla recounts the story:

> We were going to track the vocal for another song and there was something screwy happening with the headphone mix ... We were having problems, so I said, "Ben, this is gonna be a few minutes. Take a break." Ben's version of taking a break while we addressed the headphone problem was to pick up this Stella guitar that he loves and start playing this song we were planning on recording some time later during the sessions. He was still coming through the vocal mic as he was playing this, and it was sounding really cool to me, so I went up and said, "Let's track this real quick", and we did and that's what's on the record. It was a mono recording with no effects. Nothing. I added a little compression and de-essed it a bit. It's really weird. It's totally there and it's happening. (Clark, 2006)

The song's official video (that with Gibbard engaging the growing hole in the bedroom floor) shows him playing a C major fingering with the capo on the fifth fret, producing a bright F major setting. Generally, chords are articulated such that his right thumb accents single-note roots on first and third beats, sometimes in alternation with weak-beat chordal fifths on the low strings, and his other fingers together strum all of the stopped upper strings. Example 1.2a reveals the song's harmonic and voice-leading structure. Like 'If I Should Fall Behind', 'I Will Follow You Into The Dark' contains two contrasting sections, but unlike the earlier song this has three verses, each followed by a chorus. Also participating in the definition of the song's form is the anomalous five-bar extension to the third verse at 2:29, sitting timelessly on a non-resolving IV chord to portray 'the blackest of rooms', perhaps a purgatory where the singer hopes to rejoin his beloved after death. (Otherwise, all three verses are of a regular 8 + 8 bars). Not shown in the sketch is the solo guitar introduction, which is identical to the accompaniment in

Example 1.2a Voice-leading sketch of Death Cab for Cutie, 'I Will Follow You Into The Dark' (*Plans*, 2005)

Example 1.1b

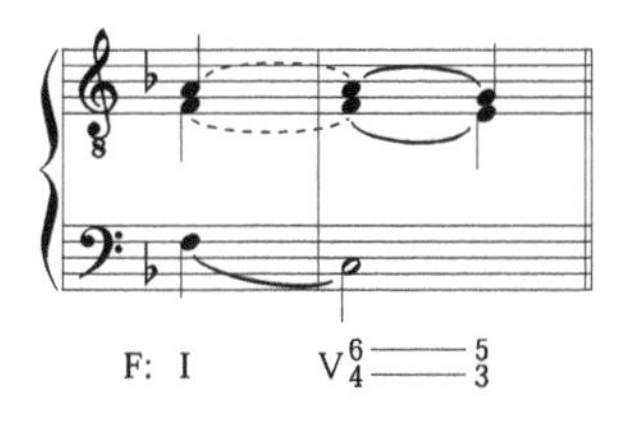

the chorus. I will present my analysis of the song's harmonic and voice-leading events in three sections, covering the three distinct phrases: that heard twice in the verse, that leading to the chorus's half cadence and that concluding the chorus with an arrival on tonic. In discussing each section, I will relate the phrase structure to the poetic text and to usages of the same or similar devices in other songs, including the Springsteen model and a wide range of contemporaneous rock songs.

In the opening phrase of the first verse, we hear the words that carry the song's main theme, 'Love of mine, someday you will die but I'll be close behind; I'll follow you into the dark'. A darkening of chord colour at 0:28 caused by a change from the opening major to minor accompanies the journey from the loving address

('Love of mine' on F major) to a prediction of the companion's dying ('someday you will die', D minor). Above the F major triad, the first note Gibbard sings is a non-chord tone, G3. (In regard to this register identification, note the example's transposing treble clef.) This happens to be the same sonority in the same key that opens the Beatles' 'Yesterday', although Paul McCartney withholds the third in his guitar there for a more mysterious air. In that song, McCartney decisively resolves the G down by step to the chord root, whereas Gibbard takes his G up to the chordal third, the primary tone, $\hat{3}$. His opening phrase does fall to the first scale degree before long, through an inner-voice descent indicated in Example 1.2a with the downward beam connecting the initial A3 to the F3 at the word 'behind', at 0:31–0:32. This first scale degree lends an air of resolute assurance to the singer's promise to remain, as did Springsteen, close by. The oath to follow his love 'into the dark' returns his voice to the fundamental line, which is interrupted on $\hat{2}$, the dark void perhaps made more mysterious by the melody's failure to resolve just yet to $\hat{1}$. This first phrase with its half cadence is not answered by a second with an authentic one, but rather is repeated, concluding the verse as an open phrase group rather than a period. In Example 1.2a, the repeated phrase is shown with its foreground detail abbreviated.

In the second verse, Gibbard's spiritual exploration returns his thoughts to painful memories of a parochial-school upbringing.[5] The sisters used corporal punishment, bruising his knuckles to teach him to associate love with fear – presumably the fear of an authoritarian God. This, despite the fact that the First Epistle of John 4:18 teaches, 'There is no fear in love; but perfect love casteth out fear: because fear hath torment. He that feareth is not made perfect in love.' Therefore, the switch from F major to D minor in this verse points up the pain and fear that the singer associates with love and with facing the supernatural.

The third verse is more hopeful; here, the change from major to minor and back only serves to underline the contrast between the extremes of all the things the couple has experienced together in Bangkok and Calgary. The two chosen cities, both large and prosperous, are quite extreme: one a tropical and polluted, densely populated city at sea-level (mentioned on a minor triad) and the other a dry, cold and environmentally clean agrarian prairie city with suburban sprawl at high elevation (set with a major chord). The repeated music is even given soothing words advocating a [D minor] sleep and soothing tears away. Thus, the three verses portray the contemplation of death first candidly, then as tied to fearful teachings and finally with acceptance as an inevitable part of a rich shared life.

To consider the accompanying pattern more closely, I will look separately at its two components: the bass-line descent in thirds from I through vi to a dominant-

---

[5] It might be recalled that as part of a long tradition of rock songs disparaging the strictness of school, the opening verse of the Beatles' 'Getting Better' begins with the line, 'I used to get mad at my school; the teachers who taught me weren't cool'. Lennon intimates that this upbringing fed a cruel streak in his love relationships; Gibbard suggests that teachers' mistreatment of him coloured his feelings about love and death.

preparatory IV, one chord per measure and the single-bar V for the half cadence that ends the four-bar phrase prematurely, not resolving on tonic. The light, flowing imperfect consonances sung against the bass – the tenth over F at 0:25 and the (sixth) over (C) at 0:34 – accompany the singer's references to his love object ('Love of mine' and 'I'll follow *you*'), whereas other harmonic intervals in the outer-voice structure – the more solid perfect fifths over vi, IV and the V at 0:35 (at 'you will die', 'I'll be close behind' and 'into the *dark*', respectively) – all contrast the grace of the couple against the weightier descent into death.[6] The underlying chord succession, I – vi – IV, is so key a characteristic of a late-1950s vocal style that I refer to it as the 'doo-wop' progression no matter the style in which it is heard.[7] This approach to a cadential V remains ubiquitous in its original form right into the twenty-first century. In this recent repertoire, the pattern is featured in such diverse songs as:

- Arcade Fire's slow-moving 'Wake Up' (2004) (in the introductory tattoo and verses, 0:22+)
- Spoon's 'Sister Jack' (2005) (in the first half of the verse, 0:08–0:22 and all of the chorus, 0:55–1:24)
- Weezer's 'I Don't Want To Let You Go' (2009) (intro and verses, 0:00–0:31) and
- Cake's 'Pretty Pink Ribbon' (2001) (repeated in the verse, 0:04–0:34).[8]

Of these, the Weezer example on its surface may be the most obvious throwback to the early 1960s style, but 'Wake Up' fills the bass arpeggiation with passing tones, $\hat{8} - \hat{7} - \hat{6} - \hat{5} - \hat{4}$, a melody that is also highly characteristic of early rock repertoire that will in turn be seen to affect the coming chorus of 'I Will Follow You Into The Dark'.[9] The many references to death in all of these songs seems coincidental,

[6] The graph's parenthetical C at 0:34 and the concomitant references in the sentences above reflect the fact that the functioning C is sometimes replaced by an actual F at this point in the bass, a point to be discussed further in regard to its voice-leading implications below. Even when F is present in the bass, Gibbard sings an imperfect consonance against it, a tenth in those cases rather than the sixth as notated, thus preserving in all hearings the overall relationship between weighty perfect intervals and light imperfect ones.

[7] Everett (2009, pp. 217–20) discusses many examples of the doo-wop progression from the 1950s and 1960s. Its frequency of appearances seems to have peaked in 1962.

[8] The lyrics of the Arcade Fire, Spoon, Weezer and Cake examples all speak of death, 'Pretty Pink Ribbon' grotesquely so. If this is not coincidental, the apparent trope – also basic to our Death Cab song – may signify a morbidity of borrowing such a done-to-death idea as the doo-wop progression, or an anxiety pervading such an influence.

[9] In addition to many recurring direct appropriations, rotations of the doo-wop progression occur throughout rock history; the bridge of the Beatles' 'I Want to Hold Your Hand' and one verse phrase in their 'Strawberry Fields Forever' is based on IV – V – I – vi, achieved by swapping the first and last pair of doo-wop triads. Another common transformation moves the doo-wop's initial I to later in the phrase, producing vi – IV – I – V, so that in repeated hearings

but it will be remembered that the I – vi – IV progression also lies at the heart of both the opening part of the verse and its refrain in Springsteen's contemplation of death in 'If I Should Fall Behind', where the change of mode from major I to minor vi (and from major IV to minor vi in the chorus's disruption) was seen to be as telling as in Death Cab's song.

Attending to the second component of the verse phrases, each back-relating half cadence is ornamented with the cadential six-four, a somewhat refined device fairly common in rock music since the Beatles featured it in 'Wait' (1965).[10] Here, the dominant harmony is decorated with contrapuntal upper voices that altogether would have the same spelling as a tonic chord with its fifth in the bass. As shown in Example 1.2b, a performer might give rise to this sonority by suspending the root and third from tonic harmony over the metrically accented arrival of the bass's fifth scale degree, after which the upper voices may resolve down into the metrically weaker chord tones, revealing the delayed third and fifth of the V chord. Preparations for the six-four other than suspensions are also possible, as with passing or neighbouring motions in upper and inner voices.[11]

Note that the sixth in Gibbard's cadential six-four is itself ornamented by its upper neighbour, the A3 moving to B♭3 and back. The slur denoting this motion in Example 1.2a is marked with an asterisk to show its relation to an idea yet to come in the chorus. The embellishment is significant in introducing the melody's first pitch outside the major-pentatonic scale (B♭ had already found work in the bass line), adding the semitone's tension to melodic proceedings. This hurried neighbour figure has long been a common voice-leading ornament to the cadential

the cadential V is heard to move deceptively to the next line's vi. This adaptation is featured in Lucenzo's 'Danza Kuduro', the topic of another chapter in this volume. See also the Axis of Awesome's 'Four-Chords' (2009), based on I – V – vi – IV, a repeated rotation of Lucenzo's pattern. See the performance reportedly from the Melbourne International Comedy Festival of 2009: http://www.youtube.com/watch?v=5pidokakU4I [Accessed 25 October 2012]. Note that at 3:21, the pattern rotates from I – V – vi – IV to vi – IV – I – V.

[10] Everett (2009) covers this cadence in pp. 208–9.

[11] Rock artists with a strong voice-leading sensibility feature the cadential six-four or substitutions for it. In the verse of 'Nice Dream' (1995), Radiohead uses traditional harmony for a mocking nostalgic look back as IV (0:27) moves to the $^{6}_{4}$ – $^{5}_{3}$ on V (at 0:35–0:39, combining a 4–3 suspension in an inner voice and a 6–5 passing motion in the vocal). As will Death Cab, Radiohead repeats the phrase for a verse that constitutes an open phrase group, and then moves directly to vi to begin the chorus. More recently, Ben Folds constructs a Mozartean preparation with a German sixth chord leading to the cadential six-four in 'Carrying Cathy' (2001) (both the sixth and fourth are suspended over the bass from the German at 0:32 and then resolve to the triadic fifth and third respectively at 0:34). Likewise, the opening phrase of 'Carrying Cathy' is repeated to give its verse the structure of an open phrase group. Elsewhere on *Rockin' the Suburbs*, in the introduction of 'The Luckiest', Folds prepares a cadential six-four with ii$^{6}_{5}$ (0:14); the $^{6}_{4}$ (0:16) is also made more complex by the inner-voice suspension of a seventh along with upper-voice sixth. The song's coda concludes with just such a decoration for the album's final authentic cadence.

six-four; it was practised as a genteel mordent in the eighteenth century, but is heard even in raucous rock music, as in the chorus-ending cadence in Weezer's 'My Best Friend' (0:47–0:50).

In Example 1.2a, the bass arrival on C3 is wrapped in parentheses. This is because although it functions in all verses as indicated, sometimes it is literally present on the downbeat and at other times its appearance is delayed by a first scale degree that supports the sixth and fourth as if a root-position tonic chord. In verse 1, I holds at first (0:34) for a full two beats before the fifth scale degree appears in the bass (0:36), but in the repeat, the first scale degree is touched for only a half-beat (0:46) before $\hat{5}$ takes over. The second verse moves from the half-beat (1:23) to the two-beat version of 'I' (1:36). The third verse dispenses with any pretence of downbeat tonic, and presents the model in its natural state, moving directly from IV to the accented cadential six-four at both 2:13 and 2:26. The performer's intention as to bass-line membership cannot be inferred with precision, because the informal nature of his thumb picking produces irregular variety, but this ear will interpret the cadential six-four as being implied in all cases, meaning that IV moves directly as dominant preparation to the V.

Often, the accompanying lyric suggests a lack of resolution also implied by the half cadence. It's already been noticed that the darkness of death is portrayed there ('into the dark', 0:36), as is the second verse's mention of a nun in her black habit (1:24–1:25). Just as one does not expect to return from death, there is no rest, no return to origins, only wandering through back-pointing half cadences: the second verse's second cadential six-four accompanies a line about not going back (1:36–1:38, there explaining why he left the nuns behind). Withholding a resolute tonic creates anticipation: the first verse ends with a reference to anticipating the spark of something new (0:45–0:49). This openness to illumination, perhaps the search for an indication as to how an afterlife is to be different from what has been known, accords with words spoken in the course of an interview in which Gibbard says that when a performance is going well, he seeks to locate and return to the (supernatural) inspiration, the 'spark', for his ideas:

> *What is going through your mind when you are up on stage?* – It varies from show to show. In the recent shows that we are playing we are still working out the kinks, so I'm thinking about stuff like the monitor mix and the transition from song to song, seeing how the new songs fit in to the set. This means that the current shows are a bit more cerebral at the moment. When it's a good show you are just thinking about the songs and getting taken back to the time the songs were written, trying to find the spark. (Klotschkow, 2011)

At the first cadential six-four in the last verse (at 2:13–2:16), Gibbard employs an image of worn-out shoes to link the notion of a lifetime of travels (recall the mentions of Bangkok and Calgary) to the tiredness with which one would welcome death. A crossing to the afterlife is suggested by the cadence-spanning enjambment that provides a different sort of a link, joining the end of one line about shoes to the beginning of the repeated phrase about their being worn out. This metaphor calls to mind one line from that other song of transcendence on *Plans*, 'Soul Meets Body': 'there are roads left in both of our shoes' (2:10–2:13), which suggests that there, death is not impending.

'I Will Follow You Into The Dark': The Chorus

The lyrics of the chorus, which are musically set with two lines in the first phrase leading to another back-relating dominant, and two in the second finally ending in tonic, comprising in all a simple parallel symmetrical period. Each of the four lines fills two bars, and the final chorus repeats the last line as coda *senza tempo*, one strum for each of the last three chords, without any final instrumental tag. Eternal purgatory (the very dark rooms) is suggested by the notion of space available neither in heaven nor hell.[12]

The chorus of 'I Will Follow You Into The Dark' features contrapuntal devices more subtle than those heard in the verse. For instance, the first three (of four) gestures in the chorus (beginning at 0:50, 0:56 and 1:02) open with a vi chord supporting the vocal upper neighbour to the fifth of tonic. This fifth, C4, then passes through B♭3 at 0:52, accompanied by a IV chord that acts as a support for the (unnotated) D – C neighbour, now repeated an octave lower in the guitar. (The 'N' under the staff indicates this neighbour function; the asterisk above the slur refers this passing motion to the neighbour ornamentation of the verse's cadential six-four. The verse idea has been developed in the chorus to connect the previously independent pitch-class C to a larger line.) The gentle neighbours and passing tones, with leading tone forestalled until the half cadence, reinforce the notion of easy satisfaction felt by the full heaven and hell. In contrast, that non-resolving half cadence is imbued with the negative quality of 'NO' vacancy, and no traveller can stop at 0:59 where there is no resolution but can only look back or keep moving. The repetition of an opening on vi – I is broken by the fourth gesture's chromaticism and mode mixture, setting the song's theme and title there with a strong poignancy.

To examine these events more closely, the vocal D4 – C4 that opens the chorus projects a motivic idea introduced in the verse as an inner-voice motive. It was

[12] A more literal emergence of the word 'vacancy' occupies a later Gibbard song, his 2010 ode to the Smith Tower, which at 42 stories was the tallest building on the West Coast when built in 1914 and remained Seattle's tallest structure until the erection of the Space Needle for the 1962 World's Fair. Apparently in response to a feature story on the apartment atop the largely abandoned building that ran in the 'Home and Garden' section of the *New York Times* on 20 October 2010 (Tortorello, 2010), Gibbard was filmed introducing the song 14 days later in a solo benefit concert at Seattle's Crocodile Cafe. The untitled song, steeped in solitude, includes the image of emptiness leading to sleep (parallel with another line in 'I Will Follow You Into The Dark'), declaring 'there's too many vacancies' in the tower. As yet unreleased, the song was not included on Death Cab's 2011 album, *Codes and Keys*.

important there both for its independence (at 'follow you', at 0:33, this figure is not part of either the fundamental line's motion from $\hat{3}$ to $\hat{2}$ or the inner descent from A3 through G3 to F3) and for its vocal completion of the major-pentatonic scale. This pitch-class pair is also featured in its high register in the extension to the third verse, at 2:29–2:30, where it's tied to the singer's highest pitch, F4. It will be shown below that it is this figure that is altered by both chromaticism (as C♯ – D) and its mirroring mode mixture (D♭ – C) in the chorus's final statement. Perhaps most notably on the surface, the D – C agent participates in a frequent play of vocal whole steps, as with the singer's first two notes (G3 – A3, soon repeated and then reversed as the primary tone falls to the interrupted $\hat{2}$). Note that the verse's fixation on G/A, as against D3 – C3 in Gibbard's lowest-sung pitches, inverts in the chorus, which opens with a high D4 – C4 (sung there three times) that alternates with an inner-voice motion from G3 to F3, heard multiple times before it is captured in the final descent of the fundamental line. This whole step is part of a pentatonic [0–2–5] collection present at several form-defining moments, as when the opening G3 – A3 moves to C4, the third verse extends through D4 – C4 – F4 and the chorus's first phrase ends (0:59) with an escape tone and a leap from the interrupted $\hat{2}$ for a rehearing of the opening G3 – A3 – C4. It is this economy and development of melodic motive that ensures the song's rich simplicity.

The chorus's opening D4 – C4 neighbour is accompanied by a D minor chord moving to F major.[13] This chord combination is given a single Roman numeral in Example 1.2b, as it may be heard as an embellished tonic function whose fifth is at first displaced by a sixth above the first scale degree. (The 6 in the figured bass is parenthesised because it becomes on the surface a true octave by virtue of the supplemental bass support, a technique that Schenker refers to as the addition of a root. It strengthens the upper-voice neighbour by giving it its own root-position triad.) This pairing reverses the order normally heard, I embellished by a vi chord that follows, as when repeated in the chorus of Nirvana's 'In Bloom' (1991), sketched in Example 1.3.

Example 1.3 Voice-leading sketch of Nirvana, 'In Bloom' (*Nevermind*, 1991), chorus

[13] See Everett (2009, pp. 219–20) for early pop-rock examples of this relationship involving I and vi.

Note that there, the fifth of tonic is followed by its upper-neighbour sixth scale degree, which is supported by a root-position vi chord. Death Cab's own 'St. Peter's Cathedral' (2011) replicates this, with a fifth over I alternating with a neighbouring octave over $\hat{6}$, but here the bass's sixth scale degree supports a IV chord in first inversion. Its function in support of the upper neighbour is the same as fulfilled by vi in other examples. (This voice leading is perhaps heard most readily when emphasised by the keyboard in 0:57–1:22). But the vi – I ordering as presented in 'I Will Follow You Into The Dark' is effectively the whole basis of Radiohead's 'How To Disappear Completely' (2000), which, however, does exchange mode assignments by alternating a major VI chord (D major) with its aeolian tonic (F♯ minor).

In a great deal of rock music, the bass-line gaps of a third in the doo-wop progression will be filled in with passing tones, effectively producing a I – 'iii^{6}_{4}' – vi – 'I^{6}_{4}' – IV progression. Elvis Presley's 'Can't Help Falling In Love' (1961) (0:07–0:13) is a good early example of the beginning of this pattern, and this inlay was also discussed above in relation to Arcade Fire's 'Wake Up' (0:44–1:04). Elsewhere, the opening of the verse of Ben Folds's 'The Ascent Of Stan' (2001) (0:21–0:30) substitutes first-inversion six-three chords ('V^{6}_{3}') for the passing six-four triads in completing this sequential model with parallel thirds moving against all bass tones. Although the doo-wop pattern is not set this way in the 'I Will Follow You Into The Dark' verse, the same bass line with passing tones appears in the chorus, divided into two parts in order to unify by correspondence the section's two phrases: the first phrase descends from F through E to D in order to connect I and vi (0:54–0:56), and then a separate but coordinated stepwise descent connects vi to the guitar's IV chord, D – C – B♭ (1:06–1:08). This correspondence connects not only the two phrases of the chorus, but also 'ties up' the bass notes of the verse's opening I – vi – IV motion.[14]

Returning to 'I Will Follow You Into The Dark', the chorus begins with death (or at least eternal rest) forestalled, with no vacancies in heaven or hell. Here, the singer's conjecture appears at first only as a weightless ornament in a reaching-over through the space existing above the fundamental line (D4 to C4, which then moves through B♭3 to recapture A3). But then at 1:05 the soul finally and dramatically embarks via the song's one pitch that moves outside the home key and out of this life, the tenor-register's raised fifth scale degree, C♯ – the key member of an applied chord tonicising the vi area that has had so much prominence through its various minor-colour contrasts against the tonic. After all of the song's half cadences, this embarkation finally discovers the path to resolution into the song's most profound tonic, and the singer's fundamental line finally descends to its peaceful end. In fact, this $\hat{3}$ – $\hat{2}$ – $\hat{1}$ motion is something I have labelled elsewhere (Everett, 1991,

[14] Recalling Gibbard's ode to the Smith Tower, it should be noted that that song features the stepwise bass descent from first to sixth scale degree in its bridge, just before the word 'elevators'. This piece also raises the third-descent ante with its oft-repeated stepwise bass connection of IV and ii in the verse and underneath the 'too many vacancies' refrain.

p. 202) a '*Gehenlinie*' because of its ubiquity in tracing goal-directed footpaths in many nineteenth-century Lieder. The design becomes a good metaphor here for the path trod in the song's title and through different motions in support of the last phrase's two nested gestures (1:03–1:07 and 1:03–1:11), each based on a $\hat{3}$ – $\hat{2}$ – $\hat{1}$ descent at diverging levels. The song's darkest moment falls appropriately at the statement of the song's title at the end of the chorus, at 1:09, when D falls to D♭, changing the colouring of the guitar's chord from major IV to minor iv, which is interpreted more inclusively – when considering the singer's sustained descent through the $\hat{2}$ of the *Gehenlinie* – as a change in sonority from minor ii to diminished ii°.

The dramatic tonicisation of vi through its leading tone (♯$\hat{5}$) and supportive applied chord (V/vi) brings prominence to a tonal area often so emphasised in popular musics of the rock age. This particular manner of emphasising vi, however, seems to have been more common in rock's early years than in recent ones.[15] Although applied 'secondary dominant' chords are still common in later rock, vi may be tonicised there more often by the home key's V acting as a modal neighbouring ♭VII chord applied to vi.[16] In many songs, the bright raised fifth scale degree is compared directly to its dark enharmonic cousin, the sixth scale degree lowered by mode mixture, which alters the underlying chord colour from IV or iv or from ii to ii° as described above.[17] Notably, Gibbard strums each occurrence of the mixture-altered B♭-minor chord – at 0:20, 1:09, 1:59, 2:56 and

---

15 Many early examples of V/vi are given in Everett (2009, p. 272).

16 I have heard more than one scholar assert that applied chords do not appear in rock music. They must be arguing without listening, because the usage is very commonplace; numerous illustrations from rock's early decades are discussed in Everett (2009, pp. 269–74). Regarding the applied chord at hand, V/vi, famous Beatle examples are heard in both 'You Can't Do That' (at 'green', 0:52) and 'I Should Have Known Better' (also introducing a bridge, at 0:38). With roots in the deceptive cadence of early rock (see Everett, 2009, pp. 230–31), examples of V ⌒♭VII/vi abound in many recent rock styles; the Red Hot Chili Peppers' *Stadium Arcadium* (2006) seems a concentrated study of this relationship. Elsewhere in this repertoire, the major triad built on the third scale degree often resolves deceptively; instead of resolving into vi, III^7 will frequently move deceptively to IV, as a chromatic substitute for I^6. For recent examples of this, see Radiohead's 'Creep' (1993) (0:05–0:14) and 'Nude' (2007) (1:19–1:27), Foo Fighters' 'Big Me' (1995) (0:29–0:34) and Arcade Fire's 'Neighborhood #1 (Tunnels)' (2004) (0:36–0:37).

The V area may be a much more proportionally common tonal centre to tonicise than other scale degrees in recent rock than it had been earlier. Examples of this can be found in Foo Fighters' 'Next Year' (1999) (ending the bridge with a tonicised retransitional V, 1:19–1:26) and the Strokes' 'Evening Sun' (2006) (II♯ moving to V right away in the verse, 0:02–0:06) and '15 Minutes' (also 2006) (in the pre-chorus, 0:50–1:06). Radiohead's 'Knives Out' (2001) tonicises iv with a passing applied V♮2 (in the chorus, 1:04–1:13).

17 The appearance of ♭$\hat{6}$ in songs of the 1950s and 1960s is covered in Everett (2009, pp. 242–3), and a listing of that era's songs featuring chromatic lines, including many that oscillate as $\hat{5}$ – ♯$\hat{5}$ – $\hat{6}$ – ♭$\hat{6}$ – $\hat{5}$, is given in Everett (2009, p. 275).

3:03 – more deliberately (that is, more slowly and/or loudly), emphasising each of its constituent notes to make them stand out from the routine, undifferentiated playing of the members of all other chords.[18]

Juxtapositions of major IV and minor iv chords remain frequent in recent rock music. They may be heard, for instance, in Ben Folds's 'Zak And Sara' (2001) (the piano's upper line in the intro and verse descends from $\hat{1}$ through $\flat\hat{7}$ and $\hat{6}$ to $\flat\hat{6}$, repeating throughout 0:00–0:20) and Suzanne Vega's 'Angel's Doorway' (2007) (with the same descent, $\flat\hat{7}$ – $\hat{6}$ – $\flat\hat{6}$ – $\hat{5}$, 0:44–0:51, here sung). The bridge of the Strokes' 'Evening Sun' (2006) (0:19–0:29), graphed in Example 1.4, is a more involved contrast of $\hat{6}$ and $\flat\hat{6}$ in moving from a major IV chord to a diminished ii°, presented in two nested levels: in the key of E, the sonority over A is thus varied (C♯ there moving to C♮), as is that of IV of A (F♯ to F♮). The idea is then immediately transposed in 0:30–0:41 to end on tonic. Just as in 'I Will Follow You Into The Dark', it's the Strokes' singer, Julian Casablancas, who adds the roots that give new identity to the inverted ii° triads.

Example 1.4 Voice-leading sketch of The Strokes, 'Evening Sun' (*First Impressions of Earth*, 2006), bridge

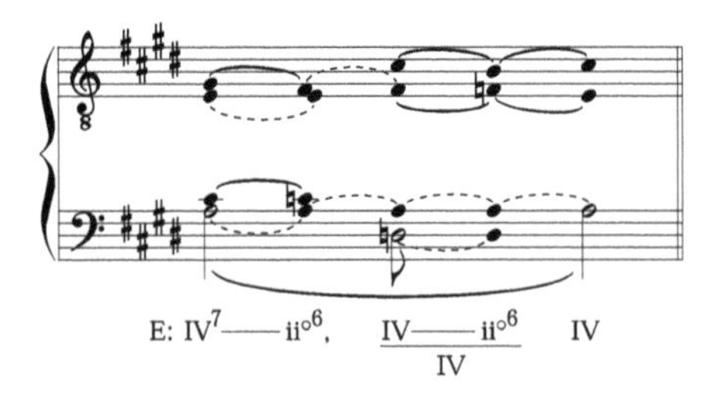

Before leaving this song, a note about the parenthetical pitches in Example 1.2a is in order. The all-important D – C whole step, sung in many guises elsewhere, does not survive in the vocal part for the song's final cadence, where they appear only in the guitar. This is why those pitches are parenthesised; Gibbard does, however, almost vocalise the D♭ between them.[19] In each chorus, Gibbard sings the pitch 23 cents below D-natural against the guitar's D♭, which is as unambiguous here as it had been in the song's introduction. (The parenthesised F3 at the beginning of the chorus is the only other treble-staff pitch shown that Gibbard articulates

[18] There is one small exception to this exclusion of emphasis that occurs in the extension of the third verse, at 2:33, where one instance of a more intense sixteenth-note rhythm (that of the opening of the Beatles' 'Things We Said Today') brings that special neighbouring IV chord to prominence.

[19] I am grateful to Ralf von Appen for applying Sonic Visualiser to this passage in order to clarify the effect here.

only in the guitar.) Of greater structural weight is the parenthetical bass C at 1:09. This does not appear anywhere in the texture, as the song ends with the dark ii° resigning directly as a neighbour chord into the final I. The C is included to show that the decisive V that would carry structural tonal weight here, and might be expected at this crucial point in many tonal styles, is in fact elided just as it was in Springsteen's 'If I Should Fall Behind'. (The same cadence – same chords, same vocal descent – will be shown in a later chapter of this book to be the basis of the ending of Fleet Foxes' 'Helplessness Blues'. That example also features the parallel-fifth doubling performed by Springsteen, as discussed above.) It should perhaps be underlined that simply because a particular song does not feature the dominant at a structural point, or anywhere at all, one should not conclude that the song is not bound by the system in which V is deeply fundamental – it simply means that the song in question does not articulate on its surface a deep part of the tonal structure. Clearly, the many back-relating half-cadential V's in 'I Will Follow You Into The Dark' make clear how conventionally this song brings out its tonal background. The tonal system is an abstract ideal independent of style that guides the ear equally as strongly in rock created by self-taught performers as it does in music once written by classical composers educated in strict methods. The lack of a final V in 'I Will Follow You Into The Dark' might be heard to add a gentle touch that an articulated dominant, with its tension-bearing leading tone, might not connote the same way. The absence carries a positive if coded message.

A Second Antecessor, from Clapton, and Conclusion

A more tragic loss of a loved one than those treated by Springsteen and Gibbard is the subject of the well-known 'Tears In Heaven' (1991), through which a grieving Eric Clapton subjunctively weighs hypothetical outcomes of reuniting with his four-year-old son Conor but concludes that he does not yet belong with the dead. In the verse of 'Tears In Heaven', the descending I – vi – IV arpeggiation familiar from the Springsteen and Death Cab examples is filled out with passing tones moving in diatonic parallel tenths above the same A – G♯ – F♯ – E – D bass line that had appeared (transposed, of course) in two portions of the 'I Will Follow You Into The Dark' chorus. For Clapton, the goal of this descent, IV, moves through 'I' to a half cadence on V; the 'I' reminds me of the sometimes cadential six-four in Death Cab. All of this is repeated as the first two phrases within a Statement – Restatement – Departure – Conclusion (SRDC) form, again corresponding with Gibbard's verse structure.[20] Despite the use of applied V's, modal alteration and parallel tenths above the moving bass (all characteristic of the final phrase of the Death Cab chorus), the remainder of 'Tears In Heaven' goes its own way. Its departure phrase ('I must be strong and carry on') features vi moving to its back-

[20] The SRDC form is shown to be the basis of many rock songs from the 1950s and 1960s in Everett (2009, pp. 140–41).

relating applied V chord, and then a moody minor dominant seventh moves to a forward-looking ('carrying on') V of ii, as parallel thirds move over a *chromatically* descending bass line, A – G♯ – G♮ – F♯ descending over F♯ – E♯ – E♮ – E♮. The verses' concluding phrase ends in an authentic cadence, but V^7 here is always made complex by a suspended fourth that, at 'I don't belong', resists resolution. Despite the heartbreaking tragedy on which it is based, Clapton's song is set in the same hopeful major mode that graces the Springsteen and Death Cab ballads. This permits an elegant and stately fall from $\hat{8}$ to $\hat{4}$ that is not characteristic of the more tortuous minor mode's lamento bass line, which characteristically ends with the arrival on $\hat{5}$ rather than gravitating to the dominant-preparatory $\hat{4}$ that appears in all of my examples.

In many ways, Death Cab for Cutie's 'I Will Follow You Into The Dark' is simple in terms of formal structure, instrumental and vocal setting, harmonic progressions, rhythmic articulation, counterpoint and deep-level voice leading. Even in its details, the song remains conventional, even conformist in nearly all regards. That does not make it a nondescript or uninteresting song. Such qualities lend strength and immediacy to its message, and connect the ballad to its broad heritage of musical and poetic expression. Making this case has required a close reading of the brief song's many characteristics: attending to aspects of the surface rhythm, timbre and texture of its vocal and instrumental parts; finding melodic invention in its outwardly calculated growth of scale membership, motivic development, implied tones and polyphony, registral contrast and ornamental finesse; noting its juxtapositions and alterations of chord colour and strategic use of chromaticism and mode mixture; being sensitive to its changes in phrase rhythm and surface patterning; parsing its poetic text in ways that at times go beyond the objectively stated words. Along with a consideration of the artists' and critics' statements, and by comparison with earlier recordings by Bruce Springsteen, Eric Clapton and with many more contemporary ones by their peers, this interpretation of harmony and voice leading as practical embodiment of a more abstract system may hopefully facilitate a deep appreciation of the love and devotion that has motivated Ben Gibbard and his team to question the power of death. The conventions on which the music depends only make the singer's profound lesson more universal.

References

Christgau, R., n.d. Death Cab for Cutie – Consumer Guide Reviews, *Robert Christgau: Dean of American Rock Critics*, [online] Available at: www.robertchristgau.com/get_artist.php?name=Death+Cab+for+Cutie [Accessed 12 May 2012].

Clark, R., 2006. Growing in the Studio, Making Plans, *Mix*, [online] Available at: http://mixonline.com/mag/audio_death_cab_cutie_2/index.html [Accessed 12 May 2012].

Everett, W., 1991. Text-Painting in Mozart's Three Lieder (K. 596–598) of 14 January 1791. In: R. Angermüller (ed.), *Mozart-Jahrbuch 1991*. Kassel: Bärenreiter, pp. 201–5.

Everett, W., 1997. Swallowed by a Song: Paul Simon's Crisis of Chromaticism. In: J. Covach and G. Boone (eds), *Understanding Rock*. New York: Oxford University Press, pp. 113–53.

Everett, W., 2004a. Making Sense of Rock's Tonal Systems, *Music Theory Online*, 10(4) (December), [online] Available at: www.societymusictheory.org/mto/issues/mto.04.10.4/toc.10.4.html [Accessed 12 May 2012].

Everett, W., 2004b. The Abstruse and Ironic Bop-Rock Harmony of Steely Dan. *Music Theory Spectrum*, 26(2) (Fall), pp. 201–35.

Everett, W., 2007. Pitch Down the Middle. In: W. Everett (ed.), *Expression in Pop-Rock Music: Critical and Analytical Essays*. 2nd edn. New York: Routledge, pp. 111–74.

Everett, W., 2009. *The Foundations of Rock from 'Blue Suede Shoes' to 'Suite: Judy Blue Eyes'*. New York: Oxford University Press.

Klotschkow, P., 2011. Interview with Ben Gibbard, *LeftLion*, [online] Available at: www.leftlion.co.uk/articles.cfm/title/death-cab-for-cutie/id/3760 [Accessed 12 May 2012].

Tangari, J., 2005. Review of Death Cab for Cutie – Plans, *Pitchfork*, [online] Available at: http://pitchfork.com/reviews/albums/2233-plans/?utm_campaign=search&utm_medium=site&utm_source=search-ac [Accessed 12 May 2012].

Tortorello, M., 2010. Making a Home in a Pyramid, 462 Feet above Seattle. *New York Times*, 20 October, [online] Available at: www.nytimes.com/2010/10/21/garden/21who.html [Accessed 12 May 2012].

Discography

Arcade Fire, 2004. 'Wake Up'; 'Neighborhood #1 (Tunnels)'. *Funeral*. Merge, MRG 255.

Beatles, The, 1963. 'I Want To Hold Your Hand'. Parlophone, R 5084.

Beatles, The, 1964. 'You Can't Do That'. *Can't Buy Me Love*. Parlophone, R 5114.

Beatles, The, 1964. 'Things We Said Today'; 'I Should Have Known Better'. *A Hard Day's Night*. Parlophone, PCS 3058.

Beatles, The, 1965. 'Yesterday'. *Help!* Parlophone, PCS 3071.

Beatles, The, 1965. 'Wait'. *Rubber Soul*. Parlophone, PCS 3075.

Beatles, The, 1967. 'Strawberry Fields Forever'. Parlophone, R 5570.

Beatles, The, 1967. 'Getting Better'. *Sgt. Pepper's Lonely Hearts Club Band*. Parlophone, CDP 7 46442 2.

Cake, 2001. 'Pretty Pink Ribbon'. *Comfort Eagle*. Columbia, CK 62132.

Clapton, Eric, 1991. 'Tears In Heaven'. WEA, W0081.

Death Cab for Cutie, 2005. 'I Will Follow You Into The Dark'; 'Soul Meets Body'. *Plans*. Atlantic, 83834-2.

Death Cab for Cutie, 2011. 'St. Peter's Cathedral'. *Codes and Keys*. Atlantic, 527251-2.

Fleet Foxes, 2011. 'Helplessness Blues'. *Helplessness Blues*. Sub Pop, SPCD 888.

Folds, Ben, 2001. 'Carrying Cathy'; 'The Ascent Of Stan'; 'The Luckiest'; 'Zak and Sara'. *Rockin' The Suburbs*. Epic, EK 61610.

Foo Fighters, 1995. 'Big Me'. *Foo Fighters*. Capitol, CDP 7243 8 34027 2 4.

Foo Fighters, 1999. 'Next Year'. *There Is Nothing Left to Lose*. RCA, 07863 67892-2.

Harvey, PJ, 2011. 'The Words That Maketh Murder'. *Let England Shake*. Island, 2753189.

Lucenzo feat. Don Omar, 2011. 'Danza Kuduro'. Yanis, 0060252777154 0.

Nirvana, 1991. 'In Bloom'. *Nevermind*. Sub Pop, DGCD-24425.

Presley, Elvis, 1961. 'Can't Help Falling In Love'. RCA Victor, 47-7968.

Radiohead, 1993. 'Creep'. *Pablo Honey*. Parlophone, CDPCS 7360.

Radiohead, 1995. 'Nice Dream'. *The Bends*. Capitol, CDP 529626.

Radiohead, 2000. 'How To Disappear Completely'. *Kid A*. Capitol, CDP 7243 5 29684 28.

Radiohead, 2001. 'Knives Out'. *Amnesiac*, Capitol, CDP 7243 5 32764 2 3.

Radiohead, 2007. 'Nude'. *In Rainbows*. XL, XLCD 324.

Red Hot Chili Peppers, 2006. *Stadium Arcadium*. Warner Bros, 9362 49996-2.

Spoon, 2005. 'Sister Jack'. *Gimme Fiction*. Merge, MRG265.

Springsteen, Bruce, 1992. 'If I Should Fall Behind'. *Lucky Town*. Columbia, CK 53001.

Strokes, The, 2006. '15 Minutes'; 'Evening Sun'. *First Impressions of Earth*. RCA, 82876764202.

Vega, Suzanne, 2007. 'Angel's Doorway'. *Beauty & Crime*. Blue Note, 0946 3 68270 2 5.

Weezer, 2005. 'My Best Friend'. *Make Believe*. Geffen, B0004617-12.

Weezer, 2009. 'I Don't Want To Let You Go'. *Raditude*. Interscope, B0013510-02.

Chapter 2
Ear Candy: What Makes Ke$ha's 'Tik Tok' Tick?[1]

Ralf von Appen

Friday, 5 p.m., Conway Recording Studios, 5100 Melrose Ave, Los Angeles, CA

The yellow flashing light on the telephone silently signals an incoming call. Luke clicks on the pause icon to stop the music and answers the phone. 'Mr Gottwald, there's a Ms Sebert at the reception. Says she's got an appointment with you.'

'Oh, right! Please hand her the phone. – Hey Kesha, it's great you're here! Just come downstairs, I'm in Studio A.'

Moments later Kesha throws her bag on the producer's armchair and flings her arms around Luke's neck: 'Hi Luke! How are ya? I'm so sorry I'm late. But you know what traffic is like on the Hollywood Freeway this time of day …'

'No prob! I've just been messing with some sound settings. I'll play some ideas to you in a minute … Hey, you're looking cool today. I like that crazy hairdo!'

'Thanks, Luke. – Well, I've been working on the lyrics for that party song I told you about. It's almost finished. Shall we start with that one? But first, I'm dying for a drink!'

'You mean this "Around the Clock"-song?' Luke hands her a can of Dr Pepper from the fridge.

'Yeah, that one. Except it's not called "Round the Clock" anymore. I mean, that just reminded too much of this fifties guy with the hairdo. But the idea is the same: having a ball, complete carelessness, getting smashed, foolin' 'round with boys. Dancing! Sun! Don't give a shit about tomorrow! Nothing but fun, fun, fun!'

'Cool! Actually, Katy's on the same trail right now. Just yesterday she showed me some lyrics for her upcoming album. One song's gonna be called "Teenage Dream", another is "California Gurls" – like that Beach Boys tune, except she's spelling it with "u": *Gurls*. In times like these you can always rely on the teens to spend some dough on music, I guess. There's always money to be made.'

'Really? Well then maybe we should stick with "Around the Clock" and get that golden days of teeny pop thing workin' for us. Actually, I'm already calling out to Mick Jagger in the lyrics, 'cause I couldn't come up with anything else rhyming with "swagger", he he. – But seriously, this song definitely shouldn't

---

[1] Music and lyrics to 'Tik Tok' reprinted with kind permission of Kobalt Music.

sound like something parents might like. It's gotta be super fresh! No ABBA sample like in that Madonna tune, no rock guitars, no acoustic drums. This has to be the bubblegum du jour! Something that only belongs to the kids!'

'Got ya! Then listen to what I got here, you might like it. It's a little riff that just came to me when I was goofing on this old Yamaha toy keyboard trying to come up with some ideas for this "California Gurls" song I'm working on with Katy.'

Example 2.1 'Tik Tok', (fictitious) initial idea

Luke glances at Kesha: 'This sound is really trashy, isn't it? Maybe I'll pimp it a bit in Pro Tools. But this cheap kinda 8-bit sound – that'll drive parents nuts! But make teenagers feel at home – it's got that arcade game, Nintendo, ring tone, you name it feel. It's kinda dirty, but modern dirty.'

'Yeah, that's phat! Play it again!' Kesha flops down on a leather couch and closes her eyes.

'It should really stay this trashy, don't polish it! – What key is it in? Does it fit my range?'

'It's B flat major, C major and D minor – an aeolian cadence. You would need to sing in D minor.'

'D is fine, but why minor? It's supposed to be a party hit!'

'Doesn't matter. If it ended on D major it would sound like shit because the F sharp doesn't go with the B flat chord and the G natural in the C chord. And if the loop ended on F major instead, it would sound too orderly, dead boring. You couldn't repeat that again and again. To me this D minor chord makes it colourful, it gives it this little something it needs. Doesn't it sound like it *needs* to be looped over and over? – Besides, this half step from e to f at the end is just beautiful, don't you think?'

'Well, okay.'

'Let me just add a kick drum and then let's see if you can sing to it. Any idea for a melody yet?' Luke chooses a bass drum from the library and loops it.

'Hold on! It's gotta be faster if you wanna dance to it. At least 120bpm!'

'Sure, here you go.'

'That's better. – At the beginning I'm going to rap, I think. Not that I'm a rapper, I can't do it at a breakneck pace or with tangled rhymes and stuff. But if I do it half singing, half rapping it might sound *real*. Like when you get up in the morning and are still a little bleary. You're not yet ready to sing elaborate melodies, you don't wanna push yourself. Just sing some lazy words that sound casual.'

'Sure, just give it a try!'
'Let it run, I'll show you what I got in mind.'

Example 2.2 'Tik Tok', verse 1, 0:00–0:08

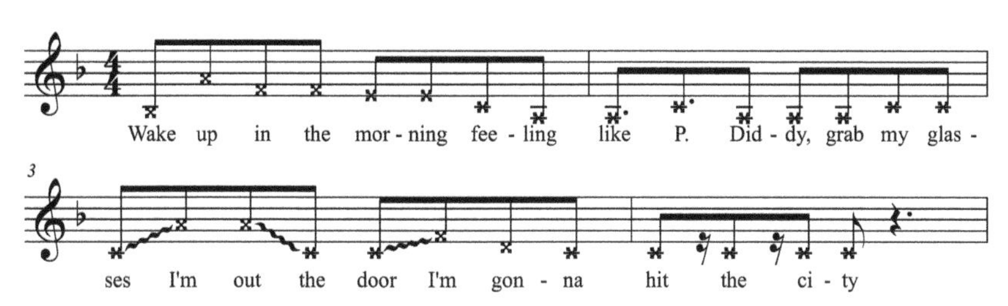

'Whoa! That's awesome! – The way you overemphasise the accents of the eighth notes it resembles a nursery rhyme a bit. Gives it the impression of a sassing teen. – And it's really weird how you end up with the second syllable of "glasses" on the "one" but then stress the next eighth note much more strongly. That's off the hook! You *gotta* keep that in! Metrical confusions like this wake them up and they keep it going even if you listen to it for the tenth time!'

'Eh, to be honest, that was not intentional …'

'Keep it in! – But tell me more about the lyrics. I mean, I get what you're talking 'bout. But if you just expand the scope and explain what you have in mind in more detail, I'll get the whole picture. I wanna understand what kind of atmosphere the song needs, what kind of vibes we're trying to make real.'

'Sure! – So this whole party thing really needs to be described from the girl side! Not just another: "all the chicks have a crush on me, I'm so super duper cool, I'm free to do whatever I want" kind of song. Instead, the girl in my song is totally in control and self-confident. She don't take shit from no one. She don't depend on no boy. On the contrary: they line up for her! She's kinda pretty, but no cheerleader bitch. She's into dress-up and nail paint and stuff, but in a freaky way. She doesn't do it for boys; she does it to make herself feel good. She likes getting bombed and doesn't care what others think. – There's this line about brushing her teeth before leaving. Just like her mother always told her – except she does it with a bottle of Jack. And that rhymes with "ain't coming back" in the next line. – This song is meant to play the parties! You have to give it a real phat dance beat. You're listening in the car or getting up in the morning and feeling like the party has started! It should make the girls feel like "I don't need no invitation from the football captain to get my night right, I'm gonna paint the town red with my gal pals."'

'Alright. So we need a dance beat, of course, we'll hold down the verse and then get them hooked with a powerful, sing-along chorus. And nothing but synthetic sounds. No rock guitars, not what Avril Lavigne and Pink are about. Then we don't need to bother with an intro, any solos or instrumental parts to show people how tight we can put the chords together or how good we can play. It's gonna be all about Kesha vocals and Kesha being Kesha. Young, modern, but not too far out. I guess you don't wanna aim at the indie niche, you wanna hit the top spot, right? So we don't wanna put off anyone or make them switch the station. It's supposed to pay off!'

'Yes! That's exactly where I'm at, Luke! And that's why I came to you. That *is* you, man! I could have chosen David Guetta – but I don't want all these electro gimmicks and I don't want this longhaired dude with all his turntables grinning beside me in the video clip or on stage! He always wants to be mentioned first on the cover and I would only be "featuring" again, like with FloRida's "Right Round". No, I'm with you, here. Let's get started!'

'Okay, so you've written two verses, each followed by a chorus that we can repeat and vary at the end. Any ideas for the middle section?'

'No, nothin' yet. Maybe I should write a third verse? Or some rapping? Maybe we'll find some female rapper. Or a guy who's rapping about how fucking sharp I am, he he.'

'We'll think about that later. Now let's just see how far we get with what you've already got. I'm gonna record the synth and loop it for three and a half minutes. Then we'll record your singing so that I can use that for reference and tonight I'll make some beats and come up with something for the chorus. Then we'll meet early next week to lay down some vocals.'

'Let's go then! Shall I use that mic over there?'

Kesha gulps the remainder of her Dr Pepper, puts her lyrics on the stand, puts on the headphones and takes a deep breath.

***

'Wow Wow Wow! This totally blows me away! You're the shit, Luke! This is definitely gonna be a hit. A number one hit! Wow Wow Wow!'

Kesha jumps around the control room and gives Luke a high five. 'I mean, I don't get it. You did that in only three days? That's impossible! You're out of control!'

'Easy, Kesha, relax! We still need to record your vocals; this was just your demo track. But honestly, I am quite happy with what I've done over the weekend; it was fun! But I didn't get much sleep the last days, I was hardly at home.'

'Stop your whining! This track is worth it, I mean totally! – Let's listen to it close. I wanna understand how you did this. Eh, you got another Dr Pepper?'

'Help yourself!' Luke hits 'play'. 'So you already know the synth-riff that's opening the track. I did process it a little, however. It sounds like an old Juno synthesiser but actually it is an Access Virus TI programmed via the virtual instrument plug-in. I started with a square wave, reduced it to 8 bit, played around with the equalisers, added a 42 ms delay and finally used some compression to make it stand out in the mix. I played the dyads in a wide position, 'cause that sounds tighter, more distinct. I also tried full chords but with the delay and everything the sound is full enough anyway. Triads tended to sound a bit mushy. In the stereo field you can hear the upper voice more to the right, the lower is more to the left.'

Example 2.3 'Tik Tok', bars 1–8, 0:00–0:16

'And why does it sound so wobbly?'

'There's a vibrato effect on both voices. On the upper one the effect is rather strong, 30 per cent detuning both up and down with a frequency of only 8 Hz. It supports the impression of a cheap arcade game sound. Makes it more lively and colourful. – And I spent quite some time to get the rhythm right. First, I played those three strokes at the beginning as triplets, but that sounded too comfy, somehow laid back and too smooth. By using these dotted eighth notes we get some tricky syncopation. The main accents are on the first and *seventh* sixteenth note, which is quite unusual. Sounds edgy, very driving and active, doesn't it?'

'Totally.'

'But I don't want listeners to get accustomed to that irritating sixteenth off-beat and that's why the bars alternatively begin either with or without an *eighth*-note pickup. And you would expect the two D notes at the end of bar 2 and 4 to appear on the two last eighth notes of each bar. Instead, I put them on the 11th and 14th sixteenth note. Thus, nothing appears on its proper position. That's what makes it driving, varied and interesting. Or do you think that's all too quirky?'

'No No No, I like it that way. – But do I have to sing these complicated rhythms or can I sing in even eighth notes?'

'We'll think about that later. Maybe the contrast between even vocals and irregular synth can make it even more captivating. – Another thing: if I understood you correctly, this song is about moments in which you just don't care what time it is. So it is about freeing yourself from the clock … making your own life tick – and if you think about it that means liberation from social expectations, from the demands of your boss and from bourgeois notions of order in general. This is exactly what this rhythm does right from the start: it overrides your ordinary sense of time. Both, the order of the hand on your watch and the common four-four metre lose their authority. Instead, this song follows its own crooked time, at least at the beginning. Nothing conforms to the rules.'

'Oh, will you stop your philosophical blah blah! I wanna make people dance and enjoy themselves – not think!'

'I'm sorry, it was just an idea … – So did you notice that little melodic variation I built in? In every second iteration of the riff there's an A instead of the D listeners have become used to, just for the sake of variation. And as we talked about on Friday the song's gonna start without an instrumental intro. You begin singing immediately, right over this part. The focus is not on the music; it's all about you and your message. Imagine this being played on the radio: you recognize the song right from the start – and the DJs won't be able to keep on yapping while your song starts.'

'That's hot!'

'At the beginning there aren't any beats yet; it's just you and the synth. If this is playing in the club everybody will immediately know what it is, and run to the dance floor. – Then in the last bar of this intro there's this sudden break – the synth stops and it's only your voice that's left. To be honest, I just forgot to delete the eighth-note pickup in the bar before – now it's hanging there all alone, without the expected notes following. But it sounds pretty cool and striking that way, doesn't it? I think I'll keep it in.'

'Definitely! Otherwise it would get boring.'

'Next, of course, the beat sets in. Its entry has an even stronger dynamic effect because of the previous breakdown. I'm looping the same synth-riff as before; however, I increased the treble of the upper synth voice, just to give it a bit more presence and to vary the sound a bit.'

'Yeah, I noticed that.'

'I worked on those beats all through the night. Actually, I asked Benny Blanco to help me with that. We tried more than a hundred analogue bass drum samples from my library. What sounds like a single mega phat monster kick is in fact built up from five different ones: each has been filtered in a way that only a small frequency range is left and then we layered one above the other and adjusted them on the time grid. Plus we compressed them, of course. No single bass drum can ever sound wicked like that. First, it's slightly restrained but in the chorus it comes in with full force.'

'Phat!'

'And the snare sounds are not half bad either! Just listen to the first few bars after the drums come in! – Instead of a snare we put some handclaps on the second quarter note. Everything below 440 Hz has been filtered out, then we added compression and a 160 ms reverb. In every odd bar the claps are answered by a low, dry snare drum on the second backbeat. And only in every other bar there's a real splashing snare with a short 50 ms delay effect. We put that one both to the far left and far right of the stereo panorama to give it more punch and distinction while the claps are always right in the middle. Add to that a darting synth glissando on every first and fourth sixteenth beat. It took ages of fumbling to construct each of these sounds and to perfect the resulting texture! But that's what makes the difference.'

Example 2.4 'Tik Tok', bars 9–14, 0:16–0:28

'So for the beginning I built an asymmetrical, kinda halting rhythm: the kick is not on the usual downbeats but on the first and then advanced, on the *fourth* eighth note. First, because it parallels the off-beat of the synth and, second, because this gives us the possibility to cut it loose when the chorus starts. It's like going with the handbrake on in the verse and then going full force, with the bass drum on every quarter note, in the chorus. – And it's the same after the chorus, only slightly varied: in the second verse we're returning to a lower energy level but we're not cutting it down to zero. In order to keep people dancing the kick drum continues its four-to-the-floor beat. But to keep it from getting boring this time I added some very low, noisy strokes on every first and fourth eighth note. They seem to be in the background because there's reverb on it. In addition, the darting synth glissandi I used in the first pre-chorus reappear. This time however, they're not heard throughout but only in every second bar.'

'Reminds me of the noise my cell phone makes when the battery's dying.'

'When we get to the second pre-chorus the four-to-the-floor kick from the verse continues. But now it's combined with a low tom stroke on the fourth sixteenth note, with a backbeat on the snare drum and some off-beat hi-hats. And I added a weird little "beep" sound from the synth. Listen!'

Example 2.5 'Tik Tok', bars 41–6, 1:20–1:32

'Awesome! – But why are you calling it pre-chorus? I only gave you four verses ...'

'Yeah, but because it's always two verses following each other I wanted the second one to differ. That's why the beats change slightly and why there's a pause right before the chorus just like in the intro. And then it needed a new chord at the end because some tension has to be built up before the chorus kicks in. You don't have any tension if the verse ends on B flat and the chorus starts on B flat. So instead of B flat major I played G minor right before that little break. And, voila, these little changes turn this verse into a proper pre-chorus! I've already got some ideas for some far out special effects on your vocals to make 'em stand out in this little solo spot.'

'Can't wait to hear it!'

'Just let me continue to show you what kind of beats I used in the chorus. We don't need that halting effect there, of course. So there's a rolling and pounding combination of kick and snare drum. But that's not all. Listen to this!'

Example 2.6 'Tik Tok', bars 17–32, 0:32–1:04

Chorus 4x 4x

'At first glance it's only your standard backbeat. But again, there are many details to keep it fresh and attractive: first, I added some restrained hi-hats on every quarter note and included the additional tom stroke on the fourth eighth note again which makes for a nice combination of the syncopated synthesiser rhythm and the backbeat of the drums. And don't you think that the snare sounds are all the same! No, they're heavier than in the sections before 'cause I gave them some more bass. In addition, the snare sounds vary: the strokes on 2 have a 90 ms reverb, the ones on 4 got 210 ms which gives them more punch and which invigorates the whole beat. To gain even more momentum in the second half of the chorus the steady hi-hats get replaced by a syncopated, hi-energy disco-like tambourine sound. Sounds really propulsive! Last but not least this off-beat is picked up by a high A5 from the synth that's played on every second eighth note. It's slightly detuned and sounds a bit like this machine they have in operating rooms.'

'It's awesome, makes me wanna da-ance!'

'Go ahead! – What I'm particularly proud of are the synth tracks in the chorus. They're based on the riff from the beginning but this time they're not harmonised in thirds. Instead I only played the roots and doubled them one or sometimes even two octaves lower. Furthermore, the notes are not played in the same register but they slide up and down all the time. These jumps are so full of energy 'cause they're so wide and quick. And they reach out higher and higher: in the last bar they cover a range from G2 to C6!

'The upbeat sixteenth notes in every other bar add even more energy. So regarding the beats, the range and absolute pitch the chorus is clearly the climax of the song – just as it's supposed to be. This also true for the density of the texture. I even programmed some ultra rapid outbursts *within* the notes. On the first beat of the fourth bar of the chorus for example, the tone shoots up and down again in only 130 ms. Sounds a bit like a DJ scratching his records. Totally synthetic, hyperactive and freaky. You can't play anything like that on a traditional instrument. Or listen to those sudden dives starting on B6 on the last quarter notes of bars 7 and 8. And did you notice how I mixed it? The synth is to the far left and right, the beats are dead center. This way they don't compete for aural space and you can hear every little bit of it.'

Example 2.7 'Tik Tok', bars 17–32, 0:32–1:04

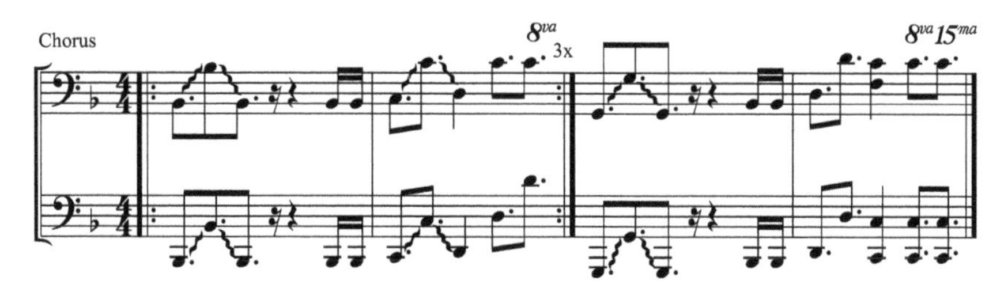

'And that's not all! In the second half of the chorus I added some extra synth chords to beef up the texture.'

Example 2.8 'Tik Tok', bars 25–32, 0:48–1:04

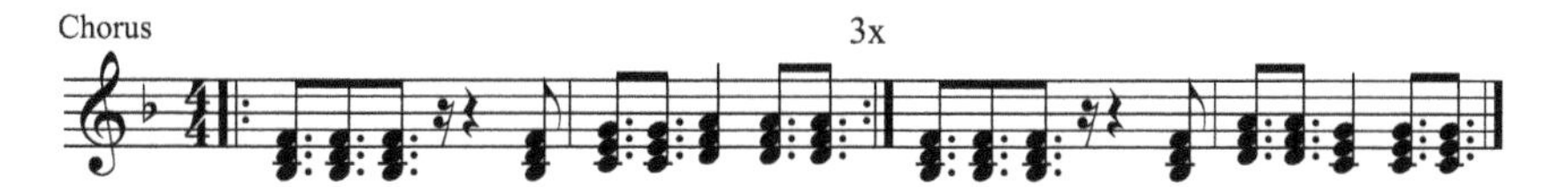

'All those different accents that go on at the same time add up to quite a crazy groove. If this doesn't make you dance you must be dead.'

Example 2.9 'Tik Tok', rhythmical structure of bars 25–6, 0:48–0:52

'So that was the chorus. Now follows the bridge that I just had to include. Otherwise the song would have been too short cuz we have no intro and no instrumental sections whatsoever. After the second iteration of the chorus we have to present something fresh to keep them awake. So I came up with this breakdown: the energy decreases, the beats pause completely. Suddenly all that's left is your voice and these soft synth pads. Unlike before the chords change only once every bar. And in contrast to the rest of the song they change on the "one" instead of on some irregular sixteenth note. No more syncopation, time to relax and for the dancing crowd to draw a breath.'

Example 2.10 'Tik Tok', bars 65–80, 2:09–2:40

Bridge 1, 2, 3. 4.

'And what am I supposed to sing here?'

'Well, rapping would be too hectic, of course. We will need some more lyrics, maybe something where you refer to the dancers in the club directly. Get a clue! –

If you listen to the chords, you'll notice something new is happening. Well, not really. The chords are the same but now they're sequenced differently: B flat major, G minor, D minor and C major. In this sequence there's always at least one note that doesn't change. That's why we need the suspended fourth in bar 4, by the way. The result is quieter and much less dynamic than before where subsequent chords didn't share any notes and where the chords always ascended without ever reaching any goal. In this section there are no dominant/tonic-relationships to be found and thus you somehow get lost, you don't know for sure where you're at home – harmonically speaking. But of course this is only the calm before the storm and everything gradually builds up again: the filters slowly open and the treble on the synth increases more and more – everything lightens again just like the sun going up or recharging your batteries. Starting with bar 2 you can hear a little hissing noise that runs backwards. It's on every beat just like that synthetic beep that comes in in bar 4. The kick drum re-enters in bar 9 and you can hear a very restrained snare with a low-pass filter on the backbeats beginning with bar 13. One more general rest – and here we go for the final chorus! This is of course where even more has to be happening – rhythm- and soundwise. New snare sounds and a whole bunch of little noises and beeps. A shower of confetti!'

'I'm thrilled! It's unbelievable how much work went into this. You've really done a world class job here, Luke! But … do you really think this is all necessary, those zillions of details? I mean, you really need headphones to notice 'em.'

'Sure, you only catch the tip of the iceberg when you're listening to it on the radio. But if you go to a well-equipped club or if you're listening on your iPhone like most people do these days then you'll get some new bits and pieces with every listen. I promise it won't get boring! And in the end it is all those little details that make the difference. It's a production like this that lets it stand out.'

'I see.'

'What's important for me when I'm producing stuff for the teenager market is that there needs to be something new happening all the time. You need to grab their attention, you need constant change and constant intensification – otherwise they'll lose interest and turn away. Our song will be in competition with thousands of other distractions and people's attention spans seem to get shorter and shorter. So you have to work hard to keep them in line. You need to offer some ear candy, that's what it is! – Additionally, all those little rhythmical details are important to produce a tight groove. And this is nothing you hear consciously. The groove will go straight into your legs and make 'em move – at least when it's programmed the right way. Most of it happens subconsciously.'

'Awesome!'

'Just wait until the mastering is finished. This is when everything will be polished and all the details can be heard more distinctively using more equalisers, limiters, maximisers, multiband compression …'

'Stop it. You're a crazy nerd! I don't even wanna hear of it, don't understand it anyway. The main point is that it sounds great. And you've definitely done a fantastic job here! But now I wanna record the vocals!'

***

'One more time? Really? I must have sung it six times already! There should be one useful take among them. Or just finally tell me what I'm doing wrong all the time!'

'No No, Kesha, you're doing fine! You get across the feeling really well: it sounds cheeky, self-assured, dynamic, vivacious and with ease. I just need all these different takes to tinker with. Tonight I'm gonna listen to all the tracks very closely and I'll reassemble the best parts to create the lead track. Like the first four syllables from take 1, then two words from take 5 and then some more from take 3 ... That's how I'll get the best results. For the chorus I will need at least two lead tracks on top of each other anyway to make it sound fuller and more powerful. And it's no problem if your timing is not perfect. I'm using this software called VocAlign. It identifies rhythmical differences between the tracks and automatically aligns them. Same with the pitch: if it's not perfect we'll auto-tune it. However, slightly different nuances in timing and intonation are in fact necessary to invigorate the sound. Sometimes I even detune the vocals I've recorded a tiny bit just to get this effect. Makes it richer and livelier, especially in the chorus. Therefore: please try again. We need another take of the pre-chorus!'

Example 2.11 'Tik Tok', bars 9–11, 0:16–0:22

'OK, that's fine. By the way, I like this contrast between the fast sixteenth and those long accented quarter notes. Not least because we mainly have strings of eighth notes in the verse.'

'Yeah, that way it's building up energy and quickening the pace towards the chorus. But do you really think it's a good idea to double all those words at the end? Phones, phones, toes, toes, clothes, clothes ... I'm not sure. They don't even rhyme properly!'

'Even if it makes you feel stupid now: these are hooks! These repetitions will stick in peoples' minds like glue. Imagine how a bunch of girls sings this part all together in the schoolyard or on the PlayStation! To make this part stand out

I'll arrange some of your vocal tracks to form some background chants. If there are many voices repeating these words people will feel encouraged to sing along as well. Just like in hip hop, they often double the last words of a line with two rappers. And then I'll put the lead vocal to the centre and the backing vocals to the left and right with some reverb. That'll make it sound like a whole gang of girls singing those words.'

'Yeah, that's good. For the same reason I tried to include the words "we" and "our" as often as possible: "our phones", "our clothes", "our CDs", "we got swagger", "shut us down" and so on. It creates a sense of togetherness, like, "together we're strong, we don't need to hide". So, yeah, make me sound like a whole gang!'

'Sure. In the second pre-chorus we can turn it around: the clique sings the words first and then you repeat them alone – By now you know how I love these variations ...'

'You're so crazy! Wait, I'll drink something and then we can proceed to record the chorus. You said I should sing it higher, like mainly on F4?'

'Right. It's always good to sing the chorus higher than the other sections because it makes the chorus stand out and increases the emotional intensity. But Kesha, are you really sure about the melody? Almost everything is on the same pitch except for little steps to G and D? That's not exactly what song-writing guidebooks teach you.'

'Who cares? This way everybody can join in. And a huge anthem-like melodic arch wouldn't really fit the song, would it? The chorus already has so many different rhythmic accents in the synth and the beats. I think we need a very simple vocal melody! Give the melodic stuff with a wide range to Katy – she's the better singer anyway!'

'If you think so ... The good thing about it is that you can concentrate on the stage choreography when you're doing it live. You'll manage those few notes even doing the wildest dance moves. Besides, I'll pimp it out with some effects to make it more interesting. Like delay ... we haven't used any delay yet! That's very fitting when you're singing about time and clocks. If you set it right a delay will remind you of the seconds hand and delay really shows you how time moves with the repetitions fading away ... For the second and third chorus we'll need some harmony vocals to enrich the sound and to achieve the effect of a whole gang singing. So I'll need several takes. Let's go!'

Example 2.12 'Tik Tok', bars 17–24, 0:32–0:48

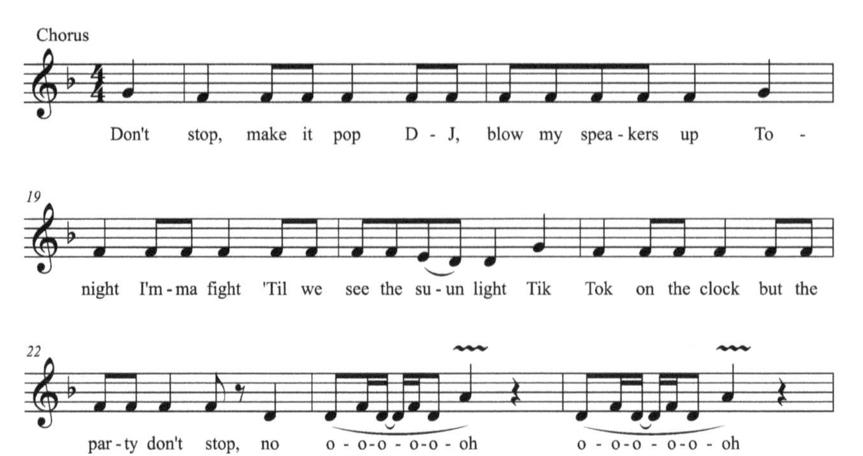

'The "o-o-o-o-o-oh" at the end is just perfect, Kesha! It's worth a mint, I mean, literally! This is the hook that clings to your ear and that will come back to you in your sleep. Take my word! Its rhythm is really interesting and the A4 at the end is the highest note you sing in the whole song. That will attract attention, of course. Very good idea, Kesha!'

'Yeah, thank you. It's hard for everyone who writes lyrics but what sticks and what people tend to sing along with are always these nonsense syllables. It's always been like that: "A-wop-bob-a-loo-bop, a-lop-bam-boom," "Yeah Yeah Yeah," the "naaa-naa-naa-na-na-na-na" at the end of "Hey Jude," the "lie-la-lie" in this Simon & Garfunkel song, Axl's "ay ay ay ay" in "Knockin' On Heaven's Door" …'

'They're not as easy to come up with as one might think.'

'So what are we gonna do with the bridge, Luke? Did you see the lyrics that I added for that section?'

'Sure, they're perfect! It's a declaration of love to the man with his fingers on the faders, I like that of course, he he.'

'Dream on! Well, you said that everything should relax in the bridge. So I came up with the idea to sing these short melodic phrases that are always falling to the root note – doesn't that have a calming effect?'

'Yes, sure. But please try to give it a different emotional expression. Less aggressive, maybe a bit exhausted, relaxed – and carrying a torch for the DJ …'

'I'll try – but forget about the last thing!'

'OK, let's try the bridge again.'

Example 2.13 'Tik Tok', bars 65–8, 2:09–2:16

'That's it, Kesha, excellent! All that's left to do is recording harmony vocals for the final chorus.'

'And then we're done?'

'Then *you're* done. For me, the real work starts now. You can't imagine how much work it'll be to produce the final vocal tracks. I've got to listen closely to all you've recorded in the last two hours, find the best parts, edit them, adjust them, equalise and compress them, mix them and all that stuff. And then I've got some very special ideas …'

'Like what?'

'Well the day after tomorrow P. Diddy booked the studio upstairs. I'm gonna ask him if he would be so kind to record two or three interjections for the intro – the part where you mention his name in the lyrics. That would surely provide some extra attention for the single.'

'Hey that's really phat. What a fantastic idea! Tell him I said hi!'

'And then, there are these one-bar pauses right before the choruses. In the first one, where you sing "tipsy" I want to apply a tape stop effect. You know, like slowing down an old reel-to-reel machine? Or I'm gonna use some psychedelic effects, something that sounds drunk or trippy. Same for the line "police shut us down", we need something special there as well. And then I'm gonna use some auto-tune.'

'Really? Why? Didn't I sing in tune?'

'No no, you're perfect! I don't use it for pitch correction but for special effects. *You* wanted it to sound artificial and modern, you wanted something for the kids that scares off their parents. That's exactly what auto-tune is for. I'm gonna make it sound as artificial as that Dr Pepper stuff you're drinking all the time. Don't be afraid, I only use it at a few selected spots to fly the freak flag. I don't want it to be annoying. Just like I used those mini scratches on the synth.'

'I definitely like artifice; I don't want to have anything to do with that authenticity crap. I'm not planning to sit on a barstool with an acoustic guitar and a buckskin jacket, singing about my ex. May Taylor Swift keep on doing that!'

'That's what I thought you would say.'

***

Friday, 11 p.m., Osteria La Buca, 5210 Melrose Ave., Los Angeles, CA

'So, Kesha, I spoke with that woman from RCA records this afternoon and she insisted that we change the title. No way we're calling it "P. Diddy". People might have problems finding it on YouTube and iTunes. They might end up buying P. Diddy's songs instead. Or maybe he would sue us for royalties. She might be right, whaddaya think?'

'I thought it was funny and would get us some attention. But why not call it "Tik Tok"? That's the obvious choice; it's easy to remember, it's international and you'll find it on YouTube.'

'Then let's have a toast for "Tik Tok"! May it hit the top, may people get crazy for it, and may it make us rich, he he!'

'Yeah, let's drink to "Tik Tok"!' Both of them clink their champagne glasses.

'What's your gut feeling, Luke? Is this gonna be a hit? Do you know it ahead of time? Did you know it when you finished producing "I Kissed a Girl"?'

'Yes, this is gonna be a big one! My guts are not always right but by and large I know what's gonna work and what isn't. This song is good, your performance is good and Benny and me did what we could production-wise. To me it sounds very, very promising. I played it to my little cousin to put it to a test – she thought it was awesome and wanted to keep a copy!'

'Well that's how I feel about it, too. But on the other hand I'm afraid that it flops and nobody cares for it at all! I mean, summer's in full swing, it's pretty late for a summer hit. Somewhere I've read that September is the month in which the fewest singles are sold.'

'Just rely on the quality of our work!'

'Honestly? Are you really that optimistic and think that quality will come out on top? Most of the time people turn their back on the good stuff and run after the crap. Besides, I'm not really sure about the lyrics. You need to be in the right mood for them. "Don't stop, make it pop, Tik Tok, on the clock" – sounds pretty gaga if you think about it. Not exactly Walt Whitman or Bob Dylan …'

'So what? Nobody listens to the lyrics anyway. Or can you remember the last time a Bob Dylan single appeared in the top ten? What's number one right now? "Boom Boom Pow"! Or: "I gotta feeling/That tonight's gonna be a good night." Songs have words to give people something to relate to and spark some associations. You only pick up one phrase or another and your imagination starts running wild. This song just conveys a cheerful atmosphere and a positive self-esteem. And who doesn't have some demand for that? You might use it to escape from a bad time you're havin', or to remember the good old days; you might use it to hype yourself up for the weekend or you just dance to it on a Saturday night … You don't have to be ashamed of the lyrics, they're not supposed to be poetry.'

'Well, thank you. But neither is the melody, like … Mozart and stuff. It's only five notes!'

'Come on, that's fine. That's why anybody can join in! Pop songs are not about utilising the most chords. Nobody wants to listen to jazz anymore! We focus on *sound production* instead. That's what takes most of the work and where the most interesting stuff happens. We want to make the dance-floor tremble and we want the kids to identify with your persona ... – so ... a video clip would be very useful ...'

'Of course. But they said they would only pay for it if the downloads in the first two weeks are promising and if the radios add it to heavy rotation.'

'Fair enough, Kesha. Videos are extremely expensive and the companies have become really careful. That's why they publish debut singles as download only, 'cause that reduces the financial risk. Being an established producer I'll make sure that my work is paid for properly. Benny and me are gonna get a nice six-figure sum for that job. I've had number one hits with Kelly Clarkson in February, with FloRida in March ... Your advance however won't be that exorbitant. If the song doesn't gross enough to meet the production costs then that's it for you. You'll owe money to *them*! But as you've written the lyrics you'll at least get royalties every time the song gets airplay.'

'And how do we get the song on the radio?'

'That's the promo department's job, they have their own staff for radio promotion. If those guys get some encouraging feedback from the clubs and if they believe in your song they'll find a way to get the song on air. Believe me, those folks at the radio, they enjoy their lives. They always did. I've heard some rumours about very expensive dinner invitations or free coke or getting invited to a "listening party" on a luxury yacht over the weekend ... I mean, sure, record companies don't have that much money to spend nowadays. But the radio people are the most important gatekeepers. If you want a number one hit you'll need to be played on the radio first! Otherwise it's all in vain. Except you're big on YouTube – but then you need a video clip ...'

'Wow, I didn't know that ... Well, I already had to learn the hard way that I won't be able to make a living with the music that I really love. By the way, did you know that I started out busking in Nashville? Like, the real thing, playing guitar, this harmonica thing 'round my neck and a hat for the money? "I've been to Hollywood/I've been to Redwood/I crossed the ocean for a heart of gold ..." I can still do that, see? I've always sung that one with my Mum and my sister. And now I'm sitting here in Hollywood myself ... and still I'm flat broke. Earning some real money would be sweet! Eh, thanks for the dinner, by the way.'

'No prob. I'm sure you're gonna make it, Kesha. I'll keep working at that. First you had this little scene in Katy's video, then the mega hit with FloRida – that got your name and face well known already. Now the radio hosts and the journalists have a little story to tell when they introduce your song: "The girl you know from 'Right Round' – now presenting her own debut single!" – And we can use that Nashville story for the press kit, it's good! I know a good copywriter, he'll write a nice CV for the kit and the website. People need a little story linked to you. And then you'll pee into the sink backstage at some award show. This will make for a little scandal that will get you into every newspaper and every blog. Then you'll officially apologise on Twitter, which will get you a million followers for free … That's how it goes. Cheers!'

Reflection: How Can Pop Songs be 'Understood' Anyway?

In a way, analysis is synthesis turned backwards. When we try to understand a piece of music, we often imagine how the people involved came to the decisions that lead to the final product rather than choosing different options. At least for some of the questions an artwork poses we believe that the artists have the answers. However, even if the artists were willing and able to disclose all their thoughts, intentions and motivations, there would still be no guarantee that they mean what they say, that their memory serves them well, that they were fully understanding what they were doing in the first place nor that their own interpretation didn't change over time. In addition, it is highly improbable that everybody involved in the making shares the same ideas about their creation. Nevertheless, the 'author's intention' remains a vital construct that many people turn to – though what is believed to refer to something objective might in fact tell more about the interpreter himself.

To broach the issues of subjectivity vs objectivity, interpretation vs understanding and reading vs ascribing of meaning I chose to change the perspective and present my analysis as a fly on the wall at 'Tik Tok''s creation. It is obviously fiction – although, on the other hand, it's not less the result of thorough research than a 'proper' analysis would have been (see the last part of this reflection for information about sources and methodology).

But first, the notion of regarding pop songs as art and the aims of their analysis need some reconsideration. Many analyses treat pop songs as meaningful works of art – and rightly so, as for example the chapters on songs by PJ Harvey, Fleet Foxes and Death Cab for Cutie in this collection show. However, the strong academic interest in the intricacies of immanent meaning has often left open the question of how to make sense of songs that have less ambition to be regarded as art. By choosing 'Tik Tok', the best-selling single worldwide in 2010, I tried to figure out how we can deal with songs that many people love to listen to 'just for fun'. Though if they are heard 'just for fun' – then why analyse them in the first place? What's the musicologist's business here? What is there to be understood?

If a musicologist considers herself not only in charge of 'high art', she might impartially study what it is that attracts listeners and what kinds of functions songs fulfil for them. What kind of reception does the music provoke and which reactions are rather unlikely? How do the songs accomplish what they are supposed to? Why do they sound the way they sound? Unless proven otherwise, we should suppose that the music is *not* interchangeable and that it's not only the lyrics, the public image or the video clip but also the actual sounds that play an essential role in how people react to songs, why they dance or sing along, chose songs to represent their identity and so forth. I shall illustrate this shortly (see Appen, 2007a; 2007b for a more detailed discussion).

A first important function of pop songs is to temporarily relieve people from being bound to the routines of everyday life. For three and a half minutes 'Tik Tok' does everything to grab your attention in order to make you forget what you've just been up to and to give yourself over to its own time and space. The everyday uses of our senses – to provide information and guide us through our day – take a back seat as our attention focuses on what is happening in the words and the sounds. Like playing a game, watching TV, having sex or doing sports, listening to 'Tik Tok' lets us concentrate on the very present, and thus forget about any worries about the future or past. This can only succeed if listening neither feels like work nor gets boring. That is why within the song's effortlessly palatable structure there is a growing and constantly changing fireworks of sonic events coming up. Producer Lukasz Gottwald comments on his work correspondingly: 'In the songs I produce I try to make it sound interesting, you know, I try to keep new elements coming in all the time, so it's just ear candy, basically' (see footnote 3, page 49, and page 50). Not only the sound production but also the rhythmic structure has been designed to demand attention and thus hijack listeners from their daily routines. The punch of the bass drum and the interwoven rhythmical netting are supposed to take command over your body and make you dance. The same goes for the melodies: they aim at seducing you to sing along and thus to completely arrest your attention as well. By these means 'Tik Tok' manages to lure its listeners into a different world. For three and a half minutes they are happy to give themselves over to the control of the song. Surrendering like that can, paradoxically, evoke a sense of freedom; freedom, that is, from anything else. This is part of what 'Tik Tok' is all about.

A second function pop songs can fulfil is to positively influence the listeners' mood. 'Tik Tok''s rhythms and melodies are set out to have a positively activating effect. The interplay of all the features outlined above has the potential to convey a party atmosphere. Depending on your personal and cultural disposition as well as your current spirits you may characterise the song as being full of energy, freaky, juvenile, modern, cheeky – or simply annoying. If you are inclined to feel like any of this, you may want to play 'Tik Tok' to evoke a corresponding atmosphere to reflect or even boost these emotions. This is part of what 'Tik Tok' is about as well.

Closely linked to this is a third function. People do not only play pop songs to reflect how they feel in a particular moment but also to express who they are (or want to be) in general. For a young female listener for instance who wants to be seen (or sees herself) as a perky, urban, attractive party girl 'Tik Tok' can serve this purpose. The song's confidence projects onto her own self-image, first boosting it, then helping to present it to others when she listens in public. A 30-year-old heterosexual man might on the other hand conceal his fondness for the song as a guilty pleasure and rather not sing along in his open convertible nor play it when his buddies come over to watch the ball game. Sharing the same music preferences strengthens the feeling of togetherness. At the same time we use music to deliberately distinguish ourselves from others. Hence, teenagers might play 'Tik Tok' to show that they don't have anything in common with the Taylor Swift fans in class. In this manner music adds to our self-concept and plays a part in defining ourselves within society. This is another part of what 'Tik Tok' is about.

Fourth, just like any other piece of art we can interpret 'Tik Tok' regarding the view of the world that it presents. The way all its musical and lyrical parameters communicate can evoke a persona characterised in manifold ways (see Moore, 2012, Chapter 7). It can lead us to imagine how the life depicted in the song might feel like and to compare this to our own values and outlooks – or as David Byrne of the Talking Heads has put it nicely:

> Music, and I'm not even talking about the lyrics here, tells us how other people view the world – people we have never met, sometimes people who are no longer alive – and it tells it in a non-descriptive way. Music *embodies* the way those people think and feel: we enter into new worlds – their worlds – and though our perception of those worlds might not be 100 percent accurate, encountering them can be completely transformative. (Byrne, 2012, p. 94)

One should, however, realise that the world 'Tik Tok' depicts is in all probability a very artificial one that does not necessarily have anything in common with the real life of Kesha Sebert. The song is credited to three authors (Kesha and producers Gottwald and Blanco) who have very different biographical backgrounds; other people involved had an influence on the final product as well. It surely was not their highest aim to paint a realistic picture of their own views and experiences but to create a product that gets as much airplay as possible, that many people are willing to spend money for and, thus, to deliver work that will foster their further careers. Therefore, 'Tik Tok' conveys an idealised vision rather than a realistic individual experience ('ain't got no care in the world, but got plenty of beer'). Nevertheless this *does* tell us something – although it reveals more about the (assumed) wishes and needs of the listeners than about the inner life of its creators.

A further level of understanding – one that is in most cases not intended by the authors – deals with the question of how pop hits reflect current developments in culture and society. An answer with regard to 'Tik Tok' can only be touched on very superficially here as analyses like these should never rely on one song alone. Considering Billboard's (or German Media Control's) top hits of the early twenty-first century it shows that 'Tik Tok''s topic is in no way exceptional. The lyrics, music and video clips of a large body of songs like 'Get the Party Started' (Pink, 2001), 'Bad Influence' (Pink, 2009), 'Just Dance' (Lady Gaga, 2008), 'I Gotta Feeling' (Black Eyed Peas, 2009), 'Danza Kuduro' (Lucenzo feat. Don Omar, 2010), 'Last Friday Night' (Katy Perry, 2010), 'Dynamite' (Taio Cruz, 2010), 'Hangover' (Taio Cruz, 2010), 'Party Rock Anthem' (L.M.F.A.O., 2011) or 'Don't Wanna Go Home' (Jason Derulo, 2011) promote hedonism, individualism, physical attraction, luxury, big egos, getting blasted on weekends and rather conventional heteronormative gender stereotypes. Thus, they are presumably reflecting the ideals and yearnings of today's US teenagers or what the major concerns of the entertainment industries try to sell as such. That might be valid from an economic point of view but in sum it endorses highly questionable ethics: the life that speaks from these songs is a never-ending party full of winners where everybody is concerned with nothing but his own fortune. Social responsibility, worries about the future, protest against the status quo or support for social movements are neither cool nor sexy and thus, not surprisingly, rarely topics of chart-topping hits.

Getting finally back to the issue of subjectivity vs. objectivity: to understand a piece of music from an academic point of view cannot mean being able to formulate or even prove any 'true' meaning. There is no 'complete understanding' as all our readings are necessarily interpretations influenced by our cultural and individual backgrounds. And yet, this subjectivity does not imply that our interpretations are arbitrary, as long as they are relating to the piece's features. What musicologists *can* aim to understand is why people react to it in certain ways. If an analysis considers both, musical structures and socio-cultural contexts, it can help us understand our own and other listeners' responses.

Sources and Methods

Telling the story from the creators' point of view made it impractical to give any references in the text. So I will quickly supply them separately to allow the reader to reconstruct the validity of the analysis.

First of all, focusing on Lukasz 'Dr. Luke' Gottwald as the mastermind behind 'Tik Tok' seems justified: whereas Ke$ha[2] has not yet been able to follow up on the enormous success of her debut single, Gottwald has been writing and producing many more hits since 2010. Songs he recorded with Taio Cruz ('Dynamite', 'Hangover') and Katy Perry ('California Gurls', 'Teenage Dream', 'Firework', 'E.T.', 'Last Friday Night', 'Part Of Me') all topped the Billboard Top 100. Gottwald has been awarded 'Songwriter of the Year' (Billboard 2009, ASCAP 2010 and 2011) and 'Producer of the Year' (Billboard 2009). I was not able to identify the exact input of co-producer and co-author Benjamin Levin (aka Benny Blanco) with whom Gottwald frequently joins forces. For the song's analysis, however, it's not crucial to know which producer came up with which idea.

To understand how Dr Luke works it has been very helpful to watch clips from the master sessions he gave at conferences of the US performance-rights organisation ASCAP in 2010[3] and 2011.[4] In the former clip he concretely talks about the creation of 'Tik Tok': about recording and editing a large number of vocal tracks and using the VocAlign plug-in (at 1:14 and from 5:27), about basic

---

[2] I am spelling her name with the '$' sign when I am talking about her as a mediatised brand and a simple 's' when referring to Kesha Sebert as a human being.

[3] http://www.youtube.com/watch?v=uNI1qvXU6f.Y ('Lukasz "Dr. Luke" Gottwald: 2010 ASCAP "I Create Music" Expo (Master Session)', accessed 22 August 2013).

[4] http://www.youtube.com/watch?v=AWVJkokLbzQ ('Dr. Luke Shares Music and Production Tips at ASCAP "I Create Music" EXPO [2011]', accessed 22 August 2013).

ideas that guided working on the song (from 2:02), about the process of song-writing and Kesha's input (from 3:50), about P. Diddy's injections and the fact that the song had actually been called 'P. Diddy' for a long time before the record label intervened (from 4:49). This clip also contains the 'ear candy' quotation (see p. 47, at 7:10) from which this chapter takes its title. In the 2011 master session Gottwald demonstrates how he programs bass drum sounds (at 1:46). A third ASCAP session[5] and a short TV feature[6] provided further insight about his equipment and the way he works.

An instrumental version of unknown origin that is available online made it easier to identify many details of the production without the vocals overshadowing them.[7] The Sonic Visualiser software was used to reduce the tempo and provide spectrogram visualisations of both versions. Furthermore, it was instructive to listen to some amateurs' attempts to recreate the synthesiser sounds of 'Tik Tok' with their own equipment.[8] Differences between their versions and the original made it easier to precisely describe the sounds. The same goes for a commercially distributed karaoke version[9] as well as clips of live performances by Ke$ha herself.[10] The musicologist, producer and songwriter Frank Riedemann pointed out some features of the production to me that I would otherwise have ignored. Insights into the financial background of today's hit singles are offered in a report by the National Public Radio (Chace, 2012). Information on Ke$ha and the public image she tries to convey has been taken from her homepage.[11] For those who want to research Ke$ha's well-publicised urge to relieve herself into basins not designed for that function, the rich resources of the Internet will provide them with sufficient references.[12]

---

5 http://www.youtube.com/watch?v=CERtLdq_BHU&feature=related ('Dr. Luke Mastering Session 2011 ASCAP Expo', accessed 22 August 2013).

6 http://www.youtube.com/watch?v=KhNGU_ujT10&feature=related ('Artist Interview – Dr. Luke' [abc news.com], accessed 22 August 2013).

7 http://www.youtube.com/watch?v=ycFw9ko-Dqc ('Ke$ha – Tik Tok Instrumental (Regular)', uploaded by 'bluntbeast' on 23 November 2009, accessed 21 March 2012).

8 http://audio.tutsplus.com/tutorials/production/quick-tip-how-to-create-the-lead-sound-from-kehas-tik-tok/ ('Quick Tip: How to Create the Lead Sound from Ke$ha's "Tik Tok"', accessed 22 August 2013) and http://www.youtube.com/watch?v=nqymEUCucdo ('Logic Pro Tutorial – Ke$ha Tik Tok Lead Synth HowTo', accessed 21 March 2012).

9 http://www.karaoke-version.de/custombackingtrack/kesha/tik-tok.html [Accessed 22 August 2013].

10 http://www.youtube.com/watch?v=rKM9YyjiWh8 ('Ke$ha – TiK ToK (Live at 2010 ECHO Awards', accessed 22 August 2013) and http://www.youtube.com/watch?v=GDvwZGIGs-Q ('Ke$ha – Tik Tok (Rock in Rio 2011) – HDTV (1080i)', accessed 21 March 2012).

11 www.keshasparty.com [Accessed 21 March 2012].

12 See http://www.contactmusic.com/news/toilet-animal-kesha_1130363 and http://www.zimbio.com/Kesha/articles/qmskwdehPq4/Ke+ha+Explains+Relieved+Herself+Sink (both accessed 22 August 2013).

References

Appen, R. von, 2007a. On the Aesthetics of Popular Music, *Music Therapy Today*, 8(1), pp. 5–25, [online] Available at: http://www.wfmt.info/Musictherapyworld/modules/mmmagazine/issues/20070330122710/20070330122906/MTT8_1_vonAppen.pdf [Accessed 9 September 2013].

Appen, R. von, 2007b. *Der Wert der Musik. Zur Ästhetik des Populären*. Bielefeld: Transcript.

Byrne, D., 2012. *How Music Works*. Edinburgh: Canongate.

Chace, Z., 2012. *Katy Perry's Perfect Game*, npr – Planet Money. [podcast] 20 January 2012. Available at: http://www.npr.org/blogs/money/2012/01/20/145466007/katy-perrys-perfect-game [Accessed 22 August 2013].

Moore, A.F., 2012. *Song Means: Analysing and Interpreting Recorded Popular Song*. Farnham: Ashgate.

Discography

Ke$ha, 2009. 'Tik Tok'. *Tik Tok-EP*, iTunes Download (6.9MB, 256kBit/s, published 27 November).

Chapter 3
Metrical Ambiguity or Microrhythmic Flexibility? Analysing Groove in 'Nasty Girl' by Destiny's Child

Anne Danielsen

Traditionally, research into rhythm in groove-based music has concerned itself with issues of microtiming (understood as relationships between points in time), including attack points, durations and/or Inter-Onset-Intervals (IOI). Furthermore, the reference structures that have formed the basis for identifying microtiming – that is, for determining whether a beat is early or late – have been conceptualised as a given metric grid consisting of series of isochronous points in time. Microtiming has, accordingly, been regarded as a matter of *expression* rather than structure, probably because many researchers have not been able to move beyond the traditional divide between structure (notation) and expression (performance) in notation-based music. The word 'groove' itself directs our attention to some important limitations regarding such an approach. When used to denote a particular rhythmic pattern (a swing groove, a funk groove and so on), groove encompasses the particular prescribed *manner* in which this pattern should be played – that is, the timing as well as the sound and shape of the rhythmic events. Traditional analytical approaches also tend to neglect the fact that a groove is a temporal phenomenon. A second limitation thus concerns the temporal or, rather, experiential aspect of a groove. This is pertinent when the word groove is used in a normative manner to judge (in an aesthetic sense) the quality of a groove: a groove is not a groove until it *actually grooves*, and this cannot happen outside time. In short, groove is performed and unfolds in time.

In this chapter, I address these two important aspects of groove analysis through a discussion of the song 'Nasty Girl' by Destiny's Child (*Survivor*, 2001). First, I problematise the very notion that the metric norm for measuring microtiming deviations (the metric grid) is a given, showing instead that it is in fact a matter of artistic exploration. Second, I discuss how a particular micro-rhythmic design establishes itself as an important structural layer over the course of a song. I begin by presenting a theoretical framework for analysing rhythm in groove-based music that relies upon a notion of rhythm as an interaction between two analytically separable levels – virtual reference structures and actual sounds. Then I apply this framework to the groove in 'Nasty Girl', using both auditory analysis and various visual representations of sound, such as waveform curves and spectrograms, to explore the rhythmic design of the song in detail. I focus my analysis upon the ambiguities surrounding the virtual reference structures that are embedded in this particular groove. These ambiguities can be conceptualised in turn as belonging to three levels of virtual reference structure: basic pulse, stylistic figures and subdivisions. I discuss how the artists and producer of 'Nasty Girl' alter the experience of the song's basic rhythm from section to section by adjusting the balance between its various sounding rhythmic layers, thereby foregrounding particular reference structures at the expense of others. I pay particular attention to the role of the vocal parts in these rhythmic machinations, and more precisely how the vocals mediate between the different structural schemes, sometimes smoothing out the tension between them, sometimes tilting the overall rhythmic feel in the direction of a particular one. Ultimately, I demonstrate how some important experiential aspects of the groove are probably better understood in the context of a more holistic, gestural notion of rhythmic structure that, in parallel to the notion of groove itself, incorporates systematic features at the micro-rhythmic level.

Rhythm: Virtual Reference Structures and Actual Sound

With regard to the complexities of groove, much work to this day has concentrated on the relation between norm and deviation, based upon the assumption that what constitutes the 'dynamic' dimensions of a groove – that is, what makes a groove *groove* – is the presence of minor deviations from a presumed norm (for example, a metric grid). Following this line of thought, as did Bengtsson, Gabrielsson and Thorsén (1969) more than 40 years ago, we end up with the question: what constitutes this norm? For that matter, what constitutes a deviation? Both terms must be defined if we are to analyse rhythm in groove-based music with any claim at all to an acknowledgement of the source of the groove itself.

The question of what constitutes the norm is closely related to what we find to be the basic structure of the rhythm. One way of approaching this is to understand rhythmic structure as the aspects of a given rhythm that make us recognise it as the same rhythm in different contexts. A related but distinct notion of rhythmic structure derives from those reference schemes that listeners apply to a song in order to structure its sounds via the act of listening. The former approach concerns the structural identity of the rhythm and aims at identifying, for example, the rhythmic figures that are typical for a given piece of music or a particular style, whereas the latter concerns more general structuring principles such as hypermetre, pulse, metre and various layers of subdivision. In the following analysis, I focus on both the role of rhythmic figures and more general structuring principles – in particular, pulse and subdivision – in constituting the norm (from which possible deviations deviate). I will now present and discuss these three levels of reference structure in more depth.

In the literature, pulse as a reference structure is termed 'regulative beat' (Nketia, 1974, p. 131) or 'subjective beat' (Chernoff, 1979, p. 50). Both of these labels direct our attention to the fundamental fact that the main pulse of the music may not be present in the sounding fabric of the rhythm. The regulative or subjective beat is an *internal* beat in the sense that a structuring scheme is applied to the sounds by the listener or performer. For groove-based music, this pulse 'behind' the music is a fundamental virtual reference structure for *both* the production and the perception of rhythm, to such an extent that if one fails to catch the correct or intended pulse, the groove can change character completely or even fall apart. This highlights the subjective aspect of virtual reference structures in general. A listener who is not confident about a given musical style might structure the rhythm she hears according to a pulse that is different from the expected pulse and thereby develop an utterly different 'understanding' of the music. Usually, however, the relevant reference pulse is quite clear to the listener.

The subdivision of a given pulse also has an internal counterpart in the listener; Nketia (1974, p. 126) calls it the 'density referent', and it may be understood as the virtual reference structure regulating the density of the fastest running level of pulsation. This subdivision also provides a reference structure for syncopations and other rhythmic events that involve notes with short durations. The density referent is also not present in the sounds as such but is suggested by rhythmic layers whose important events take place at the sub-tactus level.

In musicology, the interplay of sounding and non-sounding aspects has often been framed as a relationship between rhythm and 'metre'. However, the structuring principles at work in a groove comprise much more than musical metre, in the sense of time signatures and subdivision. When it comes to groove-based music, it is crucial to account for the intermediate level of *figure*, a style-related concept that is akin to metre in poetry. To distinguish between a sounding figure and figure as a virtual reference structure, I label the former 'gesture'. Figure, then, represents a proposal or schema for structuring and understanding the musical gesture.

A gesture implies its own structuring principles. Following J.J. Gibson (1986, Chapter 8), one might say that a given gesture *affords* the listener certain possibilities for structuring its sounds. Gesture is not sound as such (that is, a matter of physics); it includes the virtual aspects informing that sound. Paraphrasing Gilles Deleuze, the virtual must be defined as strictly a part of the real gesture – 'as though the object had one part of itself in the virtual' (Deleuze, 1994, p. 209). Gesture, then, is sound as it is understood and structured according to its affordances and the pre-understanding of the listener. Moreover, even though one analytical parameter – such as timbre, rhythm or melody – might be the primary characteristic aspect of a given gesture, it transcends in principle any traditional division into parameters.

What unites all of these different levels of structure is that they do not exist as sound per se. Rhythm therefore comprises an interaction between virtual reference structures and actual sounding rhythmic events.[1] This interaction works in two

[1] This interaction resembles the interaction of syntax and actual speech or writing in linguistics. For linguistic theory conforming to this theoretical premise, see Saussure, 1986; Ricoeur, 1973; Bakhtin, 1986. This theoretical premise is today widely accepted in the

directions: music always generates some form of reference structure, and reference structures are always applied to music.[2]

Rhythm as a Play with Reference Structures

A sounding rhythmic gesture normally carries with it implications for both a main pulse and a particular subdivision, thus inducing an internal beat and a density referent, respectively, in the listener. In genres where much of the music-aesthetic work is concentrated on rhythm and groove, performers and producers play with these implications in different ways. One alternative is to start a song with one gesture (and one internal beat and density referent) in the rhythmic fabric, then introduce a second gesture that 'turns the beat around'. This strategy can disorient the listener and necessitate a process of reinterpretation, whereby, for example, the feeling of the downbeat must be relocated from beats 2 and 4 in the measure to beats 1 and 3 (for analytical examples, see Butler, 2006, chapter 3). Another alternative is to use a given rhythmic gesture, or combine several gestures, in a fashion that simultaneously proposes more than one alternative for the internal beat and density referent. One example of a figure (or gesture, if played) that is constructed to evoke a double set of reference structures for the basic pulse is this classic time line in West African music (see transcription in Example 3.1), which may be heard equally convincingly according to a $\frac{4}{4}$ or a $\frac{3}{2}$ metric matrix.

Example 3.1 Timeline structured according to a basic pulse in three (to the left) and four (to the right)

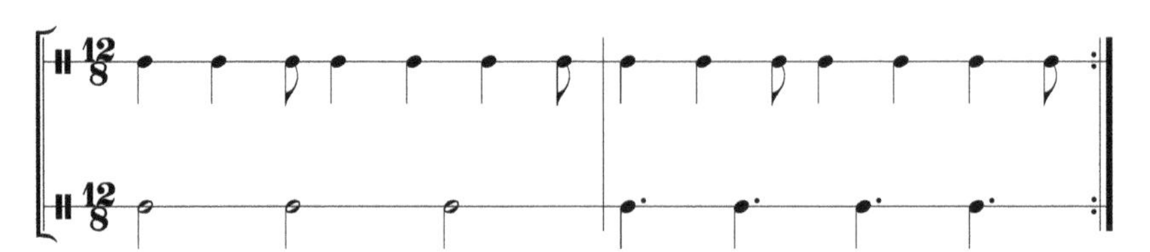

The fabric of rhythm can also be made ambiguous as to its virtual referent regarding the fastest possible subdivision in the song (the density referent). The most common strategy in this regard involves introducing the possibility of aligning the fast/short notes according to a matrix of either two or three, so that a

various strands of research on rhythm (see, for example, Clarke, 1985; Desain and Honing, 2003; Keil, 1995; Kvifte, 2004; Iyer, 2002).

[2] Interestingly, researchers in neuroscience have started to identify brain functions linked with the processing of these two (interacting) aspects of rhythm (Snyder and Large, 2005; Nozaradan et al., 2011).

given groove, for example, will work in both a duple and a triple subdivision at the same time. In the John Hiatt tune 'Thing Called Love' (1987), Ry Cooder plays the guitar riff with a swung (triple) feel to it, while drummer Jim Keltner follows a straight (duple) subdivision.[3] In this way, layers conforming to both duple and triple density referents share almost equally prominence in the groove. Potentially conflicting duple or triple patterns of subdivision also announce themselves via an obvious shuffling of the subdivision, so that the next smallest unit (after the internal beat) in the groove – for example, the quarter note – is broken into two uneven but still fixed durations, one longer and one shorter. If the ratio between the longer and the shorter notes falls somewhere between 1:1 and 2:1, then, this presents two possibilities: either the same rhythmic layer induces a double set of reference structures consisting of both duple and triple subdivisions or this particular shuffled feel supplies the necessary density referent in and of itself. Swing in jazz, like shuffled grooves, also involves ratios that are both below (that is, closer to 1:1) and above (that is, closer to 3:1) the 'mathematical' triple feel of 2:1 (Waadeland, 2001; Friberg and Sundström, 2002; I will return to this towards the end of this chapter).

One further alternative for exploiting ambiguities regarding reference structures for aesthetic purposes is to design a musical gesture that can easily be understood as one of two rather different rhythmic figures. In my previous work on Parliament's funk grooves, I locate this strategy at times in their songs built up around one central riff, parts of which are located safely more or less in the middle of two competing figures of reference – that is, because the gestures on the level of figures are both the one and the other (Danielsen, 2006, pp. 132–3).

As we shall see in the following analyses, the rhythmic fabric as a whole in 'Nasty Girl' seems to suggest more than one virtual reference structure when it comes to both the basic pulse (is the internal beat $\frac{4}{4}$ or $\frac{2}{2}$ – that is, half tempo?) and the subdivision (is the density referent in a matrix of two or three?). There are also rhythmic gestures that relate to more than one figure, and I focus here in particular on the ambiguities associated with the cross-rhythmic gesture in the synth bass. My intention is first to reveal the multiple sets of reference structures embedded in this groove, and second to demonstrate how the various parts of the song have been shaped aesthetically and purposefully via this rhythmic ambiguity.

Three Instances of Virtual Ambiguity in 'Nasty Girl'

The song 'Nasty Girl' was released as the fourth single from the immensely popular Destiny's Child album *Survivor* (2004) and became a moderate success on

[3] I thank Nils Harkestad for drawing my attention to this feature of this song.

the charts in Australia[4] and some European countries.[5] The album was produced by lead singer Beyoncé and Anthony Dent, who co-wrote the song with Maurizio Bassi and Naimy Hackett.

The different sections of 'Nasty Girl' conform more or less to the traditional overall form of a pop song. An introductory chorus (A) is followed by a verse (B), then by what might be heard as either a pre-chorus or a chorus (C) (see Table 3.1). In what follows, I refer to the latter as pre-chorus and reserve chorus for the intro/chorus section (A). The song alternates these three main rhythmic textures throughout. In the second verse, however, a quote from the hit 'Push It' (1987) by Salt-N-Pepa is 'pasted' into the tune.

Table 3.1 Schematic outline of sections in 'Nasty Girl'

	Pulse		**Subdivision**
	Bass/Bass Drum/Snare	*Percussion*	*Vocals*
Chorus (A)	Slow	Slow	Mostly duple
Verse (B)	Slow	Mostly slow	Triple
Pre-chorus (C)	Fast	Fast	Duple

The harmonic material is almost the same in these three main sections of the tune, and they mostly share instrumental sounds and accompanying rhythmic figures as well. What distinguishes them, then, is their melodic material and the respective balances among different rhythmic layers. As a consequence, the overall rhythmic feel is pulled in slightly different directions as the three main sections rotate. There are, in turn, three essential ambiguities at play here, as we will see below.

Ambiguity Regarding Internal Beat: Fast or Slow Basic Pulse?

The two introductory bars of the song suggest a main pulse in $\frac{4}{4}$ at a tempo of 130 beats per minute (bpm). In the chorus (part A) immediately following them, however, an instrumental sound that resembles a snare drum establishes a main pulse in a half tempo by marking only the third beat in each $\frac{4}{4}$ measure, suggesting it in turn as the *second* beat in a pulse that is half as fast as the $\frac{4}{4}$ at 130bpm. (In most rhythmic music, of course, bass drum strikes on beats 1 and 3 and snare drum

[4] See http://www.australian-charts.com/showitem.asp?interpret=Destiny%27s+Child&titel=Nasty+Girl&cat=s [Accessed 1 March 2013].

[5] See http://www.swisscharts.com/showitem.asp?interpret=Destiny%27s+Child&titel=Nasty+Girl&cat=s, http://www.dutchcharts.nl/showitem.asp?interpret=Destiny%27s+Child&titel=Nasty+Girl&cat=s, http://www.danishcharts.com/showitem.asp?interpret=Destiny%27s+Child&titel=Nasty+Girl&cat=s (all accessed 1 March 2013).

strikes on beats 2 and 4 are prominent indications of the internal beat itself.) The lead vocal's chorus melody also underlines the new, slow pulse through its eighth notes (which would be sixteenth notes in the new pulse), singling out this level as the density referent for this part of the groove. In the next section (part B), the basic pulse indicated by the instrumental accompaniment is still slow, but the lead vocal now accentuates the second and fourth beat of the *fast* basic pulse, recalling the initial internal beat from the two introductory bars. In addition, fragments of a very fast hi-hat pattern are heard towards the end of the bar, likewise pulling the overall feel of the song in the direction of the fast basic pulse in this part of the section. In the pre-chorus section (part C), finally, the internal beat is unambiguously presented as $\frac{4}{4}$ at 130bpm in the accompanying rhythmic layers, the vocals and the percussion parts. The hi-hat particularly advocates for the fast pulse here through its exaggerated, even virtuoso, high-speed pattern. This gesture was typical of drum and bass music of the late 1990s and is one of several stylistic elements borrowed from electronic dance music-related genres on this album.[6]

In sum, there are both a fast basic pulse and a slow basic pulse at play in this song, and their relationship to the actual (or rather virtual) internal beat varies with each section, depending on the particular combination of basic rhythmic layers that is employed. The vocals clearly contribute to inflecting the internal beat in one direction or the other. Even more interesting when it comes to the vocals, however, is the ambiguity they represent regarding subdivision.

Ambiguity Regarding Density Referent: Straight or Shuffled Feel?

A second case in point when it comes to ambiguity at the level of reference structures in 'Nasty Girl' is the fact that the fabric of rhythm implies two different and possibly clashing density referents. This feature appears in various groove-directed musics, both played and programmed, and may take different forms. The John Hiatt example discussed above is played music and thus depends upon the skills of outstanding performers. In a computer-based groove like 'Nasty Girl', several of the rhythmic layers were probably programmed as entries in a sequencer, and the task is more straightforward: one can experiment with different patterns of subdivision, as well as combine different and potentially conflicting patterns, without having to account for the perceptual limitations of human beings. Either way, of course, ambiguity at the level of subdivision contributes strongly to a groove's characteristic feel.

---

[6] As I have discussed in more detail elsewhere, one effect of this computer-based 'exaggerated virtuosity' was to draw attention to the tools involved in the production process and the particular machine aesthetics they could provide (see Danielsen, 2010, Chapter 1).

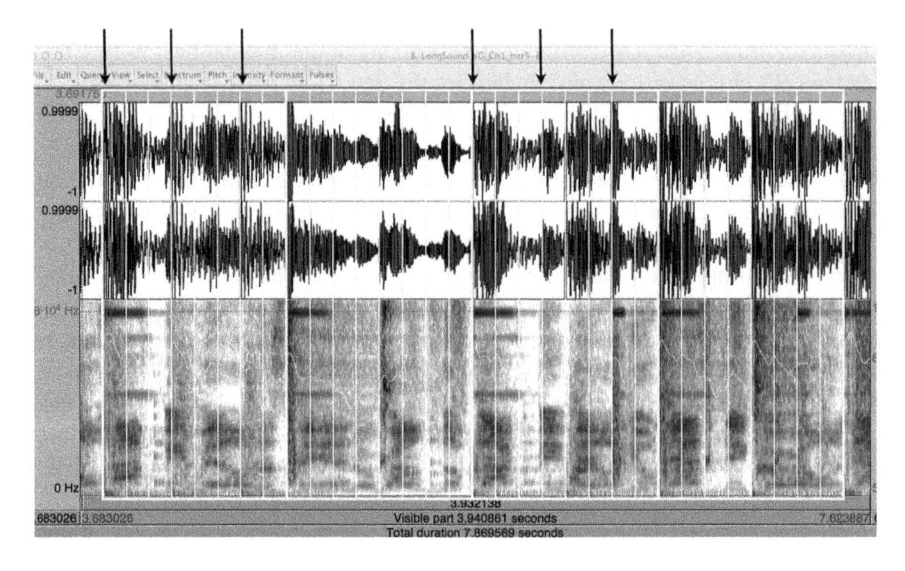

Figure 3.1 Waveform (amplitude/time) and sonogram (frequency/time) of bars 1–2 of the chorus (A) of 'Nasty Girl' (extract from first chorus). Grid on straight sixteenths (thin lines) and slow basic pulse (thick lines). Synth bass pattern indicated by arrows

As shown in Figure 3.1, in the beginning of the chorus most rhythmic events fit well with a metric grid of sixteenth notes. For example, it handily encompasses the attacks of the cross-rhythmic synth bass pattern (more on this below) and the percussion parts. However, there are also rhythmic events in the programmed groove that fit well with a metric grid of triple subdivision, such as, for example, the pick-up to the one in bar 5 (fast pulse). We also see how the slow basic pulse manifests through the snare drum-like sound on beat 3 (fast pulse).

Towards the end of the chorus, the triple subdivision tends to dominate the sound as illustrated in Figure 3.2.

This shift to shuffled feel is achieved by changing the phrasing of the vocals. Generally, the lead vocal (including its overdubs) drifts between duple and triple subdivisions: in the chorus (A), it is straight or duple in its feel for the first three phrases, then it tends towards shuffling the upbeat to the beats in the fourth phrase (the transition is illustrated in Figure 3.3).

In the verse (B), on the other hand, the lead vocal underlines a triple feel throughout. In the pre-chorus (C), the vocal(s) is again unambiguously duple. Overall, then, the lead vocal supports both a duple and a triple set of reference structures for subdivision but also occupies the limbo between them. It is also remarkably stable in its impact, in the sense that it is characterised by the same rhythmic shaping each time a phrase is repeated. These varying vocal patterns, then, are not accidental. They instead reveal an accurate inaccuracy in timing

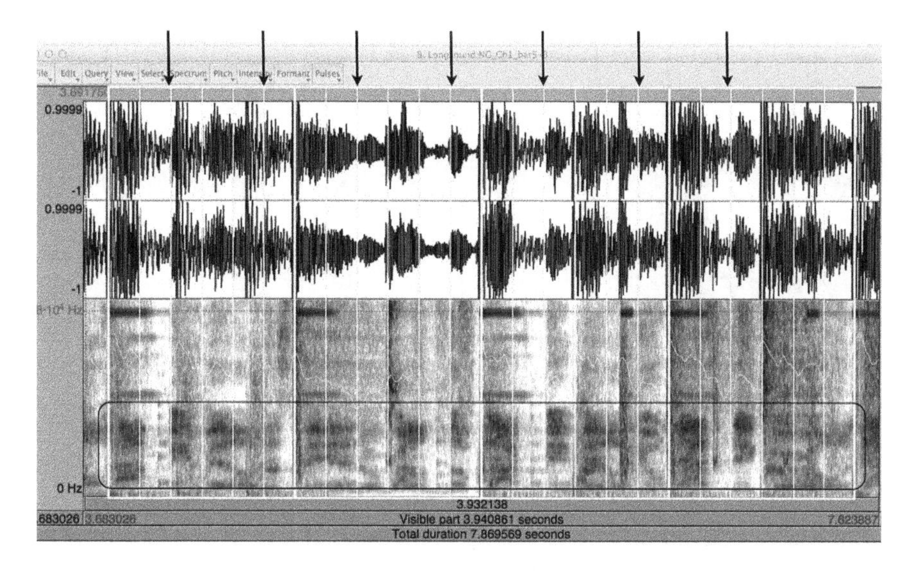

Figure 3.2 Waveform (amplitude/time) and sonogram (frequency/time) of last vocal line in the chorus (A) of 'Nasty Girl' (bars 7–8 in the first chorus). Grid on triplets of eighths (thin lines) and slow basic pulse (thick lines). Arrows indicate shuffled subdivision in vocals. Frequency area of vocal parts indicated in sonogram

that both sustains and mediates between two different and potentially conflicting suggestions for a subdivision of the song.

Such an understanding of the particular feel of this groove returns us to the idea discussed above that the groove produces a double set of virtual reference structures at the level of density referent. Locking into this groove by way of this double set of density referents might be compared to walking in a narrow corridor without touching the walls, using the distance from either wall to chart one's course, sometimes leaning towards one wall, sometimes towards the other. In short, the vocals both contribute to establishing those walls and explore the space between them. There are other ways of conceptualising this as well, to which I will shortly return.

Ambiguity Regarding Cross-Rhythmic Tendency: One Gesture – Two Figures?

I have now shown how the groove in 'Nasty Girl' can be understood as producing a double set of virtual reference structures at both the level of the basic pulse (internal beat) and the subdivision (density referent). The song's third ambiguous aspect concerns the way in which the synth bass seems to alternate between alternative counter-rhythmic figures that relate to duple and triple subdivisions, respectively.

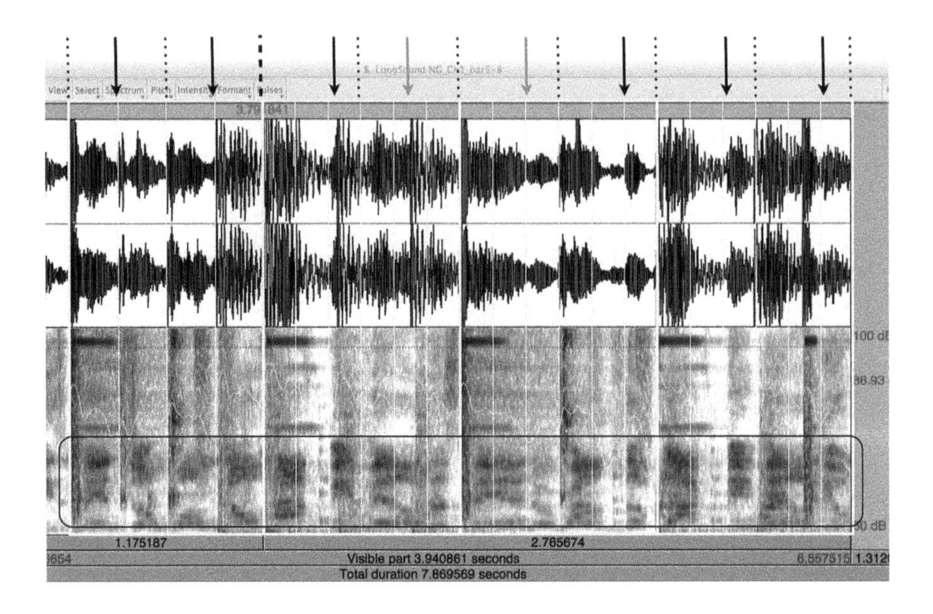

Figure 3.3 Waveform (amplitude/time) and sonogram (frequency/time) of transition from duple to triple feel in vocals in the chorus of 'Nasty Girl' (bars 6–8 in the first chorus). Grid on duple eighth notes in bar 6 and triplets of eighth notes in bars 7 and 8 (thin lines) and slow basic pulse (thick lines). Arrows indicate subdivision in vocals. Dotted lines mark the fast basic pulse

The inclusion of a counter-rhythmic element in the groove occurs regularly in dance-related popular music. This element can be organised around the same basic pulse as the main rhythm but displaced so that its stress falls on the off-beats, or it can be set up in a competing pulse scheme in a ratio of 4:3 or 2:3. In groove-directed musical styles such as funk and EDM, the latter form of counter-rhythm is almost mandatory. The synth bass in Nasty Girl is yet another example of this. Elsewhere, I have named such variants *cross-rhythmic* counter-rhythms, because they derive from a competing pulse that, if it were carried throughout the groove, would generate a true cross-rhythm (Nketia, 1974, p. 134). However, in most popular music styles where this feature is common, this competing pulse is never allowed to take over the main metre, so there is only 'a tendency of cross-rhythm' (Danielsen, 2006, pp. 62–6).

Generally, cross-rhythmic gestures, which introduce a competing pulse in parts of the groove, seem to have a certain driving, dynamic effect on a groove, always propelling it forward, probably because they provide a structurally unstable element to the pattern. In typically multilayered funk grooves such as James Brown's, this instability is often introduced in the second part of the basic unit – that is, in exactly that phase of the process when the metrical structure directs the pattern towards a mini-'closure' of sorts (Danielsen, 2006, p. 165). The effect of the cross-rhythmic synth bass figure in 'Nasty Girl' is somewhat different, however. Here, a tendency towards cross-rhythm is present at the beginning of every second bar and takes the form of a figure of four against three (4:3), with the three here referring to the fast basic pulse in quarter notes (see Figure 3.4).

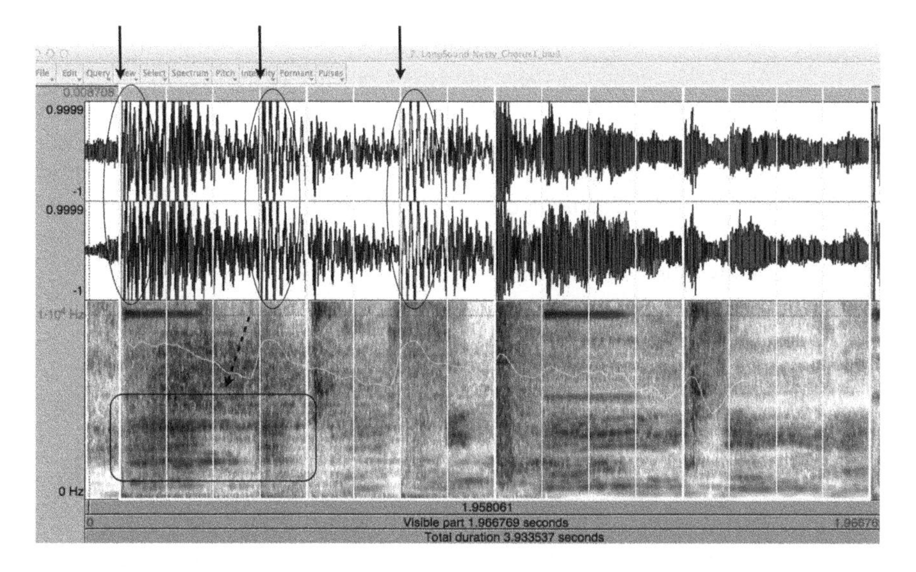

Figure 3.4 Waveform (amplitude/time) and sonogram (frequency/time) of bar 1 of the first chorus (A) of 'Nasty Girl'. Grid on straight sixteenth notes (thin lines) and fast basic pulse (thick lines). Cross-rhythmic gesture played by synth bass indicated by circles. Virtual reference figure (4:3) indicated by arrows. Dotted arrow illustrates the influence of the synth bass pattern on the vocals

Most cross-rhythmic gestures in played music are phrased so that they clearly signal their contrast to a main pulse in $\frac{4}{4}$ – they gesticulate, so to speak, that the cross-rhythmic tendency they represent is counter to a main rhythm. In 'Nasty Girl', we find an EDM-derived variant of the cross-rhythmic tendency that is located exactly on the metric grid. These programmed, on-the-grid 4:3 figures positioned at the beginning of the bar are found in numerous house and techno tracks (for examples, see Zeiner-Henriksen, 2010, pp. 189–93). The presence of such stylistic features on the *Survivor* album shows the ways in which Destiny's Child, originally a contemporary R&B group, borrowed stylistic elements from electronic dance music, anticipating the mixture of R&B, hip-hop and electronic dance music that was to come.

As mentioned, these programmed, on-the-grid cross-rhythmic gestures contain no phrasing that hints at the basic pulse. In 'Nasty Girl' – at least in those sections dominated by rhythmic layers proposing a slow basic pulse – there is likewise no clearly articulated $\frac{4}{4}$ pulse to counterbalance the cross-rhythmic strokes. The initiated listener will likely remain aware that this kind of figure, by convention, is used in contrast to a pulse that is twice as fast as the slow basic pulse. However, due to the absence of sounding manifestations of this fast basic pulse, in tandem with the lack of any micro-rhythmic *hints* of the fast basic pulse, the cross-rhythmic gesture in 'Nasty Girl' seems to shake free of this (implied) layer of the figure. Also relevant here is the synth bass's salience to the overall sound and its association with a register and musical function that are often understood to carry the basic pulse. The figure that is suggested by the synth bass, then, does *not* reveal the anticipated multilayered polyrhythm of four against three but is instead a simple pattern of three, sometimes two, dotted eighth notes in the first part of each bar (again, measured in the fast pulse). This virtual reference structure is illustrated in Example 3.2.

Example 3.2 Virtual figure implied by synth bass and vocals in the chorus section A in 'Nasty Girl'

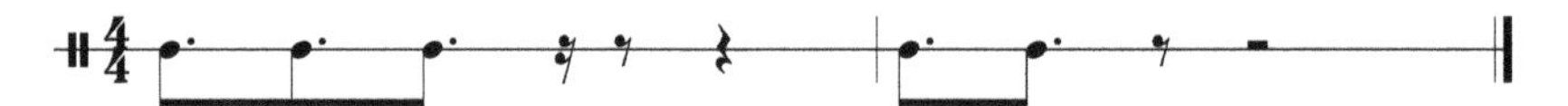

A fascinating consequence of the dominance of the cross-rhythmic gesture in the overall sound is that we tend to hear the duple eighths in the vocals as slightly swung. In other words, the dotted eighths of the cross-rhythmic gesture establish a matrix that affects how we hear the duration and timing of the vocals. This also affects the actual timing of parts of the performed vocal line – in particular, the placement of the two first syllables is tilted towards this grid (see Figure 3.4). In the verse (B), it is the other way around. The rhythmic feel of the vocals affects the entire rhythmic feel of the groove, further complicating how we hear the figure of the synth bass. The presence of a triple subdivision in the vocals alters, not the actual sound, but our *perception* of the cross-rhythmic figure, in fact, so that we tend to hear it as a triplet in quarters (see Figure 3.5 and Example 3.3).

If the synth bass pattern had been recorded live in the studio, this interaction between vocals and bass would most likely have affected the timing of the pattern.[7] In a programmed groove, of course, this is not the case, but at the level of

[7] The plasticity of the perceptual understanding of this feature's timing has an interesting parallel in the role of the *clave* figure in Latin American dance music. This figure is also structured with a three side and a two side, the former of which consists of eight eighths grouped in a 3+3+2 figure. For an empirical investigation of how the three side and the two side affect timing, respectively, see Chor, 2010.

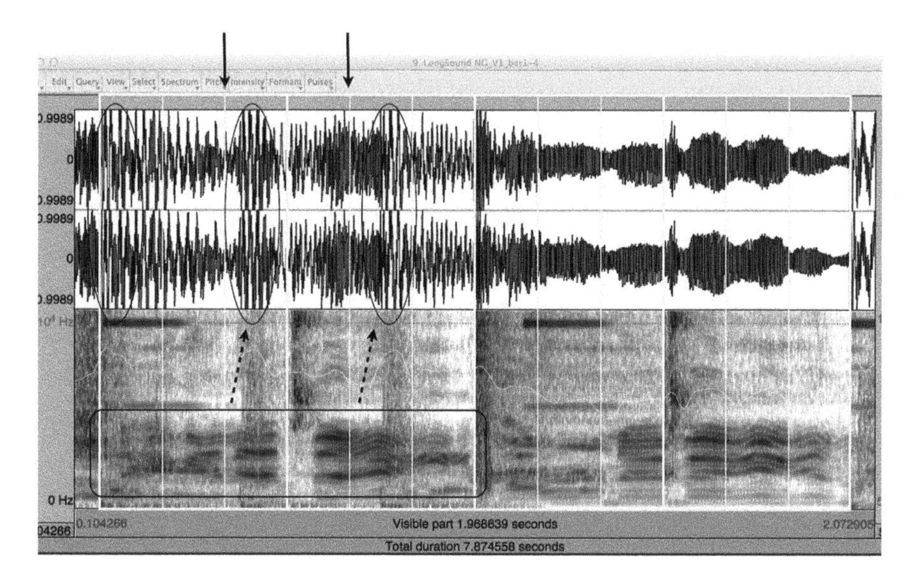

Figure 3.5 Waveform (amplitude/time) and sonogram (frequency/time) of bar 1 of the verse (B) of 'Nasty Girl' (extract from first verse). Grid on triplets of eighths (thin lines) and fast basic pulse (thick lines). Cross-rhythmic gesture played by synth bass indicated by circles. Virtual reference figure (3:2) indicated by arrows. Dotted arrows illustrate the influence of the vocals on the synth bass pattern

Example 3.3 Virtual figure implied by synth bass and vocals in section B in 'Nasty Girl'

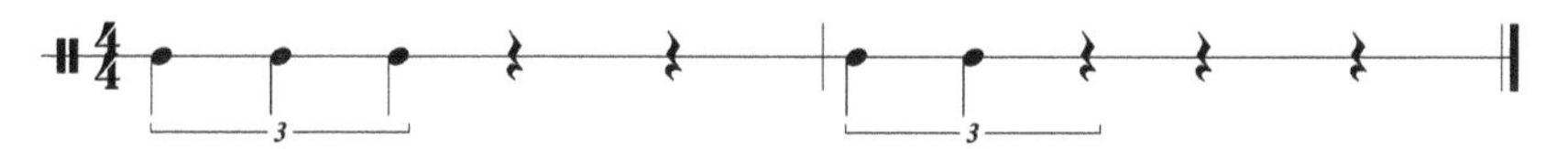

perception, it might still be claimed that we actually *hear* the synth bass pattern as a triple-based figure. If this were true, this might represent an instance where the virtual structure (the density referent) overwhelms the actual timing of the sounds, underlining the way in which virtual reference structures can in fact transform what we actually hear.[8]

Summing up, in the chorus (A), the four part of the cross-rhythmic 4:3 figure dominates so strongly that the gesture almost fails to uphold its virtual three-part. As a consequence, we tend to hear the duple eighths in vocals as slightly swung.

[8] For experimental work investigating the impact of preconceived virtual reference structures (so-called metric priming) on the formation of rhythmic categories, see Clarke, 1999; Desain and Honing, 2003.

Conversely, in the verses (B), which are dominated by triplets in the vocal, the vocal acts to alter our perception of the timing of the cross-rhythmic gesture. The triplets in the vocal perceptually 'deform' the figure so that it aligns, more or less, to three beats played against two beats of the main pulse (a 3:2 figure).[9] Furthermore, when the fast basic pulse is present in the sound (C), the cross-rhythmic gesture works as a straight 4:3 figure, inducing both of the pulse layers equally in the listener.

The difference between these three variations upon the 4:3 figure is significant when analysed in relation to the metrical system, because, understood within such a framework, these are three very different figures. When heard as part of this groove, however, they appear closely related. We must then ask, if we were to suspend the metrical matrices of the notational system, what kind of figure rises to the surface?

The Structural Aspect of Microrhythm: Gesture as Figure

Whereas it is easy to identify *in analysis* the two different metrical reference structures of subdivision in the structural aspects of this song, they are not necessarily very pronounced when we listen to it. The sound of the vocal is a crucial aspect to consider here. If the vocal were a less flexible instrument in relation to when its rhythmic events actually start – if it were, for example, an instrument with a sharp, more precise, attack – its effect on our experience of these potentially clashing patterns of subdivision would have been different. Most likely, we easily accept the many metric shifts in the song because of the mediating character of the vocal. (The smooth attack of the synth bass contributes to this as well.)

This in turn brings to the fore the fact that the characteristic feel of the song cannot be explained by purely temporal aspects alone: instead, it is a consequence of the interaction between aspects of timing and qualities of sound. More generally, it raises the question of which virtual reference structures are actually (that is, virtually) at work in our structuring of the basic elements of this song? What are we to regard as the underlying figures for the performance of, as well as the listening to, such a rhythmic design? Are the metrical schemes, which are commonly regarded as the structuring principles of such layers of subdivision, really the structures at work in the *experience* of this music?

An alternative way to approach the absence of the experience of conflicting schemes of subdivision is to claim that – apart from the analyses – they do not exist, even on a virtual level: neither duple nor triple subdivisions are to be regarded as the operative schemes for the understanding of this groove, at least not in their metrical forms. It is instead the very gesture *as heard* that forms the basis of the figure here. In my previous work on 1970s funk grooves, I discuss this

[9] In this regard, the ways in which the vocals influence our overall experience of the other rhythmic layers resonate with Serge Lacasse's notion of the supradiegetic voice (see Lacasse, 2010).

issue in relation to one of the core features of funk, namely the snappy or clipped phrasing that I – inspired by James Brown – named 'the downbeat in anticipation' (Danielsen, 2006, Chapter 5). The point here is that it is not the downbeat as such that acts as the virtual reference for playing a typical 'One' in funk in an anticipated manner. When established, the reference is rather the anticipated downbeat itself, including its particular timing. And not even this new entity or figure is stable as such; it is constantly transformed by tradition – that is, by each new realisation of itself.[10]

From this perspective, one might claim that the synth bass in 'Nasty Girl' is not really alternating between a duple-based and triple-based figure in our perception. Rather, the synth bass produces its own particular virtual figure, one that is modified by and also may be said to contain both these variants of its realisation: it is the same figure that is induced by the cross-rhythmic gesture in sections A and B and C, but it gains a certain flexibility as part of its (emergent) structure, which allows it to be heard as part of either of these rhythmic contexts. The lead vocal's variations between straight duple and shuffled duple phrasing may also be approached from this perspective. Instead of representing two fundamentally different virtual references of subdivision, they can be seen as representing two different realisations of the same flexible structure.

What I propose here is that these virtual figures are not determined by metrical properties alone but must be related to other forms of pattern recognition. More precisely, this concerns the ways in which the musical gestures themselves, over time, establish a set of figures that is unique to this song. When playing or singing or listening to a rhythmic gesture like the cross-rhythmic pattern in the synth bass, one does not necessarily recognise a certain virtual organisation of durations in an isochronometric system as such. Instead, one recognises yesterday's gestures, so to speak – which, in 'Nasty Girl', might in fact be the gesture of the previous measure.

More broadly speaking, then, we must extend the general concept of structure in rhythmic music to include aspects such as the timing and sound: a way of playing a certain gesture on a particular instrument can, in a given context, become so striking and so systematic as to form an identifying pattern in itself. The gesture, that is, becomes a figure.

[10] This important theoretical point, which I derived from my analyses of the funk grooves of James Brown and Parliament (Danielsen, 2006), is laid out in a quite lucid, and perhaps more pedagogical, manner than I achieved in a recent article by Robert Fink. In a discussion of my work, he presents this deconstructive relationship between reference and sounds in the following way: 'Persistent, structured "deviations" from a constantly implied reference structure do not negate its syntax; they actually create a new syntax by subjecting the reference structure itself to constant syntactic pressure' (Fink, 2011, pp. 193–4).

The Temporality of Grooves

The shortcomings of the traditional theoretical framework of rhythmic structure (isochronous pulsations at different levels) are clear when we confront this abstract notion with the ways in which we in fact *experience* a track like 'Nasty Girl'. We do not 'count out' such grooves – at least, not at the level of subdivision. Rather, we hear the rhythmic gestures in one piece, including properties like microtiming and the shape of the sound. At the same time, there is no need to abolish metre as a potential structuring principle in rhythm. Particularly at the level of the basic pulse, regularly recurring beats (and the grouping of such beats according to metrical matrices) play an important role in our experience of rhythm. Accordingly, when we analyse rhythm as well, it can be relevant to employ metrically related reference structures, at least in relation to certain layers of rhythm or stages in the process of listening. What I have argued here is instead that metrical reference structures cannot account for *all* of the phenomena in a groove.

The basic pattern of a groove-directed rhythm is usually designed to activate an inner dynamic that keeps the listener or dancer constantly engaged in the groove, and in this regard, the micro-rhythmic features of the groove seem to be particularly important. Sometimes the close analysis of such subtle micro-rhythmic designs eludes traditional notation-based representations of rhythmic structure. Moreover, micro-rhythmic features have a structural impact as well. If we overlook this, we risk losing both crucial aspects of a groove's structural identity and the critical interaction between this virtual structure and the actual sounds. Ultimately, as demonstrated through my analysis of, for example, the role of the cross-rhythmic gesture in 'Nasty Girl', the categories used in these structuring processes have a certain built-in flexibility in their application. Thus the categories used in the production and reception of groove also involve a level of 'rhythmic tolerance', to use a concept coined by Mats Johansson.[11] The metric grid simply does not allow for this flexibility.

A related factor in rhythm analysis that is often overlooked in analytical approaches is the basic reality that a groove is neither played nor experienced all at once but rather *over time*. Previously, I have argued (Danielsen, 2006, Chapter 8) that when we are in the participatory mode (Keil, 1995), we move together with the groove, in a sense co-producing it. This is in marked contrast to how a groove appears when we approach it from an analytical distance. If we take a phenomenological position regarding the experience of 'being in the groove', rhythm is not a given pattern as such. It unfolds in time, and we have to move together with it in time, so to speak, to be able to say how it actually works as we experience it. This is a hugely important aspect of understanding the effect of the shifts in balance between different virtual reference structures from section to section in a song. These shifts are experienced *in time*, and each new

---

[11] Johansson applies the concept to Norwegian folk dances to account for the flexibility of the categories used to structure these grooves (see Johansson, 2010).

section acquires its characteristic feel on the basis of the pattern established in the previous section.

The same kind of dynamic is at work within the chorus when the vocal, after three phrases of straight duple time, starts shuffling the subdivision. Here as well, time must be taken into consideration: the fourth phrase has to be analysed in light of how the immediately preceding rhythmic gestures influence our hearing of it. From this perspective, it might be claimed that this fourth shuffled phrase is likely to be experienced as largely similar to the previous ones, even though, from a metrical perspective, it belongs to a radically different virtual reference structure.

This shows the importance of taking the temporality of the groove experience into account when analysing rhythm. No part of this groove happens in a vacuum: every rhythmic gesture, new bar, and new phrase or section gets its meaning from what has gone before. Ongoing events unavoidably induce virtual reference structures in the listener that work as a form of priming in the listening process: they are used for predicting (When is it likely that this rhythmic event will happen? What kind of event or sound is it likely to be?), understanding (What happened?) and assessing (Did the event confirm to the expectation? Does this event belong to the same category or a different one?) the events to come.

These processes are also affected by cultural expectations and tradition, which means that different listeners may hear the same rhythmic events – for example, the shift from straight to shuffled subdivision in the vocal discussed above – in different ways. Some listeners may perceive this as a change of figure (due to the change in subdivision), while others may hear it as a variation of the same figure. Put differently, every new rhythmic gesture gets its meaning from what immediately preceded it, but it is also affected by the larger cultural and historical context and the listener's previous history with music, in the sense of preferences, listening experience and musical training. So while the actual sounds may remain the same, the perceptual response will vary – with time and place.

References

Bakhtin, M., 1986. The Problem of Speech Genres. In: M. Bakhtin, C. Emerson and M. Holquist (eds), *Speech Genres and Other Late Essays*. Austin, TX: University of Texas Press, pp. 60–102.

Bengtsson, I., Gabrielsson A. and Thorsén, S.M., 1969. Empirisk rytmforskning [Empirical Rhythm Research]. *Svensk tidskrift för musikforskning*, 51, pp. 48–118.

Butler, M.J., 2006. *Unlocking the Groove: Rhythm, Meter, and Musical Design in Electronic Dance Music*. Bloomington, IN: Indiana University Press.

Chernoff, J.M., 1979. *African Rhythm and African Sensibility: Aesthetics and Social Action in African Musical Idioms*. Chicago, IL: University of Chicago Press.

Chor, I., 2010. Microtiming and Rhythmic Structure in Clave-Based Music: A Quantitative Study. In: A. Danielsen (ed.), *Musical Rhythm in the Age of Digital Reproduction*. Farnham: Ashgate, pp. 37–50.

Clarke, E.F., 1985. Structure and Expression in Rhythmic Performance. In: P. Howell, I. Cross and R. West (eds), *Musical Structure and Cognition*, London: Academic Press, pp. 209–36.

Clarke, E.F., 1999. Rhythm and Timing in Music. In: D. Deutsch (ed.), *The Psychology of Music*. New York: Academic Press, pp. 473–500.

Danielsen, A., 2006. *Presence and Pleasure: The Funk Grooves of James Brown and Parliament*. Hanover, NH: Wesleyan University Press, in association with the University Press of New England.

Danielsen, A., 2010. Introduction: Rhythm in the Age of Digital Reproduction. In: A. Danielsen (ed.), *Musical Rhythm in the Age of Digital Reproduction*. Farnham: Ashgate, pp. 1–18.

Deleuze, G., 1994. *Difference and Repetition*. Translated from French by P. Patton. London: Athlone Press.

Desain, P. and Honing, H., 2003. The Formation of Rhythmic Categories and Metric Priming. *Perception*, 32(3), pp. 341–66.

Fink, R., 2011. Goal-Directed Soul? Analyzing Rhythmic Teleology in African American Popular Music. *Journal of the American Musicological Society*, 64(1), pp. 179–238.

Friberg, A. and Sundström, A., 2002. Swing Ratios and Ensemble Timing in Jazz Performance: Evidence for a Common Rhythmic Pattern. *Music Perception*, 19(3), pp. 333–49.

Gibson, J.J., 1986 [1979]. *The Ecological Approach to Visual Perception*. Hillsdale, NJ: Lawrence Erlbaum Associates (originally published 1979; re-published 1986).

Iyer, V., 2002. Embodied Mind, Situated Cognition, and Expressive Microtiming in African-American Music. *Music Perception*, 19(3), pp. 387–414.

Johansson, M., 2010. The Concept of Rhythmic Tolerance: Examining Flexible Grooves in Scandinavian Folk Fiddling. In: A. Danielsen (ed.), *Musical Rhythm in the Age of Digital Reproduction*. Farnham: Ashgate, pp. 69–84.

Keil, C., 1995. The Theory of Participatory Discrepancies: A Progress Report. *Ethnomusicology*, 39(1), pp. 1–19.

Kvifte, T., 2004. Description of Grooves and Syntax/Process Dialectics. *Studia Musicologica Norvegica*, 30, pp. 54–77.

Lacasse, S., 2010. Slave to the Supradiegetic Rhythm: A Microrhythmic Analysis of Creaky Voice in Sia's 'Breathe Me'. In: A. Danielsen (ed.), *Musical Rhythm in the Age of Digital Reproduction*. Farnham: Ashgate, pp. 141–58.

Nketia, J.H.K., 1974. *The Music of Africa*. New York: Norton.

Nozaradan, S., Peretz, I., Missal, M., and Mouraux, A., 2011. Tagging the Neuronal Entrainment to Beat and Meter. *Journal of Neuroscience*, 31(28), pp. 10234–40.

Ricoeur, P., 1973. The Hermeneutical Function of Distanciation. *Philosophy Today*, 17, pp. 129–43.

Saussure, F. de, 1986. *Course in General Linguistics*. 3rd edn. Translated from French by R. Harris. Chicago, IL: Open Court Publishing Company (originally published 1972; re-published 1986).

Snyder, J. and Large, E., 2005. Gamma-Band Activity Reflects the Metric Structure of Rhythmic Tone Sequences. *Cognitive Brain Research*, 24(1), pp. 117–26.

Waadeland, C.H., 2001. 'It Don't Mean a Thing if It Ain't Got That Swing': Simulating Expressive Timing by Modulated Movements. *Journal of New Music Research*, 30(1), pp. 23–37.

Zeiner-Henriksen, H.T., 2010. 'The PoumTchak Pattern: Correspondences between Rhythm, Sound, and Movement in Electronic Dance Music'. PhD, Dept. of Musicology, University of Oslo.

Discography

Destiny's Child, 2001. 'Nasty Girl'. *Survivor*. Columbia, COL 501783 2.

Hiatt, John, 1987. 'Thing Called Love'. *Bring The Family*. A&M, SP 5158.

Salt-N-Pepa, 1987. 'Push It'. *Tramp*. Champion, CHAMP 51.

Chapter 4
Pragmatic 'Poker Face': Lady Gaga's Song and Roman Jakobson's Six Functions of Communication

Dietrich Helms

I confess: I feel a very strong aversion to Lady Gaga's song 'Poker Face'. To me it sounds like the zombie of late 1970s disco raised from its grave where I had hoped it would remain forever with a wooden stake in its heart. From years under the surface it has lost some of its glamour, but it has become extremely strong and irresistible. When I started to think about this song, I definitely wasn't thinking about its meaning, but about this irresistibility I experienced whenever the piece was played. I simply couldn't help paying attention to the song although at the same time I utterly disliked it. And I wondered is there any way for me as a musicologist to pinpoint those means in the song, which get hold of my attention and will not let it go again? And why do I dislike it so much? Or, to speak more generally, is there any analytical way to study the effects of a particular song on its audience?[1]

The standard tools of traditional music analysis that are taught at schools and universities aim at two things: form (usually) and meaning in terms of semantics (sometimes). But neither form nor meaning are parameters that are in the centre of interest for a majority of listeners to a globally mega-selling mainstream dance-hit. I am not denying that 'Poker Face' does have a meaning for the members of its audience and I am not disputing that Lady Gaga is expressing something through her music. What I am arguing is that to understand properly a piece of popular music in general and a mainstream song in particular we have to broaden not only our idea of what a song is made of but also the aims of our analysis. It took musicology quite a time to recognise that the qualities of popular music are not only located in those parameters that can be written down in a score: text, melody, harmony and rhythm, but also in parameters like the sound of a voice or

---

[1] My occupation with 'Poker Face' began in 2009, when ASPM organised an informal two-day workshop on the analysis of popular music at the University of Gießen. The song was one of two we discussed then. It was 'Poker Face' that started me looking for something that, then, I thought must be something like a new rhetoric of music, a way to explain how signs in a piece of music have an effect on listeners. I wish to thank all the participants in the workshop for our fruitful discussions.

an instrument, the mix of a record and the performance on stage or on video. Now, I suggest, we also have to adapt our ideas of the aims of a musicological analysis to the necessities of the medium of the sound recording.

The traditional medium through which we study music, the score, indeed suggests mainly issues of form and meaning. It makes the description of form easy as you can browse back and forward – a thing you can't do in a performance. A score is supposed to be the manifestation of a composer's will without interference from a performer; and it needs interpretation – by musicians or by musicologists – as it is only an image of music but not the thing as such. Scores are a very intellectual form of communication; they are not particularly good at producing a feeling in their readers or in making them dance, though. Records can make them dance or dream, laugh or cry, love or loathe a song, but they are not suggestive of questions of interpretation. It is all there: the recording is the interpretation. A machine or a piece of software do the job that in the case of a score is done by human interpreters. Listening to a recording can make sense without wondering about aspects of form or meaning or execution – fortunately. A piece of music on a record does not raise a different, but a larger set of questions, some of them may be more important to listeners than others. In my example, why can't I resist listening to 'Poker Face'? How does the song make me want to move? What are the exact lyrics Lady Gaga is singing? How come the song reminds me of late 1970s disco and conjures up all those memories? Who is this Lady Gaga anyway?

Music in performance has a much larger spectrum of functions in communication than creating a certain form and suggesting a certain meaning. When I am talking about 'functions' I do not refer to the sociological or psychological sense of the word, meaning for example that group- and identity-building are functions of popular music. I am referring to the functioning of signs in communication. The study of the functions of signs in relationship to their users is part of a discipline within semiotics that is called functional pragmatics. In his article 'Linguistics and Poetics' Russian-born linguist Roman Jakobson (1960) developed a pragmatic model of the functions of language that has become very influential, although its potential for music analysis has not yet been fully recognised (see Tagg, 2013, pp. 145–7). Jakobson's basic idea is very simple and does not need a long theoretical introduction to semiotics.[2] Based on an older model by Karl Bühler, Jakobson identifies six functions of language. Each of these functions refers to one of the six constitutive factors of a speech act: the *addresser*, the *addressee*, the *context* to which the speech act refers, the *code*, as the repertoire of signs that constitute the message, the *message* as such – as a selection of signs from a certain code in a certain form, and finally the *contact* between addresser and addressee.

[2] I will not be able to deal with the theoretical background of semiotics in this article, which concentrates on the practical usage of Jakobson's six functions as an aim of analysis. For an extended view on semiotics and the analysis of popular music see for example writings by Philip Tagg (Tagg and Clarida, 2003; Tagg, 2013 and others).

A single speech act can inform the recipient about each of these constitutive factors. And each of these factors has a particular function: a speech act, Jakobson (1960, pp. 354–7) writes, refers to things and facts of the context of the conversation, and therefore has a *referential* function. It may also appeal to the addressee to do something and therefore can have an appellative or in Jakobson's words *conative* function. It may also express the condition the addresser is in, for example his or her feelings about what is said, and therefore has an *emotive* function. These three functions had already been described by Bühler (1982, p. 28) in 1934. Jakobson, who tried to bridge linguistics and poetics in his model, added three new functions to Bühler's model. Jakobson's fourth function, called *metalingual*, helps to ensure that the recipient understands the code 'right', that is as intended by the addresser. In language, for instance, the paraphrase of a difficult word may have such a metalingual function. Speech acts can also have a *poetic* function. This poetic function brings the form of a message to the addressee's attention emphasising its beauty or constructedness. Finally a speech act may also contain signs that signal the beginning and the end of a communication and that help to secure the contact between both sides. Jakobson calls this function *phatic*. The following illustration combines the constitutive factors of a communication act and their functions:

	referential function	**> context**	
emotive function > addresser	phatic function	> contact	conative > addressee
	poetic function	> message	
	metalingual function	> code	

Figure 4.1 Functions of language and what they refer to (Jakobson, 1960, p. 353 and p. 357)

Jakobson's functional categories have been developed for a description of language. They work, however, universally well with all kinds of media, including the many sign systems constituting music in performance: pitch, rhythm, sound, language and visual media like gestures, dress, and many more. This makes them ideal for the description of recorded music as multimedia communication. They may, however, also be applied to the analysis of notated music, as I have shown elsewhere (Helms, 2014). Jakobson's model is a good basis through which to make sense of forms of communication, which exist although they are free of semantics and transport no verbalisable information. It may help to describe for example dance music that communicates extremely well without any verbal 'message' on the one hand, and absolute music on the other that makes sense mainly because its form is considered to be special, beautiful or artful.

Different types of music have different communicative functions. In a piece of art music one might expect more signs with a poetic function, raising questions of form. The same may be true for popular music with a certain affinity to art, like for example the lyrics of songs by singer-songwriters or the harmony and voice leading of progressive rock. In dance music one would expect a dominance of signs with a conative function, appealing to the audience for example with the help of a micro-rhythmical groove or shouts from the singer to 'get up and dance!'. In this music signs with a poetic function that would raise questions of form would rather endanger the social function, that is dancing. Pondering about formal problems is definitely not what you want to do on a dance floor. Songs that try to install the image of a pop star in her audience's minds should contain many emotive signs, informing the listener about her persona and creating an image. For musicians of popular music it is of a fundamental importance to attract and to arrest their audiences' attention, much more than for example to make sure that everybody understands the lyrics the same way.[3] Therefore, especially in mainstream music that tries to reach as many listeners (and buyers) as possible, phatic signs that make people listen and keep them interested in the song are of a high importance.

In what follows I will discuss Jakobson's six functions of communication using the example of Lady Gaga's 'Poker Face'. The song was published in 2008 on Lady Gaga's first album *The Fame*. It is my aim to explain why the song has the effects on me described above. For the sake of the length of this chapter I will restrict myself to an analysis of the album version of the song and not consider the music video.

Poetic Functions

Form is definitely not the problem in 'Poker Face', or rather the form of 'Poker Face' does not function to give its interpreters a hint to think about the poetics of the song. If my object of study were the score of a sonata by Beethoven I would have to muse a lot about introduction, exposition, development and recapitulation and the fact that Beethoven troubles me to find out where the one formal element begins and the other ends. The individual form of the composition and its deviations from the standard model of sonata, its use of harmony and the thematic and motivic work would be important starting points of my interpretation.

Here, however, everything is obvious; this 'Poker Face' can be read like an open book. The formal parts of the song are easily recognised: the beginning of most parts is marked by a beat on a crash cymbal, the beginning of the chorus is

[3] Musicians produce fairly complex communications. However, as they are communicating via mass media they have no opportunity to control how their listeners on the other side of the communication circle will understand and interpret the message. Musicians can only perceive the degree of attention their song receives, with the help of charts, airplay statistics, record sales or the reaction of their audiences during concerts. For the communication system of popular music attention is much more important than to deliver a message (Helms, 2008, pp. 83–6).

marked by what I call a synthetic chimes sound: a high pitch sliding down about one and a half octave while the other instruments pause. All parts except for the chorus have a characteristic two-bar bass pattern (Example 4.1) as their fundament.

Example 4.1 Bass line of 'Poker Face' (not in chorus)

The chorus is chordal (four repeated bars of G♯m, E, B and F♯) while the other parts have a linear structure: the space between bass pattern and vocal line is filled with a repetitive melodic line played by a synthesiser for the second part of the verse and the pre-chorus (Example 4.2) and with an angular line that is derived from the vocal line of the pre-chorus for the bridge (Example 4.3).

Example 4.2 'Poker Face', melodic line 1 (intro, verse, pre- and post-chorus)

Example 4.3 'Poker Face', melodic line 2 (bridge)

The overall form is two repetitions of verse and chorus, followed by a bridge and a long finale with repetitions of the chorus and finally the post-chorus (Table 4.1). In many songs of a similar form there is a third verse after the bridge before the song ends with the chorus. I suppose listeners would miss a chorus at this stage of a song but not a verse. The two verses of 'Poker Face' with a total length of 16 out of 116+1 bars are perhaps the least important parts of the overall form.

Table 4.1 Form of 'Poker Face'

Bars	No. of bars	Formal part
1–12	12	Intro
13–20	8	Verse
21–28	8	Pre-chorus
29–36	8	Chorus
37–40	4	Post-chorus
41–48	8	Verse
49–56	8	Pre-chorus
57–64	8	Chorus
65–68	4	Post-chorus
69–80	12	Bridge
81–104	24	Chorus (3×)
105–116	12	Post-chorus (3×)
117	1	Final note, echo/fade out

So much for statistics. I have not even mentioned other elements in the song that create form: lyrics (repetition of text as sign for the chorus), rhythm (longer note values in the vocal melody of the chorus), melody (parlando in the verse, a lively melodic structure with larger intervals and a higher pitch in the chorus), sound (full harmonies, sound filling the whole spectrum, brilliant sounds in the chorus), mix (instruments filling the whole width of the back of the sound box in the chorus). Tagg and Clarida (2003, p. 101–2) would call these signs 'episodic markers'. A musicologist may see in all these elements signs with a poetic function, signs that inform her about the formation of the piece. Still, I maintain that the poetic function in 'Poker Face' definitely is not strong. Other than in my example of the Beethoven sonata the form of 'Poker Face' confirms the standard rather than challenges it. Its form does not raise any issues like 'Why did Lady Gaga compose it this way and not the way all other songs are composed?', 'Why do I feel irritated when listening to the chorus?'. Even as a musicologist you may listen to the song without wondering about its form. A musical form that fulfils all expectations, that is in line with the standard, loses its informational value like a sentence in a speech act loses informational value with every repetition (except for the information that the message in the sentence must be of great importance for the person repeating it). We may analyse and describe it, but it does not offer any clue for further interpretation.

This means that it may be difficult to describe 'Poker Face' as a piece of art music, as in most definitions of art the original, individual formation of a medium seen on the background of formal models and expectations of the public plays an important role. This does not mean that 'Poker Face' is composed badly or primitively, though. For most listeners the changes in the structure of the song simply fulfil a different function: they are not meant to be poetic but phatic. We will consider this function later.

Referential Functions

Older linguistic models of communication and especially of language have maintained that the foremost function of verbal signs is to refer. The word 'tree' refers to an object and therefore gains its meaning. Musicology has for a long time doubted that music can be seen as communication at all. Scholars were of the opinion that musical signs hardly ever refer to things other than themselves. This is not the place to sum up a long and intricate discussion. However, I like to point out that again the medium, that is the musical score (preferably of 'absolute' instrumental art music), and its context, that is a musicologist's study and not the concert hall, influenced scholars' ideas of what music may signify. Who (besides musicologists), I ask, would care for music if it merely were a self-referential system? Why does music make sense to billions of people, although only very few can perceive its structure according to the laws of music theory and therefore come up to Adorno's ideal of an expert listener (Adorno, 1997, p. 182)? On stage, the stage decorations, the costumes of the musicians and their gestures, the sound of an instrument or its particular form may refer. And even the music itself does refer more than some scholars would admit: with every piece of music that we listen to, we associate our individual history and situation at that time: just consider the phenomenon of 'our song' – the song that was playing while we first dated a lover and from then on reminds us of her or him. In this case the whole piece of music becomes a strong single sign that refers to an experience in the past. It is true, music has no semantics comparable to language. You cannot write a dictionary of music–English/English–music. The fact, however, that music as such has only few inter-subjectively fixed meanings does not mean that it has no meaning at all.

Songs from the popular mainstream are supposed to make sense to as many people as possible all over the world. To reach this aim, mainstream songs have to be adaptable to the minds of people with a great variety of experiences and learning. They do not have to refer to something in particular as long as they refer at all; they do not need to have a particular meaning as long as they mean something to someone. This is why signs in many pop songs rather refer to global semantic fields. In many cases their metaphors and symbols will not add up to a single, clearly definable 'deeper meaning'.

The imagery of mainstream pop is often trite. Comparisons, metaphors and symbols used in the lyrics are well known as they either make use of the worn traditions of poetic symbolism or of topics which are currently in the public's awareness. This guarantees that they are widely understood. To give the words a certain ambiguity that makes them interesting, two semantic fields may be combined. In the case of mainstream pop lyrics it has proven helpful to start the interpretation of lyrics with a word class analysis:

- Nouns: Texas plays, baby, luck, intuition, cards, spades, heart, poker face, nobody, pair, gambling, fun, Russian roulette, gun, love, muffin, love glue, chick, casino, bank, hand;
- Verbs: to hold them, to fold them, to let someone (s.o.) hit s.o., to raise it, to stay with s.o., to love s.th., to play, to start, to be hooked, to show, to get, to read, to have to love s.o., to want to roll, to tell, to kiss, to hug, to bluff, to lie, to stun, to gun, to take s.o.'s bank, to pay s.o. out, to promise, to check;
- Adverbs and adjectives: hot, hard, little, rough, marvellous.

It is easy to group these words under a common heading. An astonishingly large number of nouns and verbs in 'Poker Face' refer to gambling. The text is highly original in combining these words with a few words from a second semantic field: love (love, kiss, hug, baby, pair) and sex (muffin, glue, gunning).[4] The second line of the first verse, for example, lists a number of verbs that are used in poker. The last verb, 'to love', however, cannot be referred to gambling but to the second semantic field. In this particular combination the words change their meaning: 'hit me' and 'raise it' gain a fascinating double entendre. To stay, a term used in poker 'when a player remains in the game by calling rather than raising'[5] changes into the plea of many a love song: 'stay with me.' Although the words as such are all rather 'harmless' in combination they refer to sex. To show someone what one has got, as Lady Gaga sings in the pre-chorus, is part of a game of poker. The adverb hot, however, gives the line a sexual reference.

The listener has problems in deciding on what the lyrics are actually about: is it about gambling or about sex or both? Not even the old phrase that 'love is a game' seems to fit precisely. Most lines in the text would be considered absurd if used in everyday language. They are, rather, sequences of words from the same semantic field than meaningful sentences. The text achieves its coherence through the relatedness of the words, not through the logic of its sentences. It is rather a stream of related stimuli than a narrative expressing a larger whole. This fact is not due to a deficiency of its authors.[6] As we can see in comments on Internet forums like songmeanings.com this technique ensures that listeners may adapt the song to their individual experiences, ideas and beliefs. The song may assume many meanings and none of it may be proven wrong (or right). Not even the singer herself seems to feel the necessity to be consistent on what the song is actually about.[7]

---

4 See www.urbandictionary.com.

5 See 'Poker Terms – Poker Dictionary' on http://www.pokernews.com/pokerterms/stay.html [Accessed 10 October 2013].

6 Sung lyrics have the general problem of comprehensibility. Therefore, it is useful for authors rather to concentrate on a strong, coherent imagery than to try to unfold a detailed narrative or complex arguments.

7 See for example the quotes in the article 'Poker Face (Lady Gaga song)' on

Not only the lyrics but also the music may have a strong referential function. Especially in popular music with its quotations, imitations and emulations, its sampling and covering, referential functions are of a much greater importance than poetic functions. One of the reasons why I dislike the song can be found in the fact that its music reminds me of a pop group I utterly despised in the late 1970s and early 1980s. Boney M was all I detested: disco, highly commercial, German (at least it was produced by a German). 'Poker Face' quotes the 'Mum mum mum mah' hook from the chorus of their 1977 hit 'Ma Baker' in its intro and post-chorus. As soon as this association was on my mind, I also heard Boney M's dialogic vocal style of a deep male voice commenting on female lead vocals in the chorus of 'Poker Face' that is sung by a similarly deep, slightly rough male voice. Although the sound of 'Poker Face' is far from 'Ma Baker' with its leading strings and its fast, contrapuntal bass line, the reference may suggest that 'Poker Face' is part of a tradition of dance music. Its synthetic sounds, however, make clear that it comes from and aims at the clubs of 2008 and 2009. Not only words and sound-bites can have a referential function. The timbre of a voice or an instrument can help to classify a song as belonging to a certain genre.[8]

Emotive Functions

Signs with an emotive function do refer too, namely to the addresser. However, it makes sense to distinguish them from the referential function I have just described. In Jakobson's words the emotive function aims at 'a direct expression of the speaker's attitude toward what he is speaking about' (Jakobson, 1960, p. 354). In spoken language interjections like 'I'm sorry, but ...' or the articulation of a sentence for example in a sarcastic tone have an emotive function. I suggest extending Jakobson's definition: a communication act can say more about the addresser than his or her 'attitude'. In the sound of a voice for example we cannot only hear attitudes like irony or emotions like anger. I suppose it is a common experience that voices of unknown people heard on the telephone or the radio conjure up images in the listener's mind: voices are representatives of bodies. We associate with them a speaker's sex, size, age and character. We can hear if the speaker is smiling, crying or frowning, shaking with fear or conscious of his power. We may perceive a nationality, the colour of skin and sometimes we even fancy ourselves to hear the colour of hair (see for example Frith, 1996, pp. 183–202). All this information is part of the message (it does not refer to something outside it) and can make a great difference: just imagine the sentence 'I'm gonna make him an offer he can't refuse' either spoken in a female, high, girlish, smiling voice or in a male, very hoarse, mumbling voice with an Italian accent.

Wikipedia (http://en.wikipedia.org/wiki/Poker_Face_%28Lady_Gaga_song%29, accessed 27 September 2013).

[8] Tagg (2003, p. 102) would classify this type of referential signs as 'style indicators'.

I suggest that communication acts not only inform the recipient about the attitude but also about the identity of the addresser. Therefore I would prefer the term 'self-revelation' ('Selbstkundgabe') introduced by the German psychologist Friedemann Schulz von Thun (n.d.). For the sake of coherence, however, I will stick to Jakobson's term emotive.

The voice is definitely the most suggestive carrier of emotive signs in a recording of popular music (in a video or on stage it would be the image of the body). Before I consider Lady Gaga's performance of 'Poker Face', however, I will have a quick glance at the lyrics. They contain a few direct expressions of emotions: in the first verse she sings, 'I love it', obviously alluding to the game of poker. In the bridge she reveals that she won't tell her lover that she loves him. In the second verse she tells her listeners that she has fun gambling and that she loves it rough. More revealing is the way she expresses her ideas. In many mainstream love songs the singer pleas from a subordinate position, for example in using the subjunctive: 'I would do everything for you' or telling a 'you' how it would be, if only 'you' would love him. The persona of 'Poker Face', however, knows exactly what will happen. The verbs she uses are those of active action,[9] she uses the imperative and many sentences begin with a determined 'I will'.

(Will) power and determination are also expressed in the sound of the voice, or to be precise, in one of the three female voices in the song. The first two and the last line of the verses and the solo lines in the pre-chorus (the second and the fourth) are performed in a monotonous voice, rather spoken than sung, mostly staccato in equally accented eighth notes on a B4, sometimes dropping to a A♯4, the lowest range of the solo female vocals in this song. It sounds distanced (without high frequencies, although no echo or reverb are used except at the end of a line), harsh and nearly snarling. The vowels in 'hot' and 'got' are sung with a pronounced American accent: with an open and very long [a:].[10]

The voice in the chorus is completely different in character: it has the highest range of the song – from B5 down to D5. It is sung in a loud, clear voice with more energy than in the verse; the sound is much more brilliant, friendly, nearly smiling. This is the voice you will recognise on other recordings on Lady Gaga's album *The Fame*.

In the bridge we find a third vocal character: it can perhaps be described as baby talk. The lyrics are spoken, not sung, in a high, girlish voice. The voice sounds nasal. All high frequencies are filtered away. The words 'naïve' and 'Lolita' come to my mind to describe this voice.

The three voices are so different that if it were not for the credits one might assume the presence of three singers. If we consider the voice in the chorus as Lady Gaga's 'normal' voice, the expression of her persona, we may say that she

---

[9] In contrast for example to those of rather passive perception like 'I feel', 'I hope', 'I think' used especially in love songs.

[10] In the spoken parts of Boney M's 'Ma Baker' we may find another variant of the voice of a 'tough lady' with a strong American accent.

sings in character in the verse and the bridge. Both characters, the tough, dominant gambling lady and the Lolita, fit the lyrics. The two verses are full of words from poker and gambling in general, they mention Russian roulette and revel in the roughness of the game. Here the dominant lady is in her right place. The Lolita in the bridge is sullen: she won't tell that she is in love and shoots with a love-glue gun that on first view seems to be a toy and only for insiders is an allusion to a sexual practice.

A pop singer's voice is the core of her brand. It has to make her products recognisable and identifiable. Therefore the chorus at least has to be sung in a voice she uses in other songs as well. Starting 'Poker Face' in the role of a tough, dominant lady and performing the bridge with a Lolita voice is perfectly in line with Lady Gaga's image of playing with identities. She uses her voice(s) like the many costumes she wears.

Phatic Functions

'Poker Face' is an exemplary collection of phatic signs. For me it is a model case for how to grab an audiences' attention. Signs with a phatic function help to keep up the contact between the two sides of communication; they secure attention and signal the beginning or the end of a message. In spoken language 'hello!' or 'listen!' or an 'er' to fill a pause in a sentence would be signs with a phatic function. For listeners to music, I suppose, phatic signs are of even higher importance than in spoken language. They make a piece of music interesting without being thought provoking. Elements with a poetic function raise issues. They interrupt what some call 'passive listening' (what is a highly active, though subconscious process) and induce listeners to think about a piece of music on the meta-level of communication about communication. Phatic elements do not interrupt direct communication between musicians and listeners, they provoke attention, not thoughts. Instead of causing irritation they draw the audience even deeper into the music.

In performed music phatic signs are of high importance for the success of a piece. In the communication systems of a concert hall or a sound recording the musicians are not in the position to control whether their audience does understand them right. They cannot control the transfer of meaning. Referential signs therefore play a secondary (although important) role in the communication system of popular music. The same is true of form. What musicians *can* control, however, is attention. Musicians on stage perceive very well, whether or not they are fascinating and moving their audience, and they may react accordingly. Musicians who produce sound recordings find it even harder to control meaning or formal listening as they have hardly any chance to perceive their listeners' reactions to their songs; they can observe attention though, via charts, airplay or sales. For a musician and recording artist therefore attention is an aim that is much more important than being understood right.

Songs of the popular mainstream need repetition: they have to imprint themselves on their audiences' minds. But repetition increases the danger that a song might get boring or simply get lost in the background noises of whatever the listener is doing while the song is playing. 'Poker Face' is made up of a small number of repeated formal elements (verse and pre-chorus repeated twice, chorus and post-chorus repeated five times), which consist of an even smaller number of musical elements (the bass line for example is running through the whole piece except for the chorus). Phatic signs help to keep the listener interested at least for the time span of three to four minutes.

Elsewhere (Helms, 2014) I have classified phatic signs in four categories: (1) elements that produce tension, (2) variations of the already known, (3) contrast and surprise, and finally (4) symbolised calls for attention.[11] In 'Poker Face' we can find elements of the first three categories.

Tension is produced by denying the audience information that it expects to receive. Relaxation or perhaps even a catharsis is reached when all information is there: for example when all instruments are playing, the most catchy tune is sung, the sound box is filled with sound, the text is easily understood and the song communicates the highest energy. 'Poker Face' begins with a classic means to produce tension: a build-up that extends over 12 bars. After two bars of the bass line played in a rather clear synthesiser sound the sound becomes noisy, raspy and more exciting with added high and low frequencies. Then follow melodic line 1 and four bars later the bass drum, marking a first point of (slight) relief. When the voice starts, tension goes up again, as melodic line 1 is subtracted. It comes back in the middle of the verse after four bars. This is exactly the same place where the voice, that for the first two lines has sung in a low register and in a monotonous parlando, jumps up a sixth and becomes more melodic. For the last two bars of the verse the voice gets back to parlando style, but the loss of energy is now substituted by a doubling of the voice and enlarging it with the help of reverb. The song pushes toward a chorus, but relief is postponed: all the listener gets are two bars of a choir, singing vocalises on 'oh' (reducing information again) and a return of the parlando vocals. All this is repeated before a tutti pause of all instruments and the falling 'synthetic chimes' sound push up tension to a climax. Then, in the chorus everything is there: the vocal melody starts with the highest note and is sung with a maximum of energy, its sound is full and clear and has a large amount of high frequencies (in verse and pre-chorus the voice was filtered). The sound broadens and fills the whole sound box, harmonies are played out in full, the harmonic rhythm slows down (the turnaround needs four instead of two bars in the verse). The lyrics of the chorus are repeated and easily perceptible. The metaphor used in the chorus (to read a poker face) is much more common and intelligible than the imagery of verses and bridge.

---

[11] In certain contexts symbolised calls for attention are for example a horn signal as a symbol for a signal at a hunt, a drum roll as a symbol for a public announcement or a minor third played downward as a symbol for a call ('Rufterz' in German).

After this climax, the post-chorus is used as a starting point to build up tension again. The sound gets narrow again, there are no chords played, the bass line is the only melodic element as the voice repeats 'p-p-p-poker face' on a single note. What follows is more or less a repetition of the build-up via verse and pre-chorus, so I do not have to go into details here.

The 12-bars-long bridge builds up tension in a similar way: we have to wait for four bars for the entry of the voice. The sound gets slightly fuller to the end: a cymbal crash and a short chord fill the space in bars 73 and 77, the voice is multiplied, especially at the end.

Directly after the bridge the final climax starts with three repetitions of the chorus (as the chorus consists of two identical halves this means six repetitions of the same material). But the climax is suspended again: like the pre-chorus the bridge ends with the by now well-known synthetic chimes sound. This time, though, the bass drum and the other instruments run through to the end of the bar. The bass drum stops at the beginning of the chorus and only starts again after a run through of one half of the chorus, indicated again by the chimes sound.

The climax is then extended as long as possible. That the song closes with three repetitions of the post-chorus means a considerable lowering of the energy curve at the end that is unusual for mainstream pop songs. An explanation for this phenomenon will be offered in my analysis of the conative function.

To build up an energy curve up to the chorus is a high art, but after this first climax the production will not become easier. Now that the listener knows the largest part of the material, the producer has to fight against boredom for the rest of the track. Lady Gaga and her producer RedOne do that with the help of a few surprises, contrasts and some variations. I will not enumerate all phatic signs here, but rather refer the reader to Table 4.2 below. Here, I will only mention a few examples.

Already the introduction is rather a chain of varied material than the presentation of one long and slowly unfolding unit. It is mainly the presentation of the two-bar bass line that is introduced as the basis of the song and supplemented with further sounds, a second melody and a beat. The construction of the song from only a few elements of characteristic material and its varied repetition helps to give the song an identity. You only need to hear a few seconds of any section of the song to recognise it as 'Poker Face'.

The verse with its mechanical repetitions of notes of the same length is not only made interesting by the above mentioned jump of a sixth in the third line of the lyrics but especially by the sound of the voice that is varied twice. The first two lines are sung with a filtered nasal, dry sound (without reverb). In the third line ('luck and intuition') the sound of the voice becomes even more nasal through filtering out the higher frequencies. It appears more distanced and has a fast vibrato effect. The voice of the fourth line is comparable to the first two lines. However, it sounds broader as reverb and an echo at the end are added, and the fact that it is doubled is now clearly audible.

Little surprising 'attention grabbers' make the verse even more interesting: it starts (like all formal parts) with the sound of a crash cymbal and a brilliant B–G♯

harmony with a long reverb. The crash cymbal to mark the beginning of a formal part is commonplace in popular music but is still a very effective way to raise attention. At the end of the first line a male voice alarmingly shouts 'hey!' and at the end of the second line a female 'choir' (made up not of many voices but filling the whole breadth of the stereo panorama) interjects: 'I love it'.

Most listeners will consider the music of the second verse to be identical to the first; little variations, however, help subconsciously to enhance their interest. In the second verse the voice is clearly doubled from the beginning, the voice of the third line sounds less distanced, it is less filtered and has no vibrato effect. The whole second verse has a brighter sound than the first. This time the 'hey!' returns not only at the end of the first line but also after the second, simultaneously with the 'I love it' interjection.

Contrasts have a strong phatic effect: new material offers new information and binds the listener's attention: 'Poker Face' not only consists of intro, verse and chorus but also has a pre- and a post-chorus as well as a bridge. As we have seen, repetitions of formal elements are often slightly varied. Only the chorus as the hallmark of the song recurs unchanged. After two repetitions of verse and chorus, however, the balance between the familiar and the new, aiming at the one extreme to anchor the song in the listener's mind and on the other to entertain and excite him or her, tends too much towards the well known. The bridge brings new material and raises interest again. We have a new vocal sound, irritating lyrics about bluffing muffins and a synthesiser melody with a fast ping-pong vibrato that jumps from left to right. The vibrato is slightly out of time with the song's metre, thus at the end of the bridge it produces irritating interferences.

While the bridge is a 'teaser' that secures interest, the chorus at the end has to make sure that the song will be remembered. It is repeated as often as possible without losing the listener's attention. 'Poker Face' does without a third verse that the audience would expect after the bridge. But the first run through of the chorus functions like a rudimentary verse. It begins without drums. The energy curve starts on a lower level to build up the climax. This allows repeating the two identical halves of the chorus three times. Differing from the first two occurrences of the chorus, the synthetic chimes sound is now added between the two halves. In the first part of the song the listener has learned that this sound signals the advent of something new. In the final chorus this expectation is cheated but its effect is nonetheless to raise attention.

After three repetitions of the chorus the listener has had enough of it. The producers use a trick to extend it even longer: they add three repetitions of the post-chorus. This means a slight lowering of the energy curve. But here the post-chorus is blended with the chorus. The sound no longer is reduced to bass and drums but the chordal accompaniment of the chorus plays on and fills the sound box. Only the vocal line loses energy. This slight loss, however, is made up by the conative function of the 'Mum mum mum mah' interjection as we shall see later on. With the help of a multitude of phatic signs the producers manage to make 'Poker Face' a song that presents its chorus (including pre- and post-chorus) in

77 of a total of 117 bars. The final choruses and post-choruses extend over nearly one third of the song (37 bars). 'Poker Face' is an ideal example for the craft of branding without boring the audience.

Table 4.2 Phatic signs in 'Poker Face'

Formal element	Bars	Variations, contrast and surprises
Intro	1–2	Bass line only
	3–4	Bass line doubled with noisy, distorted electro sound (lower octave added) bar 4, 6th eight: 'Mum mum mum mah' (rep. every 2nd bar from here to b. 12)
	5–6	Start melodic line 1: rough, distorted sound (up to b. 12)
	7–8	
	9–10	Start of drums, first beat emphasised by crash cymbal and B G♯ chord
	11–12	End of b. 12: stop melodic line 1
Verse	13–14	Start of vocals (Voice 1) – crash cymbal, B–G♯ sound on first beat Change of bass drum sound (more precise) B. 14, 4th beat: single male voice shout 'hey!'
	15–16	B. 16, 6th eighth: female chorus 'I love it!'
	17–18	Start melodic line 1 (up to b. 28) Change of vocal sound (doubled, higher range of melodic line, melody more lively, close to voice 2)
	19–20	Change of vocal sound (voice 1, back to parlando melody, but added voice)
Pre-chorus	21–22	Crash cymbal and B–G♯ harmony on first beat of b. 21, Female chorus (of voice 1, vibrato) sings vocalises
	23–24	Solo vocals (voice 1, sound of b. 17–18)
	25–26	Female chorus (ref. b. 21–22)
	27–28	Solo vocals (voice 1) B. 28: all instruments end abruptly after 1st beat, 'electronic chimes' sound
Chorus	29–30	b. 29, 1st beat crash and B–G♯ harmony, Solo vocals (voice 2) start with highest note of song, drums: add. open hi-hat chordal accompaniment (b. 29 in staccato eighths, bs. 30–32 sustained chords, sound fills the whole sound box
	31–32	b. 32 male vocals ('She's got …')
	33–34	bs. 29–30 repeated
	35–36	bs. 35–36 repeated

Formal element	Bars	Variations, contrast and surprises
Post-Chorus	37–38	Crash cymbal and B–G♯ harmony on 1st beat Reduction of instruments to bass drum only, melodic line 1 and 'p-p-p-poker face'-vocals, Sound concentrated on single places in the soundbox, b. 38, 6th eighth: 'Mum mum mum mah'
	39–40	Ref. 37–8, but no crash cymbal and harmony at the beginning
Verse	41–42	Vocals voice 1 (not like bs. 13–14 but doubled like bs. 17–18) Crash cymbal, B–G♯ harmony on first beat Drums: bass drum only B. 42, 4th beat: male voice shouts 'hey!'
	43–44	B. 44, 6th eighth: female chorus 'I love it!' and 7th eighth: male 'hey!'
	45–46	Melodic line 1 (up to bar 56) Drums: Bass drum and hand claps Change of vocal sound (voice 1–2, doubled, higher range of melodic line, melody more lively)
	47–48	Change of vocal sound (back to parlando melody)
Pre-Chorus	49–50	Chorus (voice 1) sings vocalises (vibrato!), crash and B–G♯ harmony on first beat of bar 21
	51–52	Vocal sound of bs. 17–18
	53–54	Chorus
	55–56	Vocals B. 56: all instruments end abruptly after 1st beat, 'electronic chimes' sound
Chorus	57–58	b. 57 1st beat: crash and B–G♯ harmony chordal accompaniment, bar 29, 2nd eighth in staccato eighths, bs. 30–32 sustained chord
	59–60	b. 60 male vocals: 'She's got …'
	61–62	See 29–32
	63–64	
Post-chorus	65–66	Crash cymbal and B–G♯ harmony on 1st beat Reduction of instruments to bass, melodic line 1 and 'p-p-p-poker face'-vocals, bar 38, 6th eighth: 'Mum mum mum mah'
	67–68	See 37–38, but no crash

Formal element	Bars	Variations, contrast and surprises
Bridge	69–70	Crash cymbal and B–G♯ harmony on 1st beat Melodic line 2, Change of sound of hand claps B. 70, 6th eighth 'Mum mum mum mah'
	71–72	Melodic line 2 becomes increasingly wobbly, vibrato gets out of rhythm Start vocals (voice 3) on 4th beat Bar 72, 6th eighth 'Mum mum mum mah'
	73–74	B. 73, 1st beat crash cymbal and B–G♯ harmony
	75–76	
	77–78	B. 77, 1st beat crash cymbal and B–G♯ harmony change of vocal sound (doubled)
	79–80	B. 80 chimes, but instruments run through
Chorus	81–82	no drums, voice 2
	83–84	B. 84 chimes, but instruments run through
	85–86	B. 85 drums added
	87–88	
Chorus	89–90	B. 89 crash and B–G♯ harmony
	91–92	B. 92 chimes, but instruments run through
	93–94	B. 93 crash and B–G♯ harmony
	95–96	
Chorus	97–98	B. 97 crash and B–G♯ harmony
	99–100	B. 100 chimes, but instruments run through
	101–102	B. 101 crash and B–G♯ harmony
	103–104	
Post-chorus	105–106	B. 105 crash and B–G♯ harmony chordal accomp. from chorus
	107–108	B. 108 male voice 'she's got …' from chorus (instead of 'mum mum …')
Post-chorus	109–110	B. 109 crash and B–G♯ harmony B. 110 male voice 'mum mum mum mah' (every second bar to end)
	111–112	
Post-chorus	113–114	B. 113 crash and B–G♯ harmony
	115–116	
	117	'mah' echo and fast fade out

Metalingual Functions

The metalingual function draws attention towards the code used in communication. In some forms of communication, that is in language, it is important to make sure that the addressee understands the message the way the addresser has intended. An example for the metalingual function would be a sentence like: 'By the way, you are singing about love glue gunning, but what is love glue?' Like Jakobson's poetic function the metalingual function induces communication about communication, therefore it interrupts the original communication and raises it to the meta-level. For mainstream popular music or dance music such an interruption would endanger its social or psychological functions. The editor of a work by Beethoven might wonder whether a dissonance he finds in an autograph is intentional or just a scribal error. A dancer, however, should not have to ponder about wrong notes or chord progressions. 'Poker Face' does not give its listeners too much to think about while the music is playing. The music itself does not raise any issues of code. For instance, the few notes foreign to the scale (see for instance Example 4.3) are heard as blue notes. The lyrics, however, have a few instances that may induce questions on the metalingual level. As listeners to music are used to problems with the intelligibility of lyrics this will not reduce their fun while the music is playing (and dancers hardly care for the words of a song anyway). But some listeners may wish to find out more about the lyrics after the song has ended. Heavy, unintelligible and ambiguous words are a helpful way of keeping listeners occupied with the song *after* the performance and to raise the interest of the media – especially if they touch taboos. 'Poker Face' uses strange words and unintelligible passages as well as ambiguities. How successful the lyrics are in raising interest in the song may be seen in interviews with Lady Gaga[12] but also in various forums[13] discussing the text and explaining its words. Those who do not play poker (or do not know the English technical terms) may have problems already with the first line which alludes to Texas hold em', a variant of poker. The following lines contain many more technical terms. Even more questions are raised by the bridge and its phrases about bluffing someone with a muffin and stunning him with love glue. Both phrases make sense as vocal sounds in this passage that is close to rap. Both sound suspiciously of taboos. And indeed, the 'Urban Dictionary' of slang (www.urbandictionary.com) informs us about the sexual meaning of these phrases.[14]

In three instances in the lyrics, Lady Gaga produces ambiguities by pronouncing words unusually. In the pre-chorus the vowel [a:] in 'hot' is sung with a little touch of a [r]. The phrase may thus be heard as 'I get him hard'. Her singing of 'poker face' in the post-chorus has raised some discussions in various forums on the

---

12 See for example Lady Gaga in interview with Jonathan Ross on BBC One (http://www.youtube.com/watch?v=ZxHTtNWdAns, accessed 10 October 2013).

13 'Bluffin' with my muffin' for example is discussed on Yahoo!Answers (http://answers.yahoo.com/question/index?qid=20081226214335AA92A8l), on gutefrage.net (http://www.gutefrage.net/frage/was-bedeutet-i-m-bluffin-with-my-muffin), on answers.com (http://wiki.answers.com/Q/What_does_bluffin%27_with_my_muffin_mean) and on many other sides (all accessed 10 October 2013).

14 The two entries on 'glue-gunning' may be influenced by the song as they were added to the dictionary in 2009 while 'Poker Face' was in the charts.

web. When repeating the phrase 'p-p-p-poker face' the singer puts emphasis on every syllable. Some listeners stated therefore she would sing 'poke her face',[15] interpreting the phrase as an allusion to oral sex. Another phrase that is discussed on the web is the beginning of the third line of the first verse. Most lyrics websites give 'luck and intuition', some, however, transcribe it as 'Love game intuition'.[16] Having listened many times to the passage, I am still convinced I hear the rather nonsensical 'love game intuition'. By the way: 'LoveGame' is the second song on the album *The Fame*. Lady Gaga and her producer RedOne are ingenious in not only drawing attention to a song but also greatly extending this attention beyond the end of the song.

Conative Functions

Songs of the popular mainstream and especially of dance music are not made for a passive audience that lets the music simply pass by. They want to get their audiences involved. In Jakobson's six categories of the functions of communication conative signs appeal to the addressee to do something; to choose some examples from the history of popular music: 'Twist and shout!' or 'Get up, stand up, stand up for your rights' might have a conative function in certain contexts.

Music can have a strong conative function. It goes without saying that metre and rhythm are extremely strong conative signs. They appeal to the listeners to move in time. The whole structure of 'Poker Faces' is concentrated on the expression of a straight, clearly perceptible, danceable rhythm: the four-to-the-floor beat of the bass drum builds a massive basis, the bass line and the accompanying melodic lines and chords all run through in (mostly repeated) eighth notes. The 120 beats per minute are comfortably danceable.

Since childhood we have learned that an audience may signal its involvement in the music by clapping its hands to the beat. We all have had the experience that clapping hands is contagious. Producers of popular music make use of this conditioning and add virtual hand claps on the back beats. In 'Poker Face' the claps completely replace the less appealing snare drum.

We all have also learned that we may get involved in a song by singing along whenever the musicians tell us to do so: 'All together now!' Usually the audience joins in at the chorus (as the name implies). In some songs the chorus is sung by all members of the band or the leading voice is accompanied by a choir. Usually the chorus uses 'choral' instruments like strings or string-like sounds that fill the

---

15 See for example http://rock.rapgenius.com/Lady-gaga-poker-face-lyrics#lyric or http://de.answers.yahoo.com/question/index?qid=20090724011921AAnVDBo (all accessed 10 October 2013).

16 See for example http://songmeanings.com/songs/view/3530822107858738230/ [Accessed 10 October 2013].

whole breadth of the sound box. They virtually embrace the listener and make her a part of the song.

In the chorus of 'Poker Face' Lady Gaga's voice is doubled and spread over the horizon of the sound box with the help of reverb. In some instances (the second 'can't read my' and 'poker face') the voice and the keyboard accompaniment blend so much that to me it sounds as if the voice would split up into two parts. Compared to the verse and pre- and post-chorus with their parlando the chorus has the most melodic, singable vocal line. To me it has an elevating (and phatic) effect but not a strong conative character. Starting with the highest note of the song the chorus is rather uncomfortable to sing.

Much more appealing to me as a man is the 'Mum mum mum mah' of the post-chorus. It is much easier to join in with – and it is familiar since 1977 and Boney M's 'Ma Baker' (where it had the same effect). The fact that 'Poker Face' does not end with the chorus as many mainstream songs do, but with three repetitions of the post-chorus suggests that I react exactly as intended by the producers. They must have trusted so much in the conative effect of the 'Mum mum mum mah' that they risked ending the song not on the energetic climax of the chorus. 'Mum mum mum mah' is echoing on beyond the end of the last chord of the song: the audience is supposed to sing on.

Positioning Addresser and Addressee

I find Jakobson's six categories of functions of communication very useful in focusing my attention on all the elements in a piece of music that may have an effect on the audience, be it to transport a message, to inform them about the singer or to make them dance. There is, however, a group of signs in a song I have problems to assign to one of his six categories. As far as I can see my problem is specific to art, that is to literature and to music, and is especially obvious in sound recordings although it is present in the face-to-face situation of a concert as well. This information refers to something that is part of the communication act, therefore we cannot group it among signs with a referential function. They do not appeal to the addressee nor are they an expression of the addresser's emotional state and identity. They have to do something with the relationship between addresser and addressee but their function cannot precisely be described as phatic: recorded music does not only carry information about addresser, addressee, context, code, form and contact but also about the virtual space in which communication with the listeners is to take place. Space not only means a particular room like for example a concert hall but also the spatial relationship between musician and listener and this also implies their role and position in a communication act.

Let me start with the role: literature assigns various roles to its readers and audiences (and song lyrics are literature for singing): the role may be passive, like for example in a drama, where other people act something out for the audience.

In popular music this dramatic position is rare.[17] Another position of the listener also is quite passive: someone tells the story of a third person (and perhaps his relationship to him). In popular music this position, which I call narrative, can be found for example in ballads. In the third position the reader or listener is assigned an active role: the lyrical I expresses his or her feelings and addresses the listener directly as a 'you'.[18] This position can be found in the majority of mainstream popular music, especially in romantic love songs. The fact that 'baby, I love you' may be interpreted as real or as fictitious is part of the fascination of the pop star. I suggest we might call this position 'lyrical'. A fourth position is perhaps the most active. It is more common in music than in literature: in this position the boundaries between addresser and addressee are abrogated, musicians and listeners melt into one large unity. This 'we' position that can be found for example in many party hits (for example 'Live Is Life' by Opus), in political songs ('We Shall Overcome') and in some hymnal love songs (for example 'United We Stand' by Brotherhood of Man).

In 'Poker Face' we find a mix of the three positions mentioned first: the lyrical 'I' narrates how she will play (or gamble) with an unnamed 'him'. But every now and then the position changes to a directly addressed 'baby' or 'you'. The means of changing positions may prevent listeners to identify with the 'you' in the lyrics. Addressing the 'you' will at most have a phatic effect appealing rather to the listener's subconscious. 'Poker Face' turns the balance of power in traditional love songs between the pleading protagonist and the worshipped 'you' upside down. If a listener should identify with one of the characters in the lyrics at all it may rather be the strong and attractive lyrical 'I' than the passively suffering 'he' that is blended with the 'you'. The situation is made even more complicated by the three distinct voices Lady Gaga uses and the additional male voice. Whom are we actually observing to communicate with whom?

The song does not conjure up a close relationship between singer and listener and you can hear this in the mix of the song very well. The four positions I have mentioned cannot only be found in the lyrics but also in the music of a song. Songs in the 'we-position' often use a choir and have a hymnal chorus that is especially inviting to sing along with. Their sound fills the sound box and embraces the listener to make him or her a 'protagonist' of the music. The dramatic and narrative positions are reflected in the music by a spatial distance between singer(s) and listener; the singer may produce a feeling of distance by singing in a loud voice, or reverb may be added to simulate a large room. The listener remains a distanced 'observer'. The lyrical or 'me and you' position can be supported by the music for example through singing in a low or even whispered voice to produce the feeling of closeness and to exclude other listeners. Allan Moore would call this

[17] Frank Loesser's song 'Baby It's Cold Outside' of 1949, sung among many others by Bing Crosby and Doris Day, comes to my mind.

[18] An extreme version of this position only speaks of the 'I' implicitly assuming that a 'you' is feeling addressed.

position 'antagonistic' (Moore, 2012, p. 185; see ibid., pp. 179ff. for a more detailed discussion).

In the music of 'Poker Face' we can hear the same 'mix' of positions we have seen in the lyrics. Lady Gaga's voice, or rather voices, appear at a medium distance. The tough voice in verse and pre-chorus sounds pretty close, it is brought forth with the intensity of a strong speaking voice (as would be used for example by a teacher in a class room). At the end of phrases we hear a light reverb or echo simulating a larger room but at the same time in the pre-chorus we perceive breath sounds at the end of the line that indicate a short distance. The fact that the voice is doubled in most passages of verse, pre- and post-chorus except the beginning of the first verse adds to the feeling of distance, but at the same time this effect has a (very) slight tendency towards embracing the listener.

The 'Lolita' voice in the bridge is performed with a lower intensity and recorded without any reverb. It would sound close if the producer had not filtered out all the high frequencies so it creates the indirect and distancing effect of listening to a voice in an old radio.[19] Higher frequencies are only added in the last four bars of the bridge, but again at the same time the voice is doubled and retreats audibly a step into the back of the sound box. The voice of the chorus is definitely at the greatest distance from the listener. It is sung loudly, with much energy and a fair amount of reverb. But the singer does not retreat completely to the back of the sound box to give the listener a chance to join in. Her voice remains focused on the middle of the stereo panorama and only the sharp consonant[s] of 'poker face' reaches out into its extremes to the right and the left. The embracing effect is produced by the keyboard and not by the voice.

An effect approaching an embracing 'we' position is only produced in four short instances: the 'I love it' interjections at the end of the second line of both verses, the little female choir with 'oh' vocalises in the pre-chorus, the male answer in the chorus and most prominently the 'Mum mum mum mah' of the introduction and the post-chorus. None of these instances may be called a choir. The two male interjections and the female 'I love it' are rather heard as solo voices. The effect is particularly clear in the 'Mum mum mum mah': the voice echoes between both extreme sides of the panorama, but the middle of the sound box is left empty. The listener is invited to fill this void; as I said before, the 'mum mum mum mah' produces a strong conative effect. The 'we' that is created, however, is not that of a large mass of people but of the female singer and her male counterpart. The listener is free to choose one of the two roles.

---

[19] A classic instance of this sound is the lead voice of The Buggles' 'Video Killed the Radio Star'.

What's It All about?

My analysis in terms of the six functions of communication developed by Jakobson (and a seventh proposed by me) helped me to explain why I do not like 'Poker Face': its references to Boney M, but also its strong power to get me involved singing – at least in my mind – 'mum mum mum mah', although I do not want to be involved. It showed me that the power of the piece to arrest my attention is produced by carefully planned phatic signs. The reason why I do not feel close to Lady Gaga (as for example I feel close to Norah Jones – although I do not fancy her songs either) can be shown in an analysis of the emotive elements that signal a multiple identity of the singer in this song. At the same time the song positions me as a listener at a certain distance and keeps me hanging between the roles of an observer and a protagonist. I watch Lady Gaga performing the tough gambler, the Lolita and her core persona from a distance but cannot help taking a part in the song myself softly humming 'mum mum mum mah'. 'Poker Face' is a brilliantly produced piece of dance-oriented mainstream pop. It perfectly fulfils all the functions it is supposed to.

Jakobson does not offer a new methodology for analysis. His functions of communication, however, broaden the mind of the analyst and make clear that the analysis of music in performance may have a much wider aim than asking for form and meaning only. They can help us understand how music actually works beyond a description of the scaffolding of its construction and the referential function of its signs. A song does not have to have an inter-subjectively valid deeper meaning, it does not even have to have a subjective meaning. I still cannot tell what 'Poker Face' is all about. I do, however, know how the song makes sense to me, how it functions in communication with me.

Jakobson's ideas have a highly integrative power. They can be applied to interpret scores, recordings, music videos and live performances. The categories can be filled with acoustic, verbal and visual signs. They can be used for 'high' art and the most 'banal' mainstream song; they may show up that the 'banal' song is as complex as the piece of art music, but only that its intricacies refer to another category and aim at another communicative function. It may also show up that the most renowned piece of art music can appear simple and unoriginal, if you only choose a function other than the poetic.

References

Adorno, T.W., 1997. Typen musikalischen Verhaltens. In: R. Tiedemann (ed.), *Theodor W. Adorno. Einleitung in die Musiksoziologie* (= Gesammelte Schriften 14). Frankfurt/M.: Suhrkamp, pp. 178–98.

Bühler, K., 1982. *Sprachtheorie. Die Darstellungsfunktion der Sprache*. Stuttgart and New York: UTB 1982 [Reprint of Jena 1934].

Frith, S., 1996. *Performing Rites: Evaluating Popular Music*. Oxford: Oxford University Press.

Helms, D., 2008. What's The Difference? Populäre Musik im System des Pop. In: C. Bielefeldt, U. Dahmen and R. Grossmann (eds), *PopMusicology*. Bielefeld: Transcript, pp. 75–93.

Helms, D., 2014. 'Von Interesse ist die Wirkung'. Musikalische Pragmatik und notierte Musik, z.B. Sibelius' 'Finlandia'. In: S. Hanheide and D. Helms (eds), *'Ich sehe was, was du nicht hörst.' Etüden und Paraphrasen zur musikalischen Analyse. Festschrift für Hartmuth Kinzler zum 65. Geburtstag*. Osnabrück: epOs, pp. 153–84.

Jakobson, R., 1960. Closing Statement: Linguistics and Poetics. In: T.A. Sebeok (ed.), *Style in Language*. Cambridge, MA: The MIT Press, pp. 350–77.

Moore, A.F., 2012. *Song Means: Analysing and Interpreting Recorded Popular Song*. Farnham: Ashgate.

Schulz von Thun, F., n.d. Das Kommunikationsquadrat, [online] Available at: http://www.schulz-von-thun.de/index.php?article_id=71&clang=0 [Accessed 10 October 2013].

Tagg, P., 2013. *Music's Meanings: A Modern Musicology for Non-Musos*. New York and Huddersfield: The Mass Media Music Scholars' Press.

Tagg, P. and Clarida, B. 2003. *Ten Little Title Tunes: Towards a Musicology of the Mass Media*. New York and Montreal: The Mass Media Music Scholars' Press.

Discography

Lady Gaga, 2009. 'Poker Face'. Interscope/UMG, 00602517964990.

Boney M, 1977. 'Ma Baker'. *Love For Sale*. Hansa, 28 888 OT.

Chapter 5
Can't Get Laid in Germany – Rammstein's 'Pussy' (2009)

Dietmar Elflein

Analytical Approach

My analytical approach is a comparative one. Songs are embedded in a network of influences; they are influenced by other songs and influence other songs themselves. These influences exist on a general level regarding the whole song but also regarding the voice of every instrument involved. Songs are thus complex utterances that are composed of other simple and complex utterances. According to Mikhail Bakhtin 'the first and foremost criterion for the finalisation of the utterance is the possibility of responding to it or, more precisely and broadly, of assuming a responsive attitude toward it' (Bakhtin, 1986, p. 76). As a consequence utterances intercommunicate in an endless dialogue (see Bakhtin, 1986, p. 69). Sound, the 'expressive intonation' of an utterance as Bakhtin (1986, p. 90) calls it, is a necessary part of his definition of the utterance. In accordance with Bakhtin I understand songs as being comparable to the concept of *parole* and not to the concept of *langue*. Because of their dialogic character songs are able to influence other songs, that is, they are able to act like the non-human actors suggested by Bruno Latour (2010, pp. 121–42) and other authors of actor-network theory. It is important to recognise that the song and the artist should not be treated as something familiar but as something different that we have to learn to understand. We do not necessarily speak the same *parole* as the song does.

Therefore, it is necessary to relate a song to the larger body of work of the given artist and to work with any association turning up when listening. A primary goal of my analysis is to discuss the network surrounding the song by first, relating it to a network of relations surrounding the artist, and second, by carefully describing associations related to the song as a piece of art.

Consequently, I will begin with the artists, Rammstein, and their biography and image. A second step is to identify the idiolect of the artist to see whether the song in question is supporting or countering it. A third step is to consider the various forms of the song's commodification, that is to integrate the analysis of the cover art, the video clip and different release formats. If the song is part of an album, the song's relationship to the album as a whole and to the neighbouring songs should be taken into consideration. In a fourth step I try to give a thick description of my impression when listening to the song and counter these impressions with the analyses of form, harmony, sound, rhythm and lyrics. As a consequence, my analysis should enable an understanding of the music in its cultural context.

A GDR Tale

To understand Rammstein it is important to realise that the band is a kind of supergroup of the former GDR punk underground or what, in capitalist surroundings, would be called the independent scene (see Galenza and Havemeister, 1999). In addition, the majority of the musicians stem from an at least partially academic and/or artistic GDR background.

Being an artist in the former GDR meant that you could only make a living if you did not oppose the political system. Contrary to that, being a punk meant that you were treated as a public enemy and had to live your life under constant surveillance and repression (see Horschig, 1999). GDR ideology regarded punk as a product of capitalist decadence that by definition could not exist in socialism and, therefore, GDR officials fought punk (see Wicke, 1996).

Concerning the GDR popular music scene, German reunification is a specific watershed. Only a small selection of Western popular music had been released in the GDR via the state-owned Amiga label and only a few Western artists had been allowed to play concerts in the GDR. GDR audiences bought records and attended concerts of national bands because international alternatives were unavailable. As a consequence, the careers of the majority of GDR popular music artists suffered after reunification. Record sales and the number of people attending concerts of GDR bands declined dramatically once international originals had become available. The economic perspectives of many East German musicians broke down. In addition, the process of coming to terms with the GDR past showed that a lot of popular music bands (whether punk or not) had been objects of constant surveillance by the GDR state security STASI. Members of various bands had been so-called off-the-record contributors of state security and had constantly reported internal matters to the STASI. For example this is true for the GDR punk band Die Firma,[1] named after the GDR vernacular of the STASI. Die Firma was the former band of Rammstein drummer Christoph Schneider (see Galenza and Havemeister, 1999, p. 49). Rammstein guitar player Paul Landers also played occasionally with Die Firma but, together with keyboard player Christoph Lorenz, had his own band called Feeling B. Because of being punk Die Firma had no official GDR releases while Feeling B were allowed to contribute to official compilations (*die anderen Bands*; [the other bands], 1988) and to release their debut album *Hea Hoa Hoa Hea Hea Hoa* in 1989.[2] Bass player Oliver Riedel played with a folk-based

[1] Not to be confused with the West German hip-hop crew of the same name.

[2] Feeling B were also part of the official documentary of the GDR predecessor of an independent rock scene *Flüstern und Schreien – Ein Rockreport* (Schumann, 1999 [1988]). Landers was credited as the musical consultant of the film. He apparently knew how to

punk band called The Inchtabokatables prior to his Rammstein involvement. The Inchtabokatables were founded in 1991, two years after German reunification, but for Riedel all members of the band had already been involved in the GDR underground. Thus, four out of six Rammstein members had been members of well-known underground bands, while one, singer Till Lindemann, sang in a less widely known GDR punk band. Guitar player Richard Kruspe is said to have started his musical career after reunification.[3]

When Rammstein was founded in 1994 all members knew the problems GDR popular music had to face after reunification. They knew they had to face the new economic and political situation. From the very beginning Rammstein was designed for success in a capitalist surrounding. Being personally involved in the Berlin popular music scene of the nineties I remember the spreading rumours that ex-members of Feeling B and Die Firma were soon to come up with something special.

Provocation as a Means to Success

Calculated provocation accompanied Rammstein's story from the very beginning. The Slovenian band Laibach provided the role model for forming their public image. Laibach was founded in 1980 in what was then still Yugoslavia and named itself after the German name of the Slovenian capital Ljubljana – a provocation considering the Yugoslav suffering from Nazi occupation during World War II. Rammstein took their name from the Ramstein air-show disaster[4] – a provocation to the victims and survivors of the disaster as well as the German public. The air-show disaster happened in 1988 in West Germany when all of Rammstein's members were still citizens of the GDR. Laibach have often been accused of flirting with fascist ideology and iconography; Rammstein tried the same when they used Leni Riefenstahl footage in the video clip accompanying their cover version of Depeche Mode's 'Stripped' (1998).

But contrary to Rammstein, Laibach is an intellectual art project, a part of the New Slovenian Art Collective (NSK) stemming from the Slovenian punk

---

work the system. Musicologist Sabine Binas-Preissendorfer, who has been part of the GDR underground scene herself, stated in a personal conversation with the author, that the release of the Feeling B album was possible since GDR authorities were already in demise in 1988/89 (see also Wicke, 1996, pp. 24–7).

[3] Regarding biographical information on Rammstein see Mühlmann (1999) and http://en.wikipedia.org/wiki/Rammstein#Founding_and_Herzeleid_.281989-1996.29 [Accessed 30 April 2013].

[4] 'Aircraft of the Italian Air Force display team collided during their display, crashing to the ground. 67 spectators and 3 pilots died. 346 spectators sustained serious injuries in the resulting explosion and fire, and hundreds of others had minor injuries' (http://en.wikipedia.org/wiki/Ramstein_air_show_disaster, accessed 30 August 2013).

scene, which has been extensively described by Alenka Barber-Kersovan (2005). Journalist Wolf-Rüdiger Mühlmann (1999, p. 39) analyses the relationship between Rammstein and Laibach in his book *Letzte Ausfahrt Germania* [last exit Germania] as follows: Laibach is a political discussion, Rammstein a tabloid.

Not only have Rammstein copied Laibach's flirtation with fascist and totalitarian ideology and iconography but also their militaristic on-stage look and their on-stage behaviour without any interaction with the audience.[5] They have added an emphasis on male fantasies of sexual dominance as well as on sexual perversions in general to counteract, and at the same time play with, homoerotic connotations connected with the aggressive male bonding of their image and performance. In terms of authenticity the band should be treated as an example of authentic inauthenticity (see Grossberg, 1992, p. 226). Although Rammstein are not an art school band, their main influences stem from art school bands like Laibach and Depeche Mode. Robert Burns (2008) misses this point in his analysis of German symbolism in rock music. But with the restriction that Rammstein present an art school-informed performance and design concept he gives fruitful insights in 'comparisons between Rammstein's stage settings and costumes and the mechanical-kinetic constructivist movement in Germany of the 1920s' (Burns, 2008, p. 458).

But it is also necessary to state that the over-the-top image and stage shows always contain elements of sarcastic or black humour normally personified in the character of keyboard player Lorenz who for example gets cooked by singer Lindemann during the performance of 'Mein Teil' [my piece], walks on a treadmill while playing or dances awkwardly on stage.[6]

The Rammstein Formula

Laibach's musical work, especially the *Opus Dei* album released in 1987, can also be regarded as a big influence on Rammstein's musical output. The album included cover versions of 'Live Is Life' by Opus, a 1985 number one chart hit in Germany and Austria, which peaked at number six in the UK charts, and 'One Vision' by Queen, both delivered with German lyrics in almost literal translation

[5] The camera-work on the concert DVD *Völkerball* (Smith, 2006) regards every possible human emotion by a band member (for example smiling) as an invitation to zoom in on the particular face apparently in order to humanise the band members.

[6] There are more keyboard players in (German) heavy metal bands that tend to get used and abused by their fellow musicians to emphasise that keyboards are kind of dubious instruments within heavy metal music; see for example the Thuringian band Die Apokalyptischen Reiter [Riders of the apocalypse].

and a vocal style similar to Lindemann's inchoate singing style in Rammstein, including the trilled 'r'.[7]

Therefore, Burns's (2008, p. 458) argument that German interwar cabaret singers influenced Lindemann's singing should be considered as mediated through Laibach. In the above-mentioned songs Laibach combine distorted guitar sounds with electronics and marching drums ('Live Is Life') or a powerful backbeat without hi-hat or cymbals, respectively ('One Vision'). This is contrary to their usual sound, which is much more dominated by electronics and drum machines. Rammstein concentrate on this *Opus Dei* formula throughout their whole career but they add electronic sounds that are much more rooted in club culture. Laibach moved in the same direction with their following releases but soon got rid of rock-based guitars and drums. Rammstein even cite Laibach's German lyrics to 'One Vision' in the bridge of 'Rammlied' from their 2009 album *Liebe ist für alle da* [love is for everyone] – which includes the song 'Pussy'.

Other obvious musical influences are Depeche Mode and Ministry – the latter in their combination of metal based guitars with industrial music resulting in stoic heavily quantised guitar riffs and drumming as well as an aggressive use of digital editing and cutting where artefacts of the editing process are supposed to be noticed. Ministry changed their musical style from electronic-based industrial to the incorporation of electric guitars in 1987 with their *The Land Of Rape And Honey* album but broke into the mainstream with their *Psalm 69* release of 1992. Therefore, Ministry provided a useful way to combine a Laibach-based concept with commercial success at a time when Rammstein's concept was in the planning stage. Rammstein have never denied the influences of these bands on their music.

Therefore, in contrary to Burns's (2008, p. 457) argumentation the band has never been rooted in 'extreme' metal. Rammstein are mainly influenced by industrial music and related genres varying from pop music to heavy metal. The resulting Rammstein formula is based on heavily edited stoic distorted guitar riffs based on power chords in dropped tunings, stoic backbeat-based drums (also heavily edited), highly modulated electronics including club culture-based drumbeats and Lindemann's Laibach-influenced singing style. These modules are used in various combinations to create different tensions and contrasts between opposites like soft and strong, quiet and loud, verse and chorus, et cetera. In general, Rammstein use four different textures: electronic drums and keyboard; drums and keyboard (with or without electronic drums); guitar and drums, and; all instruments together. All four textures exist in combination with bass and voice as well as without. The keyboard is the only instrument that is allowed to move or even improvise freely on the given texture. Therefore, instrumental solos are usually keyboard solos. Few

[7] The Laibach version of 'One Vision' is entitled 'Geburt einer Nation' [Birth of a nation]. They have been accused of flirting with Facism first, because people did not recognise the cover version, and second, because they have replaced some strategic words in the German translation; for example they changed 'bone' into 'blood' or 'decision' into 'will'.

guitar solos occur, some of which are heavily processed by effect devices that make them sound synthesised.

Facts about 'Pussy'

'Pussy' is the first single from Rammstein's sixth studio album *Liebe ist für alle da* and was released as CD single, limited edition 7″ and 12″ vinyl single and digital download in September 2009 one month prior to the album release. The song was the first Rammstein release after a three-year hiatus and also their first number one single in Germany. In addition, the song charted in 10 European countries including the UK singles charts and the UK rock charts. 'Pussy' is one of the most successful singles of the band in terms of chart positions.

Regarding songwriting and production credits there is nothing unusual about 'Pussy'. Music and lyrics are credited to the whole band, which is Rammstein's common way of dealing with songwriting credits. Jacob Hellner from Sweden produced the track, as he does all Rammstein's singles and studio albums. The cover of the CD single shows a montage of six naked female bodies with the head of one band member on each of the bodies in front of a black background with the trademarked typography of the Rammstein lettering on top and the title 'Pussy' in a kind of pixelated old-style console typography below the montage. The typography of 'Pussy' relates to the album logo while the cover montage relates to the video shot by acclaimed director Jonas Åkerlund.[8] The video provoked a scandal because of its explicitly pornographic scenes showing all of the band members having sexual intercourse with women. It was released parallel to the single on a Dutch adult video chat portal.[9] Visual German signifiers in the video are limited to the bridge and breakdown section. During the bridge the band plays in front of a German flag with Lindemann shouting 'Germany'. The following breakdown continues the use of the German flag and sees Lindemann behind a speaker's desk equipped with historical and contemporary microphones. This is followed by a cut with Lindemann waving the flag.

To underline Rammstein's sense of humour the video portrays keyboard player Lorenz as a transgender she-male. This montage makes it obvious that the pornographic scenes are played by body doubles and not by the band members themselves. In addition, the colouring of the 7″ vinyl single in Viagra blue vinyl as well as the montage of the head of the band member with the most chunky body,

[8] Amongst other awards he has won two Grammys for his work with Madonna (see http://www.thesmile.tv/directors/jonas-akerlund/ [Accessed 8 April 2013]).

[9] The website still advertises the video release: 'Noch nie hatte eine Video-Präsentation weltweit so viel Aufmerksamkeit erregt wie diese' [never before has a video release gained so much world-wide attention] (http://www.visit-x.net/rammstein [Accessed 8 April 2013]).

singer Till Lindemann, on a pregnant female body on the single cover emphasises the importance of a wicked sense of humour as a part of Rammstein's image.

Of course, a non-explicit version of the video was released replacing the pornographic scenes with heat-image style footage of the scenes to emphasise censorship issues. Supporting access to pornography for minors is still illegal in most countries no matter how easy it might be for them to access pornography via the World Wide Web. Therefore, any censorship accusations are causeless. But in the end, this marketing campaign succeeded. Rammstein managed to provoke the scandal they needed to promote the single and thereby proved that they are still controversial. Rammstein were back with a bang after their three-year hiatus.

During the *Liebe ist für alle da* tour (2009–11) following the release of the album, 'Pussy' marked the end of the regular show.[10] During the *Made in Germany* tour starting in 2011, 'Pussy' has moved to the position of the last encore.[11] The performance repeats the usual Rammstein performance style of static band members staring at the audience while playing, with the exception of singer Lindemann who occasionally moves around. The performance contains no connotations to the video. No German flag is waved during the breakdown section. Instead, this particular part of the song is extended to use a foam cannon aiming at the audience that is ridden by Lindemann. This metaphor of ejaculation has to be seen in the context of the contemporary common use of such cannons supplying foam, confetti or something similar at the end of stadium performances of popular music. There is nothing erotic nor provocative about them – just pure patriarchic entertainment and spectacle. The song and the show end with the band members paying homage to their audience like aristocrats pay homage to their king.[12]

Facts about *Liebe ist für alle da*

As already mentioned, the album *Liebe ist für alle da* was released one month after the release of 'Pussy' as a lead single. The album peaked at number one in the German, Austrian and Swiss charts and at numbers 16 and 13 respectively in the UK and US charts.

The album cover shows a photo of the band members arranged around a table with a naked women lying thereon – in the style of a renaissance painting. The booklet contains variations of the cover theme. The back cover of the booklet shows a heart-shaped logo of the album title with pixelated typography related to

---

[10] See http://en.wikipedia.org/wiki/Liebe_ist_f%C3%BCr_alle_da_Tour [Accessed 29 April 2013].

[11] See http://en.wikipedia.org/wiki/Made_In_Germany_1995-2011_Tour [Accessed 29 April 2013].

[12] See for example http://www.youtube.com/watch?v=qC-TRyGMkf8 [Accessed 29 April 2013].

the 'pussy' typography in trying to generate an idea of a corporate image for all releases connected to the album.[13]

Liebe ist für alle da contains 11 tracks with 'Pussy' being the eighth. Like on every Rammstein album the majority of the tracks are riff-based (tracks 1, 2, 3, 5, 7, 9, 10). At least one power ballad is included (track six 'Frühling in Paris' [springtime in Paris]) and at least one track is designed to be different – the closing track 'Roter Sand' [red sand]. The remaining two tracks, including 'Pussy', are based on the repetition of harmonic formulas whereby track four 'Haifisch' contrasts a synthesised sequencer-based verse largely inspired by Depeche Mode with a guitar-driven harmonic pattern in the chorus, while 'Pussy' is entirely based on the repetition and variation of one harmonic formula.

Regarding song structures, *Liebe ist für alle da* differs from the previous albums since all of its songs use the standard rock song formula of verse-verse-break-(verse)-playout as described by Allan F. Moore (2001, p. 150) whereas on the previous albums Rammstein mixed standard rock songs with song structures based on the sequencing of riffs common in both heavy metal and electronic dance music. As usual in Rammstein's lyrical universe, the majority of the lyrics on *Liebe ist für alle da* deal with sex.

Therefore, *Liebe ist für alle da* contains all Rammstein trademarks and presents artists who know what their audience expect. Modifications occur only in the exclusive use of professionalised pop song structures and in the details used within these structures.

Listening to 'Pussy' – The Music

The following chart shows the formal structure compared to the standard rock song formula.

Table 5.1 'Pussy', formal structure

Standard Rock Song	**Intro**		**Verse**			**Verse**			**Break**	**Playout**	
Pussy	*Intro*	*Chorus (instr.)*	*Verse*	*Pre-chorus*	*Chorus*	*Verse*	*Pre-chorus*	*Chorus*	*Bridge*	*Break-down*	*Chorus*
Length (bars)	4	16	16	4	16	16	4	16	8	16	16

[13] One month after release, the album was indexed in Germany because of violent and misogynist lyrics (in the track 'Ich tu Dir weh' [I hurt you]) and pictures (http://www.bundespruefstelle.de/bpjm/die-bundespruefstelle,did=132562.html, accessed 29 April 2013). The indexation was cancelled in October 2010 (http://www.bundespruefstelle.de/bpjm/jugendmedienschutz,did=140998.html, accessed 29 April 2013). In Germany indexation means that the album is available to adults only.

'Pussy' starts with four bars of a drum machine beat, a typical backbeat variation common in all backbeat-based popular music. There is a delay effect on the bass drum and the sound of the beat recalls analogue drum machines of the post-punk era. The tempo clocks in around 135bpm. A loud and compressed snare roll played by the drums in constant semiquavers dominates the fourth bar of the introduction. Throughout the entire song this fill is used to mark the beginning of the chorus. Unsurprisingly the chorus follows in its instrumental version. A single chorus lasts 16 bars and is formally divided in two eight-bar halves which are further divided into two four-bar patterns.

Table 5.2 'Pussy', chorus

Bar	**1 & 9**	**2 & 10**	**3 & 11**	**4 & 12**	**5 & 13**	**6 & 14**	**7 & 15**	**8 & 16**
Guit, bs, keys (roots)	D	C	A	F G	D	C	A	F E
Drum rhythm	I	I	I	II	I	I	I	III

According to the Rammstein formula the chorus uses the fourth texture: all instruments together. The heavily distorted guitars play a harmonic pattern using power chords. The bass doubles the roots while the keyboard sometimes adds the missing notes to form full major or minor chords using two related sounds – probably a string and a choir pad. The sound is heavily compressed. Bass and guitars are tuned down a whole step with the lowest string detuned a further step down (full step down and dropped tuning: C – G – C – F – A – D) to provide an even heavier sound. The two guitars are panned to the right and left side of the soundbox, while bass, drums and keyboard sound more or less in the middle. By using a lot of reverb the keyboard seems to be put on top of the compressed wall of sound produced by guitars and bass and therefore sounds in the foreground. As usual within the Rammstein formula the keyboard plays the only pattern that does not consist of regular quavers by adding a little syncopation on beats three-and and four-and.

The four-bar harmonic pattern adds up to eight bars because of two differing fourth bars. In a similar way the drum rhythm is varied every fourth bar (see Table 5.5). Such a pattern variation is a common means in hip-hop and other dance music styles (see Elflein, 2012, pp. 260–66). In contrast, the rhythmic structure of the melody added in the other choruses consists of two patterns of 8 bars' length to support the 16-bar structure of the chorus as a whole.

Table 5.3 'Pussy', chorus, formal structure

	Chorus (16 bars)			
Harmonic pattern	*A (8 bars)*		*A (8 bars)*	
Harmonic and rhythmic variation in beats 4 and 8	A (4 bars)	A' (4 bars)	A (4 bars)	A' (4 bars)
Melodic structure	A	A	B	B
	single time one bar voice, one bar rest		double time continous voice	

The tonality of the harmonic formula is not that important to this analysis. It is a common pattern in popular music centred round D. The structure is I – ♭VII – V – ♭III – IV or II. Interestingly the roots (except the passing E in bar 9/16 of the chorus) correspond to the open strings of the down-tuned guitar. The goal of the pattern is to sound as heavy as possible. Therefore, Rammstein use two of the lowest possible notes on the down-tuned string instruments as starting points of the pattern: C and D. The chorus of 'Pussy' wants to be of high energy with the steady feel of a lively and fast backbeat. This impression of power is generated by compression, distortion, down-tuned power chords and playing in unison. The keyboard adds a more melodic feel. The introductory snare roll in semiquavers emphasises the idea of something full of energy coming up. This is designed for jumping around.

The beginning of the first verse is marked by a breakdown of the energy level by using the first texture of the Rammstein formula: drum machine and keyboard. The keyboard replaces the bass with a bass synthesiser based on a square wave playing also in constant quavers. The length of the verse corresponds also 16 bars. The harmonic structure of the verse is a variation of the chorus pattern. In bar 9, that is in the middle of the verse, the drums return with a variation of the chorus backbeat. Now the second texture of the Rammstein formula can be heard.

Table 5.4 'Pussy', verse

Bar	**1 & 9**	**2 & 10**	**3 & 11**	**4 & 12**	**5 & 13**	**6 & 14**	**7 & 15**	**8 & 16**
Root	D	C	A	F G	D	C	A	A
Drum rhythm	IV	IV	IV	V	IV	IV	IV	V

Whereas in the chorus the bass drum variations lead to beat four, the variations in the verse emphasise beat two.

Table 5.5 'Pussy', drum rhythms

		1	+	**2**	+	**3**	+	**4**	+
I	Snare drum			x				x	
	Bass drum	**x**				**x**	**x**		
II	Snare drum			x				x	
	Bass drum	**x**					**x**		
III	Snare drum			x		x		x	
	Bass drum	**x**			**x**				
IV	Snare drum			x				x	
	Bass drum	**x**	**x**		**x**				
V	Snare drum			x				x	
	Bass drum		x			x	x		

Therefore, there is plenty of room for the voice. We hear Till Lindemann's signature *sprechgesang* including the trill on almost every German word containing the letter 'r'. The first two lines of both verses are sung in English, the rest is in German. The melodic pattern has a length of four bars and the range of a fifth. The scale tones correspond to the harmonic roots provided by the keyboard. The rhythmic structure of the melody starts in the first two bars with a quaver rest and returns to a rest of varying length at the end of each bar, while bars 3 and 4 are sung in constant quavers with a pickup and a crotchet rest at the end of bar four. Therefore, slight tension is built up and also released in the melody of the verse.

In terms of production, the singing voice is constantly doubled. In the first two lines a breathy and soundless voice is added, which is replaced by simple doubling of Lindemann's voice until the drums are added. In the second half of the chorus Lindemann is doubled by a voice in a higher register that is either the voice of another singer or processed by a vocoder. Besides the breathy voice, all other doublings are of backup character.

A pre-chorus of four bars length follows the verse.

Table 5.6 'Pussy', pre-chorus

Bar	**1**	**2**	**3**	**4**
Git (root)	F	F	G	G
Bs (root)	B♭	B♭	G	A
Keys (melody)	E♭ D C D			
Drum rhythm	I	I	I	Snare Roll

The harmonic structure differs from the verse and chorus to avoid boredom. The vocals are delivered by a quite different and higher-sounding voice, which could be another lead singer, for example guitar player Kruspe, who usually sings backing vocals on stage. This higher-sounding voice is also featured as a backing voice in the following chorus. The pre-chorus arrangement adds one guitar and the bass both playing in constant quavers, while the guitar plays in a higher octave with a less heavy sound. The keyboard adds a short melody as usual in the Rammstein universe. The pre-chorus is a variation on the third texture of the Rammstein formula.

The instrumental arrangement of the chorus is similar to the introductory instrumental chorus. This is also true for the two other vocal choruses of the track. However, the vocal production of each chorus differs as different-sounding voice doublings and backing voices can be heard. The second verse adds only the slightly varied keyboard whistle motive of the pre-chorus to the already specified arrangement of the first verse. The second pre-chorus is identical to the first.

A bridge section follows the second vocal chorus as usual in a standard rock song. It is build around a heavy metal-inspired guitar riff of two bars' length whose harmonic structure differs from verse and chorus. Its first bar builds up tension by starting from D and ending on B♭ on the second half of beat two, while the second bar releases the tension by ending on an A power chord on beat four. The guitar riff is accompanied by double bass drumming and singer Lindemann shouting out the word 'Germany' parallel to the first part of the riff. The voice is not doubled but sounds in a higher register two octaves up, heavily processed with telephone-like equalisation and distortion. In terms of energy levels the bridge part is the climax of the song.

The bridge is followed by a breakdown which is harmonically based on the chorus section. Drums and bass are muted while the guitars are way in the background on a low intensity level and the processed voice of the bridge section continues. In bar 9 of the breakdown, drums, loud guitars and bass re-enter on every first beat until the usual snare roll leads to the closing chorus.

As already mentioned, 'Pussy''s three choruses differ only in voice production. The backup voices in higher registers become more and more dominant climaxing in the final chorus with the processed bridge voice and the differing pre-chorus voice both still audible. To emphasise the climax in the final chorus both the song and the final chorus end with a short use of double bass drumming.

'Pussy' is a carefully crafted standard rock song, like all tracks on *Liebe ist für alle da*. The formula is diversified by the extension of the bridge via a breakdown section as is common in both electronic dance music and heavy metal. Rammstein use the established textures of their formula described above to contrast verse and chorus in terms of energy and volume, a common feature since the rise of grunge and metal core. The pre-chorus is responsible for a slight harmonic variation to prevent boredom because verse and chorus basically work with the same formula. To contrast this harmonic movement the arrangement of the pre-chorus remains the same while verse and chorus are varied at every appearance. The bridge uses a different harmonic structure and is riff-based to mark the energetic climax. The drums and/or the drum machine provide a steady and danceable backbeat throughout the whole song with variations in the bass drum figure to further distinguish the formal sections without disturbing the dancers on the dance floor. Voice production also distinguishes all sections by register and sound and is used to lead the song to its final climax. Therefore, 'Pussy' is a successful attempt to craft a hit single within the universe of the Rammstein formula. Within the album context 'Pussy' is furthermore framed by two tracks that are based on heavy metal guitar riffs with occasional double bass drumming, reminiscing the style of Ministry. This builds up a powerful contrast to the use of harmonic formulas and emphasises the pop song character of 'Pussy'.

Listening to 'Pussy' – The Lyrics

The lyrical theme of 'Pussy' is a bilingual request to enjoy casual sex. In fact, the protagonist is eager to go abroad to enjoy casual sex, because he 'can't get laid in Germany' (any more?).

Both verses start with two lines in English followed by six lines in German. Lines three and four translate the first two lines in German with the exception of line four of the second verse. Here, 'one size fits all' is loosely translated as the need for an erection using the metaphor of a turnpike. Such unsubtle metaphors characterise all German parts of the lyrics. As a metaphor of sexual intercourse the bratwurst (alias the penis) should be stuck into the sauerkraut (alias the female pubic hair) and sexual intercourse is characterised as 'Blitzkrieg', using a gun made of meat.

Other German metaphors relate to the title song of Rammstein's fourth album *Reise Reise* (2004) and the German word for motorway ('Autobahn'), which is also the title of one of Kraftwerk's signature tunes. The following phrase 'Fahrvergnügen' [joy of driving] emphasises the Kraftwerk reference of 'Autobahn'.

The lyrics of the pre-chorus contain a sexist wordplay replacing 'bit' with 'bitch'. The chorus is a simple and unsubtle request for sexual intercourse in English since the protagonist misses possibilities of casual sex in Germany.

Within the album context, track number eight, 'Pussy', is framed by 'Wiener Blut' [Viennese blood] and the title track in position nine, with lyrics talking about true crime incest ('Wiener Blut') and rape from a rapist's view ('Liebe ist für alle da'). This emphasises further the poppy feel of 'Pussy' within the Rammstein universe mentioned above regarding the music.

German Signifiers – Conclusion

Metaphors in 'Pussy' relate either to Germany as the protagonist's homeland or to the need to leave Germany. The latter include the turnpike, the motorway, the self-referential 'Reise Reise' as well as line six of verse one, which translates as 'going abroad alone'. Rammstein work with images of the (West-)German tourist pop song, a tradition that started in the 1950s broaching issues of wanderlust and holidays especially related to Italy. These tourist pop song lyrics are always connected to the possibility of sexual adventures during holiday, especially with imagined hot-blooded residents of the European south. In addition, this illusionary destination is regarded as a place of authentic feelings and authentic environment in relation to the alienation experienced through daily routine in Germany. Tourist pop songs started during the West German economic miracle, which was also the age of the beginning of labour migration to West Germany. In the lyrics of 'Pussy' Rammstein, having an explicit GDR background, make use of an explicitly West German imagery dealing with the stranger in order to try to caricature the subject. They do so by lowering the tourist pop song to a narrative of sexual desire and horniness as well as relating German sex tourism to military invasion. They also caricature East German desires to travel to Western lands of milk and honey that played their parts in the organisation of the reunification process. Potentially the lyrics also deal with the population structure in rural parts of the former GDR from which well-educated young women migrate to economically prospering parts of Germany and Europe, while poorly educated young men stay. They can't get laid in Germany if they are heterosexual because there are no more women around. Rammstein make fun of them by chanting 'Germany' in the bridge section, but that may be over-interpreted. In fact, chanting 'Germany' in front of a German flag during the energetic climax of the song exemplifies Rammstein's sense of humour, since there is nothing less sexy than nationalism. This is confirmed by the live performance of 'Pussy' that replaces the flag waving by riding on a foam cannon.

Burns (2008, p. 458) reasons about Rammstein's use of the German language as a matter of 'restating the national in German rock music' (Burns, 2008, p. 458). He misses the point because he ignores Rammstein's GDR background. Such a discourse can be deduced from West German discussions since the advent of kraut rock at the end of the sixties, but not from an East German background. In the GDR you were not allowed to use the English language in rock lyrics (see also Rauhut, 1993; 1996; Wicke and Müller, 1996). You had to sing in German if you wanted your record to be released or to get the official licence to perform in public. Therefore, I argue that Rammstein vocalist Till Lindemann does not sing in German within an Anglo-American heavy metal context to prove his integrity (see Burns, 2008, pp. 459–60) or what Allan F. Moore (2002, p. 214) has called first-person authenticity of expression. Instead he does so simply because he is used to sing in German and maybe also because English has not been part of the GDR school curriculum. Moreover, 'Pussy' is Rammstein's second effort to incorporate

English lyrics. Their first effort ('Amerika', 2004) still emphasises Rammstein's awkwardness with the English language in its bridge section: 'This is not a love song, I don't sing my mother tongue.'[14] 'Pussy' has overcome this indisposition. Instead, Rammstein use every possible German signifier in the German parts of the lyrics to counter possible international image problems related to the use of the English language. They know that their international success is built upon German stereotypes and they have to aim at an international market. Therefore, we hear the likes of 'Bratwurst', 'Sauerkraut', 'Mercedes Benz', 'Autobahn', 'Schlagbaum' and 'Blitzkrieg'. The majority of these utterances should be understood internationally. Metaphorically speaking, the German parts of the lyrics scream: 'Hey, it's Rammstein again and you still can rely on them. Their three-year hiatus didn't change anything in terms of music and image; they just update their successful formula in a platitudinous way.' But that again may meet Rammstein's sense of humour.

As already mentioned, 'Pussy' is a successful effort to craft an international hit single within the limits of the Rammstein formula. In addition, within the album context 'Pussy' stands out as the closest approach to a pop song that is possible in Rammstein's universe. It should be seen as a successful endeavour to relaunch an international career built upon the use of German signifiers. But now these German signifiers aim at the international market only. Regarding the national market the text can only be understood as kind of joke.

References

Auslander, P., 2008. *Liveness: Performance in a Mediatized Culture.* 2nd edn. London: Routledge.

Bakhtin, M., 1986. *Speech Genres and Other Late Essays*, ed. C. Emerson and M. Holquist. Austin, TX: University of Texas Press.

Barber-Kersovan, A., 2005. *Vom 'Punk-Frühling' zum 'Slowenischen Frühling'. Der Beitrag des slowenischen Punk zur Demontage des sozialistischen Wertesystems*. Hamburg: Reinhold Krämer.

Burns, R.G.H., 2008. German Symbolism in Rock Music: National Signification in the Imagery and Songs of Rammstein. *Popular Music*, 27(3), pp. 457–72.

Elflein, D., 2012. Riffs, Beats und der Reiz der variierten Wiederholung. In: M.S. Kleiner and M. Rappe (eds), *Methoden der Populärkulturforschung. Interdisziplinäre Perspektiven auf Film, Fernsehen, Musik, Internet und Computerspiele*. Berlin: Lit, pp. 247–72.

[14] The first line is a reference to the 1984 hit single of the same name by Public Image Ltd., the band of former Sex Pistols vocalist John Lydon. Lydon's lyrics are a cynical discussion of leaving the underground music scene and becoming a part of the music business.

Galenza, R. and Havemeister, H. (eds), 1999. *Wir wollern immer artig sein ... Punk, New Wave, HipHop, Independent Szene in der DDR 1980–1990*. Berlin: Schwarzkopf und Schwarzkopf.
Grossberg, L., 1992. *We Gotta Get Out of this Place: Popular Conservatism and Postmodern Culture*. New York and London: Routledge.
Horschig, M., 1999. In der DDR hat es nie Punks gegeben. In: R. Galenza and H. Havemeister (eds), *Wir wollern immer artig sein ... Punk, New Wave, HipHop, Independent Szene in der DDR 1980–1990*. Berlin: Schwarzkopf und Schwarzkopf, pp. 17–40.
Latour, B., 2010. *Eine neue Soziologie für eine neue Gesellschaft*. Frankfurt am Main: Suhrkamp.
Moore, A.F., 2001. *Rock: The Primary Text*. 2nd edn. Aldershot: Ashgate.
Moore, A.F., 2002. Authenticity as Authentication. *Popular Music*, 21(2), pp. 209–23.
Mühlmann, W.-R., 1999. *Letzte Ausfahrt: Germania. Ein Phänomen namens neue deutsche Härte*. Berlin: Jeske/Mader.
Rauhut, M., 1993. *Beat in der Grauzone. DDR-Rock 1964 bis 1972 – Politik und Alltag*. Berlin: BasisDruck.
Rauhut, M., 1996. *Schalmei und Lederjacke. Udo Lindenberg, BAP, Underground – Rock und Politik in den achtziger Jahren*. Berlin: Schwarzkopf & Schwarzkopf.
Wicke, P., 1996. Zwischen Förderung und Reglementierung – Rockmusik im System der DDR-Kulturbürokratie. In: P. Wicke and L. Müller (eds), *Rockmusik und Politik. Analysen, Interviews und Dokumente*. Berlin: Ch. Links, pp. 11–27.
Wicke, P. and Müller, L. (eds), 1996. *Rockmusik und Politik. Analysen, Interviews und Dokumente*. Berlin: Ch. Links.

Filmography

Schumann, Dieter, 1999 [1988]. *Flüstern & Schreien – Ein Rockreport*. 1999 [1988] [DVD]. Icestorm Entertainment.
Smith, John, 2006. Rammstein – *Völkerball* [DVD]. Universal.

Discography

Depeche Mode, 1986. 'Stripped'. *Black Celebration*. Mute, STUMM 26.
Feeling B, 1989. *Hea Hoa Hoa Hea Hea Hoa*. Amiga, 8 56 477.
Kraftwerk, 1974. 'Autobahn'. Philips, 6305 231.
Laibach, 1987. 'Geburt einer Nation'. *Opus Dei*. Mute, STUMM 44.
Ministry, 1988. *The Land Of Rape And Honey*. Sire, 9 25799–2.

Ministry, 1992. *Psalm 69: The Way To Succeed And The Way To Suck Eggs*. Sire, 9 26727–2.

Opus, 1984. 'Live Is Life'. Polydor, 881 792–7.

Public Image Ltd, 1984. 'This Is Not A Love Song'. *This Is What You Want ... This Is What You Get*. Virgin, V 2309.

Queen, 1985. 'One Vision'. EMI, QUEEN 6.

Rammstein, 2004. 'Amerika'; 'Mein Teil'. *Reise Reise*. Universal, 06024 9868150.

Rammstein, 2009. *Liebe ist für alle da*. Universal, 06025 2719511 7.

Rammstein, 2009. 'Pussy'. Universal, 2718736.

Chapter 6
An Analysis of Space, Gesture and Interaction in Kings of Leon's 'Sex On Fire'

Simon Zagorski-Thomas

The aim of this chapter is to examine some specific ways in which features other than melody and harmony can be incorporated into the analysis of recorded popular music. The three features I shall be looking at are the spatial staging, the gestural activity of the participants and the relationships and interactions between the participants. These three features could, of course, also be characterised in terms of rhythm (perhaps more accurately as micro-timing) and timbre. In choosing to describe them in terms of the activity involved in the production process and its environment, I am reflecting my use of an ecological approach to perception (Gibson, 1979; Clarke, 2005) and embodied cognition (Damasio, 2000; Feldman, 2008; Lakoff and Johnson, 2003). Using the example of the Kings of Leon's 2008 track 'Sex On Fire' from the album *Only by the Night* I will investigate how a track's construction can suggest certain forms of meaning or interpretation and how some of this meaning may be more or less universal whilst other aspects may require culturally specific prior experience. This notion of suggestion, that meaning and interpretation are subjective and internal to the listener but that certain characteristics only afford a range of possible interpretations, is central to my methodology.

One crucial aspect of this investigation is the premise that recorded music is very different from live performance. Two key differences are the split between hearing and vision in recorded music and the notion that recorded music is a representational art form rather than a strictly performative one. Both the nonlinear method of production, with multi-tracking, overdubs and editing, and the various forms of mediation applied to the performed (and constructed) elements mean that recorded music is a schematic representation of musical performance, much like film, photomontage and even animation in relation to drama. Since the 1950s (and even earlier) recording artists have been bending this representational form into abstract forms: we have become used to more and more schematic representations as opposed to realism, something that I have described elsewhere in terms of 'sonic cartoons'.[1]

Above I described the example as a 'track' from an 'album' and not simply as a song. The conventional tools of musicology are geared towards analysing melody,

[1] These ideas are expanded and explained further in Zagorski-Thomas, 2014; 2015.

harmony and form with the possible addition of the idealised (and simplified) approach to rhythm that western musical notation affords. I have deliberately chosen an example where these features are the least interesting aspects. The (vocal) melodic material is restricted to five notes and is composed entirely from two basic patterns. The harmony is also very simple and repetitive, comprised mostly of alternating four-bar sections of E major and C♯ minor chords where sometimes an A major chord replaces the last two bars of the C♯ minor section. The form is a straightforward alternation of verse and chorus with an extended verse as an introduction and an extended chorus as an ending. The rhythmic patterns are not much less simple than these other aspects: an overall feel of continuous eighth-note rhythms with variations in density, a solid backbeat on two and four, and a little rhythmic syncopation every now and then.

As I have said, my methodology has its basis in ecological perception and embodied cognition. These have been used in the past mainly to examine music from a reception focused perspective (for example Moore, 2012; Clarke, 2005) but I will examine the way in which this track was produced and performed, as well as the musical output. Aside from the interest this may hold for students of performance and production, it also allows me to examine how factors that may not be consciously perceptible, like subtle changes in the amount and type of ambience for example, may contribute to our interpretation of a piece of music. Also, the types of artifice chosen in the production process reflect the cultural language, the various strands of cultural heteroglossia,[2] through which the artists and their audience communicate.

Narrative Structure

To return then to the notion of form, I will begin by looking at this from the perspective of narrative structure and through an extension of Smalley's (1986) term spectro-morphology. In a development that seems entirely unrelated to the work on embodied cognition and ecological perception mentioned earlier, Smalley uses the term spectro-morphology to explain the ways that electronic and electroacoustic music can suggest meaning through our perception of the type of energy expenditure over time that would create an acoustic sound with a similar frequency profile (and through the ways in which they differ from such acoustic sounds). The spectro-morphology of the 'Sex On Fire' recording can be looked at in terms of the kinds of energy expenditure that produced this changing pattern of intensities. The introduction starts at a relatively low level with a solo guitar and then the rest of the rhythm section enter and establish a rhythmic momentum.

[2] Bakhtin (1982) explored the ways in which centrifugal and centripetal forces, those of rebellion and conformity, can be seen in the structure of language and scholars such as Monson (1997) have applied the idea of multiple, competing forms of language, heteroglossia, to music.

The energy drops slightly as the verse starts and then builds up over the next 16 bars to an 8-bar chorus which presents the song's highest energy level: virtually continuous eighth-note rhythms on the drums, bass and both guitars. This verse/chorus energy morphology is then repeated almost exactly except that the chorus is double the length, and it's then repeated again with the eight-bar chorus. There is then a 16-bar 'break down' chorus in which the drums reduce to a quarter-note bass drum pattern. The guitars and bass start with the sparsest verse rhythm and build in intensity towards a final 16-bar chorus at the previously continuous eighth-note rhythm. The song ends on two eighth notes played by the whole band. I will talk in more detail later in the chapter about the way that the individual instrumental parts work together to create these changes in perceived energy expenditure but, for the most part, these changes occur in four-bar or eight-bar chunks with important structural boundaries marked by drum fills and cymbal crashes: in other words, we have a very conventional approach to popular music song writing structure.

When we look in more detail, however, there is more to be said about the precise nature of this narrative structure. Mark Butler (2006, pp. 121–37) has discussed how many introductions in dance music create ambiguity by taking a rhythmic pattern out of its song context. Many of these work because they place an accent on a beat other than 'one' and, when heard without a drum pattern establishing the 'real one' unequivocally, we interpret this accent as a 'false one'. Caleb Followill's[3] guitar introduction creates this kind of ambiguity: it is a rhythm that starts with an accent on the off-beat of four (the last eighth note of the bar) and then plays entirely on the off-beats of the bar. This creates a very strong 'false one' which is then overturned when the drums and bass enter, a perceptual flip which is aided by the fact that Caleb Followill's guitar also gets quieter in the mix.[4]

The notion of our perception being 'aided' by the mix brings us to the issue of how gestalt principles (see Deutsch, 1998, pp. 183–236) can influence our 'subject position' (Clarke, 2005, pp. 91–125). In this instance the change of volume, along with the structure of the rhythm section parts, encourages us to interpret this guitar part in a different way: as a component of the rhythm section 'background' rather than as a separate melodic figure. By 'moving' the guitar from a position of prominence our perceived position in relation to it is altered and it becomes an 'extra' rather than a 'lead actor'. As we shall see in the next section there are various ways in which the spatial staging of all the recorded elements contribute to this, but there are two additional aspects that I will cover now.

The first of these is the clean guitar riff that enters after the first four bars of the first verse. By establishing this as a melodic motif in a relatively 'empty' part of the arrangement our attention is drawn to it and then, when it returns later in busier sections where the detail of the part is more difficult to discern, we already

---

[3] Kings of Leon are the brothers Caleb (vocals, guitar), Nathan (drums, backing vocals) and Jared Followill (bass) as well as their cousin Matthew Followill (guitar).

[4] See the chapter on PJ Harvey's 'The Words That Maketh Murder', pp. 175–98, for the discussion of another example of such a 'metric fake-out'.

have a mental picture that allows us to recognise it when partly masked by other parts (such as in the last eight bars of each verse). Thus the gestalt principle of continuity encourages us to 'hear' the part we heard when it was unobscured because we assume that the other parts are masking the notes we cannot hear, rather than that Matthew Followill is now playing an incomplete version of the riff. The way that the arrangement and the mix work together, the order in which various motifs appear, their volume and the way they are built together, help to create a logic to the narrative structure that affects our perception, that affords greater clarity. This idea that knowing what we are searching for helps us to find it in more complex musical textures may seem intuitively obvious, but it is much more easily accommodated to the ecological approach to perception than into traditional psychology. It is also another instance in which our subject position in relation to this recording is influenced by the production process as well as the arrangement, and our perception of the clarity of the narrative structure (as well as the clarity of the sonic structure) is at least in part determined by how that subject position influences the way we construct our mental map of the piece.

The second aspect is that of the 'break down' chorus. The bass drum in this section is obviously both busier (being on every beat of the bar) and more exposed (because the other instruments are leaving bigger gaps in their parts) but it is not noticeably louder than in the rest of the track. It is, however, different in tone and I think this is due to two factors:[5] additional high frequencies and some stereo widening effect on the bass drum.[6] This provides another example of how the production techniques can be used to manipulate the subject position of a listener. For evolutionary reasons our perceptual system is tuned to detect change and this works on a subliminal level as well as a conscious one. Minor changes in the spectral and spatial make-up of a sound will draw our attention to it: as sound engineers say, it makes something jump out of the mix. This is an example of one of the many strategies that sound engineers have developed to make an element more noticeable without actually making it louder. This is also a moment that draws on the cultural language of the intended listeners. The device of stripping the instrumentation down to the main vocal hook and a minimal rhythmic accompaniment has particular connotations of a live rock show and a participatory moment in such an event: getting the crowd to sing along to the chorus of the hit single. The incorporation of this culturally loaded concert device in the recorded

---

[5] I have attempted to contact Jacquire King, the producer of the track, to clarify this point but was unable to get further than his management company who 'respectfully pass(ed) on taking part' (personal email communication from Jeff Castellaz at Cast Management, 21 December 2012).

[6] If you separate the left and right channels of the stereo mix and invert the phase of one channel and play them back in mono, the kick drum in this section doesn't disappear as much as it does in the rest of the track. This indicates that the two sides of the stereo image are more different at this point as the more similar they are (that is a mono track panned equally between the two sides) the more the inverted phase version will cancel the other side out.

version of the track can be seen in terms of Bakhtin's (1982) heteroglossia: that it is a centripetal form of musical language for those who frequent this type of rock concert. It also stands as a cultural marker that brands the Kings of Leon as musicians who see their identity as a live band rather than a studio band – or at least weighted towards 'liveness' rather than 'studio-ness'.

The final aspect of the narrative shape of this track that I will address is the changing tempo. The move towards constant tempi, with drummers playing along to a click track, is a frequently remarked upon feature of music since the 1980s.[7] Not playing to a click track is not only a further marker of the value the band attribute to playing live but also relates to two further tropes: one being freedom and the other being the historical golden age of rock in the 1960s and 1970s. Performing to a metronome or click track has a relatively obvious potential metaphorical connection to submitting to external discipline or control and the Kings of Leon have a fairly well established reputation for wildness.[8] Further to this, though, is the notion of artistic freedom and the idea that their integrity as musicians is enhanced by not only refusing to be constrained by a click track but that their control over tempo is part of their artistic expression (see p. 129 for more details on the tempo changes in this song). The other trope, that of reference to a supposed golden age of rock, would not be so obviously connected to the issue of a click track if there weren't other ways that the band make this reference. One such way is that this album and the three that preceded it were all made using analogue tape and a wide range of vintage audio equipment that privilege the sound of that historical period (Tingen, 2008). Interestingly though, this recording, which was transferred from analogue tape into the digital audio workstation software ProTools to allow further overdubs and mixing, was the album that gave the band their first hits in the USA. Prior to that they had been better known in Europe than in the US. *Only By The Night* certainly has the more expansive spatial feel and more clearly sculpted frequency and dynamic content (in comparison to their earlier CDs) that are more commonly found in high selling US rock albums. The 'home movies' that the band put on their website about the recording[9] maintain some of the illusion of an unmediated, straight to tape recording process that may have been seen as important in not alienating their existing fan base.

Spatial Staging

Another crucial aspect that contributes to the meaning of the musical material, the detail of the narrative structure and to the clarity of the arrangement is the spatial staging. This covers a variety of factors that have been explored from different

---

7 See for example Zagorski-Thomas, 2010a.

8 See for example Kaufman, 2011.

9 See http://www.closertokol.com/apps/videos/videos/show/14213289-obtn-home-movies-2008-all-24-days [Accessed 14 August 2013].

perspectives since Allan Moore's (1992) introduction of the term 'the sound box' and William Moylan's (1992) use of 'staging' in sound recording. Peter Doyle (2006) has looked at some of the more associative and metaphorical forms of meaning that echo and reverberation can suggest and I'd like to go further down that road. Indeed, the more expansive spatial feel and the more sculpted frequency and dynamic content that I have just mentioned are a very good example of the type of 'sonic cartoon' that I have written about elsewhere (Zagorski-Thomas, 2015). Far from being concerned with 'realism' this recording creates a schematic version of a live rock band's sound with some features exaggerated and others inhibited.

The stereo staging, by which I mean the way the various instruments are spread across the stereo image, works more to create separation and clarity rather than realism. Caleb Followill's guitar, the riff that starts the song and continues throughout, is panned to the right with a delayed version quietly on the left. Matthew Followill's guitar parts are on the left. There are two of these in the verses and one in the chorus. Jared Followill's bass and Nathan Followill's drums are panned centrally (although the hi-hat and cymbal microphones are panned a little to the left and right). Some additional percussion samples (snare drums and a tambourine) are stereo in the verse and mono in the chorus. As I've mentioned already, the kick drum becomes stereo in the break down (as do the toms, but the break down and the last two notes of the song are the only times the toms play). Caleb Followill's voice is panned to the centre. This creation of a stereo spread doesn't mirror the visual layout of the band on stage – not least because Caleb can't be centre stage singing and stage right playing guitar at the same time, but also because bass player Jared stands to the side of the stage in live shows.[10] It is, as I say, a schematic representation of the visual experience of a band on stage (although the audio experience would be unlikely to involve such extreme panning of the guitars), which facilitates the separation of the audio stream into individual components.

Alongside this stereo separation – the directions from which the various component sounds seem to be coming from – there are two other spatial parameters: the distance from us they appear to be and the size of the space we appear to be in. In the first instance, that of distance, our hearing system works with three parameters. The first is the high frequency content. High frequency content in sound dissipates more quickly over distance and therefore the brightness of a sound when it reaches our ear is usually a good cue as to distance. The other is the relative volume of the direct sound and the reverberant sound reflected off the listening environment. The closer the signal, the louder it will be in relation to the reverberant sound (no matter how long or short the reverberation is that is how large the space appears to be). The third factor is volume, especially when we have a clearly established idea of the 'normal' volume of a sound source – the human voice for example. The technologies of amplification have, of course, clouded the issue of volume for us.

[10] See the concert footage at the end of the 'home movie' on the band's website (see footnote 9).

We are all very used to hearing quiet sounds such as a soft singing voice being amplified to the point where it competes easily with a drum kit or a jazz big band. We are also used to the way that microphone technique and dynamic compression in the recording process are used to reduce the volume differences between loud and quiet parts of a performance.[11]

In the schematic, representational world of recorded sound, just as in the schematic, representational world of painting and two-dimensional visual images, we are more concerned with generating a useful interpretation than with realism and accuracy. Of course, the further a representation is from reality, the more we are aware of how much of a leap this act of interpretation is. In fact there is a schism here: we are seldom, I would say never, persuaded that a representation is the real thing and yet we often respond momentarily as if it was. Discussing the notion of representation in relation to the ecological approach to perception, James Gibson wrote:

> I insist that what the draughtsman, beginner or expert, actually does is not replicate, to print, or to copy in any sense of the term but to mark the surface in such a way as to display invariants and record an awareness. Drawing is never copying. It is impossible to copy a piece of the environment. Only another drawing can be copied. We have been misled for too long by the fallacy that a picture is similar to what it depicts, a *likeness*, or an *imitation* of it. A picture supplies some of the information for what it depicts, but that does not imply that it is in projective correspondence with what it depicts. (Gibson, 1979, p. 279)

Another basic principle of the ecological approach is that perception is proactive and responsive: I do not see or hear something passively. I instinctively move my body to generate a richer set of information. If I hear something that I cannot see, I will move my head to get more accurate positional information. The conventions for a representational form that provide 'some of the information for what it depicts', like perspective in drawing or using the balance of direct and reverberant sound in recorded music, allow us both to create an interpretation of what is being represented and recognise and assess the level of realism to the depiction, through what is missing from that depiction and from the context (for example seeing speakers instead of a band).

To return to the question of distance depiction in 'Sex On Fire', there are a range of contradictory cues about the precise detail and some of them vary from section to section, but the strongest impression for me is that everything is closer in the verses and further away in the choruses. As we shall see in a moment, this is reinforced by the fact that the perceived size of the spaces also gets larger in the choruses. However, before we discuss that, let us look at the distance cues

[11] For an example, listen to Alanis Morissette's 'Ironic' (1996) whilst watching a visual display of the volume: there is virtually no difference between the 'quiet' verses and the 'loud' choruses.

in more detail. As we have already mentioned, the volume of the guitar in the introduction reduces as soon as the rhythm section starts. This is, in itself, a cue for something getting further away but the direct sound of the guitar also seems to recede into room ambience and lose some of its brightness: it is probably the case that the intro guitar has been put through different processing than the rest of the performance. The basic positioning of the instruments in the rest of the introduction and the verses stays quite similar: the kick drum, hi-hats, bass, Caleb's guitar (the introduction guitar) and Matthew's off-beat distorted guitar chords seem to be a similar distance away, something that Edward Hall (1966) in his theory of proxemics might call a 'far phase' version of social space or a 'close phase' version of public space.[12] Hall's categories of distance relate to the types of social activity that occur at these distances, from the very intimate to the very formal and communal and, although the specifics of his ideas are very dated and riddled with dubious national stereotyping, these broad categories do reflect the way that staging in record production reinforces ideas of intimacy and communality. The elements in the verses that feel closer than these others are the voice, the tambourine, the snare drum and the clean, melodic guitar that enters each verse after the first four bars. The cues for the voice are possibly the most contradictory as there is quite a lot of ambience and yet the detail in the high frequency sound suggests proximity. On the one hand the tone of the voice is quite energetic and these social clues – at what kind of distance would that be appropriate – seem to take precedence. The tambourine and, to a lesser extent, the clean guitar and the verse snare drum, on the other hand, seem closer partly because they do not appear to be particularly energetic in comparison with other components like the drum kit. I have already mentioned that there were some additional percussion samples played over the track and the tambourine is definitely one of them; it is quite a light tap that is not very reverberant and has lots of high frequency content. I cannot be sure, but I think that the verse snare is doubled with a snare sample that sounds to me like a gently hit piccolo snare. This combines with the heavier snare from the drum kit but the tonal quality lightens the sound slightly and seems to bring it closer to the listener. The clean guitar, partly by having plenty of high frequency content but more importantly by seeming to be amplified with a lot less power and volume,[13] also seems to be closer. In the choruses the distorted lead guitar and the vocals recede to a more distant public space, almost entirely because both the reverberation and delay used get longer and so do not fade in volume in relation to the direct signal as quickly.

---

[12] Hall (1966, pp. 113–29) characterises space in terms of Intimate Distance, Personal distance, Social Distance and Public Distance. The 'far phase' of Social Distance is from 7 to 12 feet (2 to 4 metres) and the 'close phase' of Public Distance is from 12 to 25 feet (4 to 8 metres).

[13] Of course, this may be an illusion as digital signal processing or overdrive through a pre-amplifier may be distorting the other guitar sounds without a more powerful amplifier being necessary.

That brings us to the perceived size of the space that we hear. As with most forms of popular music, the answer is not straightforward. As we have seen, different instruments have different reverbs and echoes applied to them and some instruments (and the voice) have different reverbs and echoes applied at different points in the song. When Jacquire King and Angelo Petraglia produced the album they recorded the drums in the main room at Blackbird Studios, Nashville (Tingen, 2008) and also left the doors from that room open into an adjacent echo chamber where they also recorded some of the ambient sound. This natural room ambience is mixed with the close microphones on each of the drums and cymbals and an overhead microphone in the main room itself. Thus before any electronic ambience has been added there is already a mixture of the ambience from two rooms. However, the room ambience appears to have been filtered to remove some of the low frequency content to maintain greater clarity, a common occurrence in recording of this sort but one which demands a little explanation.

The sound of a large concert hall has several characteristics that are strong cues of size. The first is the length of the reverberation time: the longer the reverberation tail, the larger the space. There are also other characteristics such as the delay between the direct sound and the first reflection from the walls reaching the listener – it is only a slight simplification to say that the longer the delay the larger the space. Another feature of acoustic ambience is that the higher frequency content decays more quickly than the low frequencies and so, in a large space, low frequencies become disproportionately louder. If we add to this the fact that lower frequency sounds are, in the physical world, created by larger, more powerful entities than high frequency sounds, then our association of loud low frequency sound with power becomes a matter of ecology rather than culture. However, the increase in low frequency content that stems from reverberation in a large space also reduces clarity because the noise floor from this reverb masks the onsets as well as the detail of the frequency content of the direct sound. Record production has long utilised schematic representations of the acoustic properties of large spaces which provide some of the features of this type of reverberation but without the accompanying reduction clarity (Zagorski-Thomas, 2010b; 2012). In 'Sex on Fire', as in many other examples, the long reverb tails that are characteristic of large spaces are applied only to the voice and the lead guitar in the chorus. Jacquire King states that 'the Altiverb works primarily on the snare, kick and toms, just to give them a little bit more space. I set it to a room at Ocean Way Studios, so it's not a big splashy reverb' (King, cited in Tingen, 2008). At the same time, the enhanced bass frequencies that are also a sign of size are created through a device that doubles the bass guitar an octave below the pitch that was played[14] plus compression and equalisation that also raises the perceived volume of these bass frequencies.

[14] 'I also used a very old subharmonic synthesizer, the Dbx Disco Boombox, on the DI. Jared plays a lot of melodic stuff very high up the neck of his bass, and to be able to keep the weight of the track I synthesized some additional low end' (King, cited in Tingen, 2008).

Another perceived feature of large room ambience is a reduction in dynamic range, which is also due to the raised noise floor that the low frequency ambience introduces. This is because differences in dynamics in the direct sound are less noticeable when there is a continuous low frequency rumble in the background caused by this ambience. However this type of perceived reduction in dynamic range is also accompanied by a reduction in clarity. King uses a technique called parallel bus compression on the drums whereby the uncompressed drum signals are combined with a parallel copy of the signals, which is heavily compressed[15] (and probably equalised to emphasise the low frequencies). This again provides a single feature found in the ambience of large spaces (a reduction in the dynamic range) without the lack of clarity: a schematic or 'sonic cartoon' version of the concert hall.

As I have mentioned, there is also a dynamic manipulation of the spatial staging across the different sections of the arrangement. There is a digital delay added to the vocal, which is in time with the rhythm of the track in different ways. In the verses the repeat comes a sixteenth note after the original signal, in the choruses it is an eighth note (that is twice as long) and in the break down chorus it is a quarter note (that is twice as long again). This delay creates an artificial but schematic impression of the first reflection cue to room size that was mentioned earlier – and the longer the delay the greater the impression of size. Thus, this use of delays creates the impression that the size of the performance space gets larger in the choruses and smaller in the verses. Of course, this is a highly artificial treatment, but its purpose is to reinforce the dynamics of the arrangement without there having to be an actual change in the sound level: the peak level is exactly the same throughout the song (not including the guitar introduction). The increased level of perceived activity (see the following sections) in the choruses increases the average level rather than the peak level and the spatial changes add a metaphorical level of 'big-ness' to these changes in dynamic. Matthew Followill's chorus guitar, playing higher register lead lines, is saturated in a very synthetic sounding reverb[16] during the chorus to further emphasise these dynamic differences and the way that the tail of this reverb fades away over the sparser arrangements at the start of verses two and three serves to highlight the change in texture.

---

[15] Dynamic compression is an automatic volume control which very quickly turns down the level of a signal whenever it rises above a given threshold. While this reduces the volume of the peaks in the signal it allows the overall volume of the signal to be turned up and increases the average level, a much stronger indicator of loudness to humans than peak level.

[16] King states, 'The synth-like reverb you can hear on the guitar was done at Blackbird on an Eventide DSP4000' (King, cited in Tingen, 2008).

Gestural Activity

I now want to discuss how the perceived gestural activity of the various players suggests particular forms of meaning. However, before we progress with that, a short diversion into the nature of what we perceive as performers is in order. There are four people who played on this track but the question of how many actors we perceive is more complex. Most listeners to popular music are familiar with the notion of a drum kit and that a single agent is responsible for the multiple sounds that it produces. However, on this track:

> there's also a drum loop that Matt [Followill, the band's lead guitarist, S.Z.] overdubbed. He played it on a keyboard, and it felt really good and we used Beat Detective for some manual editing to line it up better with the drums. I also overdubbed an old Simmons snare drum in the choruses. (King, cited in Tingen, 2008)

Neither of these additions to the drum kit performance, though, are perceived as separate activity in the final mix. Even the tambourine, by replacing the expected snare on the fourth beat of each verse bar, seems to be part of the kit drum performance. Matt Followill's guitar parts, as we have mentioned, are separated into three elements: the off-beat distorted chop in the verses, the clean melodic line in the verses and the distorted, higher register lead guitar in the choruses. On the one hand, the melodic line and the chop maintain their separate coherence in the verses. On the other hand, Caleb Followill's guitar line in the chorus, which moves from the distinctive hook of the verse riff to a straight eighth-note rhythm on the chords, seems to merge with the bass at that point and become the result of a single agency. However, when Matt Followill's distorted guitar doubles the rhythm of the bass in the second four bars of the second verse, for the first eight bars of the third verse and in the break down section, the two sounds maintain their separate identity more strongly; principally because they have such different timbres. Also, when the lead vocal is doubled in the chorus, we hear single 'thicker' voice. In this instance, it seems to have been a deliberate choice as King says:

> There's also a distant lead double in the chorus. I call that a performed effect. Instead of using a delay and modulation to get something in the background, you record a second performance in a different space and with a different microphone. You get something more deliberate and unique that way. (King, cited in Tingen, 2008)

In any event, Warner (2005) has proposed that a recorded doubling by a single singer always produces the impression of a 'special' voice rather than of multiple individuals.

The way that the arrangement works, therefore, is further complicated by this notion of multiple agencies. While the verses are characterised by a lower dynamic level and a sense of closer proximity in a smaller space, they are also characterised by having more perceivable agencies at work. The choruses, on the other hand, involve fewer components and more conceptual fusing: the sense of concerted and coordinated activity that flows from the whole ensemble playing eighth-note rhythms creates a metaphorical sense of a single organism. The first half of the lead guitar's line in the chorus falls in step with this rhythm (underneath the vocal) and then breaks away during the gap in the vocal to play the discordant melodic line with the note bends. I shall return to this notion of interaction in the next section, but first I want to look at how the gestural shapes of the individually perceived actors contribute to our interpretation of the musical structure.

One of the strongest gestural shapes in a rock song of this kind is the heavy accentuation of beats two and four by the snare drum. Indeed, I would argue that this is one of main stylistic features that marked the split in the 1970s between rock music and dance music styles with their emphasis on a 'four-on-the-floor' bass drum. While there are numerous exceptions and several stylistic developments that countered this trend[17] the backbeat remains an ubiquitous gesture in rock music. In 'Sex On Fire' the lack of a snare hit on the fourth beat in the first half of each verse creates an asymmetrical feel to the rhythm – a kind of limp or stumble in the forward momentum of the track. And this too, of course, contributes to our emerging narrative: of a less energetic but more complex and detailed verse building up to the more simplistic energy of the chorus.

And on this notion of the limp or stumble, I want to return to the main guitar riff in the verse. We have already noted the rhythmic ambiguity that it creates in the introduction by offering a plausible interpretation of the accents in this pattern (all off the beat) as being on the beat. Once the main rhythm section pattern enters the ambiguity disappears but the strongest accent of this guitar part is the second eighth note of beat four: it is not only louder than the other notes but it is further accentuated by being approached through a slide up from below which also gives it a more dramatic gestural shape as well as slightly brighter timbre than the other notes of the riff. This accent, while the fourth beat is less markedly hit by the tambourine in the introduction and the first half of each verse, creates an even stronger asymmetry: we not only have a weaker four than our two but the off-beat is stronger than the four. This riff continues into the second half of the verses where the snare does also hit the four and continues to create an imbalance in the rhythmic feel, which is only relieved by the even eighth-note rhythm of the chorus. In many ways, this type of gestural asymmetry followed by symmetry creates the same kinds of feeling of tension and release that is often described in harmonic analysis. In a similar way, the asymmetric rhythmic feel of the clean guitar that enters in the second four bars of the first verse (0:32) creates an even more complex rhythmic lilt to the rhythm track. This however, is countered four

[17] For example, from the 1980s onwards many bands such as the Police, U2 and others have walked a middle road and dance music styles such as jungle and drum and bass involve a heavy backbeat. That said, it remains an important marker of separation.

bars later (0:38) by the distorted 'chop' guitar, which, while playing on the off-beat, is symmetrical in that it plays with equal weight throughout the bar. This symmetry coincides with the snare hit starting to fall on the fourth beat of the bar and creating further momentum: part of the build towards the more unrelenting momentum of the chorus. The lead guitar line in the chorus starts with a rising eighth-note rhythm figure of broken chords that, as we have said, leads to the discordant lead guitar line. The discord is of two notes a tone apart with the lower note being bent in pitch up towards the higher one until they are almost in unison[18] before resolving to a lower note: two briefer moments of tension and relief in our larger narrative.

The lead vocal provides a similar morphology of tension and relief through a variety of mechanisms. The first is that of melodic shape. We mentioned the limited range of the melody: based around five notes of the E major scale (C♯, D♯, E, F♯ and G♯). We once again find asymmetry: the first line of the melody rises, the second line falls, the third line rises but then, instead of falling, the fourth line is a repeat of part of the rising third line, even down to having the same lyric. The melody in the verse reaches up briefly to the G♯ in the first line of each eight-bar section but the sustained high note is saved for the chorus and resolves downward: a similarly brief moment of tension and relief as the one on the lead guitar that we have just mentioned.

Perhaps a more nuanced mechanism for creating narrative interest can, however, be found in the rhythmic and timbral gestures of the vocal performance. Caleb Followill's vocal style involves extensive use of the kinds of emotional breaks and gravelly timbres that are common in rock music performance. This was, of course, in keeping with the band's reputation for wildness and intensity that was mentioned earlier. One major difference between the verses and the choruses is that the verses are sung in a much more rhythmically clipped style and more off the beat whereas the choruses are more legato and more on the beat. Also interesting is the way in which his voice breaks. The last note in the first line of each eight-bar verse section is the point at which he reaches up for the high G♯ and each time his voice fails to hit the note cleanly: there is a squeak, reminiscent of uncontrolled sobbing. At the start of the third line (0:30 – 'I know they're watching'), he uses a technique described by Rossing, Moore and Wheeler (2001, p. 339) and known as 'vocal fry', one in which the vocal folds are prevented from vibrating normally: often a sign of exertion or tiredness. There are also lots of examples of a sharp transition between the open phase mode of vocal fold vibration (a breathy voice) and the normal singing mode (Rossing, Moore and Wheeler, 2001, p. 339) that causes the types of emotional break found in the words 'talking' (0:44), 'pale' (1:18) and 'forever' (2:05). There are also some straightforward moments of voice loss, most notably on the word 'play' (0:41) in the first verse. Overall, the verses display a good deal of tension and the physical signs of emotional distress whereas

[18] This, of course, is an archetypal lead guitar figure from rock and roll that dates back to the 1950s and earlier to the blues.

the chorus vocals are much more robust. The high sustained G♯ that starts every chorus does not break like those in the verse and the voice is much more open and powerful. Whilst there is a growl in his voice each time he sings the word 'sex' in the chorus, it is still in the context of this more open and powerful voice and does not exhibit the emotional frailty that characterises the verses. Interestingly, there is only one moment in the song where his voice relaxes into a softer tone: for the ad lib in the breakdown section (2:40).

Relationships and Interaction between the Participants

I have already touched on many of the ways in which the relationships and the interaction between the participants can be understood to influence our interpretation of this recording. The more complex and asymmetrical rhythmic structure of the verses is created by a series of interlocking but separate patterns that begin by getting more complex and then become busier but less complex in a way that builds the energy towards the chorus. In the first verse the asymmetrical rhythmic pattern of the drums and the main guitar riff are at first accompanied by a very simple bass line playing the root notes of the chord on the first two eighth notes of the bar (0:26). After four bars the clean guitar adds to the complexity (0:32) and then four bars later (0:38) the snare drum starts to play on beat four, the bass plays a continuous eighth-note pattern and the distorted guitar off-beat chop joins in. After eight bars of this comes the chorus (0:50) where the continuous eighth-note pattern is taken up by Caleb Followill's guitar and, initially, by the lead guitar: a uniform single activity with a single high note in the vocals suspended over the top.

As can be seen in Figure 6.1, at the onset of the chorus (see label in the centre of the figure) there is an increase in activity in the higher frequency range (between around 300 and 1300 Hertz). This provides a visual illustration of a metaphorical relationship: that a fuller range of frequencies creates a sensation of fuller musical space. While this may seem obvious, I think that it illustrates a complex and interesting point: a fuller range of frequencies does not reflect any actual fullness, just a more complicated waveform. We tend not to hear white noise[19] as filling up sonic space in the same way that multiple instruments at different pitches seem to. We hear fullness in terms of the number of 'things' happening and white noise sounds like a single 'thing'. We also expect different types of 'thing' to make noises in different frequency ranges: generally smaller 'things' make higher frequency noises and larger 'things' make lower frequency sounds. When we hear identifiably discrete sounds that range from very low pitch to very high, whether they be musical notes or any other sounds, we hear a lot of 'things' and we make a metaphorical connection: many 'things' fill up space.

[19] White noise is a signal which includes sound of equal amplitude (read level) across the whole range of audible frequencies (Rossing, Moore and Wheeler, 2001, p. 118).

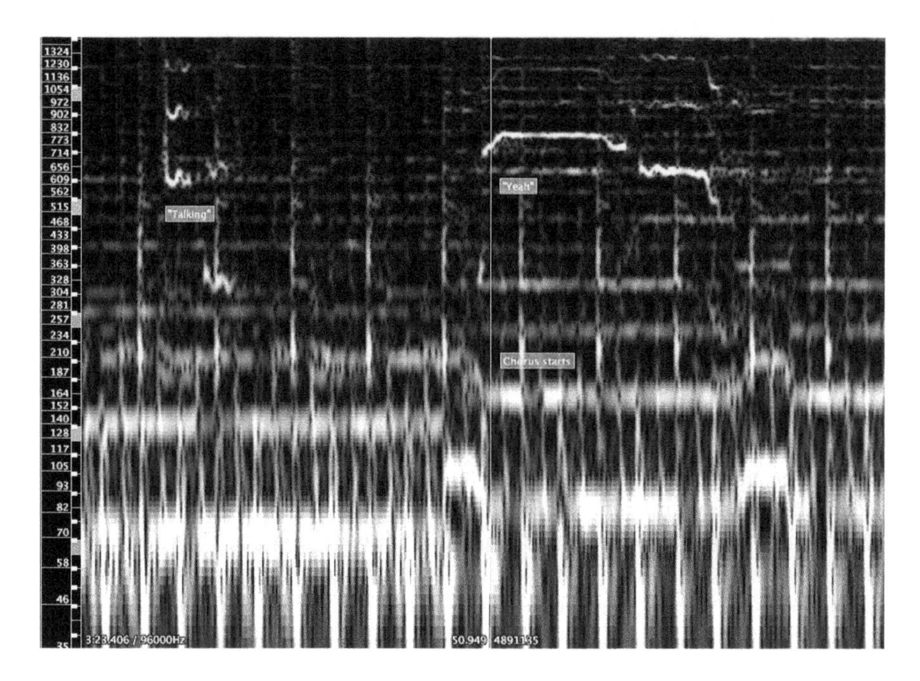

Figure 6.1 'Sex On Fire', spectrograph of the transition from verse 1 to chorus 1 (about 0:45 to 0:54) produced in the Sonic Visualiser software package

Alongside this metaphorical relationship with quantity – the number of 'things' creating this noise – is the one relating to the type of activity that is making the noise. We have already discussed the idea of unsynchronised and irregular (or asymmetrical) activity suggesting a different form of interpretation to concerted and regular activity. The affordances of synchronised musical activity are more participatory than contemplative and the affordances of more complex asymmetrical activity are the opposite. Another key indicator of the type of activity is the tempo of the music. In 'Sex On Fire' there is a slight increase in tempo (from a start of 152.8bpm)[20] into the first verse (153.2bpm) up to (153.6bpm) in the second eight bars of the verse and through the first chorus. This then slows to 153.2bpm for the start of the second verse and speeds up in the last four bars to around 157bpm before dropping back to 153bpm for the second chorus. In the second eight bars of this chorus it creeps up to 154bpm and stays at that speed until the last four bars of the third verse when it speeds up again to 155bpm and then drops back to 154 for the chorus. There is quite a dramatic drop of speed (to 148bpm) at the start of the break down section but it creeps up in speed after the

[20] These tempo markings have been created by hand using the metronome and tempo list in Logic rather than a beat extraction programme.

first four bars to the point that it reaches 155bpm for the last two bars before the full chorus returns where it slows again to 152bpm and stays at roughly that tempo to the end. Thus, the pattern of energy follows the narrative structure we have already described pretty much: the energy at the end of the verses rises towards the chorus. One surprising element is the drop of energy going into the break down section – perhaps a deliberate strategy so that there is not an inexorable rise in tempo all the way from start to finish.

One final aspect of the perceived energy level to be borne in mind is that the technology contributes to the rhythmic patterning as well. In any analysis such as this, the technology should be considered as one of the actors in that its design configures the 'user' to work within particular constraints. On an obvious level, the delays added to the bass and to the voice create additional rhythmic impetus – although the tempo is not constant the delay times work well enough to keep the momentum going. Further to that though, each of the compressors used on the various instruments has an attack and a decay time that affects the dynamic morphology of that sound – and it is fairly certain that although it is not mentioned in his interview on the topic, Jacquire King has spent time adjusting these attack and release times to match the tempo and rhythmic feel of the track. The aim would be to get all the volume levels (in as far as they are controlled by the compression) 'pumping' in time with the musical performances.

Conclusion

So while in some ways the final analysis of this track centres around its fairly obvious structure of verses and choruses, what we have discovered is that there are a great many small details that contribute to the way in which that structural narrative works. These two textures or 'feels' articulate themselves in various 'social' and 'technical' forms that suggest different levels of togetherness, different forms of activity and even different types of environment. We have examined how the types of gesture, the way that they interact, the number of perceived agents, the perceived distance they are away from us and the size of the perceived space they are in have all contributed information that is likely to influence the way that we interpret this piece of music. These seem to me to provide a much richer and more meaningful set of criteria for analysis of musical interpretation than the traditional musicological approaches of melody and harmony.

References

Bakhtin, M.M., 1982. *Dialogic Imagination: Four Essays*. New edn. Austin, TX: University of Texas Press.

Butler, M.J., 2006. *Unlocking the Groove: Rhythm, Meter, and Musical Design in Electronic Dance Music*. Bloomington, IN: Indiana University Press.

Clarke, E.F., 2005. *Ways of Listening: An Ecological Approach to the Perception of Musical Meaning*. New York: Oxford University Press.

Damasio, A., 2000. *The Feeling of What Happens: Body, Emotion and the Making of Consciousness*. New edn. London: Vintage.

Deutsch, D., 1998. *The Psychology of Music*. 2nd edn. San Diego, CA: Academic Press.

Doyle, P., 2006. *Echo and Reverb: Fabricating Space in Popular Music Recording, 1900–1960*. Middletown, CT: Wesleyan University Press.

Feldman, J.A., 2008. *From Molecule to Metaphor: A Neural Theory of Language*. Cambridge, MA: MIT Press.

Gibson, J.J., 1979. *The Ecological Approach to Visual Perception*. Hillsdale, NJ: Psychology Press.

Hall, E.T., 1966. *The Hidden Dimension*. London: Doubleday.

Kaufman, G., 2011. Kings of Leon Have Never Been Shy about Alcohol. Past Interviews Have Highlighted the Band's Love of Drinking, *MTV News*, [online] Available at: http://www.mtv.com/news/articles/1668410/kings-of-leon-alcohol.jhtml [Accessed 14 August 2013].

Lakoff, G. and Johnson, M., 2003. *Metaphors We Live By*. 2nd edn. Chicago, IL: University Of Chicago Press.

Monson, I., 1997. *Saying Something: Jazz Improvisation and Interaction*. Chicago, IL: University of Chicago Press.

Moore, A.F., 1992. *Rock: The Primary Text : Developing a Musicology of Rock*. 2nd edn. Aldershot: Ashgate.

Moore, A.F., 2012. *Song Means: Analysing and Interpreting Recorded Popular Song*. Farnham: Ashgate.

Moylan, W., 1992. *The Art of Recording: Understanding and Crafting the Mix*. Boston, MA: Focal Press.

Rossing, T.D., Moore, R.F. and Wheeler, P.A., 2001. *The Science of Sound*. 3rd edn. Reading, MA: Addison Wesley.

Smalley, D., 1986. Spectromorphology and Structuring Processes. In: S. Emmerson (ed.), *The Language of Electroacoustic Music*. London: Macmillan, pp. 61–93.

Tingen, P., 2008. Secrets of the Mix Engineers: Jacquire King. Kings of Leon: Sex On Fire, *Sound on Sound*. [online] Available at: http://www.soundonsound.com/sos/dec08/articles/it_king.htm [Accessed 14 August 2013).

Warner, T., 2005. The Song of the Hydra: Multiple Lead Vocals in Modern Pop Music Recordings. In: *Art of Record Production Conference*. Westminster University, London, 17–18 September 2005. [online] Available at: http://www.artofrecordproduction.com/index.php/arp-conferences/arp-2005/17-arp-conference-archive/arp-2005/82-warner-2005 [Accessed 14 August 2013].

Zagorski-Thomas, S., 2010a. Real and Unreal Performances. In: A. Danielsen (ed.), *Rhythm in the Age of Digital Reproduction*. Farnham: Ashgate, pp. 195–212.

Zagorski-Thomas, S., 2010b. The Stadium in Your Bedroom: Functional Staging, Authenticity and the Audience Led Aesthetic in Record Production. *Popular Music*, 29(2), pp. 251–66.

Zagorski-Thomas, S., 2012. Musical Meaning and the Musicology of Record Production. In: D. Helms and T. Phleps (eds), *Black Box Pop. Analysen populärer Musik*. Bielefeld: Transcript, pp. 135–47.
Zagorski-Thomas, S., 2014. *The Musicology of Record Production*. Cambridge: Cambridge University Press.
Zagorski-Thomas, S., 2015 (in press). Sonic Cartoons. In: M. Hanáček, H. Schulze and J. Papenburg (eds), *Research Companion to the Sound in Media Culture Network*.

Discography

Kings Of Leon, 2008. *Only By The Night*. RCA, 88697 32712 2.
Morissette, Alanis, 1996. 'Ironic'. Reprise, 9362–43700–2.

Chapter 7
Andrés's 'New For U': New for Us. On Analysing Electronic Dance Music

André Doehring

On 13 February 2012, Andrés (born Humberto Andrés Hernandez in 1975 in Detroit) debuted his own label La Vida with the release of his EP *New For U* (see Discogs.com, 2013; Kellman, 2013). The first of the three tracks[1] on this vinyl-only release is 'New For U', which was soon to be recognised by DJs, magazines, record stores and sites on the Internet devoted to electronic dance music (EDM) as a record that stood out from the mass of releases in 2012.[2] Although the first vinyl edition sold out very fast,[3] the track was voted as one of the year's 'best' tracks.[4] In spring 2013, a vinyl repress was released.

Assigning this track to the fuzzy field of EDM, as I do here, may not be the best, but is the most common way to tell other people about the sound of this recording.[5] More detailed information might be that 'New For U' is classified

---

[1] Track is the common term for a composition in electronic dance music. Usually, tracks feature a different form from songs. They tend to emphasise aspects of rhythm and sound whereas aspects of harmony or pitch are not that relevant (see also Butler, 2006, p. 9, note 7, and p. 327).

[2] A short example: 'New For U' entered residentadviser.net's DJ charts instantly and stayed there for 11 months. After the repress it charted again for two more months (see Residentadviser.net, 2013a).

[3] In the field of EDM, vinyls are released in relatively small numbers of 500–1,000 copies. Herrmann (2013) mentions an average of 200 copies for deep house labels. Regrettably, I could not get any information on the actual number of copies released by La Vida but to expect a figure within this scope would not mislead us completely. Compared to sales from other market segments of popular music, this may look small from the outside but nevertheless it has had an impact on the EDM field.

[4] To illustrate this: 'New For U' was 'best' track of the year for example in *Groove* #140 (Jan./Feb. 2013), on residentadviser.net (Residentadviser.net, 2013b) and *juno.co.uk* (Junorecords, 2013).

[5] I share this pragmatic discontent with the label EDM with Mark J. Butler who defines the 'catchall term' (Butler, 2012b, p. xii) in the following way: 'Electronic dance music encompasses a complex network of related styles, created and experienced primarily in urban and/or leisure spaces around the globe, which share practices of production and consumption that centre around dancing to and performing with recorded music in particular, dedicated sites' (ibid.).

under the genre house; those even more inside the field (for example record stores, DJs) use subgenres as 'deep house' or 'Detroit house' to give an impression of what to expect (see McLeod, 2001).

However, at this point, at the latest, I fear I will have lost most of the musicologists among my readers since neither EDM nor any of its genres have been key subjects of musicological research. Of course, there is a lot of research on EDM as I will show below, but it is fair to say that it has not been musicologists undertaking most of that work. To musicology, EDM is still a relatively new field of research where only a brave few resist the discipline's norms of standardisation (for example Butler, 2006; 2012a; Danielsen, 2010a).

What are the reasons for this neglect of a music that matters to listeners and dancers night after night in most parts of the Western hemisphere in the early twenty-first century?[6] According to Pierre Bourdieu's sociology, to enter and remain in the field of musicology you have to accept and reproduce the hegemonic rules and values of that field. As a consequence, EDM simply falls outwith the discipline's focus because it cannot claim to be accepted by the dominant definition of music.[7] Scores, common instruments or legitimate concepts of compositional development are by and large irrelevant to EDM.[8] Looking through the musicological glasses[9] that we inevitably put on once we have arrived in the field, EDM has thus become invisible. Furthermore, most musicologists, in my experience, have little knowledge of and experience with EDM because usually they are either classically or self-trained instrumentalists in the classical or rock repertoire, and they only very rarely go out to dance clubs. A last but by no means least reason for this neglect might also be musicology's mistrust of its methods' ability to cope with this 'new' phenomenon. Without any doubt, there are problems researching EDM. In the case of 'New For U', for example, its limited availability, its vinyl-only status and its integration into DJ sets as a common way of listening – and dancing! – had to be encountered (more on solving these difficulties later on). More serious, still, there is a paucity of methods among which to choose in analysing EDM. In the following pages, I will argue for a serious revision of the discipline's core method as a self-reflexive and context-sensitive approach.

[6] 'Popular music matters, and it matters to so many people we can only partially understand if we do not understand their music' (Moore, 2012b, p. ix). Unless we do not take popular music seriously in its entirety, the implication for musicology might result in a further deepening isolation.

[7] Peter Wicke (1997, p. 421) writes unequivocally: 'Die Frage, was die Musikwissenschaft mit der Berliner Love Parade zu tun hat, läßt sich kurz und bündig beantworten – nichts.' [The answer to the question what do musicology and the Berlin love parade have in common is simply – nothing; transl. André Doehring].

[8] I am far from being the first to point this out; see for example Tagg (1994).

[9] The metaphor of the glasses has been adopted from Pierre Bourdieu's *Über das Fernsehen* [*Sur la télévision*, 1996] (Bourdieu, 1998, p. 25) who describes them as the product of the journalists' socialisation and training.

After all, analysis is the only method that is capable of producing results about the structure of actual sounding elements and it is and remains musicology's unique contribution to the necessarily interdisciplinary research on EDM.

And yet, while thinking about the 'how' of analysing EDM – thereby, making it 'visible' in the Bourdieuan sense – we should not forget to address the 'why'. Here, the question of the goals of analysis is answered in two ways: analysis is well suited to learn about your individual responses to music as Allan F. Moore (2012a) has recently clarified. But it is also a method to anchor *other* people's reactions in the sounding structure. I will therefore propose analysis as a tool of music sociology. Thereby, we might learn why 'New For U' did matter to a lot of people in 2012.

(A Very Short) History of Analyses of EDM

As a general rule, academic research starts not *with* but usually way *after* the phenomenon has emerged. Thus, literature on EDM was beginning to be published more steadily in the UK around the mid 1990s when the initial acid house/UK rave movement of the late 1980s had become visible and established enough to be thoroughly investigated (and thereby historicised). In his overview of the development of the academic study of EDM, Butler (2012b, p. xiii) states that it was mostly scholars from cultural studies and popular music studies who undertook the initial research which centred on social and cultural issues (for example Thornton, 1996); Adam Krims (2000, pp. 18ff.) criticised especially popular music studies for its neglect of analysis. The first essays from a musicological viewpoint appeared in *Popular Music* in the early 1990s (Langlois, 1992; Tagg, 1994) while the first monograph from a music studies field (ethnomusicology) was published in 2000 (Fikentscher, 2000; see Butler, 2012b, p. xvii). From a statistical evaluation of the pool of literature published on dancecult.net[10] we can see that since then EDM as subject of research has advanced to a create a stable field of scholarly work in the twenty-first century.

---

[10] Dancecult.net, initiated by scholars Graham St. John and Eliot Bates in 2005, is a website dedicated to the international research of EDM. In mid July 2013, the bibliography on the website contained 328 entries; users can add new or missing literature online. Although the site wishes to limit its bibliography to 'scholarly academic works on electronic dance music' you will find books by journalists, too (for example Simon Reynolds's (1998) or Tobias Rapp's (2009) widely read books). As these were – and still are – a defining part of the history of research on EDM they are included in my evaluation.

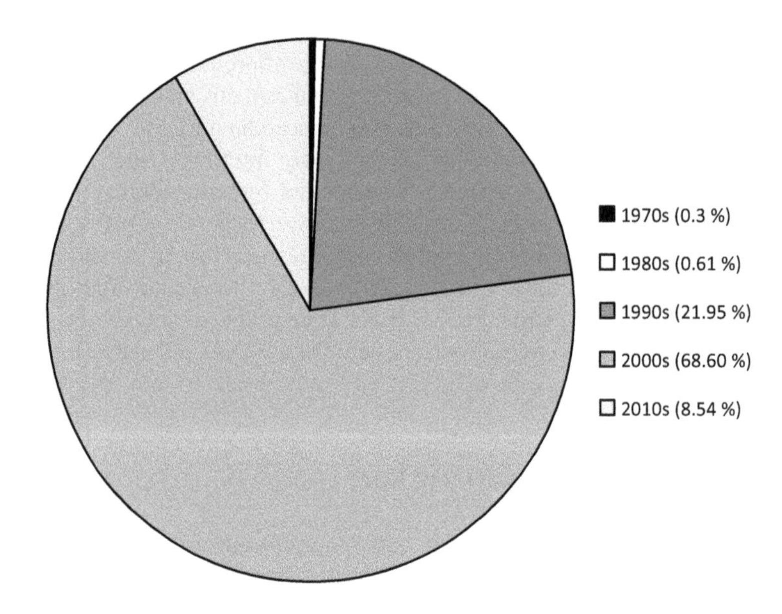

Figure 7.1 Proportion of literature on EDM published 1976–2013 (n = 328)

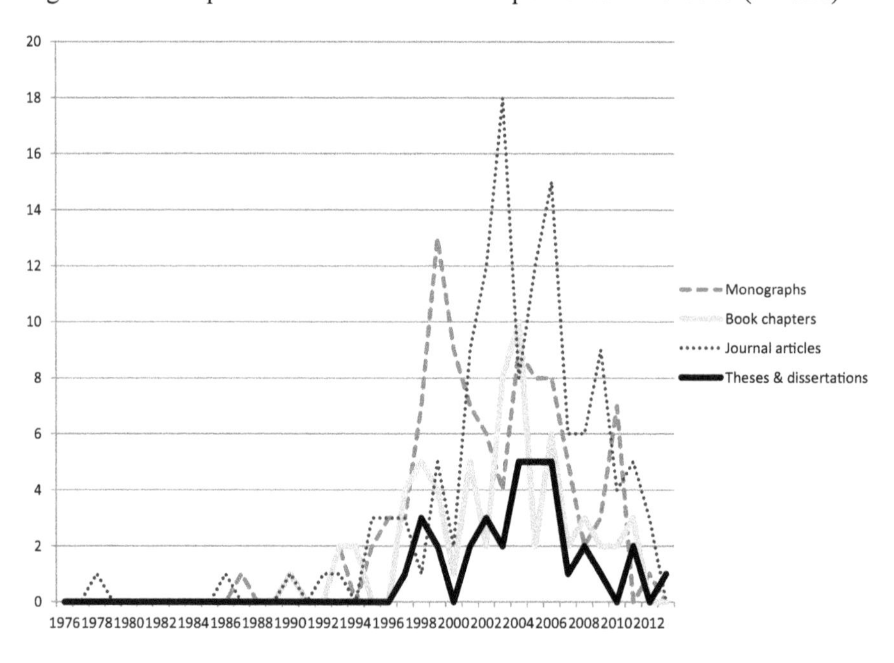

Figure 7.2 Type of literature on EDM published 1976–2013 (n = 328)

After the first monographs appeared on the scene from the mid 1990s onwards (see Figure 7.2) the vast majority of academic research (68.6 per cent) was published in their wake in the 2000s (see Figure 7.1). In recent years, interest seems to have calmed down a bit although a reader on EDM has been published lately (Butler, 2012a).[11]

Looking at the amount of work done on EDM in past years, it is worth noting that the analytical output has been comparatively small and mostly incoherent (see Tagg, 1994; Cascone, 2000; Klotz, 2002; Hawkins, 2003; Ferreira, 2008; Steingo, 2008). In the twenty-first century, though, two important analytical contributions to the field were published: first was Mark J. Butler's (2006) landmark study *Unlocking the Groove*, that undertook a survey on the existing literature on EDM and pointed to the lacuna of adequate analytical work. In response to this, he conceptualised a combined method of analytical and ethnographic work that took musical sound as being as important as the musical practices[12] of the dancers, the producers and the DJs. Furthermore, Butler, in a specifically ethnomusicological manner, was very sensitive about his role as analyst framing the 'objects' of his analyses. The second strain of research, although not limited to EDM, is the work of Anne Danielsen (2006) and her project (2004–2009) on 'rhythm in the digital age of reproduction' at the University of Oslo (the results are collected in Danielsen, 2010a). Here, fundamental work on the analysis of microrhythm and rhythmic structure is introduced. These contributions not only challenged analysts' traditional concepts of rhythm but they also considered the roles of technological

[11] In Germany, however, as a general rule, academic research starts not *with* but usually way *after* the research has been taken up in other countries. The earliest academic notions of EDM can be found at the turn of the millennium, at a time, when the Berlin love parade already attracted an estimated 1.5 million visitors and was broadcast on national public TV. A reason for this delay might be that in Germany both cultural and popular music studies were adopted years later than in the Anglophone parts of the world. As it had been in the UK, the first monographs came from the field of sociology (for example Meyer, 2000; Hitzler and Pfadenhauer, 2001) or media studies (Poschardt, 1997; Poschardt's book was one of the first German books about EDM. Although it was his PhD dissertation, it attracted a wide readership of journalists. The first edition was published in 1995 in a – probably also due to its low prices – popular left-wing bookstore and publishing house. The second edition from 1997 spread quickly among listeners of EDM; an English translation was published in 1998. From today's perspective – now that we know more and better literature on that subject – we can comprehend the demand for *any* literature about EDM at that time). To my knowledge, the first German analytical works on EDM are to be found in the annual *Beiträge zur Popularmusikforschung* (Rösing and Phleps, 1999); the first musicological monograph on techno that uses analysis as method appeared in 2003 (Volkwein, 2003).

[12] I use musical practice in the sense of the Austrian music sociologist Kurt Blaukopf who warned in 1982, 'that the word *practice* should not be taken in the narrow sense of referring only to "what is actually heard". It should be extended to include all musical acts and omissions, as well as observable behaviour patterns. Theoretical reflection on this musical practice – that is, thought about music based on each practice and capable of influencing it – will also be considered part of this practice of music sociology' (Blaukopf, 2012, p. 18; original emphasis).

aspects and corporeality in the experience of groove-directed EDM (for example Zeiner-Henriksen, 2010).

In the wake of these writings, analysing EDM today has thus become an endeavour with an, albeit admittedly short, history to build upon.[13] Still, while being rather at the beginning than at the height of its development, I think it is vital for every analytical process to debate its own discursive articulation to this body of work and thereby to clarify its resulting basic assumptions.

To begin with, in this analysis of 'New For U', the process of analysis is perceived as a social practice (see Butler, 2006, p. 16; Doehring, 2012, pp. 37–8). It is carried out by an analyst who hears, understands and interprets the music in a historically specific situation. My way of making sense of the sounds, that is the analytical results as well as my interpretation of them, have to be communicated to the readers of the analysis, thereby obeying the rules framing this communication. And second, if we consider analysis as a social practice, we might conclude that musicologists are not the only people listening intensively to music, picking out certain aspects to base an interpretation upon. By means of non-scientific[14] analyses people do interpret music for specific reasons every day. For example, focusing on the field of EDM, these analyses might ask if the music is good for dancing (even while dancing), if they want to listen to it again and buy the record (or download it from the Internet) or what might happen if the track is played at a specific time and place to a specific audience? That is to say, musical practices are – to a certain degree – based on the everyday analytical listening to and interpretation of a given music. Therefore, the goal of an analytical process can also be to connect the sound with its attributed meaning in a given musical practice. Analysis in this way becomes a tool of a music sociology that takes the sound into its account – at last, as in 1958 Theodor W. Adorno already postulated this connection in his largely overseen 'Ideen zur Musiksoziologie' [ideas on music sociology] (Adorno, 2003; see Doehring, 2012, pp. 35ff.). So broadening analysis as a social practice brings to the fore both the analyst herself and the practices of other people to whom music matters.

[13] However, if musicologists decide to use analysis it is usually not EDM they are applying it to. To give a recent example: On the mid summer 2013 'International Conference on Analyzing Popular Music popMAC' in Liverpool three out of 92 papers (plus the three keynotes, seven position papers and a roundtable address) were on the issue of analysing EDM.

[14] 'Non-scientific' does not want to denigrate other people with a different educational background. Instead, it simply indicates that in everyday evaluations of music, scientific claims for objectivity (or to be more precise and without the ideological burden: inter-subjectivity), consistency, verifiability and discursiveness are not met.

'New For U' and Me

Thinking about my first contact with the track, I must have come across 'New For U' while flipping through the bi-monthly published German EDM magazine *Groove*. 'New For U' headlined its May/June (*Groove* #136) single charts, put together from votes of DJs. I had not heard or read anything about this track before because a review had neither been published in the previous issue nor in the recent. So – curious by now – I instantly went online to listen to the track. This first encounter with the music – at home, listening to the track on a laptop computer without decent headphones and in a minor sound quality streaming from youtube.com (or rather: watching, as somebody had filmed the playing of his 'New For U'-12" on a turntable) – left me puzzled: Although I liked its catchiness, its groove and the way the strings were brought into the track right away, I wondered why anybody should want to dance to a track in 2012 that sounded dated to me and differed from contemporary productions?

By the end of April of that year (as I've tried to reconstruct), I read a particularly positive review in the online EDM magazine residentadviser.net (Ryce, 2012). This review in particular got me interested in the record. By now, I decided to purchase the vinyl to play it on my home stereo (at that time, clubbing was out of the question as we expected our second daughter soon).[15] Maybe then, I hoped, I might 'understand' why people were in favour of this record. But as it turned out, the 12" was already out of stock so I let it alone and forgot about the record – until the end of the year when 'New For U' was voted 'best' track of 2012. And now, I was among the first to get one of the represses. Writing this, I now can see that my general interest in EDM, which instigates certain practices around this music,[16] as well as my musicological interest in the sound of the track (or to be more precise: my musicological interest in the sound that others ascribe to the track) led me to buy the record.[17] But why do I have to report of this individual history of the track's reception in such detail?

From a methodological viewpoint the answer is simple: the process of analysing and the analyst form a symbiotic relationship. As 'there is no perspectiveless position from which we make an interpretation' (Moore, 2012a, p. 326), this relationship has to be reflexively examined and then communicated to the third participant in an analysis, the reader. Basically, my interpretation will only be comprehensible if I offer to the audience of my analysis the possibility of understanding my perspective on this music.

---

[15] To meet possibly arising critique in advance: yes, I have been to clubs before and since that time.

[16] In no particular order these practices include listening, DJing, producing, clubbing as well as reading, talking and lecturing about EDM.

[17] Without doubt, the latter is the male gendered behaviour Will Straw (1997) describes for rock music but which holds also true for EDM due to its materialism and its embeddedness in the same culture.

In my case, this is of particular importance since my reception of 'New For U' differs somewhat from the stereotype image of responding to EDM invoked by the literature where only dancers and DJs in one particular place (the dance floor) at one particular time (the peak time) 'really' understand the music. By concentrating on (and thereby transfiguring) this unique moment of musical reception to such an extent, research on EDM has lost sight of other – and most probably, many more – ways of dealing with EDM. Hence, the often voiced concern (for example by Kennett, 2003) about the adequacy of analysing a single 12" track outside its 'native' environment of the DJ set can be met in the same way: although 'New For U' might be called 'funktionale Musik' [functional music] (Eggebrecht, 1973), produced for the purpose of dancing in clubs together with other dancers, many people nevertheless will listen to this track as a single recording in other places while pursuing other activities than dancing. To insist on the priority of the track's (allegedly – see more on this below) sole function resurrects the notion of the composer as the creative genius against whose will thou shalt not listen. To my view, we thankfully have overcome this dated theoretical position by acknowledging that people of a different class/race/gender have valid and diverse practices of dealing with music.

Furthermore, writing about my experiences listening to the track I do not wish to imply that dancing or the club are irrelevant to the study of EDM. Quite the contrary: they remain important areas of research insofar as we acknowledge that there are also other practices that contribute to what we call EDM. Nor do I want to suggest that my way of approaching the music is necessarily in any way 'superior' to that of others. Rather, as I have said above, communication of the analyst's reception of music is indispensable to the reader. Finally, by giving account of my experiences and problems analysing 'New For U', I thereby offer possible ways for another analysis of the track to falsify my results in the most productive way.

Analysing 'New For U'

I began the analysis by transferring the vinyl into the digital copy that I am used to working with during an analysis. This activity, to some extent, has consequences for my results because I thereby create an object as basis of my analysis that is no more the original and – even more serious – whose central features: length, pitch and tempo, differ from it. However, panicking would be unreasonable, since we have to keep in mind that every analysis is a special way of dealing with music. This is inevitably done under specific circumstances by specific persons with specific interests. So the best I can do about this is to give a detailed account of my 'breadboard construction'[18] to explain the small deviations.

[18] Thy vinyl was played on a Technics SL-1200 MK2 equipped with an Ortofon Arkiv cartridge through a Native Instruments Audio 6 interface running at 24 Bit. The audio was recorded in Native Instruments' Traktor software (Scratch Pro 2.6) in the wav-format at

The tempo of 'New For U' seems to be – as every DJ will instantly feel or 'know' – 130bpm[19] by means of which it fits perfectly into the house genre. But after transfer of the record into digital audio 'my' tempo clocks in at 129.13bpm (in Ableton Live) and 129.14bpm (in Traktor Scratch Pro). An explanation for this minor deviation might be that my worn turntable did not play at the right speed although the pitch control was set to 0 per cent. Following from this, measurements of pitch are lower than they were if the record had been played at the right speed. Likewise, considering length, the 184 bars of the track in my analysis differ from other information. This means in effect that in this analysis – where it was me who decided to cut the audio at the particular points that suited my impression of the track's start and end – the runtime of 'New For U' is 5:45 minutes (in contrast to for example 5:42 min.; see Discogs.com, 2013). The sound of the digital audio also differs from the vinyl sound. And this difference increases when I play the record on a turntable equipped with an Ortofon Concorde Nightclub Mk II, often found as the standard cartridge in clubs. Suddenly, higher frequencies sound less shrill whereas the bass and the beat are foregrounded and sound more pronounced. But well, for this analysis, I worked with the digital audio described above.

My initial question was what does the music afford to my understanding of the track? Why do I want to dance to this track? Why does it sound catchy? And why do I like the strings – although the track sounds dated?

'New For U' starts with eight bars of the beat, no additional instruments or sounds can be heard. Certainly, these first bars have a function in EDM practice: they allow the DJ to adjust tempo and metre of the record to the one currently playing so that the track can be seamlessly added to the mix ('beatmatching'). But there is more to the first bars of 'New For U': The track, by its vinyl-only release, has to be played on a turntable. So eight bars of a lead-in groove at circa 130bpm will leave the DJ no more than 14 seconds to beatmatch the record. Hence, these eight bars can be read as a statement by Andrés: this record is for the professional DJ alone who not only (or in these times: still) values the 'better' sound of vinyl but who possesses the skills to cope with it in the proper and historically handed-down manner.[20]

From the first second, I am drawn into the groove of this track and it takes me through the track without any ruptures. Quite uncommonly compared to contemporary EDM recordings, Andrés did not add any editing in terms of EQ or FX manipulation to the beat over the entire duration of the track. Even at breakdowns, markers of the beat are still audible (handclaps on the backbeat,

---

+2.4 dB and cut in Audacity (2.0.3). During the analysis, I used Ableton Live 9 Suite as audio software device; additional measurements were done in Sonic Visualiser (2.1).

[19] The discogs.com database (discogs.com, 2013) confirms this impression, too.

[20] Notwithstanding its vinyl-only status, many DJs digitalised or illegally downloaded 'New For U', since today the use of DJ software like for example Traktor or Serato DJ is common. Here, the idea of beatmatching as a verification of a DJ's skills is obsolete because the software does it.

effects synchronised to the beat) so that the dancers will continue dancing. The beat of 'New For U' (see Example 7.1) consists of the steady 'four-on-the-floor' pulse of the bass drum, the bright sound of a snare drum mixed with handclaps on every backbeat as well as the sound and rhythmic pattern of the hissing hi-hat so common in house music. Playing at (more or less) 130bpm, with all sounds possibly being generated by a drum machine (or sampled from a drum machine and then played through a sampler) and with all rhythmic events mapped on a metric grid, the beat is a characteristic though not exceptional musical indicator of EDM.

Example 7.1 'New For U', one bar of the beat

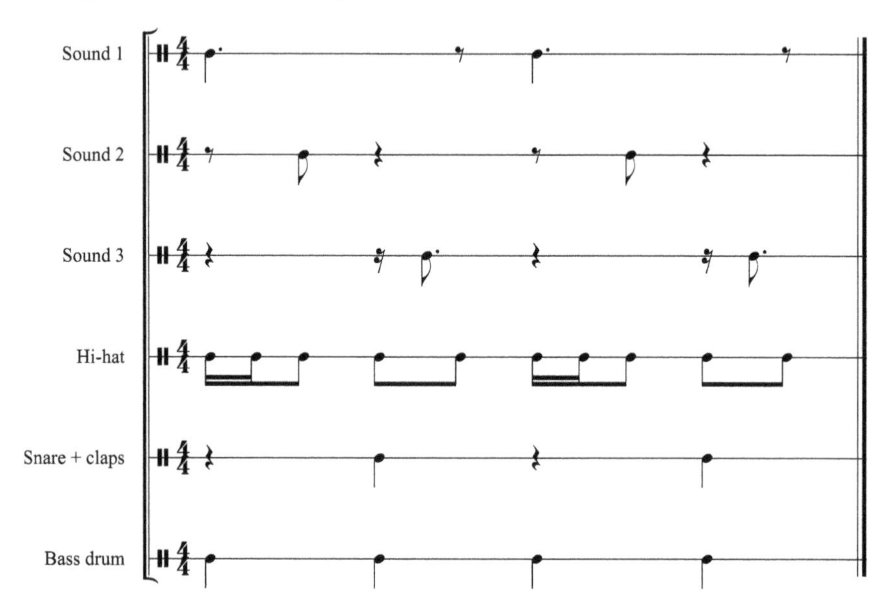

However, what *does* make the loop[21] of 'New For U''s groove special are the three extra sounds added by Andrés. First, on each downbeat he added a sound that lasts for three quavers that reminds me of a starting tape machine or of a record starting slowly on a turntable. With its breathy characteristic and its beginning on a downbeat you do not register its presence initially amidst the other more common drum sounds. Second, coming in a quaver after each downbeat we hear a hit on the snare, which is mixed to the background of the sound box and thereby nearly

---

[21] It is common practice in EDM production to loop small musical parts. Considering 'New For U', one is tempted to speak of a one-bar loop although the second half of that bar is identical to the first one. It may well be that Andrés composed/programmed only the first two quavers of the beat and looped the beat from them.

inaudible compared to the snare sound on 2 and 4. Third, a semiquaver after each backbeat, we hear the start of a scraping sound that ends with the next downbeat. All of these extra sounds are in a higher frequency spectrum. Recalling Zeiner-Henriksen's (2010, p. 128) use of the motor schemata to explain his observations of the correlation between bass drum and hi-hat sounds and the corresponding vertical bodily movements of dancers or listeners (downwards on the downbeat marked by the low frequency bass drum, upwards with the high pitched hi-hat on the off-beat), these extra sounds have microrhythmic functions due to their placement in the rhythmic structure, their shape and their sound: They make you (or at least: me) feel like dancing (see Danielsen, 2010b, p. 7).

Against the steady framework of the crotchet pulse provided by the bass drum (and supported by the rhythm of the keyboard and the bass, the latter with a slight variation on each 4 and 4+ leading you back to the next 1) the hit on the snare on the second quaver mentioned above takes you away from the heavy downward movement on the 1. This is supported by the hi-hat gesture. While on the one hand the two semi-quavers of the hi-hat on 1 emphasise the downbeat, on the other hand they already announce and anticipate the off-beat movement of the extra snare hit. In effect, as heavy as the 1 and the corresponding bodily movement may have been, this single hit on the off-beat reminds us unmistakably to move upwards again and dance on. The first and the third sound mentioned above have to be taken into account together. Their duration is longer so that together, they nearly fill the looped two quarters of the beat. The third sound starts directly after the backbeat hit on the snare. Its scraping quality is clearly audible and both signals the off-beat as well as announcing a return to the next downbeat by its duration. Here, the first sound appears again. It is obviously a counterpoint to the sharp sound heard before. As I have mentioned above, with its breathy characteristic it conveys to me a certain kind of lightness (in spite of its position on the downbeat). The image of a starting tape machine, which has been provoked by that sound, may well have originated in my first experiences in recording studios. But it is surely induced by the feeling that something – namely the loop – starts right here. And this is a nice and smooth start, not too heavy or demanding. Together with the third sound that signals the end of the loop and announces the return of its cosy beginning, these sounds add a dramaturgy to the beat at the micro-level that in its balanced design could last forever – or at least it does so for the 5:45 minutes of 'New For U'.

To return to my second question, concerning the track's catchiness[22] to me, I want to go into the deeper detail of analysing aspects of harmony, pitch, instrumentation and form. These are useful areas of research with appropriate *termini technici* for the musicological observation of sound structures – as long as the critique considering their ideological ballast is taken seriously. At least,

[22] Catchy means here that a sounding structure can be remembered and then anticipated easily due to its qualities as well as due to the listener's previous experience and familiarity with similar sounding structures.

they offer the opportunity to communicate the anchoring of my interpretation of the track in the music. In 'New For U', we have limited instrumentation (beat, bass, keyboard, strings) that sounds very warm because, for example, the higher frequencies and attacks of the keyboard (to my ears a software emulation of an electro-mechanical piano) and the soft synth bass have been reduced. Furthermore, limited musical material is used, that most listeners of popular music will surely be familiar with. There are only three different harmonic[23] loops of four bars each: The loop of $B\flat^7/Asus^4/d^9/dsus^4$ (part A^n in Table 7.1) is used in 85 per cent of the track's duration, the loop $B\flat^7/g^7/g^7/g^7$ appears in 9 per cent (part C), the four bars of part B (g/C/A/d) are played just once (2 per cent).[24] The cadence of part A^n is an essential element of 'New For U' where Andrés uses the common harmonic formula of VI – V – i that most listeners will be familiar with. The harmonic shape of the other two loops is different for formal reasons (see below) but it nevertheless stays inside the harmonic space of the D-harmonic minor scale.

Most of the chords have alterations we know from a lot of styles of popular music. The main theme of the strings is a pentatonic scale on A minor that starts over a D minor chord, which thus becomes a d^9. The strings end on A, which adds the major seventh to B♭. The pedal point on D played by the keyboard also provides an sus4 to the A-major chord and keeps the focus on D minor in the last two bars of the theme while the bass moves from D over A to G and then F.

Furthermore, the analysis of formal aspects of 'New For U' (see Table 7.1) shows that Andrés uses a structure that draws upon ways of processing form known from EDM as well as popular songs. On the one hand we have the building of larger parts from sequences of four bars by varying their texture, as found in most EDM styles (see Butler, 2006, pp. 206ff.). Here, I interpret the four bars of the bass theme as the structuring principle of parts A^n, which have in their many variations two different functions: core and build-up (see Butler, 2006, pp. 223–4). But on the other hand, a third function of part A emerges with the recurring appearance of the core from bars 9–16 that I termed 'chorus' because first, every additional rendition of the core is now accompanied by the beat and features the complete theme with the vocals. It therefore conveys more energy compared to the rest of the track, as choruses usually do. Second, memorability of the 'chorus' is supported by the fact that a 'chorus' is repeated more often upon its next arrival (until the last 'chorus' is cut off after two run-throughs). In addition, the vocal part ('turn to you') appears in the 'chorus'; this is a simple and easily comprehensible tune so that we can

[23] It would be appropriate to speak of harmonic implications since in 'New For U', the only chord is provided by the keyboard at the start of the four-bar loop (d–f–a over a B♭ in the bass). Therefore, all chord symbols represent my interpretations of the harmonic room that the bass implies together with the other instruments.

[24] The remaining 4 per cent go to the introduction where no additional instruments are used besides the beat.

Table 7.1 Form of 'New For U'

Bars	Length	Part	Function	Commentary
1–8	8		Intro	Lead-in groove for the DJ
9–16	8 (4+4)	A^1	Core	Presentation of the theme without the beat
17–32	16 (4+4)+ (4+4)	A^2	Build-up	Beat is brought back in, thinner texture building up tension by 'call-and-response' of keys/strings
33–36	4	A^3	'Breakdown'	Disorientation – feels like a repetition of A^2 at first but is then unsettled by B
37–40	4	B	'Pre-chorus'	Higher rhythmic density, new harmonies: preparation for 'chorus'
41–48	8	A	'Chorus'	Theme with the beat
49–64	16 (4+4)+ (4+4)	A^4	Build-up	Thinner texture building up tension, variation of the strings in the second eight bars compared to A^2
65–72	8 (4+4)	C	Breakdown/ 'Pre-chorus'	A breakdown is being anticipated, the different harmonies pause on G minor; the bass is building up tension through repetition; the chorus' theme in the keyboard is there; this part is leading to the chorus, hence the pre-chorus feel
73–80	8 (4+4)	A	'Chorus'	
81–88	8 (4+4)	A^5	Breakdown 'chorus'	Beat is reduced to the claps, bass is muted, dub FX on reduced keyboard; the markers of the 'chorus' (strings and vocals) are there
89–112	24 (2*(4+4))+ (4+4)	A^6	Build-up	Another variation of building up tension that leads to additional eight bars with complete strings
113–120	8	C	Breakdown/ 'Pre-chorus'	Same as above
121–144	24	A	'Chorus'	Three repetitions; keyboard in the higher register manipulated with delay and reverb
145–152	8	A^7	Breakdown	Reduction on beat and bass; Jamaican 'drum & bass concept' (Veal, 2007, pp. 57ff.)
153–168	16	A^8	'Builddown'	Usual building of tension is turned upside down; tension is reduced
169–184	16	A	'Chorus'	'Chorus' returns unexpectedly since tension has been reduced before and without its usually preceding pre-chorus

quickly sing along with on each occurrence.[25] Third, the 'chorus' is prepared by parts B and C, which have the quality of a 'pre-chorus'.[26] As part B appears only once, to me, it has the function of harmonically closing the previous build-up and preparing the listener for something different happening afterwards – the 'chorus'. However, in part C the driving motion of part A^n seems to come to a halt although the beat is playing on. But the permanent four-on-the-floor rhythm from the bass is suspended and the harmonic movement pauses for a moment on the three bars of g^7. Hence, I call part C breakdown – and 'pre-chorus' since it leads us into the 'chorus' every time. By using Philip Tagg's (1987, p. 292) idea of the hypothetical substitution, that is the imagined exchange of parts B and C, we might understand why Andrés has composed 'New For U' like this: A breakdown in the place of B would have been way too early for the dancers and the continuation of B as pre-chorus-model would have changed the overall character of 'New For U' due to part B's tonic-directed cadence. In effect, by combining these two musical form processes in a subtle manner, 'New For U' appeals to the regular clubber as well as to anybody who usually listens to other styles of popular music.[27]

What has been simply called strings so far is in fact a thoroughly edited sample of strings and synthesiser from Dexter Wansel's 'Time Is The Teacher' (1978). Although Andrés is not the first to sample from this composition[28] he seems to be the only one to sample from this very part of the composition beginning at 25 seconds (see Example 7.2). Regarding the tempo of Wansel's music (about 62bpm), Andrés had to slightly speed up the sample to use it in double time at 130bpm. Then, he cut the duration of the first two quavers by half. Additionally, he used an EQ to emphasise the upper voice of the string ensemble, which has the effect of turning the homophonic texture of Wansel's into a monophonic melody in Andrés's version. Moreover, Andrés changed the sample metrically as it now begins on the backbeat (see Example 7.3a). There is hypermetrical conflict, as well. Every listener is tempted to hear the sample beginning – due to 'New For

[25] At the same time, 'turn to you' addresses the community of dancers on the dance floor.

[26] The only exception appears towards the end. The last 'chorus' is not preceded by a pre-chorus, and since in the previous A^8 we have heard the 'builddown' process the listener in a way is ambushed by this last 'chorus' appearing without a warning.

[27] Before I started my analysis of form, 'New For U' seemed to roughly consist of intro – breakdown – build-up – breakdown – build-up. This probably relates to my expectation that I was listening to an EDM track chosen by dozens of DJs and hence, to anything else but a popular song.

[28] Most of the songs that sample from 'Time Is The Teacher' sample from 1:10 or 5:05 (see for a list Whosampled.com, 2013). 'Maybach Music 2' from Rick Ro$$ feat. Kanye West, T-Pain and Lil' Wayne (2009) is the exception because it samples the strings from the beginning of the introduction. Listening to these strings, a connection to the issue of Afro-American upward mobility is made possible, a subject Philly soul is usually associated with and Rick Ro$$'s title is hinting at. Also, Andrés was perhaps inspired by Wansel's harmonic progression of the part following his sample: $d^7/B\flat^7/d^7/B\flat^7/g^7$ a^7/C^9 $F^7/B\flat^7$ $a^7/B\flat^7$.

U"s hypermetre of the looped four bars – with the whole note above the B♭[7] chord (see Example 7.3b). But actually, his sample starts in bar 3 of the hypermetre on the backbeat and extends to the first bar of the next loop (artificially extended into bar 2 of the loop by reverb and delay). So in fact, his sample crosses the hypermetre of 'New For U'. Yet, by the way Andrés cut the sample in two parts of equal length and weaved them into the composition the other way around every listener or dancer will be unaware of that.

Example 7.2 Outline of the outer voices of 'Time Is The Teacher' beginning at 0:25

Example 7.3a Andrés's edited sample of 'Time Is The Teacher'

Example 7.3b Andrés's edited sample as heard in the hypermetre of 'New For U'

After the repeated presentation of the theme's four bars in the core, he teases his listeners in the varying build-up sections: For example, in the first build-up, after muting the strings for eight bars, he launches the sample beginning with semibreves followed by three bars of the keyboard pounding out its bouncing – or the more time passes by: impatient – crotchets on D. To me, this is a kind of 'call-and-no-response' procedure that not only builds up tension but also invites the listener or dancer to fill and use these spaces opened up by the strings. Not until three repetitions of this have passed, the complete theme 'finally' appears in the first 'chorus' at 1:14 – the release of getting back what we were exposed to in the core, instantly comprehended and now love to hear again.

Now, having analysed the track, I do understand most of my reactions to it as I tried to connect them to the sounding structure of 'New For U'. What has been left open so far is my aesthetic judgement of its somehow dated sound in 2012. Why do I interpret it this way? When I heard those strings for the first time, I was thinking of two aspects: The creation of that sound and the historic place of that sound. To me, the strings do not sound 'real' as if played by an ensemble but they also do not sound as being reproduced by a synthesiser. I was thinking of a mellotron at first, which in a way is not too far off from Andrés's use of sampled strings. While it is certainly not important what kind of instrument Andrés actually used, my connection to the mellotron opened up a link to popular music's history (for example its use in 1960s popular music) that I usually do not expect while listening to recent EDM. Furthermore, the use of strings in EDM history is tied to a period of its beginning in the 1970s where labels released many funk and R&B records with an additional string ensemble accompanying the music; these records were played in discos and entered the charts (see Shapiro, 2005, pp. 133ff.). In particular, the label Philadelphia International Records (PIR) contributed to the creation of what was to become known as Philly soul, a trademark of Afro-American dance music. As Dexter Wansel was one of PIR's producers and artists, the use of his music for 'New For U' explains my connections to dance music's past. But still, it cannot elucidate why in 2012 people want to dance to these sounds. So, recalling Robert Walser's request, 'music analysts need to be able to account for music's appeal' (Walser, 2003, p. 37), I will turn to the musical practices of other people in the following.

'New For U' and Other People

In a model taken from Peter Wicke (2004) the meaning of music is inevitably connected to its sound and the discourse surrounding this sound. Following him, every utterance about music – even calling this sound 'music' – is a consequence of the speaker's social position and history *and* her listening and interpretation process. Here, sound matters as much as the meaning we ascribe to that sound. Therefore, analysis must take into account the discourses shaping a particular meaning, too.[29]

I got in touch with 'New For U' through music magazines. Their influence on public opinion has been debated (see Jones, 2002) although a key issue has long been left aside, namely the actual processes at work inside the editorial offices of these magazines. Since it is here, at the junction of several parties and interests (the music industry, owners of the publishing house, managers, bands et cetera), where under specific conditions a few editors produce meanings of popular music for many readers, I conducted empirical research in German music magazines (Doehring, 2011). To the editors of these magazines, music possesses an objective

[29] I have published elsewhere on this in more detail (Doehring, 2012).

quality that only the expert listener (that is themselves) can assess so they feel duty bound to provide the service to readers of identifying the 'best' music available. Furthermore, they do not only reproduce, but also enforce notions of music as an artful object and of the musician as a creative genius. In their representations of both music and musicians you find a narration of a unique origin from which a style was 'born'. While this neglect of historical processes might be regrettable, it is nevertheless the dominating perspective on popular music, originating from journalistic conditions and requirements under late capitalism.

In *Groove*, a magazine devoted by its subtitle to electronic music and club culture, there are the standard feature articles about musicians[30] and reviews of album and 12" releases edited (and partly written) by the editorial staff which consists of four people. However, a selection of 125 DJs and record stores is responsible for the charts published in every issue; 54 of them are given room to present their top 10 list in print. Obviously, these charts have a function of legitimising *Groove* inside its readership as being closely connected to the musicians and to the club culture; additionally, by publishing these charts *Groove* necessarily has to stand out from competing magazines. From these charts, we can deduce that 'New For U' occupies a generic position created by – and to identify! – experts of EDM. Following from this, subsequent use[31] of 'New For U' may also transfer expert status to a wider group of people, for example DJs playing this record shortly after its release. However, the novelty of a track only lasts for some weeks, so the question remains why people still favoured the track at the end of 2012.

At this point, empirical research has to be integrated into the analysis to obtain qualitative statements about musical practice considering 'New For U'. Hence, I collected 67 statements about the track in reviews, articles, forums and blogs and interviewed six Frankfurt-based DJs about the track (all of them are also producers, two own a record store). After qualitative evaluation of this data, the following topics emerged: first, DJs evaluate the track due to their role on the field of EDM, due to its possible use and due to its status as a 'classic'. Second, the predominant tendency of evaluating the sound of this track is to connect it with a historically and locally limited place: the transfiguration of Detroit and its musical past of the last 20 years. Hence, the sound of 'New For U' is interpreted as a critique of 2012 EDM productions since it offers listeners and dancers a nostalgic impression of an era long gone by.

To begin with, most of the statements referred first to the beat and to the strings when they were talking about 'the music'. Observations similar to my own were made: the beat could last forever in its 'intoxicating energy' (Junorecords, 2013), the strings are 'gorgeous' (Poland, 2012), but 'simple' (Residentadviser.net, 2013b) or, put even more simply, 'Those violins, good lord those violins!'

---

30 Of course, the category 'musicians' covers DJs and producers, too.

31 To give an example, think of the timeline of 'New For U''s rapid rise in the residentadviser.com charts mentioned in note 2.

('Mark_Anthony', 2012). My analysis might help to understand why 'New For U' afforded such notions. But how and why did DJs integrate 'New For U' into their sets? You have to take into account that DJs are affiliated with record stores, get promotional records from labels, listen to their fellow DJ colleagues and observe the market by reading magazines (like *Groove*) or by visiting relevant sites on the Internet (like for example residentadivor.net). So they knew that Andrés had released his first EP on his new label and some of them at first played the track simply because it was new. Second, they anticipated a good response from their audience since they noticed that this track is useful for many occasions: 'That track is awesome cause you can play it everywhere and works good at every hour, from afternoon lounge, to warm up, to middle night to after, just fucking good vibes' ('djKul', 2013). Third, they played the track simply because they liked it. And they liked it, because 'New For U' to them sounds 'instantly eternal' ('Mark_Anthony', 2012) and is qualified as 'essential' ('matty_S', 2012) or a 'future classic' ('dmp', 2012). As DJs are also record collectors, 'New For U' was heard as 'absolute must have Deep house Traxx of 2012' ('paddiosf', 2012).[32] To them, 'New For U' exhibits in a way a timeless essence of dance music. In my opinion, this view is closely connected to the second point, the importance of an imagined Detroit and nostalgia for recent EDM.

Detroit is Andrés's place of birth as well as his place of living. This is not really noteworthy in itself, but in the context of meanings brought about by music journalism this suddenly becomes important information. Detroit is a place of desire for European musicians and DJs (Ingenhoff, 2013, p. 50) – as well as for journalists. And hence, the life and previous musical work of Andrés, the so-called 'Detroit house and hiphop don' (Red Bull Music Academy Radio, 2013) or 'Detroit underground hero' (Ryce, 2012), are recurring subjects in the collected statements, especially his affiliation with J Dilla's Slum Village in the 1990s and his releases on Moodymann's KDJ label. Both J Dilla and Moodymann (Kenny Dixon Jr.) are idealised inside the discourse for their musical skills and their reputation as outsiders to the music industry. Moodymann, in particular, is known for his advocacy of Afro-American (electronic dance) music and vinyl as format of choice.

To cut things short, 'New For U' emerges from musical practices inside a discourse that ascribes certain values to the music. Novelty (albeit ephemeral), originality *and* tradition as a way of continuing the imagined Afro-American dance legacy of Detroit are what made 'New For U' special, at first for many DJs, then dancers and listeners followed in their wake. Andrés, himself a part of this discourse, knows about its rules. So it could be argued that he picked 'New For U' as the first release of his debuting label La Vida because he sensed that it could

[32] At the same time, 'Mark_Anthony' (2012) describes the track as 'pure uncut house music funk soul' – so much on questions of genre categories. And he continues, 'Pure as the driven snow. 5 out of 5 stars. If you're a househead and you don't own this, your record collection is always going to be 1 title short of completion.'

afford such notions. So while the track is self-evidently dance music, its function is also to place a new economic player on the music market.

Although the ascribed 'Detroitness' of Andrés's music[33] or the influence of Dilla and Moodymann on his music cannot be found 'in' the music (for example in the way of identifying a musical quote), analysis is a tool to point out music's affordances to ascribe such meanings. We now can link, for example, the qualities of the beat described above with the statements as a part of people's musical practice. In this way, we might understand why this track matters to them when they praise its 'eroded house drums' (Residentadviser.com, 2013b) or its 'crunchy, tape-worn groove' (Ryce, 2012) and why they connect it to 'Larry Levan mixes' (Residentadviser.com, 2013b) and 'Salsoul [Records, a label where former musicians of PIR recorded, AD] in the late 70s' (Ryce, 2012). Without sensitivity to the track's context, analysis cannot understand 'New For U''s appeal inside a discourse that evaluates tradition in this way. Also, through its vinyl-only status and its crackling vinyl sound[34] 'New For U' allows interpretations of the track in which nostalgia drives the critique of contemporary EDM tracks: 'Hats off to Andrés for releasing this immaculate track amidst the sea of overproduced dance music we get fed every day' ('zevozone', 2013). 'Witnessing such a sensitive yet rough, sensual production reaching anthem status among younger crowds is indeed a blessing and gives hope for the future of house. This is the absolute anti-Swedish House Mafia[35] anthem' ('restless', 2012).

'From a good song', Moore (2012a, p. 286) writes about the goal of an analysis, 'we learn about ourselves'. Now, I know that although I am an avid reader of music magazines, I am not deep enough into the discourse to instantly understand these nostalgic ways of listening to 'New For U'.[36] And by integrating other people's musical practices into my interpretation we have also learned why people wanted to listen and dance to this sound in 2012. By its sounding structure, 'New For U' was able to establish a common set of musical values and a sense of community for the EDM discourse in the early twenty-first century, at a time when the historicisation of the genre is in full bloom.

---

[33] In an interview with the Red Bull Music Academy Radio (2013, at 6: 0) Andrés adds fuel to the fire, 'Is Detroit's musical influence in me? Definitely soul, a lot of soul, a lot of incorporating emotion into your music.'

[34] Especially during the core, where the theme is exposed for the first time, you can hear the crackling of the vinyl. If Andrés added this sound on purpose or if we hear it due to the required turntable equipment – in the end, it does not matter since the sound in itself affords notions of nostalgia.

[35] The Swedish House Mafia (2008–2013) was the project of three Swedish DJs on the EMI label owned by the Universal Music Group that had several top hits (for example, their single 'Don't You Worry Child' went to number 1 in the UK in 2012).

[36] I am not the only one with that lack of understanding. In the collected statements, you may follow a thread of debate on residentadivor.net in which 'New For U' was described as an 'undeniably retroactive record' ('marzie', 2012).

References

Adorno, T.W., 2003. Ideen zur Musiksoziologie. In: R. Tiedemann (ed.), *Musikalische Schriften I–III. Klangfiguren. Quasi una fantasia. Musikalische Schriften III.* (= Gesammelte Schriften 16). Frankfurt am Main: Suhrkamp, pp. 9–23.

Blaukopf, K., 2012. Goals of the Sociology of Music. In: T. Zembylas (ed.), *Kurt Blaukopf on Music Sociology: An Anthology*. Frankfurt am Main: Peter Lang, pp. 13–20.

Bourdieu, P., 1998. Über *das Fernsehen*. Frankfurt am Main: Suhrkamp.

Butler, M.J., 2006. *Unlocking the Groove: Rhythm, Meter, and Musical Design in Electronic Dance Music*. Bloomington and Indianapolis, IN: Indiana University Press.

Butler, M.J. (ed.), 2012a. *Electronica, Dance and Club Music*. Farnham, and Burlington, VT: Ashgate.

Butler, M.J., 2012b. Introduction. In: M.J. Butler (ed.), *Electronica, Dance and Club Music*. Farnham, and Burlington, VT: Ashgate, pp. xi–xxxi.

Cascone, K., 2000. The Aesthetics of Failure: 'Post-digital' Tendencies in Contemporary Computer Music. *Computer Music Journal*, 24, pp. 12–24 [also in Butler, 2012a].

Danielsen, A., 2006. *Presence and Pleasure: The Funk Grooves of James Brown and Parliament*. Middletown, CT: Wesleyan University Press.

Danielsen, A. (ed.), 2010a. *Musical Rhythm in the Digital Age of Reproduction*. Farnham, and Burlington, VT: Ashgate.

Danielsen, A., 2010b. Introduction: Rhythm in the Age of Digital Reproduction. In: A. Danielsen (ed.), *Musical Rhythm in the Digital Age of Reproduction*. Farnham, and Burlington, VT: Ashgate, pp. 1–16.

Discogs.com, 2013a. Andrés New For U, *discogs*, [online] Available at: http://www.discogs.com/Andrés-New-For-U/release/3395216 [Accessed 12 August 2013].

Discogs.com, 2013b. Andrés New For U – Reviews, *discogs*, [online] Available at: http://www.discogs.com/reviews?release=3395216 [Accessed 12 August 2013].

Doehring, A., 2011. *Musikkommunikatoren. Berufsrollen, Organisationsstrukturen und Handlungsspielräume im Popmusikjournalismus*. Bielefeld: Transcript.

Doehring, A., 2012. Probleme, Aufgaben und Ziele der Analyse populärer Musik. In: D. Helms and T. Phleps (eds), *Black Box Pop. Analysen populärer Musik*. Bielefeld: Transcript, pp. 23–42.

Eggebrecht, H.H., 1973. Funktionale Musik. *Archiv für Musikwissenschaft*, 30(1), pp. 1–25.

Ferreira, P.P., 2008. When Sound Meets Movement: Performance in Electronic Dance Music. *Leonardo Music Journal*, 18, pp. 17–20.

Fikentscher, K., 2000. *'You Better Work!' Underground Dance Music in New York City*. Middletown, CT: Wesleyan University Press.

Hawkins, S., 2003. Feel the Beat Come Down: House Music as Rhetoric. In: A.F. Moore (ed.), *Analyzing Popular Music*. Cambridge: Cambridge University Press, pp. 80–102.

Herrmann, T., 2013. Schocker: Universal Music entdeckt Kickstarter. Ist es nicht wundervoll, dieses Internet?, *de-bug*, [online] Available at: http://de-bug.de/musik/10729.html [Accessed 17 July 2013].

Hitzler, R. and Pfadenhauer, M. (eds), 2001. *Techno-Soziologie. Erkundungen einer Jugendkultur*. Opladen: Leske und Budrich.

Ingenhoff, S., 2013. Andrés. Hip-Hop-Head im Housepelz. *Groove*, 141, March/April, pp. 50–51.

Jones, S. (ed.), 2002. *Pop Music and the Press*. Philadelphia, PA: Temple University Press.

Junorecords, 2013. Andres – New For U, *junorecords*, [online] Available at: http://www.juno.co.uk/products/444180–01.htm [Accessed 10 August 2013].

Kellman, A., 2013. Andrés Artist Biography, *allmusic*, [online] Available at: http://www.allmusic.com/artist/andrés-mn0001856189/biography [Accessed 26 May 2013].

Kennett, C., 2003. Is Anybody Listening? In: A.F. Moore (ed.), *Analyzing Popular Music*. Cambridge: Cambridge University Press, pp. 196–217.

Klotz, S., 2002. 'A Pixel Is a Pixel. A Club Is a Club': Towards a Hermeneutics of a Berlin Style DJ & VJ Culture. *To The Quick*, 5, pp. 28–41 [also in Butler, 2012a].

Krims, A., 2000. *Rap Music and the Poetics of Identity*. Cambridge: Cambridge University Press.

Langlois, T., 1992. Can You Feel It? DJs and House Music Culture in the UK. *Popular Music*, 11(2), pp. 229–38.

McLeod, K., 2001. Genres, Subgenres, Sub-Subgenres and More: Musical and Social Difference Within Electronic Dance Music Communities. *Journal of Popular Music Studies*, 13, pp. 59–75.

Meyer, E., 2000. *Die Techno-Szene. Ein jugendkulturelles Phänomen aus sozialwissenschaftlicher Perspektive*. Opladen: Leske und Budrich.

Moore, A.F., 2012a. *Song Means: Analysing and Interpreting Recorded Popular Song*. Farnham: Ashgate.

Moore, A.F., 2012b. Series Preface. In: M.J. Butler (ed.), *Electronica, Dance and Club Music*. Farnham: Ashgate, pp. ix–x.

Poland, T., 2012. Andrés – New For U Review, *Junodownload*, [online] Available at: http://www.junodownload.com/plus/2012/02/09/andres-new-for-u-review/ [Accessed 10 August 2013].

Poschardt, U., 1997. *DJ-Culture. Diskjockeys und Popkultur*. Reinbek b. Hamburg: Rowohlt [revised and updated reprint].

Rapp, T., 2009. *Lost and Sound: Berlin, Techno und der Easyjetset*. Frankfurt am Main: Suhrkamp.

Residentadvisor.net, 2013a. Andrés – New For U, *residentadvisor*, [online] Available at: http://www.residentadvisor.net/track.aspx?408829 [Accessed 10 August 2013].

Residentadvisor.net, 2013b. RA Poll: Top 50 Tracks of 2012, *residentadvisor*, [online] Available at: http://www.residentadvisor.net/feature.aspx?1705 [Accessed 10 August 2013].

Reynolds, S., 1998. *Energy Flash: A Journey through Rave Music and Dance Culture*. London: Picador.

Rösing, H. and Phleps, T. (eds), 1999. *Erkenntniszuwachs durch Analyse. Populäre Musik auf dem Prüfstand*. Karben: Coda.

Ryce, A., 2012. Andres – New For U, *residentadvisor*, [online] Available at: http://www.residentadvisor.net/review-view.aspx?id=10893 [Accessed 10 August 2013].

Shapiro, P., 2005. *Turn the Beat Around: The Secret History of Disco*. London: Faber and Faber.

Steingo, G., 2008. Producing Kwaito: 'Nkosi Sikelel' iAfrika' after Apartheid. *World of Music*, 50, pp. 103–20 [also in Butler, 2012a].

Straw, W., 1997. Sizing up Record Collections: Gender and Conoisseurship in Rock Music Culture. In: S. Whiteley (ed.), *Sexing the Groove: Popular Music and Gender*. London: Routledge, pp. 3–16.

Tagg, P., 1987. Musicology and the Semiotics of Popular Music. *Semiotica*, 66(1), pp. 279–98.

Tagg, P., 1994. From Refrain to Rave: The Decline of Figure and the Rise of Ground. *Popular Music*, 13, pp. 209–22 [also in Butler, 2012a].

Thornton, S., 1996. *Club Cultures: Music, Media, and Subcultural Capital*. Hanover, NH: Wesleyan University Press.

Veal, M.E., 2007. *Dub: Soundscapes and Shattered Songs in Jamaican Reggae*. Middletown, CT: Wesleyan University Press.

Volkwein, B., 2003. *What's Techno? Geschichte, Diskurse und musikalische Gestalt elektronischer Unterhaltungsmusik*. Osnabrück: Epos.

Walser, R., 2003. Popular Music Analysis: Ten Apothegms and Four Instances. In: A.F. Moore (ed.), *Analyzing Popular Music*. Cambridge: Cambridge University Press, pp. 16–38.

Whosampled.com, 2013. Andrés New For U, *whosampled*, [online] Available at: http://www.whosampled.com/sample/155627/Andrés-New-for-U-Dexter-Wansel-Time-Is-the-Teacher/ [Accessed 14 July 2013].

Wicke, P., 1997. 'Let the sun shine in your heart'. Was die Musikwissenschaft mit der Love Parade zu tun hat oder Von der diskursiven Konstruktion des Musikalischen. *Die Musikforschung*, 50(4), pp. 421–33.

Wicke, P., 2004. Soundtracks. Popmusik und Pop-Diskurs. In: W. Grasskamp, M. Krützen and S. Schmitt, eds. *Was ist Pop? Zehn Versuche*. Frankfurt am Main: Fischer, pp. 115–39.

Zeiner-Henriksen, H.T., 2010. Moved by the Groove: Bass Drum Sounds and Body Movements in Electronic Dance Music. In: A. Danielsen (ed.), *Musical Rhythm in the Age of Digital Reproduction*. Farnham: Ashgate, pp. 121–39.

'djKul', 2013. Andrés New For U – Reviews, *discogs*, [online] Available at: http://www.discogs.com/reviews?release=3395216 [Accessed 12 August 2013].
'dmp', 2012. Andrés New For U – Reviews, *discogs*, [online] Available at: http://www.discogs.com/reviews?release=3395216 [Accessed 12 August 2013].
'Mark_Anthony', 2012. Andrés New For U – Reviews, *discogs*, [online] Available at: http://www.discogs.com/reviews?release=3395216 [Accessed 12 August 2013].
'marzie', 2012. RA Forum: Andres – New 4 U, *residentadvisor*, [online] Available at: http://www.residentadvisor.net/forum-read.aspx?id=191080 [Accessed 12 August 2013].
'matty_S', 2012. Andrés New For U – Reviews, *discogs*, [online] Available at: http://www.discogs.com/reviews?release=3395216 [Accessed 12 August 2013].
'paddiosf', 2012. Andrés New For U – Reviews, *discogs*, [online] Available at: http://www.discogs.com/reviews?release=3395216 [Accessed 12 August 2013].
'restless', 2012. Andrés New For U – Reviews, *discogs*, [online] Available at: http://www.discogs.com/reviews?release=3395216 [Accessed 12 August 2013].
'zevozone', 2013. Shoutbox – Andrés New For U, *last.fm*, [online] Available at: http://www.lastfm.de/music/Andrés/_/New+For+U [Accessed 12 August 2013].

Discography

Andrés, 2012. *New For U*. La Vida, 001.
Rick Ro$$ feat. Kanye West, T-Pain and Lil' Wayne, 2009. 'Maybach Music 2'. *Deeper Than Rap*. Island Def Jam Music Group, B0012772–01.
Swedish House Mafia feat. John Martin, 2012. 'Don't You Worry Child'. EMI, 8390012029.
Wansel, Dexter, 1978. 'Time Is The Teacher'. *Voyager*. Philadelphia International Records, JZ-34985.

Chapter 8
So Just What Kind of Life Is This? Amy Macdonald's 'This Is The Life'

Allan F. Moore

Situating This Life

I am not really very much interested in 'keeping up' with the 'latest thing' in music. Through the marvels of contemporary technology we now have ready access to centuries' worth of music from large parts of the globe. The assumption that something written, recorded, performed, produced, last week will inevitably be better, more interesting, more relevant (what does that really mean?) to/for me than something which appeared earlier is facile, at best, a remnant of modernism's unthinking attraction to progress at all costs, and which sees ever new versions of expensive pieces of 'kit'[1] which do the same thing as the previous version, although in a flashier, presumably more seductive way, persuading me to part with money for no reason other than that contemporary society is only kept afloat by the circulation of money. Consumption as moral imperative!

My encounter with what was, at the time, a new track, was thus entirely coincidental. What matters, of course, is how one responds to such a coincidence. In the autumn of 2010, if you were watching British commercial television, you would be highly likely to have seen advertisements for the new (of course, for why advertise something that is not new?) Fiat 500 TwinAir.[2] It's (or by now, maybe it was) a car. That much is clear, although what the '500' refers to I have no idea, nor its link to two closely related kinds of gas. I guess the advert was a failure, then.[3] As with so many lifestyle ads, its most appealing feature was the music soundtrack, a hackneyed chord sequence played by a very ordinary strummed guitar under an intriguing slide guitar upward bent note, giving way to a young guy singing. His words, "this is the life"[4] implied that driving this pretty little car in a carefree manner was 'where it's at', but what he immediately went on to sing

---

[1] That is some item of (normally) hardware which does something I/we don't need.

[2] At the time of writing, the advert can be seen at http://www.youtube.com/watch?v=uuOW4oalG70 [Accessed 2 May 2013].

[3] Nor was I able to remember, until beginning research for this chapter, even what make of car was being advertised.

[4] Throughout this chapter, I use double quotes where I am quoting lyrics, and single quotes for all other purposes.

completely changed the tone, puncturing the illusion. What? Didn't the advert's makers listen to the music, or even the lyrics, they were using? Of course not; it's only the title that such people ever hear, to my mind. I guess the advert was a real failure, then (unless viewers don't listen beyond the title either, which presumably must at least be possible). I do, though, and after stumbling across the advert three or four times I determined to listen to the entire song, for it had got under my skin.

Unless you too revel in being out of touch, you'll have had this experience, of some half-heard piece of music that you want to track down. If only we had search software that worked by sound rather than words (another piece of useless kit, I suppose). My only technique in such circumstances is to remember a line of lyric, type it into Google and see what happens, tracking down via Spotify or iTunes whatever Google finds for me. In this case, it led me to the title track from Amy Macdonald's 2007 album *This Is The Life*. But that's not right! I duly went and bought the album (I know; I'm old-fashioned like that) and listened to it, repeatedly. But where's the guy gone? Ah, the advert makers must have used a cover. Pretty good cover, though, for that guitar attack is spot-on. It was not until I accidentally saw the advert again, after having got to know the song, that I could persuade myself I had been mistaken. I had been listening to the voice of Amy Macdonald all along. For reasons I still cannot begin to fathom, perhaps I found this somewhat androgynous (to my ears), slightly unusual voice strangely attractive, slightly dangerous. A point to which I'll return. More importantly, though, what had happened to that shift from the opening guitar swish straight into the singing of "this is the life"? In the advert, these two are ineradicably linked, but in the song I had managed to track down …?[5]

Measuring This Life

The song is ordinary, conventional, unexceptional (at least to me), in so many respects, which can be discussed by focusing in turn on its form and its textures. After one 'loosening up' bar, we hear a four-chord sequence once, as the four-bar introduction, then twice, as the first verse, and then once, as the chorus. In defining the bar in this way, I'm hearing a style reference back to rockabilly, with the snare on every half-beat, contributing to the track's faux jauntiness. Thus I'm hearing a speed of 96bpm. The chorus is repeated with a new tag, leading to a four-bar transition to the second verse. The second verse and chorus follow the same pattern, while the second transition is doubled in length. We then hear two more choruses, a single transition and we're done. If I could be bothered (for this is not really a song I'm attracted to), I could probably find hundreds of songs with

[5] For the advert, we hear the introductory segment, 0:02–0:11, which is expertly spliced into the beginning of the chorus, from 0:32. The difference in timings, here, from those given in Table 8.1 are a result of the song's incessant upbeats, which I shall discuss below.

the same outline, but the feeling of familiarity is strong enough to be not worth the effort. Table 8.1 summarises its form and textures.

Table 8.1 Formal/textural scheme of Amy Macdonald's 'This Is The life'

Timing	Label	Section	Chords	Dominant textural features
0:00	P-I	pre-intro	one bar (notionally v)	soft guitar chics
0:02	I	introduction	aeolian: i – VI – III – v (one per bar)	prominent bass & standard kit, strummed guitar & hidden piano as harmonic filler, resonant slide guitar
0:12	V1	verse 1	x2	voice replaces slide guitar, Macdonald self-harmonising last line
0:33	C1	chorus 1	x2	second half has Macdonald self-harmonising
0:53	T1	transition 1	x1	acoustic guitar melody 'x' (imitating voice in V1) replaces voice, add low register slow fiddle
1:03	V2	verse 2	x2	as V1, add self-harmonising and fiddle (first half)
1:23	C2	chorus 2	x2	as C1, electric guitar has crept subtly into texture
1:43	T2	transition 2	x2	as before, piano more prominent for second half
2:04	C3–4	chorus 3–4	x4	first half of C3 drops most of texture, second half recovers most, first half of C4 adds remainder, second half adds 'x'; rit. at end
2:46	T3	transition 3	x1	as T1 but has lost 'x'
2:57	E	final ringing chord	i	

As for its texture, all the elements we might need are there: melody, rhythm and bass conventionally thickened with guitars, piano, and a subtle fiddle. These instruments alternate in that the acoustic guitar stands in for the voice in the transitions, while the textural drop away and re-build in choruses 3–4 is almost clichéd. And, even though the impression is one of oft-repeated formula, the details of soundbox use hide some subtleties. Most important, to pre-empt a later discussion, is the fragmentary electric guitar line of the introduction which I identified as a 'swish' above and, presumably because it precedes the memorable first line, I'll identify as the 'whistling' guitar. This is actually a combination of two separate guitar parts, a pedal steel on the left-hand side of the stereo space which gives way to an electric guitar on the right, both meeting (on the right) on the last note, but switches to the right, as if tracing the path of the wind relative to a perceiver. In the second verse, this guitar returns, again on the left, playing another fragmentary line which gives way to the piano, again on the left, with a downward scale consisting of repeated notes. In the subsequent chorus, a guitar switch to the right recapitulates the earlier movement. In the third chorus, this guitar is again present, while the acoustic guitar takes on the piano's counter-melody to the voice. Other than these details, the main thing to note seems to be the intense presence of the whole production – everything is 'in your face', confrontational. Even the kit does not seem to be situated behind the other sound sources. The acoustic guitar tends to the left (where it seems to be doubled by shakers), the piano to the right and the whistling guitar at mid width wherever it appears – everything else comes at the listener pretty centrally, individuated only by timbre. It is, perhaps, only Macdonald's own backing voices which appear at a little distance.

Why should I feel impelled to hear that little guitar line as a "whistling" guitar? I should take some time over this, since it becomes central to my understanding of the track. I should also note that it took me many months to realise that this was what that line 'meant' for me, and then many more months before I was able to work out why, in what follows. And, before I start, I should note that this little line hit me between the eyes the first time I heard the track, for on the advert (see above), the line leads into the chorus, and thus I had previously heard the guitar line as symbolising the presumably carefree attitude of the title.

There are two types of reason to align the guitar line with the song's "whistling", one ecological and one semiotic, and it is the combination of the two which I find so convincing. First, note that it moves, in four dimensions. It moves left to right in the soundbox. It moves upward by step, at two stages. It moves metaphorically in terms of increasing durations (short to long). And it moves closer to me, as the pedal steel fades in on that last note, giving a momentary sense of increasing volume.[6] The first of these motions specifies something moving across me. The second specifies some objective movement, which I merely observe. The third specifies movement away from me[7] but the fourth specifies a momentary shift in the opposite direction. This combination appears to capture the sense of the movement of wind in a narrow, funnelled, space, the "cold, dark streets". But the sound does not in itself specify wind (unless you hear something in the guitar's actual timbre, and I cannot be convinced that I do). Example 8.1 transcribes that little combined guitar line, as it leads into the first line of the verse. Note that the motif to which the words "whistles down" (fifth bar of the excerpt) are sung is exactly that of that guitar line (third to fourth bars), but transposed such that, instead of moving across harmonies, it is now situated firmly within the tonic chord, a gesture of clear affirmation, as if to say 'that is how to hear that guitar

---

6 My thanks to Ralf von Appen for pointing this one out.

7 This is a difficult equation, but note that sounds in the environment with length tend to be more reverberant than short sounds and, hence, are likely to be further away from the listener, all other things being equal.

line'. What is happening here is an instance of what cognitive theorists would call conceptual blending: two input mental spaces (the guitar line and the vocal melody) are projected into a blended mental space which 'develops emergent structure that is not in the inputs' (Fauconnier and Turner, 2002, p. 42), namely the identity of the guitar line and the quality of whistling down dark streets.

Example 8.1 Opening guitar and vocal motifs of Amy Macdonald's 'This Is The Life'

It seems to me that time-bound art forms have two fundamental ways of creating interest in perceivers: the first concerns what they do *with* time, the second concerns what they do *within* time.[8] In the first, the work's existence in, and relationship with, time is problematised (as in the plays of Beckett, the novels of Eco or Calvino, the music of Birtwistle, Stockhausen or King Crimson). In the second, it is taken for granted and manipulated from the inside. This is one reason why what we might call formulaic music can be so exhilarating. The implied contract with the listener drills some long way down into the song's substance, not remaining at the level of discursive repetition, but at the level of the museme.[9] Listeners to this song know roughly what to expect, both in terms of the order in which events happen (the form) and the shaping of those events (the texture) before they hear more than a few bars, and they get what it is they've been led to expect, but they get something more, too. And it is that 'more' that gradually began to interest me.

Living this Life

Let's begin at the beginning. That bar of chics is a call to attention, an announcement that the song is about to start, but not necessarily that it has already done so. The position of Macdonald's hand deadening the strings just about allows a G♯ to be identified at the top of the texture, suggesting to my ears that notional 'v' (the song is performed in C♯ aeolian), but I think this has little significance. The rhythm of the

[8] I draw this distinction from Andrew Chester's between *extensional* and *intensional* musics, but I suspect it has wider applicability (see Chester, 2007).

[9] Philip Tagg's term, to identify the smallest sonic unit, in any given context, capable of carrying meaning (see, for instance, Tagg, 2004).

chics suggests busyness, a busyness which the track will occupy but, in its clear syncopation, probably without being fussy. The chord sequence which ensues is familiar without being over-familiar. Variants appear in well-known songs, such as Alice Cooper's 'Poison' (which alters the last in the sequence, thus aeolian i – VI – III – VII) and the Beatles' 'She Loves You' (whose verse alters the mode, thus: ionian I – vi – iii – V). The avoidance of step-wise motion between successive basses is key to this sequence, and the most notable intertextual reference here is to Macdonald's own work: 'Poison Prince', from the same album, for example, is based on aeolian i – III – VI – V. This soundworld of familiarity brings a measure of comfort, of security, which is so appropriate to the track's narrative.

Both the very opening texture and the bass movement call to mind other recent indie pop–most clearly for me the Coral, and the track 'Dreaming Of You' from their debut album *The Coral* (both at the same tempo, incidentally). Like Alice Cooper's 'Poison', 'Dreaming of You' is based on aeolian i – VI – III – VII, but does not use it in the simple loop that Macdonald employs. The connotations of conviviality carried by 'Dreaming Of You' carry over to 'This Is The Life', at least in potential, but that guitar bend and talk of the "wind [which] whistles down" suggest an altogether bleaker scenario[10] which is, perhaps, explored by Macdonald's use of verbal space.[11] The process appears to be one of growing congestion such that, in retrospect, the opening of the verse appears sparse. I think this sparsity is enhanced by the idea of wind whistling, for it can do so only in bounded but uninhibited spaces. I shall return to the details of this use of verbal space in the subsequent section.

In terms of both melody and harmony, the essential motions are oppositional ones – every turn is matched by its counterweight. Melodically, the essential motion of the verse is locally upwards, but globally downwards. As a result the melody fails to achieve any real motion: the first two lines each move from $\hat{1}$ to $\hat{3}$, while the second two lines move from a lower $\hat{7}$ up to $\hat{2}$. Lines 5 and 6 eventually rise from $\hat{1}$ to $\hat{3}$, and then lines 7 and 8 simply fall from here to $\hat{2}$. This sort of motion might be held to typify attempts at action (those little local rises) which fail to persist. The chorus uses the same elements, but in a different permutation. Each half of the chorus is essentially the same, so we only have four lines to concern us. The first two each reverse the verse's initial motion, moving from $\hat{3}$ down to $\hat{1}$, but at twice the speed (four such moves across two lines). Line 3 drops further, to that lower $\hat{7}$, before rising to $\hat{3}$ and then sinking (exhaustedly?) back to $\hat{2}$. It seems to me the most striking element here is that leap of a fourth, from $\hat{7}$ to $\hat{3}$, which can only happen at this transposition level within the chord, chord III. With this exception the melodic movement is minimal throughout, although

[10] Other similarities between the two tracks are dominated by the melodic motion, particularly a shift from $\hat{3}$ to $\hat{1}$ to $\hat{3}$ over the first two chords of the sequence.

[11] Dai Griffiths's term, to identify the degree of compression of lyric syllables within the course of the singer's delivery (see Griffiths, 2003).

it is conceivable that there may be some relationship between the local upward/downward motion and the use of verbal space.

Underpinning this motion, through both verse and chorus, we have been hearing that unending harmonic pattern, i – VI – III – v. There is more than one way of parsing this simple sequence. The obvious one is to take it as it is presented to us, that is i – VI answered by III – v. However, I think its effect is better understood by construing it as two moves which contradict each other, thus: VI – III against v – i. Seen this way, the root motion reverses – a rising fifth answered by a falling fifth – while the harmonic colour does likewise – major set against minor. The effect is, again, one of the possibility of rising from the current situation (whatever that may be), but a possibility which is at every turn thwarted. Like all such loops, it activates the CONTAINMENT schema (see Moore, 2012, p. 240). In this track, that seems best understood as the constant reiteration of that thwarted possibility.

There is one more pair of oppositions I want to raise before discussing the lyrics and their delivery in greater detail, that between the two key statements of the chorus. Out of context, "this is the life" would appear to be a positive statement (although this is problematised by being set to a minor chord). However, "where you gonna go?" is rather a negative question. The presentation of this latter is particularly effective. Throughout the song, lines of lyric are characterised by carefully chosen lengths of upbeat. In the first half of the opening verse, we start with short upbeats which, for the fourth line, become no upbeat at all. In the second half of the verse, the lengths of upbeat gradually increase such that, by the beginning of the chorus, everything is upbeat, with the downbeat forming the last syllable of the line. This gradual intensification of emphasis on the upbeat contributes strongly to the emotional sense particularly of the chorus. By the time we hear the first "where you gonna go?", the upbeat has become so heavy that there is no downbeat, "go" falling on the fourth beat of the bar. This means that the next "where" actually does start on the downbeat, entirely unexpectedly, shifting a great deal of meaning on to that word, and on to the ensuing phrase. The lyrics at this point describe a somewhat unpleasant shift from drunken pleasure to its after-effects, giving way after the chorus to yet another opposition, of the rather choppy guitar and kit against the low, held violin notes.

Narrating This Life

The lyrics to the song can be readily found on the Internet – indeed, on Amy Macdonald's own site.[12] I wouldn't always recommend such a source – some singers are notorious for making changes to the lyrics they sing after initial recording or, in the days when lyrics appeared frequently on record sleeves, after

[12] See http://www.amymacdonald.co.uk/gb/lyrics/this_is_the_life/ [Accessed 15 October 2013].

the sleeves were printed. In this case, though, I think I'm hearing what the site claims Macdonald to be singing.

The key to the first verse lies in the interaction between the lyrics as they stand and how they are delivered. I have already alluded to the notion of verbal space – time now to put flesh on those bare bones. The first four lines of the first verse have the following syllable lengths: 6/6/8/5. If we remove the upbeats, then the lengths of line starting from the downbeat are 4/5/6/5 – the process is one of growth, interrupted by the lack of an upbeat to the fourth line. The process picks up again in the second half of the verse – syllables 11/11/11/2. Removing the upbeats, we have 9/9/9/1. The process of growth has reached a plateau which, again, is interrupted by the last line. The amount of empty verbal space seems gradually to be diminishing (notice how the word "chase", quite a mouthful with the opening affricate and closing sibilant, almost gets swallowed), until it broadens out at the end of the verse, as we regather our energies to be launched into the chorus.

In terms of lyrics, this delivery begins with emptiness ("wind whistles", "cold dark street"), moving towards signs of inhabitation. We get anonymous "people", who then become 'boys' and 'girls', and probably quite particular ones, since a characteristic ("curls") is described. Then a specific group, presumably of these (a "shocked too many") is isolated – a gradual process of individuation which reaches its culmination only in the chorus. The process of increasing congestion (of the delivery of the lyrics) is metaphorised in the final line, as the songs to which the chasers and chased are dancing are described as getting progressively "louder" (for louder, read denser, that is more congested).

So, the verse is not simply a description of some observation or encounter, but acts processually to propel us into the extraordinary chorus. I begin in the same way, looking at syllable lengths. The chorus' first four lines appear with the syllable count 12/15/15/2 – a marked increase on the 11/11/11/2 of the last half of the verse. Removing upbeats, though, we are left with 7/9/5/1. You can see the massive increase in the number of syllables which appear in an upbeat position, which leads us inexorably to the next downbeat (see Table 8.2).

Table 8.2 Syllable count in the first verse and chorus of Amy Macdonald's 'This Is The Life'

Timing	Section	Syllables per line	Syllables in upbeat to line
0:12	verse 1, part 1	6/6/8/5	2/1/2/0
0:22	verse 1, part 2	11/11/11/2	2/2/2/1
0:33	chorus, part 1	12/15/15/2	5/6/10/1
1:03	verse 2, part 1	13/10/10/2	2/2/1/1
1:13	verse 2, part 2	10/12/11/2	2/2/1/1

The absence of gaps in this delivery of the chorus makes the whole thing rather breathless, rather urgent. The apex of the process is on the word "feels" and, as a result of this congestion, note how the preceding word ("head") is barely audible. Certainly the final 'd' is not sounded, in the rush to reach the 'f'. This seems to be an effective sonic metaphor[13] for the pounding of a hangover headache which, while one's head may feel over-large, is still trying to escape the boundary of the skull. The process of narrowing down, from people to boys and girls to a single group reaches its culmination in the individual "you" addressed in the chorus, with a responsibility which cannot be avoided. The parallelism between this focusing and the syllable length is remarkable. In some musics, it would be the harmonic details which carry the drama. Here, the harmonies continue unabated, as we have seen, acting simply as the backdrop against which the dramatic process is enacted by the lyrics' addressees and manner of delivery. A final point to make, here, before addressing the lyrical narrative: these fast-delivered syllables in the chorus are sung to many repeated notes, as we have seen – the melody line moves minimally. The effect of these lines, as sung, is, thus, that of moving very fast to get nowhere.

So, what is the song about? It seems to be describing a situation in which, in a rather bleak setting, people both anonymous and particular are having a great time dancing, singing and (by implication) drinking. This description does not finish with the verse, but hangs over into the first line of the chorus. The remainder of the chorus then picks up with the ensuing hangover and a clear return to a bleakness of vagrancy. The security offered by having fun is clearly positioned as momentary, as illusory.

The second verse can be taken in at least two distinct ways. The first is to fill in a gap in this narrative, between boys chasing girls and the following morning. This approach does seem to me rather weak, however. A stronger approach would take this detailed description of a night out which fails to materialise as a subsequent occasion, another in which the bleak perspective comes to dominate. It is notable that this second, more obviously narrative, verse, does not have the syllabic growth of the first. It maintains the same level as the chorus, which is particularly appropriate since its last line is borrowed from the chorus.

Watching This Life

Of course, 'This Is The Life' has its accompanying video. I have my own difficulties understanding the desire to accompany tracks with videos. I don't think we understand why this phenomenon need exist. I suspect an underlying reason is often political, situated in a desire not necessarily on the part of songwriters themselves, but of other industry professionals with an investment in their work

[13] What Phil Tagg has described as an 'anaphone', some museme or collection of musemes which is congruent to some experience of the extra-musical world.

to control the meaning of the track. The sort of discussion I have outlined above indicates that such attempted control is specious, but that does not remove the suspicion of the presence of the desire to do so. It is often remarked that we are a visual rather than an aural culture, and so there is a market for people to have their understanding visually packaged for them, rather than have to work it out for themselves from purely aural signals. My prejudice leads me to be unable to recall a really good song which hasn't been ruined by its video,[14] but at least in part this is because I am not a particularly visual person. In terms of theory, a video always compels a viewer into a second-order interpretation of a recording, in other words into an interpretation of a prior interpretation. We are not here in the realm of the *gesamtkunstwerk*, where a single individual presents a unified vision, mediated through different perceptual domains.[15] On the contrary, we are in a world where the owner of the song's copyright licenses a visual interpretation in order, as I suggest, to attempt to control the way the song is read. It was from this perspective that I began to write about the track's official video. And, although I found some of my preconceptions justified, in that some of the track's ambiguities were ambiguities no longer, there are details of the video sufficiently thought-provoking to require me to see some value in negotiating between a first- and a second-order interpretation.

Before moving into the video itself, I need to make a distinction between three different Amy Macdonalds, all of whom will play a part in my discussion. There is Macdonald the singer and writer of the song, Macdonald the *performer*, who plays no obvious part in the video (but who could, if a viewer so desired, be 'written in', as it were, since she inhabits the video on three levels[16] as an actor). There is Macdonald the *persona*, adopted by Macdonald the *performer* for the purposes of this song: I shall identify Macdonald's persona as **Amy**. Then, there is Macdonald the *protagonist*, who appears inside the song's narrative: I shall identify the protagonist who, in the video, is played by Macdonald, as *Amy*.

The video can be found here.[17] It broadly makes use of three locations: (a) Macdonald alone situated in one of those "cold dark streets"; (b) Macdonald and a group of mates situated in a spacious living-room; (c) successions of stills of these mates, individually and together, shot sometimes in the living-room, but mostly in a series of locations representing a night out (leaving a block of flats, messing about in the street, going to a chippy, in a pub). Each of these three locations occupies a different time-sense. Location (c) is seen in *Amy*'s immediate past (presumably 'last night'), prior to *Amy*'s immediate present, which is when location (b) is seen, while location (a) is the narrator's eternal present, occupied by **Amy**, external to the action being recounted. In this interpretation, both verses

[14] And I certainly include 'Thriller' and 'Bohemian Rhapsody' here.

[15] The locus classicus, of course, is the music dramas of Richard Wagner.

[16] The levels of performer, persona and protagonist.

[17] See http://www.universal-music.de/amy-macdonald/videos/detail/video:89874/this-is-the-life [Accessed 31 May 2013].

occupy the same timespan, in contrast to the narrative line I suggested above (of two separate events).

Whereas the lyrics imply that the 'cold dark streets' serve simply to set the bleak tone, in the video they underpin the whole narrative – everything takes place there, which means it is crucial to identify them as British urban (I cannot identify any more particular location). On the same album, the song 'Let's Start A Band' is based on a very similar chord sequence (pairs of major and minor triads, separated by intervals of a third), opening with strummed guitar but, in this latter track, a trumpet implies perhaps somewhere near the Mexican border. I have heard the streets on 'This Is The Life' in a similar location, absent of anything more particular, but that ambiguity is destroyed by the video interpretation. The streets of the video are clearly inhabited (the car headlamps) and in an urban British location, and yet **Amy**'s audience is only the camera.

The narrative pointed to by the video seems to take the form of a night out, embarked on during the first part of verse 1, as a succession of stills follows the smiling group, which includes *Amy*. In the second verse, some of the lads are shown messing about on the street, the group are seen in a chippy and eating at tables outside, and then in the subsequent choruses are also seen in the pub. *Amy* appears to be drinking orange juice, which might account for her being able to appear at the beginning of the video as the non-hungover **Amy**, external to the action. Then, during the opening of the song, *Amy* is shown being the first to wake in the living-room, and clearly wondering, initially, where she is. That feeling of momentary disorientation is so familiar and so well captured here, and could be explained if her previous night's tipple had actually been vodka and orange.[18] The first chorus returns here – still everyone else is asleep. Under the line "where you gonna go?", it is as if nobody really cares. In the break after the first chorus, *Amy* is shown looking at photos of the 'previous' night, recollecting the scenes with a measure of pleasure.

In four distinct ways (and you may find others), the video closes out some possibilities offered by the track. First, the video fixes the location of the track, in contradiction to the lyrics (there appears to be no wind ruffling **Amy**'s hair, for instance). Immediately, if aware of the contradiction, one is forced to consider which to believe – what one sees, or what one hears (in real life, of course, the second is usually far more reliable). Second, it excises some of the pleasures of the track's narrative (no chasing, no dancing and no obvious singing) – again, a contradiction that requires some resolution. Third, it compresses the narrative into one night and the following morning, rather than the two separate occasions I have suggested might be implied in the lyric. Fourth, the bleak tone taken by **Amy** bleeds into the facial expressions of *Amy*. This last seems to me particularly notable. Whereas the track carries no implication that Macdonald is her own protagonist (she is surely commenting with some disdain not on a single event, but on a class of events which, in essence, are common occurrences to so many in

[18] My thanks to André Doehring for this suggestion.

contemporary society), the video uses this invention to personalise, to make more immediate to the audience, the change from pleasure to subsequent distaste. But does this new intervention cause us to doubt the reliability of **Amy**? I submit that this potential is now opened up by the first order interpretation that is the video. I suspect that there are other ways that the video can be seen to close down the possibilities offered by the track, but these are sufficient for my purposes here. In the first three of these, the experience of the track seems to me diminished – a subsequent secondary interpretation of the track becomes less rich as a result. In the fourth, though, a new way of hearing the track results such that a secondary interpretation is potentially enriching.

Now let me return to the presence of the whistling guitar. As I suggested by my naming of it, it seems emblematic of the wind which opens the first verse but is then forgotten. I have criticised the video because it insists on maintaining the cold streets as an ever-present feature – indeed, it is the location from which **Amy** addresses her audience throughout. However, in reading it this way I had not recognised the return of that whistling guitar in subsequent sections of the track. Once I had (eventually, after years of familiarity, perhaps assumed over-familiarity, with the track) noticed this reappearance, it made sense at least of this aspect of the video's reading of the track. This, of course, opens up some other possibilities. It is possible that my reading of the video, while it looks sophisticated, is actually rather stupid and naive (as I say, I am not a visual person) – it now becomes at least possible to me that the other ways in which I claim the video closes out possibilities of the track may result only from an inept reading. I don't actually believe that, of course, but it would be arrogant in the extreme not to recognise the possibility. This, of course, is where the negotiation of meaning is so important – would that I were working as one of a team of five and could benefit from others' insights[19] here rather than labouring over a lonely laptop on an empty train to somewhere whose location I'll remember in a moment. I hope.

Whose Life?

Such discussion could continue at great length, but I think I have presented sufficient material to enable the outlines of an understanding of this track to be seen. The key question, too often ignored, recognises as I have here the subjectivity of the enquirer. While the details I have discussed may be something that any other listener can come up with, they are nonetheless subjective details and, where they are shared, they are intersubjective, not objective – they do not exist in the absence of a perceiver. So, that key question – where am I in all this? How does this track position me? Am I an observer, an addressee, a participant? What does it feel like

[19] Although I am grateful for the loan of the ears of my co-editors, Ralf and André, at a couple of points.

to take on these roles? 'This' may be 'the life' – is it mine?; can it be mine?; should it be mine?

I have paid great attention above to diminishing verbal space, across the first verse and chorus, as a process which links these two sections together and, as with any observable process, it carries some sense of inevitability. But, this process hides an important dislocation between the first verse and chorus. In the first verse, I am positioned as an observer, as is **Amy**, but there the similarity ends. I am eavesdropping on a narrative she relays either to somebody else, or gives as voiced musings. In the chorus, however, my positioning is open to change. It is possible for me still to be eavesdropping on **Amy**, but here she is less relaying a narrative than addressing a particular individual, "you". That "you" is someone specific, and it may be me.

Those opening guitar chics are extraordinarily close, intimate. Earlier I used the word 'confrontational' to describe the presence of the entire soundscape – this guitar certainly meets me face-to-face, implying that I am not simply a distant bystander. Although I don't want to go into the theory behind my use of the term, I feel I am here *interpellated* by the track. I am drawn in, enfolded by it, seductively immersed in it. I am not permitted the choice of simply brushing it off. The texture then broadens out, amplifying my focus. By the time we come to the chorus, I am being addressed. The following break, between chorus and verse, is focused on that little acoustic guitar line. This is not an occasion for ostentatious display. The line is simple, repetitive, but perhaps slightly on edge as a result of those repeating notes at the beginning of the phrase. It is very everyday, in other words. Homely, perhaps. The second verse only intensifies this feeling. The piano, busy somewhere in the background, suggests there is something else 'going on', something not explicitly part of the narrative but which nonetheless colours it. The lyrics hint at this – the 'I' being addressed is clearly expected to know who "Robert Ragger" is, although 'I' as listener am none the wiser. I've always heard his crew as "motley", but the official lyrics describe it as "1 leg", which makes no sense to me, adding to the obfuscation.

In this second verse, my own position is again unclear, as is **Amy**'s, in that here I am potentially positioned as one of the gang. When she addresses me, and I think only me, in the chorus, she is somewhat involved in the narrative, although as somebody offering advice (which is unlikely to be taken!). Otherwise, she is offering comments on a common situation (but a specific instance of such a situation), and yet with clear insider knowledge (how else could she know it was "Robert Ragger" we were talking about, or "Jimmy"'s front door we were heading for?). This knowledge gives her delivery a certain power, which seems to magnify that depth her voice has. Perhaps this unacknowledged insider knowledge is why I heard it as slightly dangerous – it has no obvious accent, it has limited range, but a comfortable, perhaps 'understated' tessitura.

A remarkable feature of the song is its sense of tense. Although the video makes use of three different locations, each with its own time-sense, in the track itself, everything takes place in the immediate present, and with one exception there is no invitation to stretch one's consciousness outside this limited frame. That exception, of course, is the invitation to consider where I shall be sleeping tonight. So, the time period of the track is very definitely the present and, while it explores the moment, there is a sense of continual repeat, as if 'I can't learn from this experience', given by the repeated chorus and its dominant question. And yet, this repetition is definitely pleasurable, not unlike the pleasurable anticipation of getting drunk.

Oh dear. Am I pushing this too far? It's only a song, after all. It's over in three minutes and then we can simply get on to the next one. My answer to this, quite reasonable, question would be one that recalls the necessity all living creatures have to respond to their found environment. Much response is automatic, of course, but it must be made. Sometimes we have a choice how to respond, but even a decision not to respond is still a response. We cannot but respond to our environment, and I would rather do so knowingly than blindly, wherever possible. That's it, really. The song experience is framed as a song, of course, as a work of time-bound art, its as-if quality does not require me to take it seriously, but offers the *possibility* of so doing. This song, and the images it conjures up (or, more accurately, the images it enables me to conjure up, on the basis of partial recall), are as much a part of my environment as the air I breathe and the orange juice[20] I have just finished. The track reminds me of a situation to which it is all too easy to respond unknowingly, of an existential possibility of rising from the current circumstance, but a possibility which is at every turn thwarted – the only way to escape from it is not to enter it in the first place. That sense is energised by that remarkable usage of verbal space which, for me, is the song's abiding sense. And, if I can learn from that, then the time spent tussling with what's going on in my relationship to these ordered sounds is worthwhile. And the framing of the song as song gives me time to do just that.

This is the Life

So, although I am resistant to getting involved, although I would prefer to position myself as an eavesdropper on the situation **Amy** narrates, I find this an impossible position to maintain (otherwise these previous paragraphs could not have been written). What is the life? It is one where hedonism, an avoidance of considering consequences, dominates. Is it to be sought? **Amy** encourages me not to, in the swift juxtaposition of pleasure and distaste which, as the harmonic loop tells me, is an inevitable succession. (How far we have come from the 1980s!) And yet, the experience of that juxtaposition is, itself, pleasurable. And, although "this is the life" is what one says when relaxed, untroubled, perhaps in its dogged insistence on being sung to a minor chord, can "this is the life" also be said in that distaste?

[20] Without vodka – my attraction to staying down from the times extends that far.

References

Chester, A., 2007. Second Thoughts on a Rock Aesthetic: The Band. In: A.F. Moore (ed.), *Critical Essays in Popular Musicology*. Aldershot: Ashgate, pp. 111–18 (orig. 1970).

Fauconnier, G. and Turner, M., 2002. *The Way We Think: Conceptual Blending and the Mind's Hidden Complexities*. n.p.: Basic.

Griffiths, D., 2003. From Lyric to Anti-lyric: Analyzing the Words in Pop Song. In: A.F. Moore (ed.), *Analyzing Popular Music*. Cambridge: Cambridge University Press, pp. 158–72.

Moore, A.F., 2012. *Song Means: Analysing and Interpreting Recorded Popular Song*. Farnham: Ashgate.

Tagg, P., 2004. Musical Meanings, Classical and Popular. The Case of Anguish, [online] Available at: http://www.tagg.org/articles/musemeuse.html [Accessed 15 October 2013].

Discography

Beatles, The, 1963. 'She Loves You'. Parlophone, R 5055.

Cooper, Alice, 1989. 'Poison'. *Trash*. Epic, EPC 465130 2.

Coral, The, 2002. 'Dreaming of You'. *The Coral*. Deltasonic, DLTP006.

Macdonald, Amy, 2007. 'This Is The Life'. *This Is The Life*. Melodramatic/ Vertigo, 173, 212–4.

PART II
Listening Together

Chapter 9
An Ambiguous Murder: Questions of Intertextuality in PJ Harvey's 'The Words That Maketh Murder'

Cláudia Azevedo, Chris Fuller, Juliana Guerrero, Michael Kaler and Brad Osborn

'The Words That Maketh Murder' is the fourth of 12 songs on the album *Let England Shake*, which was recorded in a church in Dorset, in April–May 2010, and released in February 2011 on Universal Island Records Ltd. The album – which is a loose concept album dealing with England's wars – was extremely well-received, winning the Mercury and Ivor Novello awards. Like all the other songs on the album it was composed by PJ Harvey, and played by her and her backing band of John Parish and Mick Harvey.

Introduction (Chris Fuller)

When we gathered for our 'summer school' of popular music analysis, this was the song our group was assigned to analyse. None of the members of the group previously knew any of the other members, nor did we know the song that was to be our subject. It goes without saying that over the days that followed, we got to know each other and this song rather well.

Much group interaction went into our analysis of 'The Words That Maketh Murder', but to organise this chapter, we each took specific responsibilities as identified in the section headings, while Michael Kaler edited the whole. The result is an attempt at both a collaborative close analytical reading, bearing in mind our greatly diverse backgrounds, and an exploration of the methods of popular music analysis. We initially staged a reception test, followed by further close, often individual, listening and intensive group discussion, which enabled us to get to grips with how we as listeners perceived the song. From this we outlined five areas for subsequent analytical investigation: form, lyrics, texture, intertextuality and cognitive perception. In keeping with much popular music analysis, the methodology was designed to allow the salient empirical 'facts' about the song to provide the foundations for subsequent interpretation via an extramusical theoretical lens. Our use of intertextuality and image schemata are socially reliant inasmuch as the first relies on an external link (in the listener's mind) to be made between historically disparate songs, and the second relies on several assumptions about our perception of the world and the extent to which we are sympathetic to Lakoff and Johnson's ideas. Thus, essential to our reading of the song is the balance between the internal relations of the music and the external social world within which the song exists.

Our methodology can in no way be seen as a definitive way to 'do' popular music analysis, as the formal elements we chose to focus on were contingent on the song, and the interpretive elements were contingent on our collective backgrounds and willingness to engage in new (for us at least) theoretical ideas. This opens up a broader disciplinary question as to whether, as analysts, we should aim for sustainable and reproducible methodological models, or whether popular music analysis must remain methodologically unstable and in need of perpetual reinvention.

The answer probably lies somewhere between these two extremes. Analytical approaches to popular music are now established enough for us not to have to 'reinvent the wheel' with each new analysis, but because – as our own methodology exhibits – popular music is a social practice, each methodology needs to be flexible enough not to treat music as a stable and fixed object. Thus, as shown through our collaborative approach, the meanings we make in relation to popular music are as contingent upon our ability to comprehend its structures, forms and content, as they are on those external decisions we make as listeners based on our places within, and understandings of, society.

Instrumentation and Formal Structure (Juliana Guerrero)

The instrumentation of 'The Words That Maketh Murder' includes lead (female) and backing (male) vocals, an autoharp (PJ Harvey), a trombone (Parish), an acoustic guitar (Parish), a slide guitar (Parish) and drums (Mick Harvey). Figure 9.1 shows how they enter and where they play in the song.

An autoharp starts the song alone and it plays throughout, with only one brief pause at the beginning of verse 2. The autoharp is an instrument of German origin, popular in the United States in the late nineteenth and early twentieth century especially among folk musicians (Kettlewell and Long, n.d.). It is an uncommon instrument to encounter in rock music, but Harvey has played it on several of her recent albums.[1]

In addition to the autoharp, the foundation of the song includes acoustic guitar and drums. They start bar 3, creating the 'metrical fake-out' that will be described

[1] Harvey first recorded with the autoharp in 2004, for a song called 'The Darker Days Of Me & Him' on the album *Uh Huh Her*. Subsequently it was used on many of the songs of her album *White Chalk* (2007), and on most of the songs of her latest album *Let England Shake* (2011).

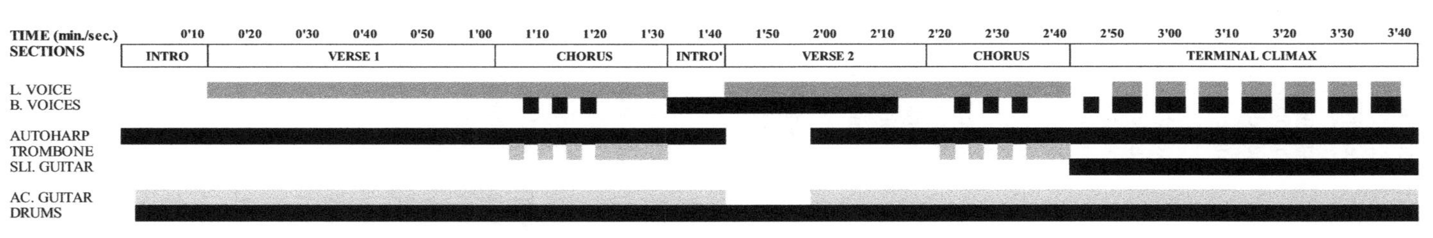

Figure 9.1 'The Words That Maketh Murder', instrumentation schema

Table 9.1 'The Words That Maketh Murder', formal structure

Section	Time	Chord progression	Description
Intro (10 bars)	0:01–0:15	Em–A–G–D/F♯	Sets up groove and instrumentation: syncopated autoharp unaccompanied, then drums and acoustic guitar enter
Verse 1 (16+16 bars)	0:15–1:06	Em–A–G–D/F♯	Voice enters over intro groove
Chorus 1 (16+4 bars)	1:06–1:34	G–Gm–D–C	Trombone enters, male voice joins PJ Harvey in singing title lyric, chords now all on strong beats. Sectional overlap/elision between verse ending and chorus beginning
Intro' (8 bars)	1:34–1:46	Em–A–G–D/F♯	Male voice chants title lyric on E3 and B2 over intro groove
Verse 2 (16 + 6 bars)	1:46–2:19	no chord, then Em–A–G–D/F♯	Guitar and Autoharp tacet, PJ Harvey voice re-enters, lyrics begin the same as verse 1, then new lyrics over recapitulated verse melody
Chorus 2 (16 bars)	2:19–2:44	G–Gm–D–C	Chorus 1 accompaniment with new lyrics
Terminal climax (33 bars)	2:44–3:45	Dm–Cm–B♭–Gm (end on Dm)	Slide guitar enters, PJ Harvey and male voice sing in unison (×8)

below (see p. 180) and play throughout the song, establishing a steady, cyclically repeating four-bar unit.

During the main body of the song, the lyrics are sung by Harvey, in the first person, while the male backing vocals support and reinforce (or comment on?) her lines. In the terminal climax, the backing vocals take the lead, singing repeatedly the last line of the lyrics, and then are joined by the lead vocal.

The first verse has a clear texture, with the lead vocal taking the melody, supported by autoharp, guitar and drums. In the following chorus, the texture is made denser through the introduction of trombone and male backing vocals, functioning as support to, and foil for, the lead vocal. The double-tracked trombone is already heard a few seconds before the first chorus and plays its repeating pattern four times, rising to a climax the fourth time. In this section, the male backing vocals closely reproduce the trombone's rhythm figure. The male voices alternate with Harvey's voice and the trombone, in call-and-response interplay.

If privileging harmony and texture, one might assert that Harvey sings the first line of the chorus at 1:06 over the trombone pattern; then, without the trombone but with the male backing vocals, she sings the second line: 'The words that maketh murder'. However, once we hear this title lyric, we can, retrospectively, hear that same melodic/lyrical statement over the verse harmony and texture at 1:03, thus creating a sort of 'sectional fake-out' (analogous to the 'metrical fake-out' in the introduction) with regard to the end of the verse and beginning of the chorus. Following this sectional elision, the trombone line in the fourth phrase finishes in a crescendo and stretches into the following section, holding its note until Harvey, alone, sings the last line of the chorus: 'Murder.'

The next section, a repeat of the introduction, gives an altered presentation of the introduction material, and thus has been labelled 'intro' on the form graph. The main differences between it and the original introduction include the presence of the backing vocals, which continue chanting the two lines from the chorus, and the uninterrupted presence of the drums and guitar.

In the second verse, the male voices continue repeating this line of the chorus while Harvey sings the new lyrics in counterpoint. Note that the intensity is now *pp*, and the acoustic guitar and the autoharp are tacet until slowly faded in during the verse. Following this verse, there is a second chorus, structured as the first one.

What effect does this choice of instrumentation have on our understanding of the song? Why did Harvey choose these instruments for her song? One possible answer might run as follows. The drums and guitar are, of course, unexceptional for rock music, while the autoharp gives the song a distinct sound, which distinguishes it from other works of the genre and also tags it as being by Harvey, since the autoharp has become something of a trademark for her over the past seven years. The trombone suggests not only military bands, but also, and more generally, the old tradition of community-based brass bands. Its presence therefore could quite possibly invoke associations of the military (linking it to the lyrics) and public gatherings, such as demonstrations, an evocation that would resonate with the song's ending, in which a group of people chant their declaration to take their problem to the United Nations.

The key to understanding this song's form can be found in its conclusion. 'The Words That Maketh Murder' exhibits a formal design found commonly in post-1990s rock music, one that Osborn (2013) calls 'terminally climactic form.' Songs that make use of this form present a small amount of repeated new material in their conclusion, rather than a repeated chorus. This final section, with its new material, acts as the song's memorable high point, a distinction usually signalled through harmonic modulation, a repeated lyrical/melodic hook and a shift from turbulent rhythm to a more relaxed groove.

The climactic ending of Harvey's song is marked in several ways. It repeats the final line eight times, which is the longest stretch of uninterrupted vocal repetition to be found in the song; it introduces a new instrument, the slide guitar, which appears to match the new lyrics and melody; it features a harmonic shift (see below); and it straightens out the groove, creating a notable contrast with the syncopations and micro-rhythmic dissonance to be found elsewhere in the song.

We will discuss the intertextual significance of the repeated final line of the song below. For the moment, it is important to note that Harvey's use of terminally climactic form gives the final line a great deal of impact. Not only is it the last thing that the listener hears, but it enters as a novelty, a surprise, rather than having become familiar through repetition, as would be the case at this point with the chorus. Indeed, the song's construction creates a nuanced hierarchy of significance. The chorus is privileged through its recurrence, and it is from the chorus that the song's title derives, thus being invoked whenever the song is mentioned. But the repetition and positioning of the final line gives it, in our view, even more weight.

Rhythm (Brad Osborn)

In 'The Words That Maketh Murder', the string instruments and Harvey's voice consistently work as a foil to the almost mechanical, metronomically precise $\frac{4}{4}$ backbeat played by the percussion, subverting its rigidity by obfuscating the strong beats. This playful subversion happens on two levels – the structural level (the level of steady pulse), and the micro-rhythmic level (the level of 'feel').

The song opens with what we have described, in Justin London's term, as a 'metrical fake-out'.[2] Generally speaking, successive strong beats tend to be interpreted as downbeats until proven otherwise; this makes it quite likely that the listener will hear the opening unaccompanied autoharp pattern as accenting beats 1 and 3 in common time. (See Example 9.1 for a transcription.)

Example 9.1 'The Words That Maketh Murder', opening autoharp pattern

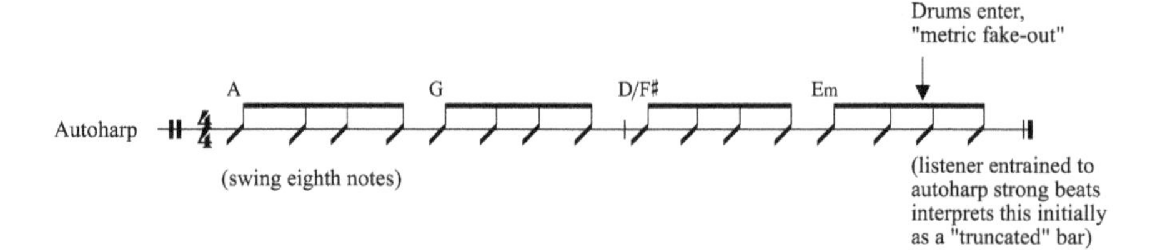

But as soon as the percussion enters – which happens directly after this figure – the listeners will be likely to align themselves with a familiar backbeat, and to perceive the autoharp accents as taking place on beats 2 and 4. See Example 9.2:

This structural, metrical clash between autoharp and percussion persists throughout the verses of the song, save for a brief moment in verse 2 where Harvey's highly rhythmically nuanced approach to the vocal melody gives the impression that she is dancing over the chanting male voice. This sudden absence of rhythmic contrast creates the sudden impression of space in the music, as well as bringing the vocals to the forefront.

There are also at least two micro-rhythmic dissonances that persist throughout the song until the terminal climax. Indeed, their resolution in the terminal climax is

[2] See London's homepage at http://people.carleton.edu/~jlondon/ for a spreadsheet listing a number of metrical fakeouts.

Example 9.2 'The Words That Maketh Murder', transcription of percussion and autoharp

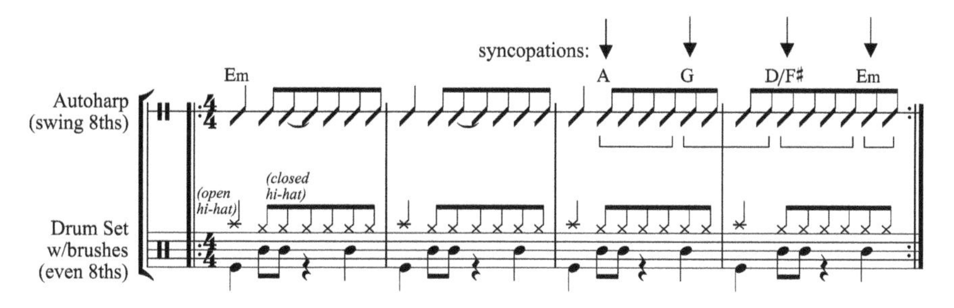

used to accentuate the impact of that section. The first of these is produced through juxtaposition of two different interpretations in eighth-note feel. As Example 9.2 shows, while the autoharp initially sets up a swung eighth-note feel, the percussion enters and persists with almost mechanically steady eighth notes played by brushes on a closed hi-hat, creating an effect different from, but comparable to, the 'half-swung' rhythm that was beloved by early rock and blues artists:[3] in both cases, tension is created through the juxtaposition of swung and straight feels. This feel persists through both the verse and chorus, and only at the terminal climax is it resolved, when the autoharp and acoustic guitar finally give in to the percussion rhythm. This rhythmic uniformity, the loss of Harvey's expressive individuality, deepens the effect of the terminal climax's lyrics, which show Harvey looking to an external, remote source of authority to resolve her problems.

The second micro-rhythmic dissonance involves the way that Harvey's vocals consistently dance around the steady underlying beat. In her singing as in her autoharp playing, then, Harvey presents herself as an individual working against a standardised rhythmic backdrop. This dissonance, too, is resolved at the terminal climax, when Harvey consistently sings in rhythmic unison with the male voice for the first time.[4] One could hear this choice as implying that Harvey is giving in to the uniformity of the backing vocals, shedding her expressive micro-timing so as to be heard together with the other vocals in unison, thus increasing their strength, and – perhaps implicitly – falling into line with the standardised 'regulations' of the UN.

---

[3] The term 'half swing' is 'often used to designate swing that is somewhere between the straight-eighth feel and triplet swing' (Ripani, 2006, p. 53). A good example of this can be found in Junior Wells's recording of 'Good Morning Schoolgirl', from his *Hoodoo Man Blues* album, in which the bassist (pioneering electric blues bassist Jack Myers) plays with a straight feel, the guitarist (Buddy Guy) plays with a swung feel and the drummer (Billy Warren) alternates between the two.

[4] There are also moments of rhythmic unison in the first and second choruses.

Harmony and Voice-Leading (Brad Osborn)

A list of the chord progressions found throughout the song is found in the Table 9.1 formal chart, but voice-leading analysis allows us to craft a narrative of the song's expressive trajectory. See Example 9.3:

Example 9.3 'The Words That Maketh Murder', middleground and background voice-leading graphs

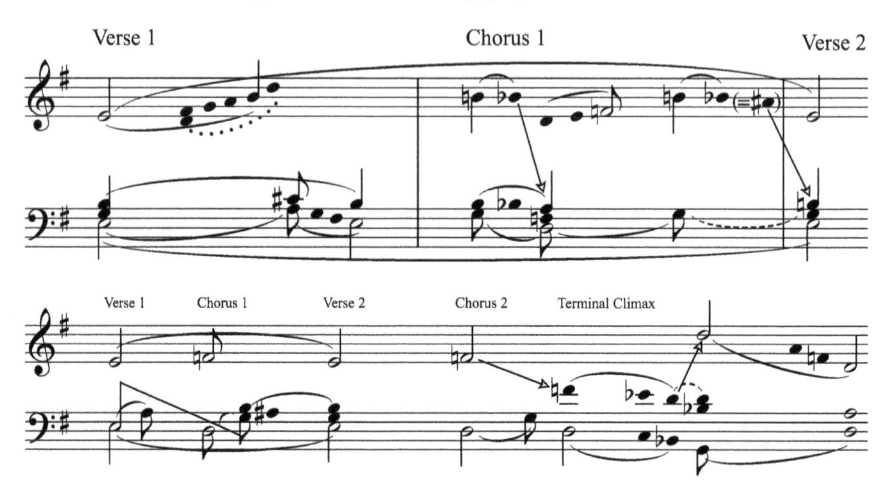

Harvey only sings over the E minor chord in the verses, and so we can regard this as an E minor pedal. Indeed, all of Harvey's vocal pitches fill in an E minor pentachord, occasionally dipping down for the lower Aeolian neighbour (D natural), but never actually choosing between the modal sixth scale-degree (C or C♯). The accompanying autoharp riff consistently presents C♯ as the raised third of an A major triad, suggesting an E dorian sound, but Harvey leaves the mode ambiguous. This is coherent with Harvey's general approach to the song – as we have seen and will see, she makes considerable use of ambiguity in many aspects of 'The Words That Maketh Murder'.

The chorus moves to a D minor collection, with Harvey's voice presenting strong emphasis on the tones B♭ and F – which are, of course, the two tones that must be altered to achieve this shift in tonal centre. She is helped in this modulation from the trombone, which echoes her title lyric ('The words that maketh murder' = D4 – E4 – F4) in canon two measures later as the 5th passing through to the seventh of the G minor seventh chord. This reinforces the song's title lyric, as well as helps to partition it from the verse by emphasising a new harmonic area.

The verse and chorus present nearly analogous cadential structures, with each tonic being prolonged through a subdominant neighbour (E is prolonged through

A, D prolonged through G). While these analogous structures present verse 1 and chorus 1 as two competing tonal centres, the move back to verse 2 gives us good reason to hear the D minor area as a lower neighbour. The chromatic slide from B to B♭ that occurs over the modally inflected G minor chord of the chorus can be enharmonically reinterpreted as B to A♯ so that G minor may voice-lead back to E minor to begin verse 2. Harvey's vocal emphasis on E4 in the verse and F4 in the chorus suggests a Phrygian double-neighbour with D and F acting as lower and upper neighbours, respectively, of the E minor tonic of both verses.

This reading, which emphasises the return of E minor in verse 2 (rather than the chorus), highlights the role of the male voice, which opens the second verse by chanting the song's title lyric using only E3 and B2. This oppressive tonic-dominant axis, presented in a rigid (militaristic) rhythm, nuances our reception of the song's title. When Harvey first sings it, she does so with modal tones and micro-rhythmic expressive timing in the 'wrong key' in the chorus, which give it the sense of being an agitated and very personal statement. This sense changes when the line is then presented by a male voice in an authoritative low register in the 'correct' key: the line then becomes a declaration, or an assertion.

The notion of a global E minor tonic is challenged after the second chorus, when the terminal climax does not return to E, as had verse 2, but instead continues in D. Harvey's F4, which had previously acted as an upper neighbour to E4, is now transferred to an inner voice to move in parallel tenths with the bass, allowing her to present D as a new tonic, outlining the tonic triad in a full octave.

It is important to note here how the parallel tenths (D/F, C/E♭, B♭/D) involve the addition of yet another flat (E♭) to distance us even further from the original E minor tonic. Earlier, Harvey's message might have felt as though it was in the 'wrong key', but here she forces the listener to hear D minor as the 'right key' by continuing the tonic of the chorus, and, in fact, by distancing us even further from E minor by the addition of the E♭. This reading is bolstered by her repeated presentation of this climactic lyric eight times with a melody that, expressive intonation notwithstanding, outlines the tonic triad of the new key.

Much of the criticism levelled at voice-leading analysis – especially that is does an inherent violence to the music – stems from monotonal applications of the theory to pieces which may otherwise be heard in multiple tonal contexts. The voice-leading analysis presented here, which highlights the two *competing* tonal centres, actually helps us create meaning in conjunction with the song's lyrical structure and rhythmic profile.[5]

---

[5] As part of his analysis of Mendelssohn's 'Venetianisches Gondellied', Poundie Burstein (2006, p. 35) notes: 'There has long been a suspicion that voice leading analysis seeks to reveal the logic of music and disentangle its ambiguities, at the expense of the individuality and intriguing paradoxes found in such great music … Yet surely this is a simplification. Indeed, a rigorous voice-leading analysis can often highlight tantalizingly illogical moments and ambiguities within specific works.'

Voice-leading analysis, viewed in this way, is a form of storytelling. 'The Words That Maketh Murder' tells a story of battle and compromise, a story whose backdrop consists of, and whose emotional impact is intensified by, the competing tonal centres and 'squashed' rhythmic expressivity present at key moments of the story. We hope to have shown that by highlighting the ambiguous and anomalous harmonic, rhythmic and formal structure of PJ Harvey's song, and by considering these aspects in conjunction with the lyrics, we lay the groundwork for the creation of a richer and more meaningful appreciation of the song than either lyrical analysis or musical analysis alone could yield.

Vocal and Lyrical Interplay (Cláudia Azevedo)

The lyrics to 'Words That Maketh Murder' are pungent from the start, displaying images of physical dismemberment and decay. Human body parts are referred to as undifferentiated lumps of meat; detached arms and legs are blown into trees; flesh quivers in the heat, swarmed by flies.

The setting evoked by these lyrics is that of a battlefield. There are references to soldiers and a corporal, which could be read as a play on words alluding to the human body as well as to a rank in the Army. But while one tends to think of *male* soldiers in battlefields, the lead vocalist is female. Is the protagonist, then, a woman? Or is Harvey singing from a masculine point of view? Harvey sings of a longing for a woman's face, but is this the desire of a male soldier in an exclusively male context, or the desire of a woman to see another woman after seeing only men? Such gender ambiguity is not unknown in Harvey's work, and hence the confusion may be intentional.

This is rendered all the more likely by the fact that the ambiguity is not restricted to issues of gender. The lyrics to the song are sung in the first person and indicate agency: Harvey states that she has seen and done things she wants to forget. Is she, then, saying that she was actually involved in some battlefield situation, one that has traumatised her and that she now deeply regrets? Who is the speaker? None of these issues are made clear, but what *is* clear is that Harvey is singing about a terrible place, associated with terrible deeds. This lack of clarity may well be deliberate – Harvey has said that in her view 'the nature of conflict is timeless', since war 'has been here since time began and will be long after we're gone' (Harvey, cited in Breihan, 2011).

In our examination of vocal delivery, the means by which Harvey tells us about this enigmatic and evil place, we will start not with the voice, but with the autoharp's introductory chords, which could be heard as forming a riff – one that will be repeated without change 11 times in this section of the song. As it occurs at the very start of the song, it creates a context for the listener. In itself, it is not particularly tense or disconcerting – in fact, Harvey has said that in her view the autoharp produces 'quite a delicate sound' (Harvey, 2011). However, the entrance of the bass drum and the revelation of the metrical fake-out (see above, p. 180), force the listener to relocate the downbeat. Thus the autoharp riff has a sense of friction, because we perceive it as starting on the first upbeat of the bar – which could be read as a metaphoric hint that in this song, things do not flow as smoothly as one might like.

The hint having been delivered, the female voice enters. In her first sentence, the words are articulated with a contour that brings them close to spoken language. With the exception of an anacrusis of a fifth, B to E, the vocal remains throughout within an interval of fourth. The descending fourth interval, from A to E, closes the sentence in an assertive way, like a full stop.

Another anacrusis, this time to the higher octave E on the downbeat ('*sol*diers ...') starts the second sentence and catches the listener by surprise. Soon after that, the voice goes higher again, to D on the upbeat of the bar. The instability of the protagonist's voice, or tale, is established against the steadiness of the metre and the tempo. This may be related to what Harvey refers to as her 'child-like responses': 'the nature of the words are often addressing very dark weighty subjects. I couldn't sing those in a rich strong mature voice without sounding completely wrong' (Harvey, 2011).

From then on, there is a prolongation of the vowels of the last word of every line. The female vocal enters sometimes anacrustically, sometimes on the downbeat, and her subdivisions are slightly flexible within sentences, although still following the rules of prosody. Five times during verses 1 and 2, she chooses to reach the higher octave and all these situations occur on the downbeat of bars. Apart from these, she moves in a range of a little more than an octave in the song. This configuration might be the result of Harvey's compositional approach to *Let England Shake*. She spent several years just writing the words before she began 'even thinking about music' (Harvey, cited in Breihan, 2011): when the time did come to develop the music for the songs, she 'would sing them until the words told me their melody ... They've already got a rhythm, the rhythm is there. When you begin to work with the rhythm then the melody just comes' (Harvey, 2011).

It is possible to see a semantic link between the autoharp riff and the female voice. Both of them sound detached from the accompaniment not only due to their pitch, but also due to the conveyance of melodic lines (considering the autoharp's riff as a melody) – in fact, they alternate in this role. In addition, the autoharp riff presents the rhythmic friction. Could the autoharp riff represent emotions that cannot be put into words, like an ellipsis mark, a pause between sentences? Harvey sings that she has seen soldiers fall like lumps of meat [riff], blown and shot out beyond belief. 'Blown' refers to 'soldiers', which is in the previous musical phrase. This situation happens at several points throughout the song. It is important to observe that verse 1 is regular, being divided in two parts with rhymes at the end of sentences. Each part starts with the statement that she has seen and done things she wants to forget. This regularity in verse 1 creates the expectation that subsequent verses will be regular as well. This expectation, however, goes unfulfilled. While verse 2 features lyrics that refer to verse 1 and similar musical structures, its lyrics do not rhyme, which for us serves to increase the song's tension, leaving us waiting for a resolution which it seems reasonable to expect, but which is never delivered.

Then she sings of the words that gather pace (second verse, 4th line) and 'the words that maketh murder', instead of which the protagonist longed to see a woman's face. Which words are these which function through the use of the verb 'to make' in an archaic form, 'maketh'? Do they refer to decisions which lead to war and treat humans statistically? Do they refer to official or legal judgements which determine what is going to be considered murder, and treat humans as examples or as test cases? Or do they refer to the passions in human nature, considered to be sinful since archaic times: lust, gluttony, greed, sloth, wrath, envy, pride?

As the protagonist mentions 'the words' in bar 45, a new section starts, featuring a male choir and brass instruments. Just as the autoharp is linked to the protagonist in instability, so too the brass instruments are linked to the male voices and 'the words' in steadiness in metre, prosody and pitch, always starting on downbeats and assertively repeating the lines, moving from V to I. Over this configuration, the protagonist's voice, when alone, enters on the upbeat of bars.

At the end of the first chorus, the male voices take over from the protagonist on the word 'murder', after a brass crescendo before the lead vocalist has wrung the full emotional expression out of the word, the backing vocalists make it clear that they are already there to stay: they repeat the lines very steadily seven times, like an *ostinato* marching under the protagonist's voice. Unlike the lead vocalist, they do not seem to be emotionally driven. Rather, they just go on, cycling from $\hat{5}$ to $\hat{1}$, as if to say that this is the way things are: war is necessary, one kills in the name of (another) one's interests. *C'est la vie*. Sad but true.

It is difficult to say where verse 2 really starts, due to the augmentation of the repeated harmony with new vocal lines and lyrics, displaying modifications which challenge the expectancy built from the formal regularity of verse 1. On the third repetition of the male voice ostinato, the texture gets less dense with the guitar and auto harp tacet, at the same time that the protagonist's voice sings the first line of the song exactly as she sang it on verse 1. As mentioned above, none of the six phrases in this verse – rather than eight as in verse 1 – have rhymes, thus frustrating the expectation of regularity created by verse 1. The corporal whose nerves were shot lost them in both ways: the impulses of sensation and the courage in a difficult situation. Here, again, soldiers fell like lumps of meat and flies were swarming everyone. Apart from the flies, one wonders precisely what entity is feeding on these pieces of humans?

Following this verse, the chorus returns with the same structure as before – that is, with the brass instruments on the downbeat, while the protagonist enters on the upbeat. The difference this time is that the male voices are with her in every other line.

As noted above, the song finishes with a terminal climax, which brings in new lyrics, new melodic and harmonic material and new instrumentation. In terms of the new instrumentation, we hear a high-pitched slide guitar playing D and in a range that had previously been the lead vocalist's domain, coming in on the downbeat of the second syllable of the word 'mur*der*', which is also the first time that the lead vocalist has deviated from the standards of prosody. This configuration happens over a D minor chord which can be heard as belonging simultaneously to the previous section, the chorus, and to the song-concluding terminal climax. The slide guitar is not steady, moving in and out of downbeats, just as the lead vocal line did throughout the song.

In this final section, the male voices ask again – eight times without variation – what if they took their problem to the United Nations? Harvey is absent the first time, putting the emphasis on the new slide guitar line; following this, all the voices sing together for the second and the third repetitions, and then from the fourth on, the lead vocalist stretches the vowel sound of the words 'm*y*' and 'nati*on*s', in a gesture that resembles the slide guitar's approach.

The musical structures in the terminal climax suggest that neither the protagonist nor the male voices believe it would be of any help to take the problem to the United Nations – there seems to be no trust in the institution. Could we hear the high-pitched slide guitar as a voice lamenting a hopeless human condition? Furthermore, can we even trust the protagonist? Might Harvey's high-pitched leaps be intended to represent hysteria in a stylised manner? While she moves irregularly over the steady beat, and while she works with the autoharp in creating rhythmic friction, nonetheless she performs the octave leaps very accurately. And when we listen on headphones, it becomes apparent that her voice is always placed in the middle of the mix's virtual space; although it sounds close, it does not invade intimate space. Male voices, by contrast, are placed laterally and from 1:50 to 2:20 seem to become slightly louder in the mix, as though they were marching closer. Finally, the overall reverb sets the events aurally in a wider space.

'The Words That Maketh Murder' leaves the listener with many unanswered questions. As we have been at pains to point out in this paper, it is, on many levels, a profoundly ambiguous song. Ambiguity is affectively uncomfortable and so is war, if we may be permitted this understatement! The combination of musical structures as employed in the song seems to embrace the idea of ambiguity through the creation of tension – not overtly dramatic tension, however, but subtle and localised tension. Ambiguity is not a blunt tool: the secret to its effective use lies in one's ability to work with details. Our experience as listeners was that Harvey was successful in her search to find a way to sing the words to her song without giving them the 'wrong feeling', making them seem self-important or dogmatic. As she said: 'I wanted the songs to be much more ambiguous than that' (Harvey, cited in Breihan, 2011).

Lyrical Intertextuality (Michael Kaler)

Questions of intertextuality usually involve the consideration of the way(s) that one text is activated within or by another text – with 'text' here being taken in a wide sense. The discussion of intertextuality can take in, at its broadest extent, the whole of a work's relationship with its past, or with its audience's past. For example, we could look intertextually at the call-and-response interplay between Harvey's vocals and the autoharp riff in the light of the whole rock tradition of voice/guitar interaction and call-and-response techniques, leading back to elements of pre-rock African American musical structuring. But for our present purposes we will take up a more narrow consideration of intertextuality, one that is restricted to a pair of verbal intertexts that are clearly signalled within the work.

The word 'maketh' in the song's title and chorus is the first of two such intertexts that we will examine. Its grammatically incorrect use of the archaic -eth third person *singular* ending with a *plural* noun subject evokes broad reminiscences of pre-nineteenth-century English literature. These evocations, in fact, rely on the '-eth' ending; the correct form of the verb, 'make', would not evoke them, simply because it is still in use today.

In addition to being declined archaically, the verb is also used in an unusual way. Normally we would expect it to be used with a noun, with an article as an object or with some sort of verbal phrase, that is 'maketh the sun to shine' or 'maketh the day and the night'. Here it is used to link the subject to an anarthrous noun object ('murder'). In so doing, 'the words' are suggestively assigned the responsibility for creating/causing not just *a* murder, or a *specific* murder, but rather *all* murder.

This suggestion that we are not dealing with one crime, but rather with fundamental moral principles, combined with the archaic phrasing, arouses associations with the King James translation of the Bible, particularly the book of Psalms.[6] The song's title may have been derived from a specific source, but if so, this source is obscure. Its general associations with old English literature and the King James Bible do, however, add to the song's air of nostalgic timelessness; they also introduce a strongly moral note.

The second intertext that we will address is much more specific, and occurs in the terminal climax section, where Harvey (slightly mis)quotes a line from Eddie Cochran's 'Summertime Blues'. In the last verse of 'Summertime Blues', Cochran sings 'I'm gonna take my problems to the United Nations'; Harvey, by contrast, turns the phrase into a question.

Now, in addition to this explicit intertextuality, a number of other features of the 'The Words That Maketh Murder' could quite easily be taken as being implicated in an intertextual relationship with 'Summertime Blues'. These features include (but need not be limited to):

a. The use of low, calm male voices alternating with the higher-pitched and more emotional voice of the lead singer. In Cochran's original, these low voices represent the protagonist's father, boss and Congressman; in Harvey's song, these voices are the backing vocals of her bandmates.

---

6 See especially Psalm 23:1–2: 'The Lord is my shepherd, I shall not want./He maketh me to lie down in green pastures.'

b. The rhythm of the autoharp strumming pattern, which seems to be similar to Cochran's broad strumming on the guitar.
c. The handclaps used as part of the percussion (as in 'Summertime Blues').

In short, the lyric quotation marks a clear intertextuality, but it is up to the listener to decide which, if any, of the other features will be understood as intertexts. However the listener may resolve that issue, it is clear that the conceptual or associative context for 'The Words That Maketh Murder' is one that includes 'Summertime Blues'.

But although 'The Words That Maketh Murder' shares a conceptual space with 'Summertime Blues', this is not to say that it simply evokes Cochran's song. Rather, 'The Words That Maketh Murder' *works with* 'Summertime Blues', most evidently in the slight change in the lyric quotation. Other changes, which may or may not be relevant to various listeners include (but need not be limited to):

a. the choice of autoharp as lead instrument rather than Cochran's distinctive guitar;
b. the tonally ambiguous, chromatic harmony in Harvey's tune (discussed above), versus the straightforward three-chord rock of Cochran's song;
c. the fact that the low male voices in Harvey's song sing a line that the higher-voiced protagonist sang in Cochran's song;
d. the way that the low male voices and the lead vocal seem to be working together in Harvey's song, rather than the former representing the voice of repressive authority opposing the latter as in Cochran's song;
e. the way that Harvey's song presents an evocative, imagistic narrative, as opposed to the very straightforward tale of *avant la lettre* slackerdom in Cochran's song;
f. the change of lyrical content from middle-class teenage angst to graphic depiction of death and destruction.

As was the case above, here again, the change in lyrics is unmistakable and explicit, while the other changes may or may not be meaningful to listeners in terms of nuancing the intertextual context shared by 'The Words That Maketh Murder' and 'Summertime Blues'. We can say, then, that 'The Words That Maketh Murder' inhabits a context that includes 'Summertime Blues', but we must also say that there is a progressive and dialogic aspect to this shared context. 'The Words That Maketh Murder' derives part of its meaning by *moving through* 'Summertime Blues' – or, at least, it does so for those listeners who recognise the intertextuality.

Now, artistic meaning is not simply discovered. Rather, it is also created, and it is plural, which is to say that everyone who perceives this intertext will use it in one way or another in his or her idiosyncratic construction of the meaning(s) of the song. In the hope of inspiring or extending such activity, we would say that for us, the most striking effect of this intertextuality is to enhance the mood of alienated confusion that, as we have seen, 'The Words That Maketh Murder' conveys through its properly musical aspects as well.

Cochran's original song, 'Summertime Blues', presented a world simplistically divided into 'us [or rather, me] versus them', in which even the low-voiced 'them' was perhaps obstructionary, but not actively antagonistic to the higher-voiced protagonist. The father, boss and Congressman may get in the protagonist's way, but they don't actively wish him ill. The world of 'Summertime Blues' is comprehensible and clear. In this world, the most extreme desire conceivable is the desire to be free to hang out with friends; the worst eventuality conceivable is that one might have to get a summer job.

In Harvey's recasting, by contrast, *all* the parties involved, high voiced lead singer and low-voiced backing singers alike, are trapped *together* in a violent and unclear world, with memories of atrocious carnage and not even an evident enemy (nor is it entirely clear what the problem is; is the war still going on? is the protagonist looking for reparations?). The only recourse that is presented in 'The Words That Maketh Murder' is the appeal to the United Nations, but how could this alter the protagonist's memory of all that she (is the protagonist female? is Harvey singing as a male? we don't know ...) has seen and done? And anyway, in contrast to Cochran's straightforward singular declaration ('I'm gonna ...'), here the appeal is no more than a suggestion, a glimpse of a possibility ('What if ...'). Within the emotional world established by 'The Words That Maketh Murder' it feels unlikely that such an appeal will even be carried out, or that it will be successful if delivered.

To us, then, it seems that the evocation of 'Summertime Blues' brings with it a whole world of adolescent simplicity and clarity, a world that contrasts strikingly with the murky, violent world into which 'The Words That Maketh Murder' leads us. This implicit contrast, it seems to us, intensifies the impact of Harvey's song, by inviting us to see it in the light of its opposite.

Thinking about Ambiguity (Chris Fuller)

'The Words That Maketh Murder' has now been discussed from a number of more or less isolated analytical categories. The conclusions to these discussions strongly suggest that the obfuscated rhythmic interplay, muggy textures, mixed messages in the lyrics, (mis-)quotes of other songs and non-goal directed harmony establish ambiguity as one of the song's fundamental themes. One problem that can arise with the use of ambiguity as an interpretive adjective is that it can often be read as overly reliant on plurality. This can result in readings of ambiguity becoming ambiguous themselves, either leading the reader to banal conclusions, or leaving her even more confused than she was before (see Agawu, 1994). However, we would argue that a reading of a more nuanced presentation of ambiguity in Harvey's song is plausible because the musical material suggests a dearth of interpretive possibilities. Thus, the following is an attempt to ground this reading of ambiguity in such a way that we are able to understand better its function in the song and how it manifests itself as meaningful.

The ideas of conceptual metaphor, cross-domain mapping and image schemata derive primarily from the work of George Lakoff and Mark Johnson who suggest 'metaphor is pervasive in our everyday life, not just in language, but in thought and action', the acknowledgement of which subsequently enables us to understand our cognitive perception of the world (Lakoff and Johnson, 1980, p. 454). To summarise briefly, Lakoff and Johnson describe conceptual metaphor as our way of 'understanding and experiencing one kind of thing in terms of another' (Lakoff and Johnson, 1980, p. 455; original emphasis). Their example of one such metaphor is our understanding of arguments in terms of war, in which there are winners, losers, attacks, defences and strategies. This also explains the notion of cross-domain mapping where the metaphor of war is taken from its home domain and transplanted into the domain of argument as a means of understanding argument as a concept. Johnson has defined an image schema as 'a dynamic, recurring pattern of organism-environment interactions [that] will reveal itself in the contours of our basic sensorimotor experiences' (Johnson, 2007, p. 136). For Johnson image schemata are 'basic structural features of all human bodily experience' (Johnson, 2007, p. 136). An example is the 'SOURCE-PATH-GOAL' schema in which we use the notion of a path to conceptualise some kind of physical or metaphoric journey from one place to another (Johnson, 2007, p. 142).

Various music scholars have taken Lakoff and Johnson's work as a means of understanding our conceptualisation of music. In the present context, it is impossible to give an in-depth exploration of the use of conceptual metaphors and image schemata in music research. However, scholars such as Allan F. Moore, Patricia Schmidt and Ruth Dockwray (2009), Janna Saslaw (1996), William Echard (1999), Lawrence Zbikowski (2005) and Michael Spitzer (2004) have all written on ways of perceiving and understanding music through various applications of Lakoff and Johnson's theories.

To give a necessarily brief summary of the musical uptake of such theories: Moore, Schmidt and Dockwray apply Johnson's theory to various popular musics, suggesting it is possible to 'consider sonic extensions of schemata in music' (Moore, Schmidt and Dockwray, 2009, p. 87). Echard suggests that Johnson's theory 'refuses mind-body dualism from the start' thus allowing 'meaning-making' to be 'a dynamic, experimental, embodied process' (Echard, 1999, p. 134). Saslaw adopts the theory as a means of 'cognitive organization' (Saslaw, 1996, p. 127). Suggesting that 'schemata are not metaphors but grounds for metaphors', Spitzer is keen to align himself with a classical Kantian approach in which schemata can be used to produce a 'transcendental mental image that synthesizes concepts and intuitions' (Spitzer, 2004, pp. 60–61). In the hope of grounding the ambiguity in 'The Words That Maketh Murder', we will provide a loose amalgamation of such applications of image schemata and conceptual metaphor.

Firstly, and stemming primarily from the sound-image presented by the song's textural make-up, one physical metaphor that repeatedly came up as we discussed this song was that of the swamp. This effect is created mainly through the high level of reverb (possibly natural considering the majority of songs were recorded in a church), the slight delay and microphone position of the recorded autoharp, and perhaps to a lesser extent the very open sound of the kick drum, which clutters the sonic space with ambient noise even after the actual musical utterance (Gerryts, 2011). We found it appropriate to describe this atmosphere as swamp-like because of its oppressive effect on the sonic landscape; if we had to correlate the feeling that the song gave with a physical activity, that activity would be trudging. Working with the collection of image schemata defined by Johnson, a suitable choice for understanding this swamp-like atmosphere would be the 'CONTAINER' which has to have an inside, an outside, and a boundary that divides the two (Lakoff and Johnson, 1999, p. 32). In essence the container schema is useful because it allows for the possibility of being trapped. We can imagine moving within the container, but the boundary always stops us from getting out.

Upon examination, we find that this containment schema also works at other levels within the song. In terms of the initial 'metrical fake-out' stemming from the autoharp's relation to the metronomic backbeat we can suggest that the autoharp is constrained by the oppressive downbeat; this is also the case for Harvey's vocal delivery, which, as we noted above, is linked to the autoharp, rather than the percussion's downbeat. There is a clear interplay between the rigid downbeats and Harvey's expression, the rigid elements functioning as the boundary of the container (the formal limits we perceive the song to set itself), whereas Harvey's voice and autoharp can be seen as trapped in the container and attempting to get out. This is also supported by the fact that Harvey eventually comes to accept the structural level of rhythm during the terminal climax.

The container schema is also interesting in terms of the song's harmony. If we imagine the container as the swamp it would be as difficult to find a centre point, as it would to locate its boundaries. Although it has been suggested that a rough tonal centre of E is plausible but ambiguous modally, we can read more into the jarring quality of the shift to the lower neighbour note D with the chorus. This move to D minor can be read as an attempt to break away from the ambiguous E, which never quite settles as dorian or Aeolian. Thus, the shift to a harmonic area with a greater sense of clarity can be perceived as a brief escape from the ambiguity of the E, which in this case is read as a container.[7]

The image schema of containment also fits in with the 'mixed' messages of the song. In what could be described tentatively as the cultural space the song occupies, there are obvious themes of conflict and war, and the main lyrical message appears to be a disagreement with such horrific events. Yet Harvey depicts war as at once horrifying but at the same time inevitable. She creates her own moral trap by being part of and simultaneously opposed to the conflict and giving an overall confusing presentation of her persona. She never settles, and thus opens up various

[7] This is based on purely verse-chorus relations; as we will discuss below, the terminal climax itself offers another image schema possibility as well.

subject-positions for both our interpretation of her persona, but also the position we can adopt in relation to the song: are we/she oppressor, oppressed, dead, alive, man, woman, observer, actor, enemy, or ally?[8] We are never made aware explicitly whether Harvey is in power, therefore a creator of atrocity, or whether she is in fact a puppet, submissive to a power that forces her to witness and take part in the atrocities. This is one of the most pervasive mixed messages throughout the song. With her vocal remaining at all times in control of tone and pitch (despite the almost virtuosic (hysterical?) upward leaps in the verses) she is somewhat detached from the 'action'. Whichever persona we attribute to Harvey or even take up ourselves, the container schema is activated by the depiction of conflict and the characters within conflict being involved in the inevitable continuation of war.

At the terminal climax it is possible to suggest not only that other image schemata are activated, but also that this intensifies the previous sense of containment and therefore gives an overall reading of containment much more impact. It would appear that the song 'opens' up at this point: rather than revert back to an E harmony, the song remains in a D minor area until the end, which if read in light of the above would suggest it has escaped the container; the prominent autoharp riff has been replaced by a slide-guitar figure that is metrically stable and aligned with the downbeats; this new focus on the slide-guitar is also significant because, although it is drenched in reverb, it produces a single tone and offers the listener more pitch and textural clarity than the autoharp had. There is also an overall change in texture as certain 'dryer' elements such as the acoustic guitar placed to the right of the sound-box become more prominent. The (re)interpretation of Cochran's 'United Nations' phrase also offers a lyrical opening up because, read as non-cynical, the United Nations can be seen as a positive power with the ability to release us and Harvey from the oppression of our previous containment. These elements could therefore be read as activating the image schema of 'COMPULSION', which Johnson defines as the 'bodily encounter with physical forces that push and pull us' (Johnson, 2007, p. 137). Thus, the emergence into the terminal climax can be read in terms of us as listeners being pushed through the boundary of the container and oppression into a realm of possibility.

This interplay of image schemata could be read as a more global indicator of containment. On one level the terminal climax gives a sense of relief because we have trudged out of the oppressive swamp and entered a lighter and propulsive atmosphere. On a second level a global sense of containment is possible if we read the Cochran quotation as cynical. It intensifies an overall sense of containment because it alludes to the notion of 'outside' intervention as ineffective, and the

---

[8] There are also various other cultural 'mixed' messages within the song: Is she female, or is she male (and longing to see a woman's face)? What are the actual words that maketh murder? In which geographic and historical location is her depiction of war taking place?

United Nations as offering a futile attempt to break from the container.[9] The reading of local level containment within individual formal areas and specific musical areas of the song can therefore be combined with interplay on a wider structural-interpretive level. Combined at the global level we can not only suggest an intensification of the local level of containment, but also an overall sense of containment within the entire song.

It seems to us that the idea of image schemata has been a useful tool in grounding and untangling an interpretation of ambiguity in 'The Words That Maketh Murder'. The song's initial ambiguity has become less ambiguous, because each ambiguous element has been read in terms of cognitive experience and therefore become more functional and, subsequently, more meaningful in an overall interpretation of the song.

In conclusion, we would like to point to two issues arising from our reading of PJ Harvey's song which are, we feel, especially in need of further exploration. Firstly, the interpretive ramifications of image schemata, conceptual metaphors and cross-domain mapping are interesting on the level of individual analyses as they offer a way of processing the salient analytical characteristics of a song to be read in terms of our bodily, cognitive and perceptual experience. Secondly, naturally difficult terms such as 'ambiguity', which are quite often overused yet under-theorised could become more significant when read in terms of cognitive experience – although the creation of a flexible yet sustainable methodology that would enable us to read music in such a way would of course be no easy task.

References

Agawu, K., 1994. Ambiguity in Tonal Music: A Preliminary Study. In: A. Pople (ed.), *Theory, Analysis and Meaning in Music*. Cambridge: Cambridge University Press, pp. 86–107.

Breihan, T., 2011. PJ Harvey Talks New Album, Let England Shake, *Pitchfork*, [online] Available at: http://pitchfork.com/news/41160-pj-harvey-talks-new-album-let-england-shake/ [Accessed 23 May 2012].

Burstein, L.P., 2006. Of Species Counterpoint, Gondola Songs, and Sordid Boons. In: L.P. Burstein and D. Gagné (eds), *Structure and Meaning in Tonal Music*. Hillsdale, NY: Pendragon, pp. 33–40.

Echard, W., 1999. An Analysis of Neil Young's 'Powderfinger' Based on Mark Johnson's Image Schemata. *Popular Music*, 18(1), pp. 133–44.

[9] Another reading of the Cochran quotation as cynical could suggest the 'CYCLE' image schema has been activated. This part of the song is most suggestive of the notion that war is an inevitable repetition of death and brutality. Even the intervention of the United Nations cannot stop war. This would not have an effect on the overall sense of containment we can interpret in the song as, the cycle could be read as part of, instead of an intensifying contrast to the containment schema.

Gerryts, R., 2011. PJ Harvey's Eype Church Album to be Released. *Dorset Echo*, [online] 12 January. Available at: http://www.dorsetecho.co.uk/news/8785310.PJ_Harvey_s_Eype_Church_album_to_be_released/ [Accessed 30 September 2011].

Harvey, PJ, 2011. Local Rock Star PJ Harvey Talks to the News [interview]. *Bridport News*, [online] 26 January. Available at: http://www.bridportnews.co.uk/news/localnews/8813041.Bridport__Local_rock_star_PJ_Harvey_talks_to_the_News/ [Accessed 23 May 2012].

Johnson, M., 2007. *The Meaning of the Body: Aesthetics of Human Understanding*. London: University of Chicago Press.

Kettlewell, D. and Long, L.M., n.d. Autoharp, *Grove Music Online*, [online] Available at: http://www.oxfordmusiconline.com/subscriber/article/grove/music/01568 [Accessed 26 September 2011].

Lakoff, G. and Johnson, M., 1980. Conceptual Metaphor in Everyday Language. *The Journal of Philosophy*, 77(8), pp. 453–86.

Lakoff, G. and Johnson, M., 1999. *Philosophy in the Flesh: The Embodied Mind and Its Challenge to Western Thought*. New York: Basic.

Moore, A.F., Schmidt, P. and Dockwray, R., 2009. A Hermeneutics of Spatialization for Recorded Song. *Twentieth-Century Music*, 6(1), pp. 83–114.

Osborn, B., 2013. Subverting the Verse–Chorus Paradigm: Terminally Climactic Forms in Recent Rock Music. *Music Theory Spectrum*, 35(1), pp. 23–47.

Ripani, R., 2006. *The New Blue Music: Changes in Rhythm and Blues 1950–1999*. Jackson, MS: University Press of Mississippi.

Saslaw, J., 1996. Forces, Containers, and Paths: The Role of Body-derived Image Schemas in the Conceptualization. *Journal of Music Theory*, 40(2), pp. 217–43.

Spitzer, M., 2004. *Metaphor and Musical Thought*. London: University of Chicago Press.

Zbikowski, L., 2005. *Conceptualizing Music: Cognitive Structure, Theory, and Analysis*. Oxford: Oxford University Press.

Discography

Cochran, Eddie, 1958. 'Summertime Blues'. Liberty, F-55144.

Harvey, PJ, 2004. 'The Darker Days Of Me & Him'. *Uh Huh Her*. Island, 986 671–1.

Harvey, PJ, 2011. 'The Words That Maketh Murder'. *Let England Shake*. Island, 2753189.

Junior Wells' Chicago Blues Band, 1965. 'Good Morning Schoolgirl'. *Hoodoo Man Blues*. Delmar, DS-9612.

Chapter 10
Interpreting Meaning in/of Janelle Monáe's 'Tightrope': Style, Groove and Production Considered

Frederike Arns, Mark Chilla, Mikko Karjalainen, Esa Lilja, Theresa Maierhofer-Lischka and Matthew Valnes

This chapter examines both potential narrative meanings of, and referential meanings in, Janelle Monáe's 'Tightrope' by analysing the track through various methods and approaches. Primarily, the analysis covers stylistic referentiality and aspects of rhythm, 'groove' and harmony as they contribute to the delineation of form and narrative meaning in the lyrics. As the title implies, special attention is also paid to aspects of production – a less frequently studied parameter of recorded music – in the investigation of possible meanings of the song. For example, in addition to the formal aspects of the music, various choices in the methods of production can be interpreted as eliciting stylistic references. Some methods and theories from cultural studies are also brought in to contextualise the analysis within a broader discourse of Black music. In addition to the recording of the song, some audio-visual sources were also used for testing certain interpretations.

The study was conducted by six participants in the ASPM International Postgraduate 'Methods of Popular Music Analysis' Summer School in Osnabrück, Germany in September 2011, and makes extensive use of the writings and comments of the invited guest lecturers. For example, our analysis draws partly on the idea of the 'sound box' – as proposed by Allan Moore (2012, pp. 29–44) – to describe aural space created through production techniques such as reverberation and panning. In the hermeneutic field such techniques may be used – or the aural outcome may be interpreted – as affecting the subject positions (Zagorski-Thomas, 2012, pp. 138–9) or 'persona' (Moore, 2012, pp. 179–214) in the song. Our melodic/harmonic analysis is mostly, but not solely, based on Schenkerian terms. Walter Everett's work (for example 2008) and his discussions with the group also greatly helped us polish our analysis. The discussion below of the rhythmic layers of the song owes much to Anne Danielsen's work on groove in funk music (2006), as well as her commentary during our Summer School sessions. The other guest lectures also contributed to our analysis and are credited below.

In order to expand our theoretical framework and to partake in a broader scholarly discourse, some further, more culturally oriented, theories are incorporated as well. The African American literary scholar Henry Louis Gates

Jr.'s Signifyin(g) as 'turn[ing] on the play and chain of signifiers, and not on some supposedly transcendent signified' (Gates, 1983, p. 688) – a widely used theory in Black music scholarship (see Floyd, 1991; 1995; Monson, 1996; Tomlinson, 2002) – is valuable for understanding African American music as a performative phenomenon. Simon Frith's conception of hip-hop as 'performance of the making of meaning' (Frith, 1996) is also a helpful conceptualisation of the hermeneutic process in African American music.

With the aid of this collection of methods and theories we aim to show that popular music can be rich in meanings, but also that the methodology needs to be kept up to date in order to meet the artistic tools and processes used in contemporary music-making. The expansion of formal and textual analysis to consider various productional aspects aims at showing how Monáe combines historical styles in an eclectic manner that opens up the hermeneutic possibilities of the track.

The artist Janelle Monáe (Janelle Monáe Robinson) was born in 1985 in Kansas City, Kansas. Currently, she is living in Atlanta, Georgia, and has signed with Sean Combs's 'Bad Boy' label. Her song 'Tightrope', featuring the rapper Antwan 'Big Boi' Patton from the group OutKast, was the first single from her 2010 album *The ArchAndroid*. The single was nominated for a Grammy in 2011 and brought her to international prominence.

Stylistic References

One of the most prominent features of this track is its abundant use of stylistic references. As discussed below, Monáe appears to be evoking a number of African American styles such as funk, hip-hop, neo-R&B/retro trends, contemporary pop, 1960s R&B (doo-wop, Motown and its derivatives), big band jazz and the Afro-futurist cultural movement of the 1970s.

The funk references are most apparent, especially in the descending pentatonic bass line (Example 10.1). The strong emphasis on beat one with the lowest note of the pattern, the high register and the prominence of the bass line in the mix give it its funk characteristics, recalling similar features in the bass player Bootsy Collins's early work with James Brown, for example on 'Super Bad' (1970), or even James Jamerson's work in Motown recordings, like the Four Tops' 'Bernadette' (1967).[1]

[1] The high register of the bass is probably due to the low end of the spectrum being filled with the prominent bass drum sounds. The practical reasons for this notwithstanding, the higher frequencies of the bass line prominently featured in the mix are a funk characteristic. Thanks to Simon Zagorski-Thomas for helping us come to this conclusion.

Example 10.1 'Tightrope', the bass pattern as it appears in (a) the verses and (b) the choruses

Rhythmically, the syncopated and cross-rhythmic patterns in the collective groove of the ensemble, as well as the micro-rhythms in the drums and vocal patterns strongly indicate a funk groove. Stylistically, the minor-pentatonic vocal melody, the percussive horn stabs and guitar strokes and the heavy backbeat in the drums create an up-tempo funk groove. At 171 beats per minute, it is faster than many funk grooves from the 1960s: Brown's classic 'Cold Sweat' (1967) clocks in at only 112 beats per minute and his 'Papa's Got A Brand New Bag' at 126 beats per minute, yet the 'nice and rough' section of Ike and Tina Turner's funky 'Proud Mary' (1971) is closer in tempo at 176 beats per minute (Everett, 2008, pp. 319–20). The groove, thus, might be better interpreted as signifyin(g) on, rather than merely referring to, grooves of the 1960s and 1970s James Brown bands.

Further James Brown references can be heard in Monáe's vocal delivery, the percussive punches of the verse and especially the gritty pronunciation of the 'ee' vowel of words like 'scene', 'screen', 'lead' or 'machine', which are similar to Brown's vocal delivery in 'Get Up (I Feel Like Being A) Sex Machine' (1970).[2] Her dance moves, fashion and pompadour hairstyle in both the video of the song and in live performances also seem to pay homage to James Brown. Her momentary insertion of the 'performer persona' at the end of the song as she directs her band might be another reference to Brown, but it could also be more of a feature of African American popular music performance practice in general. In live performances, however, Monáe even goes as far as having the signature James Brown cape laid on her shoulders in the end of the show. In general, such features referring to James Brown's performance style are apparent in the video and in live performances of the song.[3]

The pre-verse introductions of the performers, the DJ scratches at 3:40 and the insertion of Big Boi's rap are clear hip-hop signifiers. Further contributing to this hip-hop aesthetic is the collage-like production technique, and features such as a synthesised bass drum sound that becomes prominent in the chorus starting at

---

[2] Thanks to Walt Everett for pointing out this reference.

[3] For the video see the official music video on Janelle Monáe's homepage: http://www.jmonae.com/video/tightrope-ft-big-boi-2/ [Accessed 9 October 2011]. For live versions see for instance 'Janelle Monae performs tightrope live at Glastonbury', http://www.youtube.com/watch?v=wBeAwmow1eA [Accessed 16 October 2011].

2:30, perhaps from a Roland TR-808 drum machine[4] widely used in 1980s post-punk/new-wave and dance music.[5] At the same time, the insertion of a rapped verse in the middle of an otherwise non-hip-hop song is also highly indicative of a contemporary pop style and the conventionalisation of hip-hop as part of pop music's stylistic repertoire in which such rap sections are common.

The overall 'retro' sound of the recording is a common trend in contemporary pop music, particularly the neo-R&B/Soul trend popularised by Amy Winehouse (in her 2006 album *Back to Black*), Duffy (in her 2008 single 'Mercy') and Adele (in her 2011 album *21*). Such 1960s retro sounds can be observed in all aspects of the recording. Some of the timbral signifiers are quite obvious: the background girl vocals are reminiscent of doo-wop and Motown, and the use of horns also connotes Motown and other 1960s R&B music. Moreover, the method of recording seems to imply a more 1960s 'retro' feel by using some specific production techniques. The song begins with an acoustic bass drum sound – distinct from the synthesised bass drum later in the song – that is reminiscent of the unmuffled bass drums from early 1960s recordings: examples vary from jazz drummers Max Roach and Tony Williams to rock drummers Ginger Baker (Cream) and Mitch Mitchell (The Jimi Hendrix Experience). This sound is rather uncommon for a contemporary pop music recording, which typically features only synthesised bass drum sounds like those in the second and third verses and the last chorus. Additionally, the horns appear to be recorded and processed as a section instead of separate instruments, a recording technique heard in 1940s big band recordings such as Duke Ellington's 'Take The A Train' (1941) or Count Basie's 'One O'Clock Jump' (1943). This recording technique can also be heard in the 1960s film music (for example early James Bond films).

Stylistic references extend beyond rhythmic, timbral and production techniques to encompass harmonic practices, as well. The extended tertian chords in the horn, string, and the dominant 7♯9 chords[6] on the guitar parts in the chorus could be heard as evoking jazz (see Example 10.4). The latter, however, could be interpreted as referring to Jimi Hendrix, since the dominant 7♯9 chord was a commonly used chord in such songs as 'Purple Haze' (1967), 'Foxy Lady' (1967) and 'Crosstown Traffic' (1968), or merely as a now conventionalised guitar voicing, since it is also heard in a number of pop/rock songs from the same era, such as the Beatles'

[4] Thanks to Simon Zagorski-Thomas for this observation.

[5] An illustrative example of the use of such drum machines in these genres is reflected in http://www.the-sisters-of-mercy.com/tech/doktors.htm [Accessed 2 September 2013].

[6] The chord has been marked enharmonically as 7♯9 by jazz musicians and theorists, and we adopt the same manner of marking it here. For Hendrix the source for this chord was probably jazz music, but for Monáe's arranger (or guitar player) it could have just as well been Hendrix. For further discussion see Lilja (2009, pp. 161–4, pertaining to heavy metal music). In a polyphonic context the phenomenon of coinciding minor and major thirds can already be found in what has been called 'the English cadence' due to its popularity in the sixteenth and seventeenth century English music (see Merwe, 1988, pp. 174–5).

'Taxman' (1966) and the Blood, Sweat & Tears' 'Spinning Wheel' (1969). Just as with the above-discussed references to James Brown's performance style, the referentiality here can also be interpreted through Gates's Signifyin(g) as 'turn[ing] on repetition of formal structures, and their difference' (Gates, 1983, p. 686). The reference is here evoked by the formal aspects, the chord notes, while the instrumentation is far from Hendrix's distorted guitar. On top of the above-mentioned significations, references to 'computers', the 'machine', the use of electronic noises and the overall theme of the entire album all appear to be evoking the Afro-futurism movement of the 1970s – an aesthetic movement combining Afro-centrism with science fiction and fantasy elements, represented by such artists as Sun Ra and George Clinton and his Parliament/Funkadelic. In the album *The ArchAndroid*, which is part of a large suite of concept albums called 'The Chase Suite', Monáe has embodied the persona of a cyborg sent from the future back in time to free citizens from tyranny, in a plot that mirrors Fritz Lang's science fiction classic *Metropolis* (1927). This connection is alluded to in the end of the song as Monáe introduces 'the funkiest horn section in Metropolis'.

However, the references go beyond African American musical idioms. In addition to the productional aspects, mentioned above, the string and horn parts later on in the song, with their lush orchestration and emphasis on sevenths and ninths, are indicative of the 1940s big band orchestration style and subsequent film music, such as the scores of some 1960s spy and thriller films. And to complicate the matter, a ukulele is added at the end, an unconventional choice among all the inter-textual referencing to other African American musical idioms in the song (see below).

There should remain no doubt that stylistic references seem to be a defining element of the recording. But the question remains as to 'why'? And further: What effect do these aesthetic choices have on our understanding of the piece? Marketability is a potential reason: simply put, 'retro' sounds and hip-hop were profitable in 2010. Since 'Tightrope' was the leading single off of a new album, it seems plausible that marketability was a significant factor in its production. How it might play into the meaning of the work will be discussed later. Before discussing meaning and interpretation, we would like to focus on one additional parameter of the song that was a large part of our analytical focus: rhythm and 'groove'.

The Groove

When examining the funk-like rhythms of 'Tightrope', one of the first issues that arose was how to understand the groove. What makes this groove so danceable, so funky, and how do the rhythmic elements interact with one another? Although groove has acquired many definitions in popular music scholarship, Robert Walser's description of groove as 'repetitive patterns of rhythm, harmony, and counterpoint' (Walser, 2004, p. 167) proves useful for this discussion as it views groove as a configuration of multiple musical parameters. The groove itself changes in subtle ways throughout the track, particularly with reference to the bass. By listening closely, one gets the impression that the basic pulse[7] of the song is changing from one section to another, a feeling that can be explained by various musical details.

Example 10.2 'Tightrope', the first two measures of the verse

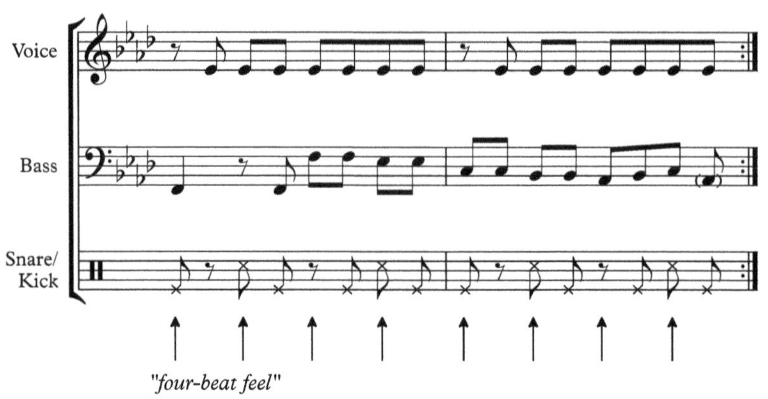

In the first verse, near constant quaver lines in both the bass and the percussive vocal delivery create a four-beat feel; crotchet pulses seem to be driving the rhythm (see Example 10.2). This is supported by the nearly ubiquitous quaver rhythm of the percussion. In the introduction, which consists primarily of percussion, this four-beat feel is established from the beginning: the loud snare drum as a crotchet upbeat leads to beat one, which, along with the bass drum and hand claps, sets the pulse. The rhythm of the guitar in the introduction complicates matters slightly.

The rhythm guitar figure from the introduction returns in the first chorus, and facilitates the change of the basic pulse in subtle but important ways (see Example 10.3). Rhythmically and harmonically, the guitar line creates a two-measure unit, and seems to change the basic pulse from the crotchet found in the verses to the minim level. In the first measure of the chorus, for instance, the guitar strongly articulates the downbeat, while lightly accenting the end of beat two with a quaver anticipating the third beat. In the following measure, two quavers on beats one and three strongly suggest that these beats receive the emphasis, while the guitar remains silent on beats two and four. At this point, Monáe's vocal line, which has

[7] We understand this term in the sense Anne Danielsen gives to it: 'In a groove, the rhythm triggers an underlying basic pulse, an internal beat … This internal beat is fundamental for playing, dancing and listening – in short, for understanding the groove. However, it does not need to be articulated as a part of the sounding music … Dancing, handclapping and stomping are, as a rule, externalizations of this internal beat' (Danielsen, 2006, p. 55).

Example 10.3 'Tightrope', the first four measures of the chorus

almost incessantly articulated quavers, slows down, coinciding with the opening of the guitar figure. The sustained notes she sings fall on (or at least very closely to) beats one and three of the guitar's two-measure unit.

Simultaneously, the rhythmic shift of the bass creates a two-measure grouping, but one that does not align with the guitar's grouping. While the descending pentatonic figure of the bass does not change (Example 10.1), its rhythmic placement creates a different grouping structure from that found in the verse. Because the descending figure now begins on the downbeat of the second measure, these two two-measure units – the guitar and vocal line on the one hand, the bass on the other – begin one measure apart. This creates a tension that propels the chorus forward. Indeed, as the song continues, more and more layers – rhythmic and harmonic – contribute to this feeling of tension and energy. Take, for example, the increased harmonic and melodic activity in subsequent verses and choruses: as more instruments enter – horns, synthesised strings and backing vocals – the harmonic rhythm accelerates, and the basic chords found in the verse and first chorus are expanded with the addition of extended tertian harmonies and altered pitches.

We 'tested' our hypothesis of the changing crotchet and minim pulse in the song by observing the dance moves in the song's video. The pulse, although not necessarily a sounding layer in the music, is a 'felt' layer among all the participants, particularly the dancers, as Danielsen argues (see footnote 7 above). The video shows clearly how Monáe's movements slow down as she sings 'Whether you're high or low …' as compared to the more active movements she gives during the verse.

What can be heard in the chorus is tension between the start of the descending bass figure, which begins in the middle of the guitar, and the vocal line's two-measure unit. That seems to be incredibly important in keeping a type of motion present. During the verse there is this almost 'nervous' energy from the constant

Example 10.4 Harmonic outline of Janelle Monáe's 'Tightrope' (2010), featuring Big Boi

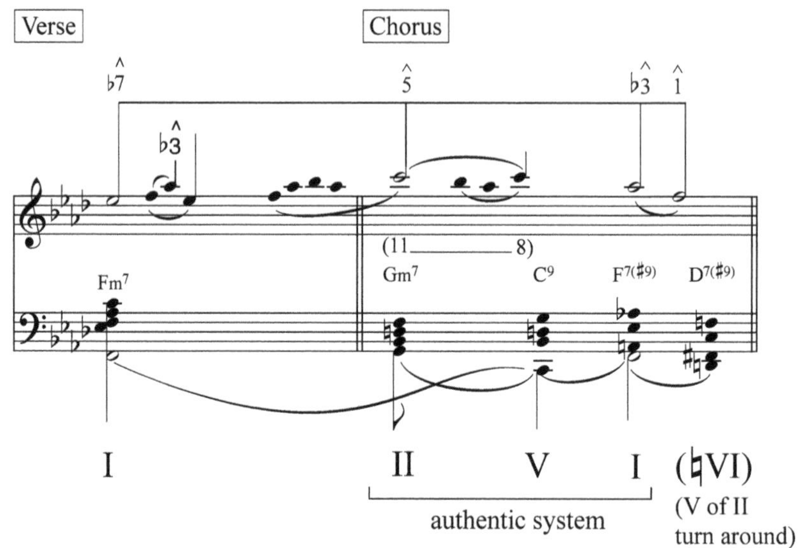

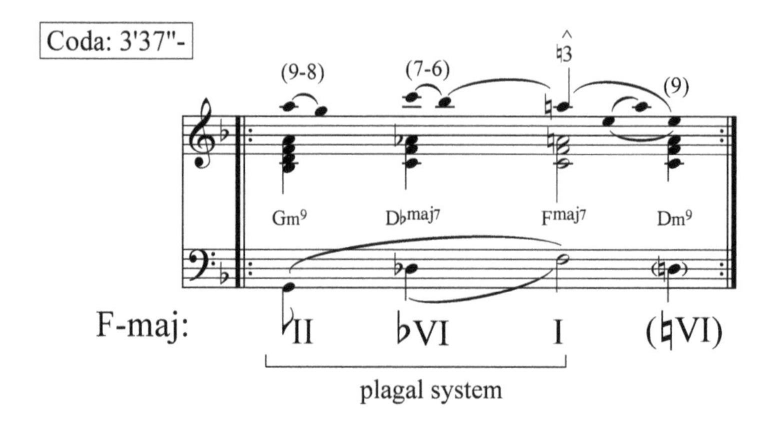

quavers, which is placated by the emergence of the half-note pulse. To contrast this, it seems like this 'unstable stability' is created by these two incommensurate layers.

But, what does this mean? Or perhaps better, how do these changes facilitate the creation of diverse interpretations? Rhythmic tension seems crucial to 'Tightrope'. Examining the lyrics can begin to provide possible interpretations of the track.

Meaning and Interpretation

In this song, Monáe uses the titular 'Tightrope' as a metaphor for dealing with the pressures of fame, as she confirms on her website.[8] When one is famous, one must negotiate both the 'highs' of praise, and the 'lows' of criticism. In 'Tightrope', dealing with these pressures is conceived of as a balancing act: you need to 'tip[toe] on the tightrope', so as to not let the highs or lows overcome you. This requires concentration, focus and perhaps most of all, confidence and self-assuredness. These themes play out in various ways in the music. The 'chain of signifiers' (Gates, 1983, p. 688) is turned on by various formal aspects of the track opening up its narrative and meta-narrative for multiple interpretations.

In the verses, Monáe sings a steady E♭, scale-degree flat-seven. This E♭ acts as, to borrow Philip Tagg's term, a 'visual anaphone' for the titular tightrope, a steady stream of notes, focused and linear (Tagg and Clarida, 2003, pp. 99–103). It may also create an expectation in the listener. Certainly, the repetition of one note cannot last forever and one might ask, 'when is it going to change?' or perhaps 'when is she going to fall off?' Amidst all of the rhythmic, harmonic and instrumental activity around her, Monáe holds her vocal position throughout the verses. Yet, her position is somewhat tenuous. For instance, she avoids the first downbeat of every measure, which creates an unstable rhythmic figure. In addition to that, her melodic focus is, after all, the flat seventh of the tonic chord, which in a traditional sense can be construed as a dissonance against the tonic F. However, at the same time this E♭ might be heard as a consonant note, simply a chord member in a Im^7 chord – the very chord that is outlined by melodic focal points of the verses and choruses (Example 10.4). If taken as a chord tone, it could be heard as yet another stylistic reference. The use of scale-degree flat-seven is, after all, rather characteristic to African American musical genres.[9]

---

[8] See the section 'Bio' on her homepage: http://www.jmonae.com/bio/ [Accessed 28 September 2011].

[9] There were some contentions in our group among how we should interpret this note – whether it should be considered a dissonance or consonance. The minor seventh has been regarded as a dissonance in Western music theory since the sixteenth century (see Zarlino, 1968). Although in African American genres like blues and rock 'n' roll, the lowered seventh has a more prominent, almost consonant, function. For more discussion of the broader issue of unresolved flat sevenths, see Averill (2003, pp. 163–8), Mathieu

The apex of this line hits the note A♭, scale-degree flat-three, three times on the word 'scene' (Example 10.4). The emphasis of the word 'scene', which, additionally, each time falls on a downbeat, draws attention to the source of her conflict: the scene, the limelight, fame. Furthermore, the responding background vocals in the chorus ('tip, tip on it') are pinched, nasal and placed in the background and to the side of the sound box in contrast to Monáe's clear and centred vocals. The character of these vocals taunts her, like a kid on the playground; or perhaps like a devil on one's shoulder.

The pressure is apparent, but Monáe – or rather her persona in the song – has her own way of dealing with fame, which is explicated in the chorus. The harmony moves from the incessant, static tonic and becomes goal-directed in the chorus. A minor ii chord (in the key of F minor or F dorian) moves to a dominant and then resolves to a tonic in the fifth measure of the chorus (Example 10.4), creating a harmonic and melodic goal on the word 'Tightrope'. The accent on beat one differs from the almost consistently empty beat one in the verses. Instead of omitting the first beat, she anticipates it in the choruses, except on the word 'tightrope'. Tipping, or tiptoeing, on the tightrope becomes the persona's central mantra in dealing with the pressures of fame.

The lyrics seem to also have a 'progression' built into them. The subject position changes during the song from a second person 'you' to a first-person 'I'. The second person seems not be referring to another, but is rather used passively ('you' as in 'one') or self-reflexively (Monáe's persona speaking to herself). In the first verse, she is outlining an obligation: when dealing with fame, one has to obey certain imperatives, is what she appears to be implying. She is also describing what others, 'they', will do to you when you are famous.

While the subject position 'you' remains in the first chorus, the second verse and second chorus have an encroachment of the active, first-person 'I'. Finally, at the end of the song with the third verse and third chorus, the subject position is entirely in the active first-person. Monáe's persona is no longer providing itself with a future imperative, but now asserting her intention. Moreover, she has completely ignored the pressures of others to focus entirely on what she is going to do, despite what others say. It is now 'I' rather than 'you' that has to tip on the tightrope.

Changes in Monáe's subject position play out musically as well, but rather ambiguously. The two-versus-four conflict in the basic pulse can be interpreted in terms of Monáe's subject position. Later verses are not consistently in two or four, but rather can be heard/felt in either way depending on the musical elements at work. The bass is nearly always variable: sometimes it projects four, sometimes two, sometimes it follows the rhythm in the bass drum, and occasionally it drops out altogether. The rhythmic conflict does not become more complicated, per se, but rather increasingly unpredictable. While the drums and guitar do not alter their

---

(1997, p. 126), Tallmadge (1984) and Lilja (2009, pp. 134–7, 197–8, pertaining to heavy metal music).

pattern, they do fall out of the texture on occasion. Monáe's vocal articulations, on the other hand, remain constant – perhaps this shows that Monáe's persona remains unaffected by the unpredictable rhythmic articulations.

Other aspects of the music do show a progression towards greater complexity. The taunting, unison background vocals first get doubled at the fifth, and then become parallel triads. The texture increases with an addition of horns (at first sustained, then as percussive stabs) as well as string counter-melodies adding further harmonic colour. Harmonically, the music moves from a rather clear F dorian with a minor-pentatonic melody towards a more complex F major with mode mixture, in cadential formulas that change from a goal-directed cadence in the Schenkerian sense (that is authentic system) towards a plagal system,[10] and towards increased use of extended tertian chords (see Example 10.4). The varied but still fundamentally root-position ii–V–i–vi progression of the chorus resurfaces as a rather sophisticated ii^9–$\flat VI^7$–I^7–vi^7 progression, with inversions and multiple spellings of scale-degree six. Stylistically, the most remote musical references – film music and the possible reference to Hawaiian music (see above) – are also heard in the end of the song.

Monáe's persona is not overcome by the pressure, but instead takes it in stride. In the final chorus, even with the bass not there to ground her, she ventures out on her own melodically by improvising additional melismas and reaching higher and higher into her range. Despite all of the increasing complexity, she has maintained her balance and even gained a self-assuredness by venturing out creatively in her vocal delivery. This is a far cry from the measured, steady and focused drone of the first verse. Her confidence comes to the fore when she leaves the song persona and enters into the 'performer' persona in the final section of the song. Instead of trying to psych herself up or declare her intention, she simply performs, and with command. She introduces the band (which is now larger and has a more complex arrangement), and tells them confidently to 'Shut up'! At this point, her vocal timbre changes radically: instead of the careful and precise articulations her 'tightrope persona' used to deliver, her 'performer persona' now literally dares to scream and shout while continuing her vocal melismas.

With a played coyness, she even implores the audience to allow her to play her ukulele 'just like a little lady'. In fact, this line, together with the ukulele sound used during this passage, can be interpreted as another inter-textual reference, for 'Ukulele Lady' was a song made famous by Vaughn DeLeath (1925).[11] DeLeath was especially known for her 'crooning style (sometimes with a little girl affectation)' (Gracyk and Hoffmann, 2000, p. 89). Monáe, however, seems to be ironically perverting this cliché of the 'little lady': her vocal timbre changes during

---

[10] The coda serves as an example where subdominant functioned chords (ii and $\flat$VI) have a greater degree of cadential independency than the Schenkerian term 'pre-dominant' would imply (see Everett, 2008, p. 222). For authentic and plagal systems, see Harrison (1994, pp. 28–42, 90–105).

[11] Thanks to Walter Everett for this reference.

the final section of coda, it gets a sort of lascivious quality and is more whispered. In contrast to verses 1 and 2, her intonation now follows the natural speaking melody. So her voice seemingly creates more intimacy, but actually Monáe is just playing with the listener, promising him or her a glimpse of her inner life, and thus certainly not being the shy little lady with her ukulele. Gates's Signifyin(g) could again provide the interpretative strategy for this performative moment. This time the 'chain of signifiers' (Gates, 1983, p. 688) turned on by Monáe's ukulele playing and verbal reference to it, point beyond the African American cultural sphere to larger questions about the position of women in the society. In musical terms, she is providing the most sophisticated harmonies of the song with her ukulele; perhaps hinting her disposition within the feminist discourse. Monáe's public persona appears to reflect this reading: she and her collective of like-minded artists, who refer to themselves as the 'Wondaland Arts Society', not only present themselves androgynously by wearing only tuxedos, but they also strive to act with the belief that 'women are much smarter than men'.[12] This reference and her performance may be interpreted as Monáe trying to challenge, subvert, or elevate women's position in society by constructing her own femininity through 'Tightrope' and the Wondaland Arts Society's rather radical view. Multiple interpretations are, however, possible depending on the listener's perspective. It could, then, be more fruitful to conceive of Monáe's performance as 'performing the making of meaning' in Simon Frith's sense (Frith, 1996, p. 115) rather than attempting to convey a clearly formed subject position. This open-ended view of the hermeneutic process is also in line with Gates's Signifyin(g), discussed above.

At the end of the song, it is as if she has, for the most part, made her peace with the pressures of fame, and is now allowing herself to enjoy her role as a performer. Yet, all the while, the mantra of maintaining her concentration stays at the back of her mind. The words 'I gotta keep my balance' echo from side to side in the stereo field in Monáe's 'own' voice. Even with all of this acquired confidence, it seems as if the persona had to constantly remind herself to maintain this focus and dedication.

So, what is the impetus for this newly found self-assuredness? The answer, we believe, lies in Big Boi's rap. It is after this rap that Monáe changes the subject position completely to 'I'. Big Boi, in a sense, provides the confidence that Monáe needs. He warns of the dangers of succumbing to the pressure and exudes a certain confidence in his delivery that only an established and personally centred artist could. At first his rhythm perfectly matches the rhythm of the bass line, in steady quavers and marking every single downbeat, in contrast to Monáe. But then halfway through the verse, he begins to stray from the bass (or perhaps 'that base') with his own self-assuredness, rapping with more rhythmic freedom by including more syncopations and his signature triplet quavers. In the same manner, Monáe

[12] See the 'about' section of the Wondaland Arts Society blog, http://wondaland.wordpress.com/about/ [Accessed 15 October 2011].

strays from her own rhythmic confines in her final chorus and the subsequent vocalisations in the break down.

A number of factors could be seen as supporting this interpretation. For one, this dynamic between Big Boi and Monáe exists not only within the song, but also with the two of them as performers in the real world. 'Tightrope' was Monáe's first major single, her first major exposure to the pressure of fame. Big Boi is the established artist who plucked Monáe out of obscurity. Her first recording was a guest spot on OutKast's 2006 *Idlewild* ('Call The Law'). It makes sense that Big Boi would be providing professional advice to his fledgling, young protégé.

Additionally, the music video could be seen as supporting our interpretation in various ways. Monáe finds herself in 'The Palace of the Dogs', an asylum where dancing is prohibited, as the introductory text in the video informs us. She slowly emerges from her private life in the Palace towards a more public atmosphere, picking up dancers along the way and performing her signature 'tightrope' dance. At one point, she enters into a performance space (the 'scene') where Big Boi is already performing to a crowd. He is reading his lyrics from a piece of paper on a music stand, which he confidently throws aside, demonstrating his own self-assuredness at the very moment when his rap leaves the strictness of the bass line and gains more rhythmic freedom. The rap inspires Monáe to jump up on the table and embrace her emergence 'on the scene' with confidence as she sings and performs her tightrope dance in the public eye. She is escorted back to her room by faceless guards who punish her for dancing, but in her mind, she escapes the confines of the asylum. The musical analogue of this could be the way she escapes the confines of the rhythm, as discussed above. By following her tightrope mantra, she has achieved a kind of transcendence above any pressures of fame. The highs or lows do not matter as much, because she knows how to remain above it all.

In conclusion, Janelle Monáe's 'Tightrope' is a track abundant with open-ended stylistic references, or significations, both in the formal and productional aspects of the music and in the ways it has been performed. Together with the formal aspects of the song, the use of contemporary production techniques has helped this track to become commercially viable in the popular music market. The narrative meanings of the track, however, also imply that its creation has not been a mere commercial endeavour for its makers. As discussed above, the narrative meanings of the track have levels that are highly personal to Janelle Monáe and others the listener can identify with, and find her/his own personal interpretations for. In short, 'Tightrope' contains many possible meanings and is open to many interpretations. Incorporating music analysis, cultural studies and African American studies, this essay has attempted to articulate some possible meanings.

Methodological Observations

The analysis displayed above is the result of a four-day working process which took place within an international group of music scholars: two male participants from

Finland, two male participants from the United States and two female participants from Germany. The two American members had some prior knowledge of the song and the artist (they could even be called fans), but had not critically examined the song, whereas the Europeans did not know the song at all.

After a first listening to the song, everybody discussed his or her first impressions. It was only in a second step that we examined Janelle Monáe's career, the concept behind the album and other background information. While these observations were not crucial to our interpretation, they orientated it in some ways. The video clip did not guide our interpretations, it only helped us to confirm various observations.

The things which struck us most at first hearing of the song upon which everyone agreed, were the stylistic and inter-textual references used in the song. At this point of our investigation we didn't know yet why they were used, but we already had a first trace to follow. During the course of our analysis, we would continue to discover more and more of them. We also had noticed the numerous changes of sound and texture throughout the piece, and in a next step, established its overall structure. After this, we split up tasks and each member of the group concentrated more closely on different things which we would discuss altogether later on: harmony, rhythms, lyrics and the organisation of the sound box.

The discussion and comparison of theses separate points quickly brought out one central question of our analysis: Why does the song 'groove' so much? In order to find an answer to this, we focused our attention on the bass line and on the rhythmic patterns that we identified as being a central driving force behind the groove. Removing the centre panning of the track allowed us to concentrate on these elements. For this we used the freely available software *Audacity*,[13] which allowed us to cancel out the sounds that were equally present on both the left and the right channels. Subsequently, we also found the lyrics important to the song and examined them more closely. With this, we were able to combine our first observations to our later findings and come to a general interpretation of 'Tightrope'.

Some general observations might be added. First, our working process might be described as an alternation of group and individual work; the group work was guided by the workshop lecturers sitting in in the sessions and providing valuable feedback. The heterogeneity of the group may have been its strong point: three nationalities, two continents, two sexes and different musical and academic backgrounds reaching from music theory to literary studies. Nevertheless, all ideas were discussed on an equal base and with respect. The actual writing of this article, based on a rough version written during the Summer School, was done via email correspondence. Much of the contextualisation of our analysis in terms of, for example, cultural studies resulted from this period of reflecting on the analysis and working on the text. The overall experience seemed so fruitful to us that we hope to continue to collaborate and share ideas across continents.

---

[13] http://audacity.sourceforge.net/ [Accessed 16 October 2011].

References

Averill, G., 2003. *Four Parts, No Waiting: A Social History of American Barbershop Harmony*. Oxford: Oxford University Press.

Danielsen, A., 2006. *Presence and Pleasure: The Funk Frooves of James Brown and Parliament*. Middletown, CT: Wesleyan University Press.

Everett, W., 2008. *Foundations of Rock*. Oxford: Oxford University Press.

Floyd, S.A., Jr., 1991. Ring Shout! Literary Studies, Historical Studies, and Black Music Inquiry. *Black Music Research Journal*, 11(2), pp. 265–87.

Floyd, S.A., Jr., 1995. *Power of Black Music: Interpreting Its History from Africa to the United States*. New York: Oxford University Press.

Frith, S., 1996. Music and Identity. In: S. Hall and P. du Gay (eds), *Questions of Cultural Identity*. London: SAGE, pp. 108–27.

Gates, H.L., Jr., 1983. The 'Blackness of Blackness': A Critique of the Sign and the Signifying Monkey. *Critical Inquiry*, 9(4), pp. 685–723.

Gracyk, T. and Hoffmann, F.W., 2000. *Popular American Recording Pioneers, 1895–1925*. London: Routledge.

Harrison, D., 1994. *Harmonic Function in Chromatic Music*. Chicago, IL: University of Chicago Press.

Lilja, E., 2009. *Theory and Analysis of Classic Heavy Metal Harmony*. Vantaa: IAML Finland.

Mathieu, W.A., 1997. *Harmonic Experience: Tonal Harmony from Its Natural Origins to Its Modern Expression*. Rochester, VT: Inner Traditions.

Merwe, P. v. d., 1988. *Origins of the Popular Style*. Oxford: Clarendon Press.

Monson, I., 1996. *Saying Something: Jazz Improvisation and Interaction*. Chicago, IL: Chicago University Press.

Moore, A.F., 2012. *Song Means: Analysing and Interpreting Recorded Popular Song*. Farnham: Ashgate.

Tagg, P. and Clarida, B., 2003. *Ten Little Title Tunes*. New York: Mass Media Music Scholars' Press.

Tallmadge, W., 1984. Blue Notes and Blue Tonality. *The Black Perspective in Music*, 12(2), pp. 155–65.

Tomlinson, G., 2002. Cultural Dialogics and Jazz: A White Historian Signifies. *Black Music Research Journal*, 22, pp. 71–105.

Walser, R., 2004. Groove as Niche: Earth, Wind & Fire. In: E. Weisbard (ed.), *This is Pop: In Search of the Elusive at Experience Music Project*. Cambridge, MA: Harvard University Press, pp. 266–78.

Zagorski-Thomas, S., 2012. Musical Meaning and the Musicology of Record Production. In: D. Helms and T. Phleps (eds), *Black Box Pop. Analysen populärer Musik*. Bielefeld: Transcript, pp. 135–47.

Zarlino, G., 1968. *The Art of Counterpoint – Part Three of Le Istitutioni Harmoniche, 1558*. Translated from Italian by G.A. Marco and C. Palisca. New York: Norton.

Filmography

Lang, Fritz, 1927. *Metropolis*. UFA.

Discography

Adele, 2011. *21*. XL Recordings, XLCD 520.
Beatles, The, 1966. 'Taxman'. *Revolver*. Parlophone, PMC 7009.
Blood, Sweat & Tears, 1969. 'Spinning Wheel'. *Blood, Sweat & Tears*. Columbia, 9720.
Brown, James, 1965. 'Papa's Got A Brand New Bag'. *Papa's Got A Brand New Bag*. King Records, KS 938.
Brown, James, 1967. 'Cold Sweat'. *Cold Sweat*. King Records, KS 1020.
Brown, James, 1970. 'Get Up (I Feel Like Being A) Sex Machine'. *Sex Machine*. King Records, KS 1115.
Brown, James, 1970. 'Super Bad'. *Super Bad*. King Records, KS 1127.
Count Basie, 1942. 'One O'Clock Jump'. *One O'Clock Jump*. Columbia, JCL 997.
DeLeath, Vaughn, 1925. 'Ukulele Lady'. Columbia, 361–D.
Duffy, 2008. 'Mercy'. *Rockferry*. Island/Mercury, 001082201.
Ellington, Duke, 1941. 'Take The A Train'. Victor, 27380.
Four Tops, 1967. 'Bernadette'. *Reach Out*. Motown, MS 660.
Jimi Hendrix Experience, The, 1967. 'Purple Haze'. *Are You Experienced?* Track, 612 001.
Jimi Hendrix Experience, The, 1967. 'Foxy Lady'. *Are You Experienced?* Track, 612001.
Jimi Hendrix Experience, The, 1968. 'Crosstown Traffic'. *Electric Ladyland*. Track, 613008/9.
Monáe, Janelle feat. Big Boi, 2010. 'Tightrope'. *The ArchAndroid (Suites II and III)*. Bad Boy Entertainment, 7567898983.
OutKast feat. Janelle Monáe, 2006. 'Call The Law'. *Idlewild*. LaFace Records, 82876752661.
Turner, Ike and Tina, 1971. 'Proud Mary'. *Workin' Together*. Liberty, LST-7650.
Winehouse, Amy, 2006. *Back to Black*. Island/Universal, 1713041.

Chapter 11
'Can't Keep it to Myself': Exploring the Theme of Struggle in the Fleet Foxes' 'Helplessness Blues'

Paul Carter, Samantha Englander, Alberto Munarriz, Jadey O'Regan and Eileen Simonow

Introduction

Much has been written about the way in which our personalities, genders, social contexts, races and educational backgrounds inform our musical choices. These parameters not only guide our decisions when it comes to the music to which we choose to listen, but they also guide the way we react to it. As we all know, the resulting experience is a highly personal one. At the same time, alongside the uniqueness of this relationship we know that there are numerous natural concurrences between our experiences and those of others. This is what allows for music's communicative power.

We rarely have the opportunity to explore the delicate balance that exists between these two inextricable sides of the musical experience. Often our non-scholarly discussions about particular songs take place among friends, colleagues, other fans and the like; in short, with 'a community' whose members share enough background, pertinent knowledge and taste as to favour considerably similar interpretations. The situation we were confronted with at the Osnabrück summer school was considerably different. In a small room of a German university, five researchers from four different countries (Australia, Argentina, Germany and the US) sat with the intention of examining a song none had a particular relationship with, the Fleet Foxes' 'Helplessness Blues'. Although most of us were all familiar with the band and their work, our relationships with them were considerably different, and understandably so: although we shared similar socioeconomic positions, racial backgrounds and levels of education within the Western tradition, our cultural backgrounds, genders, academic disciplines, interests and tastes varied.

After our initial contact with the song we floated first impressions that immediately reflected some of our differences. Most noticeable were the discrepancies that existed between our approaches to analysis. We gradually managed to reconcile our major discrepancies but, in retrospect, it is evident that these methodological differences came to exacerbate the kind of interpretative disagreements one is likely to find in a setting like the one in which this analysis was taking place. In spite of this situation, however, we soon realised that we were able to agree on the existence of one underlying theme: the idea of 'conflict' or 'struggle'. This was the theme that began to guide our analysis. Further into the research, we found out that we were on the right path. In their promotional biography accompanying the release of their album *Helplessness Blues*, Robin Pecknold, lead-singer and songwriter of the Fleet Foxes, shed light on how important for the group was the theme we had identified. He notes:

> The last thing I'll talk about is the title. It's called Helplessness Blues for a number of reasons. One, it's kind of a funny title. Secondly, one of the prevailing themes of the album is the struggle between who you are and who you want to be or who you want to end up, and how sometimes you are the only thing getting in the way of that. That idea shows up in a number of the songs. (Pecknold, 2011)

Interestingly, the theme that we initially considered central to the song was soon going to prove itself relevant outside its context. For reasons intimately tied to the above-mentioned differences, the interaction between the members of the group grew increasingly conflictive. We all agree that, as Allan Moore puts it in his introduction to *Analyzing Popular Music*, 'analysis is an issue of interpretation' (Moore, 2003, p. 6), an account of something that might be taken in a number of ways. The situation, however, required us to find a common ground between the various interpretations we had produced, something that proved to be more difficult than we would like to admit.

We can examine the theme of struggle or conflict, as expressed through the singer, in numerous ways. First, the generational conflict that might be seen in a close reading of the lyrics, is emphasised and enacted in and through the musical material. The Fleet Foxes' conflict is obvious in an additional statement by Robin Pecknold:

> I think this music draws influence and inspiration from popular music and folk rock of the mid '60s to the early '70s, folks like Peter Paul & Mary, John Jacob Niles, Bob Dylan, The Byrds, Neil Young, CSN, Judee Sill, Ennio Morricone, West Coast Pop Art Experimental Band, The Zombies, SMiLE-era Brian Wilson, Roy Harper, Van Morrison, John Fahey, Robbie Basho, The Trees Community, Duncan Browne, the Electric Prunes, Trees, Pete Seeger, and Sagittarius, among many others. I'd say it's a synthesis of folk rock, traditional folk, & psychedelic pop, with an emphasis on group vocal harmonies. Astral Weeks was a big inspiration on this album, if not always in sound then in approach. The raw emotion in Van Morrison's vocals and the trance-like nature of the arrangements were very inspiring for this album! (Pecknold, 2011)

Second, the Fleet Foxes evidence their struggle with the label 'new-folk' as an identity conflict by trying to relate to almost uncountable sounds, styles and social contexts. Central to this issue is the question of who they are as a 'new-folk' group and how they position themselves within the continuum of a genre with very loaded connotations. They have issues following in the footsteps of those who they acknowledge as their influences and mention musical connections that one cannot clearly hear in their music. One is left with the impression that they cannot reach their ambitious goals, and aside from their admired musical predecessors, they lack the social and political awareness of the folk and folk-rock movement.

The following analysis looks at the various ways in which these struggles and conflicts are apparent throughout 'Helplessness Blues'. The paper is divided in three sections that examine the poetic content of the song, its musical material and the production of the track as it appears on the album, respectively.[1] Given the specificities that guide the articulation of meaning, the set of analytical tools presented in this work would have to be re-thought and re-developed for the examination of other works. Since the Fleet Foxes themselves have pointed to the theme of conflict as permeating not just 'Helplessness Blues', the song, but also the similarly titled album, we consider that this analysis opens the door to a more extensive examination of how these themes have been explored throughout the album and the numerous implications their pervasiveness could have.

Establishing a Lyrical Narrative

There are several possible interpretations of the lyrical narrative in 'Helplessness Blues', however, one in particular seems to us to be cohesive enough to encompass the contrary nature of the lyrics across the entirety of the song. The narrative is divided into two musically contrasting sections, which will be referred to as 'Section A' and 'Section B'.

In Section A, we find the persona of the singer isolated and alone, contemplating the meaning of his life. In the first verse, he reflects on his upbringing, and recalls being told as a child that he was special and unique. However, he seems uncomfortable with this idea and presents a different lifestyle of safety and purpose, contemplating that he might become a small part in a larger 'machinery', an idea that contrasts with the ideals of being unique which were instilled into him in his youth. The singer's persona sways between two extremes throughout Section A. On the one hand he remembers the idealism that accompanied his upbringing, but on the other hand finds himself in a dystopian machinery, trying to oppose 'armies of night' and 'men who move only in dimly-lit halls'. But in the second verse, upon consideration, he starts to realise that in doing so, he must compromise his own ideals, which he feels unable to do: he does not want to 'bow down' and allow someone else to 'determine [his] future for [him]'. He admits to

[1] Although the material presented in this chapter has been read, reviewed and edited by all the members of the group, the section comprising it have been written by different pens. As a consequence, the reader may find a series of stylistic discrepancies that we hope will not interfere greatly with the flow of the argument.

his own confusion about the direction of his life in verse 1 of Section A: neither does he want to be a 'unique snowflake' nor part of a machine that restricts his freedom. This supposedly refers to a coming-of-age conflict, in which he opposes something he was told when younger, although he has not resolved the multiple conflicts that come with finding out where he wants his life to lead to.

In the third and final verse of Section A we learn that in his confusion the singer's persona finds reliability only in the fact that the world outside overwhelms him to the extent that he cannot articulate himself through speech any more, but instead expresses himself through music: 'everything that I see of the world outside is so inconceivable often I barely can speak' and instead of speaking he has turned to sing 'Helplessness Blues', but now is ready to even question the use of doing so. Later sections of this chapter will show how musical relationships express the concerns of the singer's persona.

The beginning of Section B is clearly marked with various musical changes to be discussed in this chapter's various sections to follow. The persona of the singer, in what may be a daydream, imagines an orchard, a place where he could work physically with his bare hands instead of facing an inner conflict. He conjures up the image of a woman with 'gold hair in the sunlight', with whom he apparently wants to live a simple but happy life. Throughout this article, Section B is referred to as 'dreamy', a connotation derived from a close reading of the lyrics as well as an interpretation of the musical material, which will be discussed later in this chapter. We are presented a poetic contrast between the dark and the light. Whereas the 'armies of night', the 'machinery' and the 'dimly-lit halls' refer to a dark dystopia, in Section B, we are introduced to 'gold hair in the sunlight' and 'my light in the dawn' – a hopeful dream that the singer's persona imagines.

The last line of the song is probably the hardest to interpret in terms of a coherent lyrical narrative: 'Someday I'll be like the man on the screen.' The instruments stop as if the protagonist awakens to a somewhat sombre reality. The screen functions here as the opposite to the nature-oriented dream depicted in the orchard. On the television or movie screen we are presented with ideal people, or at least we are tempted to perceive them as ideal. Being on screen might represent success or some other form of fulfilment that the singer's persona either works towards or finds himself working towards, because society makes him do so.

The conflicts presented in 'Helplessness Blues' might refer to those of an individual in a society with particular rules or obligations. It is as much about adopting other ways of living as it is about trying to establish one's own. Whereas the American folk music of the 1960s – best represented by Bob Dylan, Joan Baez and the Byrds – can be characterised as being highly political, the music of Fleet Foxes has a similar sound but is limited to self-centredness and self-adulation – perhaps being a result of the 1960s striving for individualism and freedom of choice. The song seems to remind us of the folk music of the 1960s, but lacks any political stance.

Analysis of Musical Material

Formal Considerations

In her article 'Narrative Paradigms, Musical Signifiers, and Form as Function in Country Music', Jocelyn Neal (2007, p. 41) reminds us that structural elements not only define how a song's textual themes are presented to the listener, but more importantly, she writes, they determine 'how the listener receives, parses, and comprehends the song'. Neal's clarification may seem unnecessary to many and yet, as Everett notes (Everett, 2000, p. 272), the role form and design play in the articulation of meaning often remains overlooked in popular music analysis.[2] Contrary to the template-based approaches that commonly guide the analysis of formal structures, gauging their 'communicative role' relies on a detailed examination of the particularities of each setting.

In spite their undeniable importance, form and design are features that listeners would seldom point at as saliently relevant in guiding their understanding of a song; timbre, vocal quality, mode, melody, tempo and rhythmic drive are more likely choices. There are, however, examples where the communicative weight of these parameters is unavoidably evident; songs like 'A Day In The Life' by Lennon and McCartney or Ike and Tina Turner's famous version of John Fogerty's 'Proud Mary' are clear examples. Something comparable occurs in 'Helplessness Blues'.

As previously noted, there was no agreement among the members of the group as to what the band's intended message was and we had a number of dissimilar interpretations. Despite these different readings, however, we all recognised how important formal and design considerations were in guiding them. Through the dissecting process that followed our initial exposure to the composition, new interpretative possibilities emerged. As expected, through selective listening, a deeper involvement with the text, a closer examination of the musical surface, and some background research on the band, we began to establish some connections that deepened our understanding of the song and what we considered the composer's intended message could have been.[3] Interestingly, the fundamental dichotomy that we initially sensed remained largely unaffected by the interpretative discrepancies that existed between the members of the group. This situation led us to realise that, as Neal (2007, p. 42) suggested, our understanding of the song was highly influenced by the specific way in which the story was presented through the song's form.

---

[2] Following the distinctions established by Felix Salzer in *Structural Hearing* (1962) we understand form as the organisation and division of the overall structure of a composition into definite sections, and the relation of those sections to each other, and design as the organisation of the compositional surface, in terms of its thematic and rhythmic material.

[3] We were never in a position to ascertain what this message was; efforts to contact writer Robin Pecknold and other members of the Fleet Foxes proved unsuccessful.

As previously mentioned, the narrative of 'Helplessness Blues' presents us with two divergent facets of one distraught individual. Based on the frequent real versus imaginary topos, the contrast is set between the character's existential problems and an idyllic world he imagines to escape them. The formal scheme of the composition is used to enact this main thematic dichotomy by setting the character's 'real' and 'imaginary' facets over unmistakably distinct musical textures. From the listener's perspective, the demarcation is primarily established by a conspicuous change in the metric structure of the song (2:48). Although not abrupt, the move from duple simple to compound triple metre is certainly unexpected. There is no transitional material to speak of; the last measure of the opening section is extended by two quarter notes and turned into what can be interpreted as a bar of 6/4 (see Example 11.1). Over the last four quarter notes of this extended measure two heavily articulated quarter-note triplets, setting the words '... soon, myself', disrupt the regularity imposed by the preceding duple simple-metre texture. The effect is accentuated by a notable slowing of the tempo, by approximately 20 beats per minute produced within the 6/4 bar. The perceived decrease in momentum produced by the rallentando over the quarter-note triplets is rapidly counteracted by the reinterpretation of the slowed-down quarter note that closed the initial section as a dotted eighth note in the subsequent one.

Example 11.1 'Helplessness Blues', transition from Section A into B

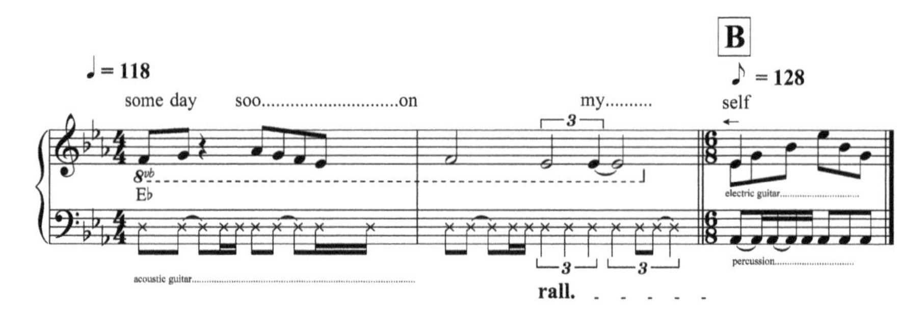

Interestingly, further examination of the sections evidenced other expressions of the three-against-two dichotomy. A hemiola appears in the last two bars of the opening eight-bar phrases in the first two verses in Section A. As in the closing of Section A, the rhythmic gesture is articulated by setting quarter-note triplets over the prevailing pulse, this time as four consecutive triplets over the span of the phrase's last two 4/4 measures. The effect is the apparent allargando of the phrase's end and a concomitant emphasis on the message: the crumbling of the character's perception of uniqueness ('... distinct among snowflakes, unique in each way you'd conceive') and his subsequent resignation to the forces of the dystopic context ('in some great machinery, serving something beyond me'). From a formal perspective, these occurrences could be interpreted, retrospectively, as hinting at the forthcoming metric change; however, such interpretations hinge heavily on our extended involvement with the song. Even if the listener does not establish this connection, it is likely that he or she would register the recurrence of the quarter-note triplets. This repetition provides a sense of formal order.

Up to this point the materialisation of the formal concept has hinged on an examination of the song's metric/formal structure. In the following sections metre, rhythm, harmony and melody will be carefully analysed. Before that, however, a brief comment on the use of texture and timbre is needed. Although established primarily by the previously examined metric shift, sectional contrast is emphasised by instrumentation. Throughout the opening section, the singer delivers his complaint over a series of overdubbed acoustic guitars. The rhythmic density of the patter articulated by the strumming varies, but this does not change the overall 'acoustic feel' of the section. At the initial downbeat of Section B, after the slowed-down triplets, electric bass, kick drum and electric guitar appear and establish a clear change of prevailing texture. This is maintained until the end of Section B, when most of the instruments fade out. Although still in triple compound metre and accompanied by sparse drumming, the song finds its end with a texture that is reminiscent of the acoustic feel that characterised the opening. Without altering the overriding binary subdivision, this invocation of the opening section establishes a connection that strengthens the composition's overall formal cohesion.

Rhythm and Metre

The rhythm and metre in 'Helplessness Blues' function on two interpretive levels. On a superficial level, they contribute to a sonic manifestation of conflict as a concept, presenting the listener with various metric contrasts and rhythmic dissonances. On a deeper level, they provide further insight regarding the *essence* of this conflict, and the complex nature of the battle between fantasy and reality.

The listener can most readily hear the superficial demonstration of conflict in the contrast between Section A and Section B in the song's overall form. Section A presents the listener with a simple quadruple metre with predictable phrase structure. Each of the three verses is 16 measures long, divided into four lines that are 4 measures each. Each verse is followed by an eight-measure refrain that is sectioned into two four-measure lines. Between each pair of verses of the strophic first section we find transitional material that is four measures long. With the exception of a brief overlap when the last bar of the refrain and the first bar of the transitional material are the same, the metric organisation of Section A is straightforward and hypermetrically predictable.

Section B, in contrast, employs a compound metre with bars of varying numbers of beats, resulting in an unpredictable phrase structure. For the majority of the section, the metre is most easily understood as compound duple, with occasional measures that are expanded into compound triple or truncated into compound single. Throughout Section B, the amount of time allotted to each line's delivery tends to be inconsistent and uneven, as demonstrated in Table 11.1. While there is some consistency – the second line of each of the three verses lasts for seven beats, for instance – Section B consists primarily of unpredictable and uneven phrases that seem to the listener to begin and end in an improvised manner that is standard in traditional American folk music.

This contrast between the two sections illustrates the lyrics perfectly. On one hand, the protagonist wants to be unique and flourish as an individual, and on the other he wants to contribute to a greater good, at the inevitable expense of his individuality. Section A, with its uniform and predictable style, sonically illustrates the 'functioning cog' that is indistinct but operative. Section B, utilising erratic hypermetre and varying phrase lengths, represents the distinct snowflake, asserting uniqueness through unpredictability. Furthermore, the unpredictable and improvised structure of Section B lends itself to the dreamlike quality of the section as a whole, as dreams are by nature uncertain and illusory.

Table 11.1 'Helplessness Blues', phrase structure of Section B

	Lyric	**Number of beats per line (♩.): natural groupings of those beats, as determined by harmonic rhythm and vocal phrasing**	
Intro	[Instrumental]	12:	2, 2, 2, 2, 2, 2
Verse 1	If I had an orchard, I'd work till I'm raw	10:	2, 2, 2, 2, 2
	If I had an orchard, I'd work till I'm sore	7:	2, 1, 2, 2,
	And you would wait tables and soon run the store	7:	2, 1, 2, 2,
Verse 2	Gold hair in the sunlight, my light in the dawn	11:	2, 3, 2, 2, 2
	If I had an orchard, I'd work till I'm sore	7:	2, 1, 2, 2,
	If I had an orchard, I'd work till I'm sore	7:	2, 1, 2, 2,
Verse 3	Oh, Oh …	11:	2, 3, 2, 2, 2
	Oh, Oh …	7:	2, 1, 2, 2,
	Someday I'll be like the man on the screen	5:	2, 1, 2*
Outro	[Instrumental]	9:	2*, 2, 2, 2, 1

*These two beats overlap

Not everything about Section B is unpredictable, however. As Table 11.1 also demonstrates, the tripartite form within the section is in no way unusual. It is, in fact, the same structure we have just heard in Section A: three verses presented strophically. The uniformity of Section B's form can be interpreted as well. Perhaps even in the dream sequence of the song, uniformity and lonely associations seep in from Section A; even in his fantasies, the protagonist cannot escape the weight of reality. This deeper understanding the music provides the listener not only illustrates the existence of conflict, but also elucidates the complex nature of it.

In addition to an unpredictable phrase structure, Section B is also different from Section A due to the shifting of metric accents upon the repetition of melodic material. Example 11.2 illustrates the beginnings of the first and second verses of Section B, at 3:05 and 3:39, respectively. The melodic material is essentially the same, but the metric strength of that material is inconsistent: in the first verse, the majority of the material is a long anacrusis with the strong arrival just before '-chard'. In the second verse, the material itself begins on a strong arrival after the substantially shorter anacrusis that consists only of the eighth note, 'gold'. The shift in strength of this material is achieved by cues in the accompaniment: arpeggios in the electric guitar during the introduction of the section establish a compound duple metre that clearly states where the strong beats fall leading up to the first verse, and a loud percussion entrance indicates where the strong beat falls in the beginning of the second verse.

Example 11.2a 'Helplessness Blues', verse 1 of Section B (3:05)

Example 11.2b 'Helplessness Blues', verse 2 of Section B (3:39)

This re-contextualisation of established melodic material is another instance where the listener can gather a deep understanding of the *nature* of the persona's conflict, not only its mere presence. There is a real crisis of identity taking place, and the listener would not know, outside the context of the accompaniment, whether certain material were metrically weak or strong. This crisis of identity occurs in the dream sequence of the song, the section during which, with a superficial understanding of the bipartite form, one would dismiss the material as existing within a fantasy, unobtainable in reality. But this identity crisis seeps into the fantasy, and the listener can understand that as an overbearing reminder; even as he dreams and fantasies about another life (either in a literal orchard, or something else that the orchard represents), the weight of reality is always present to the protagonist. This further illustrates the interpretation gained from the previously mentioned formal consistency between the two large sections of the song, that the lonely Section A leaks into the dream sequence, weighing on the protagonist's fantasies.

Finally, rhythm plays an interpretive role in 'Helplessness Blues', complicating our understanding of the nature of the protagonist's conflict. While the uniform structure and re-contextualised melodic material previously discussed can lend themselves to an interpretation that Section A is contaminating Section B in some way, the rhythm sheds a brighter light in the other direction: rhythmic patterns associated with the dreamlike Section B slip into the more solemn Section A, indicating that perhaps there is an optimistic attitude present within the protagonist, even in the darkest and most confused times. Example 11.3 illustrates an instance where we hear a measure of straight quarter-note triplets in the very first verse of Section A.

From the beginning, there is a foreshadowing of the compound duple metre that is to come, and after we hear the song for the first time, we understand that it represents something hopeful, unpredictable and not alone. In direct contrast to our other interpretations, now the dream sequence is seeping into reality, and a lighter interpretation is gained.

Example 11.3 'Helplessness Blues', triplets in Section A (0:38)

It seems obvious on first listening that 'Helplessness Blues' employs rhythm and metre to convey the idea that the song's protagonist is experiencing conflict, an idea that completely supports the lyrics. But further investigation into rhythm and metre yields a much deeper, more lucid and satisfying understanding of what that conflict is like, and how the protagonist experiences that conflict. The easily missed formal consistencies across the two sections of the song provide a deeper grasp of the recognisable hypermetric inconsistencies across the sections; the re-contextualised melodic material that begins each verse in the dream sequence sheds light on the instability the protagonist feels, even playing on the ideas of 'weak' and 'strong', which can be applied to the protagonist as well as the metre; and the triplets that pervade the first half of the song play on ideas that are most readily associated with the second half of the song, allowing for an optimistic interpretation that the protagonist is keeping his chin up in the darkest of times. This song is not just about conflict in general; it is about the unique conflict experienced by the song's protagonist. A thorough analysis of 'Helplessness Blues' allows us to gain a clearer understanding of this complex conflict that is multifaceted and experienced in several simultaneous ways.

Pitch Structure

Simple as folk music can be harmonically and melodically, 'Helplessness Blues', incorporates several devices that effectively serve to amplify certain core aesthetics and meanings the song conveys in other parameters. The song draws upon a very basic set of melodic and harmonic materials, in that, barring one instance near the end of the song, not only is the pitch set entirely diatonic, but the harmonic palette is comprised completely of tonic and subdominant harmonies, or extensions of and substitutions for them.

Melodically, the verse sees an accretion of scale degrees through its first few measures where, by bar three, scale degrees $\hat{1}$, $\hat{2}$, $\hat{3}$, $\hat{5}$ and $\hat{6}$ are used – explicitly spelling out the major-pentatonic collection on the tonic. What is quite effective in this unfurling of the scalar materials is the arrival and maintaining of $\hat{6}$ for the words 'somehow unique, like a …'. One bar later, supported by a tonic major 7 chord, $\hat{7}$ is offered, sung in repeated-note fashion over the lyrics 'snowflake, distinct among snowflakes …' followed by a fall through the scale to $\hat{3}$, supported by the phrase-ending tonic chord, over the lyrics 'unique in each way you'd conceive' (see Example 11.4).

The support for Section A's verse and chorus[4] is characterised by the tuning Robin Pecknold uses on his 1967 Gibson 12-string, but also by a small set of chords that 'deny' the dominant function in their route to deliver colouration and support to the narrative. The 'Open D' tuning Pecknold uses is one in which a root position, fully formed D chord is created without stopping any of the strings. So simply strumming the guitar's unstopped strings with a capo on the first fret will produce a richly voiced tonic chord for the key of E (see these sonorities in Example 11.1). But partly due to this tuning and the chordal possibilities it naturally suggests on the fretboard, the harmony in the verse moves only to IV (in second inversion) and back to I, with the exception of the tonic major 7 chord used in the middle of the phrases, the chord under which $\hat{7}$ gets its support. This creates an effective paradox: a somewhat moderately liberating 'flight' of the melody up through $\hat{7}$ and back, over chords always 'tethered' by $\hat{1}$ in the bass. The imagery here could easily be one of a fanciful flight in a uniquely coloured hot air balloon, but one that is always restrained by external, or in the case of the speaker here, self-imposed, forces.

The verses generally portray a conservative atmosphere during Section A; the first verse is especially spare, as it is the only part of the section where only one vocalist is heard. But the choruses offer an alter-ego bolstering of the protagonist's confidence and self-assessed stature. The two-voice, sung parallel lines beginning each of the choruses are impressive for their front-of-the-mix dominating presence, which is only made more powerful by the range these achieve in the first half of these choruses. In addition, the energetic strumming in these sections presents the arrival of full-on, root-position subdominant chords, that (finally) convey a deliberate statement of purpose. This statement is long-awaited, because in the preceding verses, all the harmonies presented in the accompaniment were either tonic harmonies or occasional other harmonies presented over a pedal 1. These

[4] After a strumming intro on the I chord, the form of Section A is almost exclusively three verse-chorus pairs, with strumming similar to the intro between these paired form units. This makes for a basic form of V1–Ch, V2–Ch, V3–Ch.

Example 11.4 'Helplessness Blues', voice leading and harmonic support for Section A

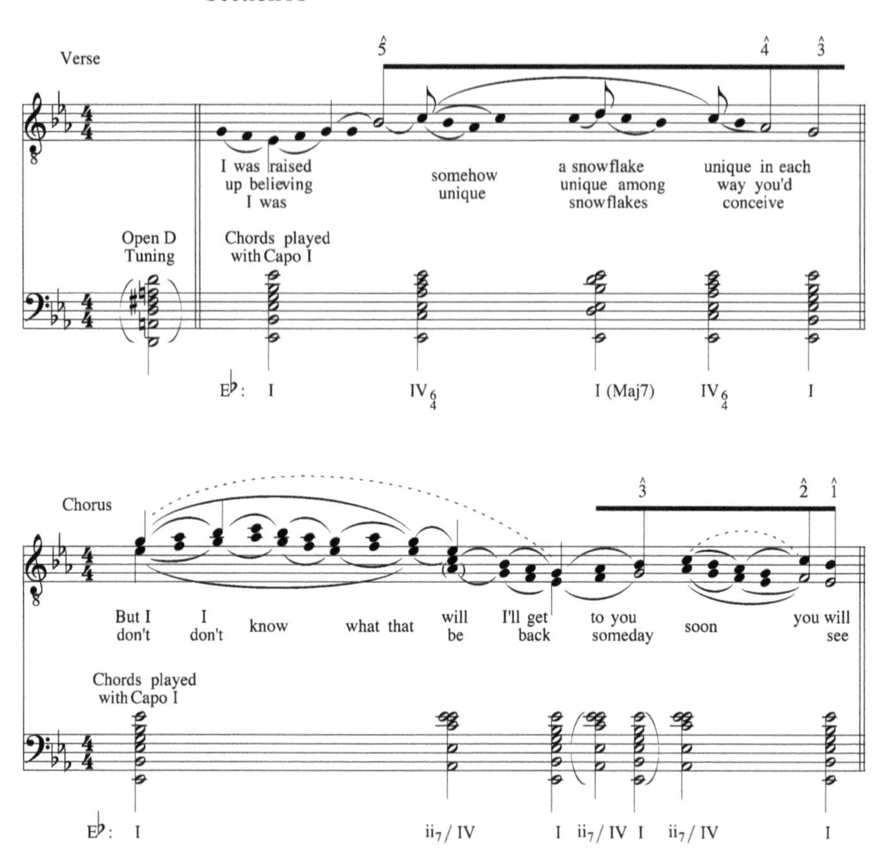

confident devices accompany lyrics that assure the listener, as well as the love interest of the speaker, that he will accomplish his goals and courageously return to her someday, completing the portrait of a man with an admitted lack of confidence, but a determination to change his situation despite this. The confidently strong moment is especially present at the start of the chorus, as it begins in a vocal register one octave higher than the verse section is sung. The sketch in Example 11.4 offers a depiction of this device, along with the voice's return to the lower octave at the end of the chorus. This high-flying feeling is mitigated, however, as the prolonged $\hat{3}$ undergoes an octave transfer downward, back to the original register, coinciding with the lyric 'I'll get back to you someday'. This 'return' to the original register signifies the continually 'tethered' state the singer lives in, whether that is a symptom of his own persona or a condition produced by outside forces.

'Helplessness Blues' can be described as a single song about both reality- and fantasy-based experiences, where Section A depicts the speaker's plight against reality and Section B portrays a fantasy world providing an escape from his dilemma, with its closing material representing a return to reality through musical and lyrical devices. The contrast between the 'worlds' of these two sections, already clearly delineated in the metrical change, is expanded further in Section B by a departure from the harmonic scheme used in Section A. After Pecknold introduces Section B by strumming for six bars a tonic chord in the new expansively slow $\frac{6}{8}$ metre, a more exotic, otherworldly effect unfolds: in bars of varying compound-unit lengths, the three strophes of this section are harmonised by non-tonic harmonies (though at times over a tonic pedal), which intensify the metric contrast already depicted in Table 11.1. For each strophe, the amount of musical time per chord function, in terms of the basic compound metre 'beat' (three eighth notes), is as follows:

Table 11.2 'Helplessness Blues', beats per strophe in Section B

Function	Number of beats in strophe
I	5
ii	10
IV	10 (14 beats for strophe 3, counting its 4-bar concluding outro)

This makes for a case where, in terms of musical time, 80 per cent of Section B is harmonised by the subdominant (IV) or ii – which often functions as a substitute for IV. Example 11.5, shown below, provides a way to see this in a score layout.

Example 11.5 'Helplessness Blues', harmonic functions of Section B

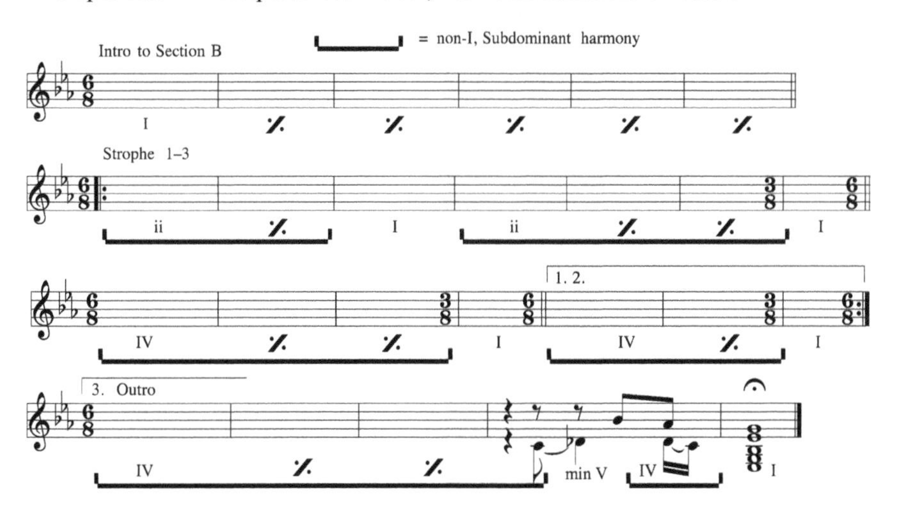

Section B, therefore, acts like a 'trip' away from reality. In concert with the groundless atmosphere provided in the rhythmic flow, the harmony creates a non-committal 'floating' atmosphere that does not benefit from cadential or functional drive. There are considerable excerpts in Section B (see bracketed sections in Example 11.5 above) where we are taken away from the tonic and arrive at emphasised root-position subdominant chords (instead of a more standard dominant-tonic cadence) to achieve arrival and create tonal grounding. These are the only points in Section B, once we move past the introduction, where it feels like there is any sense of harmonic arrival or stability. But to further question the reality of this section, these gestures come amid sporadically interspersed and short-lived tonic chords. Furthermore, where arrival-announcing gestures would be expected in the usual structuring of a pop song's form, obfuscation arises from the implementation of these 'non-cadential' harmonic devices in these locations at the same time as the previously described metrical phrasing idiosyncrasies. This produces a relationship between metre, harmony and lyrical form that is anything but conventional.

The 'outro' placed at the end of the third strophe is similar to the endings of the other strophes of Section B, in that there is only a single voice, less reverb, and a single guitar as accompaniment, harkening back to the haunting 'reality' from Section A. This third strophe of the section, if it kept the same structuring as the other two, would end with the final lyrics. Here, however, four bars are added to the end of this that consist of an extension of, or a hanging-on of, the subdominant harmony, over the $\frac{6}{8}$ strumming that has provided the background texture for all of Section B. These four bars serve to allow the singer to evade the 'reality' of his world yet again: this 'hanging' on the subdominant signifies his delusional reluctance to return to the real world fully, at least until the song's final musical gesture, a double plagal-like figure (v – IV – I)[5] in the guitar work that leads to the final held tonic harmony. This at last portrays a 'grounded' return to the real world – harmonically now, as well as in the piece's other parameters.

Production Styles

Production plays an elusive but integral role in the making and shaping of popular song. While the relationship between production and other musical elements such as harmony, melody and rhythm can be difficult to untangle, it is worthwhile,

---

[5] Walter Everett is one who recognises that minor-v moving to IV then I (v – IV – I) is functional substitute for the double plagal cadence. In his 'Pitch Down the Middle' essay (2008, p. 56), he qualifies this and gives the example of James Taylor's 'Fire And Rain', where this substitute forms the introduction of the song. In a discussion, he further explains the reason for this similarity of function and effect: the (upper) voice leading is the same, and because this is the main musical event at play, the root motion, which contains the only different pitches, is of minimal significance.

as production shapes the *sound* or timbre of a song (Moorefield, 2005, p. xiv). It is important to understand production not just as a collection of devices (for example, ProTools, EQs, Compressors and so on), but, as Paul Théberge explains, as an 'environment in which we experience and think about music ... defining, in the process, what music is and can be' (Théberge, 2001, p. 3). In this case the production reinforces and contextualises the lyrical narrative and the expression of conflict, particularly through the use of reverb and instrumental positioning.

One of the most important sonic elements in Fleet Foxes' music is the way in which the band uses reverb to both channel earlier styles and to advance the lyrical narrative. For the recording of 'Helplessness Blues', Fleet Foxes used an EMT plate reverb unit, a vintage unit that lacks the clarity of digital devices, but features a warm, grainy quality (Doyle, 2011, p. 155). Exploring how the band used this kind of reverb in different ways through the two distinct song sections can show how production styles express important parts of the song's narrative. Reverb and instrumental positioning go hand-in-hand; often the more reverb is used, the further away something sounds, while with less reverb, it sounds closer. In order to position the instruments in 'Helplessness Blues', Fleet Foxes and producer Phil Ek used the digital editing software ProTools. The combination of the use of this modern technology with vintage equipment (that is, plate reverb), defines the expression of a 'slick-organic' sound that Phil Ek has used to describe his production aesthetic when working with Fleet Foxes. As the discussion below will show, the contrast of modern and vintage equipment helps underline the conflict and tension in the lyrical narrative between wanting to be part of a machine and longing for a simpler pastoral life.

The first verse of Section A in 'Helplessness Blues' begins with the strumming of acoustic guitar, followed by the entrance of the lead vocal. The acoustic guitar is miked closely and is relatively free of reverb, which conveys an intimacy and clarity to the instrumental part. The vocals, however, resonate with reverb, which makes the singer sound as if he is singing alone in a large, empty space. This mental image of a man singing alone in such a space provides a vivid setting for the loneliness and personal confusion of the lyric. These musical choices also set up the conflict of the song, albeit on a small scale, almost immediately, with the intimate vocals reflective of the desire for a simple life, and the feeling of a large space reflective of the 'great machine' the protagonist struggles with in later verses.

In verse 2, an additional second guitar part enters, panned left, widening the sonic picture. This musical movement change also reflects how the lyrical change transitions from the personal reflection of the first verse, to the relationship between the singer and the wider world. The lead vocal is joined by a second voice, set further back in the mix. The use of 1960s-era plate reverb, along with the style of the two-part vocal harmony, heavily evokes the early work of Simon and Garfunkel (for example, 'The Sounds Of Silence' (1965) or 'I Am A Rock' (1966)), whose lyrics often share with 'Helplessness Blues' a concern for the individual's place in society expressed in literary language. The addition of the second vocal line and guitars denote the movement between the singer being 'alone' to being part of a society populated with other voices. The production choices reinforce his contemplation of his own path, whether as a 'snowflake', a 'cog in some great machinery' or neither.

Moving into Section B, the same plate reverb and instrumental positioning are now used to create dreaminess rather than loneliness. The reverb, when used on numerous double-tracked instrumental and vocal parts, makes the individual parts difficult to discern, much in the same way that a dream is difficult to explain. As such, the harmonies tend to sound like a sonic haze that feels joyous and *hopeful* in comparison to the *helplessness* of Section A. This production technique was pioneered in the 1960s in the recordings of Phil Spector, whose music, like this section of 'Helplessness Blues', featured what he termed the 'wall of sound'. This technique featured many reverbed voices and instruments playing the same part simultaneously, creating a sound where it was deliberately difficult to discern individual parts (Moorefield, 2005, p. 52). In the context of music with youthful male harmonies, however, this 'wall of sound' evokes the Beach Boys' mid 1960s period, where producer Brian Wilson used Spector's techniques to create his own utopian dream of an endless summer in order to escape his difficult reality. In Section B, Fleet Foxes are portraying a similarly utopian dream, where the 'wall of sound' effect reinforces both the dreaminess and the longing for a simpler life. This connection is also present in the lyrics, where the line 'gold hair in the sunlight' is quite similar to the Beach Boys' 'Good Vibrations' (1966), whose opening line mentions the 'way the sunlight plays upon her hair'. The use of plate reverb, both in its sonic effect and its evocation of 1960s popular music with similar lyrical concerns, reinforces the dreaminess of this section.

Production is an important part of popular music – as our relationship to music is often to a recording, rather than a song. Fleet Foxes use production to create a distinct sonic aesthetic, and they use it in order to underscore the conflict in the lyrical narrative. These production techniques can also evoke specific musical references from a particular era (the mid 1960s), and they use these techniques in combination with modern technologies and influences to create music which reflects their own concerns about being stuck between two worlds: the old and the new, the real and the imagined, being unique or fitting in.

Conclusion

At the centre of the Fleet Foxes' 'Helplessness Blues' lies a personal and generational conflict. The uncertainty and internal conflict of the singer's persona is underscored by the song's formal design, uncommon metric changes, non-resolving harmonic gestures and other sonic considerations resulting from the use of analogue production techniques. The overlapping use of acoustic and electric instruments alongside old and modern musical production techniques underpins a generational struggle and, at the same time, a conflict between a disheartening reality and an imagined world. Additionally, the band's emphasis on the 1960s folk influence underlines the group's conflictive relationship with the genre, especially with the idea of sociopolitical activism often associated with it.

Since the techniques, formal and stylistic parameters described throughout this chapter are not unique to the Fleet Foxes but shared by a number of other 'new-folk' groups – some contemporaries of Fleet Foxes – this examination may be useful to others studying new-folk. For this same reason, some of the theories and methods introduced in this work may contribute to the study of popular musics that demonstrate changing aesthetic approaches within popular music's tradition.

References

Doyle, T., 2011. Fleet Foxes – Phil Ek: Recording Helplessness Blues. *Sound on Sound*, August, pp. 152–57.

Everett, W., 2008. Pitch Down the Middle. In: W. Everett (ed.), *Expression in Pop-Rock Music: Critical and Analytical Essays*. New York: Routledge, pp. 111–74.

Moore, A.F. (ed.), 2003. *Analyzing Popular Music*. Cambridge: Cambridge University Press.

Moorefield, V., 2005. *The Producer as Composer: Shaping the Sounds of Popular Music*. Cambridge, MA: MIT Press.

Neal, J., 2007. Narrative Paradigms, Musical Signifiers, and Form as Function in Country Music. *Music Theory Spectrum*, 29(11), pp. 41–72.

Pecknold, R., 2011. Biography, *Sub Pop!*, [online] Available at: http://www.subpop.com/artists/fleet_foxes [Accessed 8 August 2012].

Salzer, F., 1962. *Structural Hearing: Tonal Coherence in Music*. New York: Dover.

Théberge, P., 2001. Plugged in: Technology and Popular Music. In: S. Frith, W. Straw and J. Street (eds), *The Cambridge Companion to Pop and Rock*. Cambridge: Cambridge University Press, pp. 3–25.

Discography

Beach Boys, The, 1966. 'Good Vibrations'. Capitol, 5676.

Beatles, The, 1967. 'A Day In The Life'. *Sgt. Pepper's Lonely Hearts Club Band*. Parlophone, CDP 7 46442 2.

Fleet Foxes, 2011. 'Helplessness Blues'. *Helplessness Blues*. Sub Pop, SPCD 888.

Simon and Garfunkel, 1966, 'I Am A Rock', 'The Sounds Of Silence'. *Sounds of Silence*. Columbia, CS 9269.

Turner, Ike and Tina, 1971, 'Proud Mary'. Liberty, 56216.

Chapter 12

How to Make a Global Dance Hit: Balancing the Exotic with the Familiar in 'Danza Kuduro' by Lucenzo featuring Don Omar

Félix Eid, María Emilia Greco, Jakub Kasperski, Andrew Martin and Edin Mujkanović

On 15 August 2010, the single 'Danza Kuduro' was released in Latin America and Europe. The song features collaboration between French pop singer and producer Lucenzo (Philippe Louis De Oliveira) and Puerto Rican reggaeton artist Don Omar (William Landrón). This particular version of 'Danza Kuduro' was a remake of an earlier version by Lucenzo – without the collaboration of Don Omar – titled 'Vem Dançar Kuduro' that was released in June of 2010 to little fanfare.[1] After a slow start, the new version of the song gradually climbed to the top of popular music charts in Europe and Latin America. By spring 2011, 'Danza Kuduro' had reached number one positions in pop charts across Europe, Latin America, Central America, the Caribbean and the Latin pop charts of the United States. The song's popularity was further bolstered by its inclusion in the soundtrack of the box office smash film *Furious Five* (alternately known as *Fast and Furious 5: Rio Heist*) released by Universal Studios in April 2011.[2] By summer 2011 'Danza Kuduro' had ascended to the status of a global phenomenon, following the path forged by past global dance hits the likes of the 'Macarena' in 1995–96 and the 'Lambada' in 1989–90. The wide-reaching success of 'Danza Kuduro' penetrated into the everyday lives of people across the globe and a quick survey of www.youtube.com

[1] Another version of the song featuring Big Ali was regionally successful in France and Sweden, reaching number one (Sweden) and number two (France) on the pop charts of these respective countries during the middle of summer 2011. For information on chart position, see http://swedishcharts.com/showitem.asp?interpret=Lucenzo+feat%2E+Big+Ali&titel=Vem+dan%E7ar+kuduro&cat=s [Accessed 4 June 2012] and http://lescharts.com/showitem.asp?interpret=Lucenzo+feat%2E+Big+Ali&titel=Vem+dan%E7ar+kuduro&cat=s [Accessed 4 June 2012].

[2] For more information on box office figures, see http://www.deadline.com/2011/05/box-office/and http://boxofficemojo.com/news/?id=3152&p=.htm [Accessed 4 June 2012].

queries displays hundreds of fan-generated videos of 'Danza Kuduro', many with viewership in excess of 2 million hits.[3]

However popular 'Danza Kuduro' was, is, and will be, the ability of the song to resonate with a massive number of people from diverse socio-economic, language and cultural backgrounds is a testament to its communicative power and/or that of the media industries. Furthermore, establishing any one specific identity for the song is problematic and several factors of the construction of 'Danza Kuduro' display an evasiveness when applied to questions of musical style, lyrical meaning and intertextual meaning. To this end, we argue that 'Danza Kuduro' by Lucenzo featuring Don Omar is a dance song created in a global pop song style, not out of any one specific musical tradition or style, but out of a desire to reach the widest possible audience across the globe. It is our contention that the song's wide-reaching success was achieved, in part, by appropriating several Latin American and European musical styles and elements (both traditional and modern) in order to create a product that displays a sense of the familiar *and* the exotic without becoming too regionally identifiable with any one culture or region.

In his landmark study of postcolonial attitudes in Europe, Edward Said (1987) redefined the term 'orientalism' to mean the prejudices, false assumptions and stereotypes that define Eurocentric attitudes toward the Far and Middle East. In the case of 'Danza Kuduro', a type of orientalism is at work, which adjusts this perspective to reflect the prejudices, false assumptions and stereotypes that define Western attitudes toward Latin American music and culture. We intend to show this modified brand of orientalism through an analysis of the musical components and styles used to create 'Danza Kuduro' and through an analysis of the contemporary and traditional cultural components that historically are represented by these musical identifiers. On nearly every level of construction, the sound design of 'Danza Kuduro' elicits a musical balance between the familiar and the exotic, allowing the listener the maximum amount of leeway for applying and imprinting meaning.

The appropriation of Latin American musical elements by major record labels, the manipulation and conversion of these elements into identifiable and simplified stereotypes, and their presentation to a worldwide audience as being 'traditional' Latin American music, are also important aspects germane to the discussion of 'Danza Kuduro'. However, the musical and cultural palette used to construct the song is vast and therefore this analysis will focus on issues regarding lyrics, rhythm, harmony, form, hooks and recording production techniques.

[3] Based on a search of www.youtube.com, 15 September 2011.

Lyrics

In launching into an analysis of 'Danza Kuduro', the first area of discussion is that of lyrical function and interpretation.[4] At the outset of this discussion, it is important to note that the original 2010 version of 'Danza Kuduro' ('Vem Dançar Kuduro') created by Lucenzo features lyrics exclusively written in Portuguese. Indeed one of the substantive changes in the version is the use of both Portuguese and Spanish lyrics. The translation of lyrics from Portuguese to Spanish appears inherently logical considering that Don Omar is a well-known recording artist and singer in the Spanish language musical genre of reggaeton. But rather than translating the lyrics entirely, certain portions of the text remain in the song's native language suggesting a marked reach towards the Portuguese speaking audiences in Brazil. Presumably, this musical choice was a market driven move and the bilingualism offers a hybrid that appeals to Latin American populations in North, Central and South America. This can also be seen as an extension of a tradition in reggaeton music developed in the 1990s in which lyrics sung in English and Spanish are mixed, translated and appropriated by audiences, most notably in Panama, Spanish-speaking United States territories (Puerto Rico, Florida and New York) and Jamaica creating new non-cognate words (Marshall, 2008, pp. 139–40). In the case at hand, the lyric translation, appropriation and creation of new non-cognates from 'Vem Dançar Kuduro' to 'Danza Kuduro' by Don Omar fits well within his comfort zone as a well-known reggaeton artist and producer.

Despite the appropriation of some key words or phrases, the bilingual nature of the lyrics in 'Danza Kuduro' seemingly might not hold the same amount of appeal for non-speakers of either language and yet the song still succeeds. In fact, if 'Danza Kuduro''s statistics on the international pop music charts of various European countries are to be utilised as a serious indicator of popular audience reception, then the language barrier had little negative impact.

Deciding which sections of 'Danza Kuduro' to convert from Portuguese to Spanish was no small task for Don Omar and Lucenzo. Spanish would arguably reach a wider audience worldwide; however, retaining the essence and character of a song which already enjoyed modest success in Portuguese speaking areas was also a factor. The compromise, then, was to use Spanish language choruses and Portuguese verses. The chorus is repeated several times throughout the song and is one of the main hooks established early in the overall structural formulaic sequence. The fact that this chorus is sung in Spanish instead of Portuguese supports the notion of audience familiarity argued throughout this essay. Besides,

[4] Due to copyright restrictions, the lyrics have been omitted from this text. The lyrics for 'Danza Kuduro' are, however, freely and readily available throughout the Internet on various song lyric websites.

most Portuguese speakers understand the core elements of the Spanish language regardless of their fluency with the language.[5]

The actual content of the lyrics indicates that 'Danza Kuduro' – if read literally – is another example in a long history of instructional dance songs. In the realm of African-based American popular music, this history reaches back several decades and 'Danza Kuduro' follows iconic instructional dance songs of yesteryear the likes of the 'Twist', 'Limbo', 'Locomotion', 'Hustle', 'Lambada' and 'Macarena'. Stylistic convention would suggest that if one were to write an instructional dance song, understanding the lyrics would promulgate understanding of the basic dance steps as one informs the other. Accordingly, understanding the lyrical instructions would appear primary to the generation of meaning in a song of this nature. Surely, if the singer is suggesting that one should 'Put your hands up/Moving only the hips/Turn half around/Dance to Kuduro' then understanding this instruction would lead to a more meaningful experience listening and dancing to the song. However, the importance of the lyrical content in 'Danza Kuduro' is put into question in light of the several fan-generated videos posted on www.youtube.com from places such as Stockholm, Berlin and Copenhagen. In these videos, the audience visibly reacts little to Don Omar's instructions in the opening lyrical section. For example, his call to arms 'las manos arriba (put your hands up)' receives little more than polite applause from the audience, but the instruction is followed precisely by the backup singers who execute the hand raising while repeating the lyric. Interestingly, the audiences in question do raise a collective hand during the song's performance, but not until the tag line sung on the vocable 'Oioioio' later in the song. It appears as though the lyrics matter little to these Scandinavian and German audiences as the videos clearly indicate that they either do not understand, or choose not to act on, the actual instructions of the song as transmitted in the chorus. It should be noted, however, that for their part Don Omar and Lucenzo themselves do not strictly follow 'Danza Kuduro''s instructions in the German and Scandinavian concert videos either. The latter seems more likely a result of audience demographics as performances in Latin America and the United States witness Don Omar and Lucenzo in lock step with the lyric instructions of the song and, for that matter, the dancing audience members.

The language barrier is present and German and Scandinavian audiences do not appear to appropriate certain words, 'Oioioio' in this case, to mean something new in Swedish, Danish or German as was noted earlier in regards to reggaeton's treatment of English and Spanish language non-cognate words. In any case, the language barrier does not seem to impact the reception of the song among non-Spanish/Portuguese speaking audiences. For those outside the language area the words become vocables that are meant more to sound than to be understood.[6] In

[5] This observation is informed by Félix Eid, co-author of this chapter and native Spanish speaker who now lives in Brazil and speaks Portuguese fluently.

[6] Another example of a song with lyrics that 'sound' is 'The Ketchup Song (Aserejé)' by the group Las Ketchup. The song's chorus 'Aserejé ja de jè de jebe tu de jebere

this sense, these vocables effectively become melodic riffs or hooks that further perpetuate the cyclic dance music form of the song and give energetic landing points for audiences without knowledge of the Spanish or Portuguese language to grasp and shout along with as the song's form presses forward. One way in which Don Omar and Lucenzo support this idea is through forced emphasis on the ending vowels of each individual vocal line. Long or enunciated vowels are an identifiable characteristic of both Portuguese and Spanish languages that distinguish the smooth flow and elegant pronunciation of fluent speakers. In the chorus of 'Danza Kuduro' we hear Don Omar emphasise the vowels 'o' and 'a' with backup vocal support from Lucenzo *à la* the interplay commonly found in hip-hop songs by American hip-hop artists. The added energy lends dramatic punctuation to the lyrics and drives home their presumed importance for those not inhibited by the language barrier. For non-Spanish speakers the added emphasis on these phrase-ending vowels appears to suggest that these words, regardless of translation, are important and should be supported by audience members.

Therefore, aided by the predominance of vowels over consonants, the simplicity of the text in the chorus, easy rhymes and relaxed flow of the language throughout 'Danza Kuduro' supply an easy listening experience for all audiences, regardless of whether they understand the text or not. However, what meaning, if any, can the vocal sound of these lyrics possibly portray to listeners who don't speak Spanish or Portuguese? The answer may lie in the character and timbre of the voices of Don Omar and Lucenzo. Such aspects of the voice have been studied in various contexts, and are strongly supported by voice anthropologists such as Steven Feld in his study of the language of musicality. According to Feld et al. (2004, p. 323) 'Language's musicality – its tonal, timbral, prosodic, and gradient dynamic qualities – highlights the role of vocal performance for linguistic meaning'.

Thus, the voices of Don Omar and Lucenzo perform a role within the song that goes beyond the actual verbal meanings of the words. Don Omar begins this process with an energetic call to dance, which is understood independent of its language. Then, in the chorus, his synthesised voice is mixed with the synthesised accordion, preventing his vocal timbre from standing out excessively, which gives more emphasis to the lyrics for Spanish speakers. For the non-Spanish-speaking audience, the soft tone of the voice (and its lost instruction to dance) reinforces the accordion's melodic hook, and its easy prosodic movements make it possible for them to relate to the rhymes, or perhaps even sing along after being better acquainted with the lyrics through several repetitions.

In the Spanish-sung first verse, the accordion disappears and Don Omar's voice gains a rhythmic role in detriment to melody. Here the voice does not mix and fade in conjunction within the accordion sound, Don Omar's vocal timbre becomes more natural and displays a more identifiable character. The lyrics of the first verse describe the figurative 'fire' and 'heat' present in those who dance

seibiunouva/Majavi an de bugui an de buididipi' contains no actual words and is a series of vocables.

the Kuduro, specifically women. However, for non-Spanish speakers this is problematic considering that the melodic phrase of the verse lyrics are no longer the short phrases found in the chorus, making it increasingly difficult to follow, let alone sing along. Therefore, it is in the verse and not the chorus where a more discernible 'persona'[7] can be detected. In this case the singer Don Omar follows a prescribed Latin American stereotype and is portrayed as a strong, seductive Latin lover, dripping with machismo.[8] Still, an understanding of the language and, by extension, such a character is neither implicit nor a necessary message for the actual lyrics to convey. The tonal, timbral, dynamic, corporal and rhythmic aspects of the voice in 'Danza Kuduro' are enough to portray such a role so successfully that little effort is needed whether or not the audience understands the language, in immediately imagining or constructing this persona.

The first of Lucenzo's interjections (Verse 2 in the form Table 12.5), all of which are sung in Portuguese, occurs following the first verse. In this new section the accordion (with a varied rhythm) is once again present as a prominent member of the sound texture. During this lyrical section, Lucenzo's voice is even more synthesised, this time with heavy degrees of echo, vocaliser-effect and delay, in an attempt to match its sound to that of other top reggaeton artists. This alternation between the highly synthesised voice, and its interplay with the accordion, reduces the natural human sound of the timbre in an effort to de-emphasise the lyrics in yet another attempt to make the song familiar to all audiences. Indeed, the large-scale lyrical form of 'Danza Kuduro' is constructed in a manner that alternates between the choruses, Don Omar's verses, and the interjections or countermelodies by Lucenzo in Portuguese. However, it is also worth noting that although both Don Omar's and Lucenzo's voices are synthesised, each has its own tonal, timbral and dynamic qualities. This brings a sense of movement and variation to the listener through vocal sound alone, even if such sense is not consciously perceived because one is a non-Spanish or non-Portuguese speaker. As for the Latin American listeners, the alternation between Spanish and Portuguese brings a familiar yet exotic touch that is intended throughout the whole construction of the song.

Rhythm

Rhythm is a key component necessary for developing musical integrity in dance music of any kind. Based especially on the work of Richard Middleton (1990; 1993) and János Maróthy (1974), Jeremy Gilbert and Ewan Pearson (1999, p. 60) further argue that any form of speech is neither entirely physical nor mental based

---

[7] This concept is taken from Allan Moore, and may be related to the concept of 'character' of Simon Frith (1998). For this theoretical discussion see Moore (2012, pp. 178–214).

[8] For more information on Latin stereotypes in reggaeton, see Floyd (2002), O'Brien Chang and Chen (1998), Lipsett-Rivera (2007).

on the way one experiences a sound. Moreover, they suggest that music is a form of speech 'more physical than others' (Gilbert and Pearson, 1999, p. 87) which inherently gives rhythm a prominent role in the experience. In this regard, the use of rhythm throughout 'Danza Kuduro', in its varied forms as a musical signifier and structural device, is consistent with popular music in a similar vein. There are, however, several key rhythmic factors employed in 'Danza Kuduro' that are altered versions of more traditional rhythmic elements and which, because of their alteration, add an exotic freshness to their configuration while also retaining elements of their regional heritage. In 'Danza Kuduro', Don Omar and Lucenzo utilise a hybrid son clave/reggaeton groove, various levels of syncopation, extreme tempos and overly busy ancillary percussion rhythms to create a unique aggregate rhythmic soundscape that enhances the song's appeal for local and global audiences.

Table 12.1 2–3 Son clave

2–3 Son Clave																
Time	1	&	2	&	3	&	4	&	1	&	2	&	3	&	4	&
Clave			X		X				X		X				X	

A hybrid son clave/reggaeton groove pattern is one of the most identifiable rhythmic elements of 'Danza Kuduro''s soundscape. The 2–3 Son clave (see Table 12.1 above), a bedrock of salsa, son and several Latin American dance music genres, is one of the more widely known Latin American rhythms throughout the world. Its popularity transcends Latin America, and casual listeners can hear the groove making its way into American popular music where it has been a part of rock 'n' roll's musical lexicon, in one way or another, since the later 1940s (Starr and Waterman, 2007, pp. 153–97).

The other equally popular and common Latin American dance groove present in the groove of 'Danza Kuduro' is the pulsating syncopated base rhythm of reggaeton dance music (see Table 12.2 below) also known as the 'dembow' rhythm (Marshall, 2008, p. 135). The dembow rhythm has roots in soca and several other regionally identifiable musical styles of the greater Caribbean region. However, since the 1990s the dembow rhythm has become synonymous with reggaeton music as the genre's popularity has risen exponentially over the past decade with hits the likes of Daddy Yankee's 'Gasolina' (2005) and Nando Boom's 'Ellos Benia' (1991).

Table 12.2 Reggaeton dembow groove

Reggaeton Dembow Groove																
Time	1	E	&	A	2	E	&	A	3	E	&	A	4	E	&	A
Snare Drum				X			X					X			X	
Bass Drum	B				B				B				B			

The son clave and reggaeton dembow grooves are combined in order to create a singular hybrid groove used throughout 'Danza Kuduro' (see Table 12.3 below). The static bass pulse that appears on all four beats of each and every measure throughout the song supplies a driving energy and propels 'Danza Kuduro' forward. The bass pulse also serves as a point of reference for aligning the syncopated grooves, hooks and counter-rhythms of the song. The use of a static bass in this fashion is very much a dance music convention and is one of the only direct similarities between the son clave and reggaeton dembow rhythmic patterns. However, one of the unique features of the hybrid 'Danza Kuduro' groove is its emphasis (and conversely de-emphasis) of signature or readily identifiable elements of the root son clave and reaggaeton groove patterns from which it is derived. For instance, the 'Danza Kuduro' grooves display an emphasis on downbeats and de-emphasis of the syncopated off-beats in the synthetic hand clap rhythm. In doing so, the new 'Danza Kuduro' groove strips away the full musical and cultural baggage associated with both son clave and reggaeton music. The resulting aggregate pattern has musical shades of the two predecessors but cannot be attributed directly and completely to either style. Here we see once again the extent to which Don Omar and Lucenzo went in order to enhance the homogeneous cross-appeal of 'Danza Kuduro'.

Table 12.3 'Danza Kuduro', groove

'Danza Kuduro' groove																
Time	1	E	&	A	2	E	&	A	3	E	&	A	4	E	&	A
Clave (2nd half)	X						X						X			
Dembow				X			X					X			X	
Kuduro	X			X			X		X			X			X	
Bass drum	B				B				B				B			

The globally recognisable nature of both the son clave pattern and the standard reggaeton groove, and their adaptation into a new hybrid rhythm by Don Omar and Lucenzo, is perhaps best understood as a play on the musical heritage of each individual style. Barbara Kirshenblatt-Gimblett suggests that theorising heritage is a three-part concept in which heritage is a mode of cultural production in the present that has recourse to the past, heritage is a 'value added' industry, and heritage produces the local for export (Kirshenblatt-Gimblett, 1995, pp. 367–80). In this sense we can consider 'Danza Kuduro' as making a concerted effort to exploit the musical heritage of son clave and reggaeton rhythmic components. Here, 'Danza Kuduro' would be a mode of cultural production (a piece of dance music) in the present (currently popular) with recourse to the past (in this case the well-established musical styles utilising son clave and reggaeton). 'Danza Kuduro', by employing the familiarity of son clave and reggaeton dembow rhythms, has created a system by which value can be added by individual listeners in a variety of geographic regions. And by its very definition as a combination of the two pre-existing popular regional musical styles, the basic rhythmic groove of 'Danza Kuduro' is fundamentally a local product intended for export globally.

The basic rhythmic groove of 'Danza Kuduro', regardless of its local or global aspirations, unfolds over a consistent and unwavering pulse; just as one would expect in a song intended for dance. In considering the functional rhythmic aspects of 'Danza Kuduro', mainly as a piece of popular dance music, the issue of tempo with which the song progresses presents another example of hybridity and utilisation of unconventional methods. The temporal referent of 'Danza Kuduro' further balances two socio-musical genres, each with competing stylistic treatments of tempo devised from the functionality and performance practice of each dance in its given culture. For example, most reggaeton songs written since 1990 have adopted 90 to 110 beats per minute (bpm) as the standard temporal referent (Marshall, 2005). As a result of this tempo choice, the ancillary and complimentary rhythmic voices tend to favour more complex rhythmic syncopation and layering. The moderate tempo allows for such latitude and the overall soundscape of reggaeton can support this increased level of rhythmic activity without over-saturating the musical texture or relegating individual melodies and hooks to a sonic whitewash. In general, the dance variations associated with reggaeton in clubs and concerts throughout North and South America suggest movements that are, because of the moderate tempo, complex in a way that corresponds to the rhythmic layering of the music.[9]

Western dance music often favours faster tempos (for example contemporary house music at 130bpm).[10] The rhythmic activity of hooks and melodies in this musical genre are adjusted for the increased speed and display a noticeably more simplistic nature when compared to their reggaeton counterparts. The increased tempo (which has implications for the overall structure of 'Danza Kuduro' which we will discuss later) results in a sonic texture that relies more on timbre and

---

[9] This observation is based on a survey of approximately 100 different fan-generated reggaeton concert videos from www.youtube.com.

[10] Personal conversation with Simon Zagorski-Thomas, 14 September 2011, Osnabrück, Germany. See also Moelants (2003).

production manipulation, such as adding sub-bass lower octave doublings to low bass notes, than it does a leveraged play of highly active and syncopated figures. 'Danza Kuduro', then, in an effort to bridge the gap between the tempo disparities among reggaeton and European dance musics, does not simply split the difference and clock a 115bpm tempo. Although hypothetically attractive, in practice this creation would serve only to alienate both socio-musical bases and feel foreign. Rather, 'Danza Kuduro' adopts the faster European dance music tempo of 130bpm while also retaining the rhythmic activity and layering of the slower reggaeton-style melodies and hooks. The resulting tempo is attractive for European dance-orientated audiences while the Latin American audience, possibly slightly alienated by the increased tempo, finds familiarity with the heavy rhythmic layering and syncopation of melodies and hooks. With no prescribed or traditional dance moves to complicate matters further, the corresponding dance of 'Danza Kuduro' is fan-generated and therefore adaptable to any tempo.[11]

The brisk tempo and dense sound texture of 'Danza Kuduro' has the potential to become too intense and overwhelming. However, several key production manipulations serve to clarify the overall rhythmic texture and focus the sound of the key melodies that subsequently become hooks and musical signifiers. In particular, Don Omar and Lucenzo clarify the sonic texture of the snare drum and hand clap portions of the overall musical texture (these figures can be found in Table 12.4 below).

Table 12.4 Rhythmic breakdown of ancillary parts for 'Danza Kuduro'

Time	**1**	**E**	**&**	**A**	**2**	**E**	**&**	**A**	**3**	**E**	**&**	**A**	**4**	**E**	**&**	**A**
Accordion	x	x		x		x	x		X		x		x		x	
Bass guitar	o ---------------										o		o		o	
Synth	x________				x________				x________				x________			
Snare/hand clap	x			x			X		x			x			x	
Bass drum	x				X				X				x			

The snare drum, bass drum and hi-hat are three key elements necessary in constructing an appropriate dance music rhythmic texture.[12] Normally, in European dance music hits, the hi-hat sound is prominent in the overall soundscape which

[11] Examples of 'Danza Kuduro' re-recorded by fans at various tempos, some as fast as 160bpm, are present in fan-generated websites throughout the Internet. For example, see http://www.youtube.com/watch?v=pVzmzZ2hBho and http://www.youtube.com/watch?v=GAtvDAzHvdw [Accessed 12 May 2012].

[12] Personal conversation with Simon Zagorski-Thomas, 14 September 2011, Osnabrück, Germany. See also Butler (2001).

provides a balance to the driving bass pulses which occupy downbeats. The snare is a distant second place and is less in volume and overall impact. In 'Danza Kuduro', however, the threat of rhythmic over-saturation is readily at hand due in part to the extreme tempo. To combat this, the hi-hat is less pronounced, even barely audible. In its place, the snare drum (which is synthetically altered with handclaps to promote the participatory nature of the song) is brought forward in volume. This alteration accentuates the reggaeton of 'Danza Kuduro' while also balancing the rhythmic complexity of the texture. The result is a dance track that is fast in tempo, rhythmically dense, with an overall musical texture that is discernible and full of recognisable hooks and melodies.

Hooks, Timbre, Form and Harmony in 'Danza Kuduro'

Throughout this analysis we have argued that 'Danza Kuduro' is hook-driven, and that the song's simultaneous balance of familiar and exotic sounds, musical styles, lyrical meaning and dance music structural conventions are at the very core of its fundamental construction. Musical hooks, however, are also largely responsible for the construction of much of 'Danza Kuduro''s form and harmony. The term 'hook', as it is understood in this study, is informed by the work of Gary Burns who defines the hook as 'a musical or lyrical phrase that stands out and is easily remembered' (Burns, 1987, p. 1).[13] Moreover, hooks appear in two basic forms throughout most popular music and are divided into 'textual elements' (rhythm, melody, harmony, lyrics) and 'non-textual elements' (performative elements and production elements). In 'Danza Kuduro', the intertextuality of hooks is of primary importance. According to Burns, melodic intertextuality (the sounds-like principle), like rhythmic intertextuality, can work as a hook if the audience is familiar with the original source (Burns, 1987, p. 10). And indeed this is an important part of the methodology at work in 'Danza Kuduro' as our impressions of the song's intertextual relationships serve to create meaning, and Don Omar and Lucenzo attempt to guide the formulation of this meaning with melodic and rhythmic hooks.

For example, one of the first musical sounds of the track, the sound of the accordion, plays a large part in establishing the song's primarily melodic hook. The instrument is a component of many Latin American traditional and popular musical styles. However, the manner with which it is used in 'Danza Kuduro' is neither traditional nor familiar to Latin Americans beyond the actual sound of the instrument, which is processed and slightly more synthetic in sound than usual. In this way it gives the song an exotic freshness equally appealing to Americans and Europeans with accordion traditions of their own, but who are ignorant of the historical context of accordion playing in Latin America. In this case, and in every case within the song, the use of a musical signifier (the accordion, for

[13] See also Monaco and Riordan (1980).

example) is not intended to be a representation of a specific style or sound; rather, it attempts to represent a variety of similar styles. Put another way, the accordion in 'Danza Kuduro' aims to *sound like* the accordion from other musical styles without sounding too much like these particular styles. And the perspective of the listener (European, Latin American, etc.) has no bearing on this process as the song's creators have identified and employed musical signifiers that transcend regional boundaries and foster the familiar/exotic dichotomy in terms of a glocal identity. In this case, the synthesised accordion is a sound so culturally variable that depending on an individual's cultural positioning, it can be heard as Mexican norteño, Argentinean chamamé, Bohemian polka, French musette, Balkan Romani music or none of the above.

According to Burns's study and topology of musical hooks, repetition is not an essential component of a hook, but is not ruled out, and the balance between repetition and change, the process of variation, is used by performers and record producers to manipulate structural elements of the pop songs and to produce hooks. The manipulation of structural elements via the use of variation and hooks is precisely the methodology at work in 'Danza Kuduro'. In the table below, the constant variation of marked sectional elements, which are themselves hooks or hook-driven, indicates a near continuous pattern of change throughout the duration of 'Danza Kuduro'.

The basic form, as indicated above, is chorus/verse with two different sets each of verses and choruses interpolated among the sections. However, the sequence of the actual verses is far less important to the overall forward motion and energy of 'Danza Kuduro' than the constant variation of the verses and choruses. The new material is still only a slight variant of familiar verse/chorus material and thus is designed to retain the interest of a dancer in São Paulo or Berlin without losing track of the core melodic and rhythmic hooks of 'Danza Kuduro'. To this end, using timbre changes in the voice (as in switches between Don Omar and Lucenzo as the main singing voice) or changes of language are more easily accepted by the listener when implemented as variation to pre-existing musical material. In its overall formulaic structure, 'Danza Kuduro' is atypical of American popular songs and Latin American or European dance music tunes in that its structure relies on variation of base forms rather than a quick succession of individual hooks.[14]

Harmony is also used as a hook of sorts in 'Danza Kuduro'; however, the way in which it impacts the listening experience is somewhat mysterious and, possibly, intentionally ambiguous. For the overall harmonic structure of 'Danza Kuduro', Don Omar and Lucenzo rely on a sequence comprising four chords [Am – F – C – G] that repeats, without variation, in a loop throughout the duration of the song. A functional analysis of this progression is problematic as the roots

[14] This generalised statement concerning European and Latin American dance music forms was presented to the authors of this study by André Doehring during a group study session on 14 September 2011, Osnabrück, Germany. For information on typical form structures in American popular songs see Summach (2011).

Table 12.5 'Danza Kuduro', form

INTROD. 00" – 0.14"	**CHORUS 1** 0.15" – 0.29" Don Omar: *"La mano arriba…"*	**CHORUS 1'** 0.30" – 0.44" Don Omar: *"La mano arriba…"*	**VERSE 1** 0.45" – 0.58" Don Omar: *"Quién puede domar…"*	**CHORUS 1** 0.59"- 1.14" Don Omar: *"La mano arriba…"*	**VERSE 2** 1.15" – 1.27" Lucenzo: *"Balança que é uma loucura…"*	**CHORUS 2** 1.27" – 1.43" Lucenzo: *"Oi oi oi…"*
	Spanish				Portuguese	
H1		H1		H1	H1	
| H2	H2	H2	H2	H2	H2	H2
H3	H3	H3			H3	H3
						H4
	E1			E1		
	E2	E2	E2	E2	E2	E2
			E3			E3
				E4		

Table 12.5 continued

CHORUS 1 1.44" – 1.59" Don Omar: *"La mano arriba..."*	**CHORUS 1'** 2.00" – 2.13" Don Omar: *"La mano arriba..."*	**VERSE 2** 2.14" – 2.26" Lucenzo: *"Balança que é uma loucura..."*	**CHORUS 2** 2.27"- 2.43" Lucenzo: *"Oi oi oi..."*	**Break** 2.44"	**CHORUS 1** 2.45" – 2.59" Don Omar: *"La mano arriba..."*	**CHORUS 1'** 3.00" – 3.14" Don Omar: *"La mano arriba..."*
Spanish		Portuguese			Spanish	
	H1		H1			H1
H2	H2	H2	H2			
H3	H3	H3			H3	H3
			H4			
					E1	E1
E2	E2	E2	E2		E2	E2
		E3				
E3					E4	E4
					E5	E5

Legend

H1: Hook 1 – Accordion melody

H2: Hook 2 – Snare drum
H3: Hook 3 – Word “kuduro”
H4: Hook 4 – Oi

E1: Element 1 – Vocal melody in accordion with distortion

E2: Element 2 – Chord sequence
E3: Element 3 – Chord sequence flashing
E4: Element 4 – Synthesizer melody 1

Vai - vai - vai - vai

E5: Element 5 – Synthesizer melody 2

of the chords form a subset of the minor-pentatonic scale. All the chords can be generated by what is called a gapped fifths cycle, meaning that if related harmonic fifths are stacked as if to generate a pentatonic scale [IV – I – V – (ii) – vi] and then one of those fifths (here, the ii chord) is removed, the progression emerges. This gapped fifths cycle progression, a progression with roots that reach to the 1950s that has become somewhat common in facets of guitar-based rock written since 1990 (Osborn, 2013; Capuzzo, 2009) has four different tonal centres depending on rhythmic and harmonic factors. In 'Danza Kuduro', these factors suggest that the tonic is either rooted in C major or A minor Aeolian, but neither tonal centre is firmly in place as an ultimate tonic destination.

Example 12.1 Harmonic voice leading of 'Danza Kuduro'

In 'Danza Kuduro', Don Omar and Lucenzo take advantage of the ambiguity of this chord progression. Since there is no harmonic resolution, regardless of tonal centre, the harmonic motion of the song barrels forward, building tension without a tangible release point; an effective tool for any dance song. Brad Osborn argues that the rotation between tonal centres in gapped fifth cycles often results in ambiguous tonal centres and that a more musical portrayal of tonality would include a comparison of the chord progression in relation to important melodic hooks.[15] In 'Danza Kuduro', the C major or A minor Aeolian chord progression can only be understood as one or the other in relation to the melodic hooks present throughout the song. For example in Chorus 1 following Verse 2 (2:00–2:13) Lucenzo varies the original chorus by singing in harmonised fourths above Don Omar's lyrics. Because of this vocal harmonisation, the resulting harmony of the song supports, at this moment, a C major tonality. Conversely, during Chorus 1 following Verse 2 (1:44–1:59) Lucenzo sings a subtle descending melodic hook using the pitch set [E – D – C – A]. This supports, at this moment, an A minor Aeolian tonality. The

[15] We are particularly indebted to Osborn for his help in describing the gapped fifth cycle. For more information see Osborn (2013), Everett (2004) and Biamonte (2010).

moment to moment ambiguousness of 'Danza Kuduro''s harmony is unlike most dance music songs of regional or global likeness. Harmonic looping of chords in dance music is, after all, common in Latin American and European dance music. However when, as in the case of 'Danza Kuduro', it is used as a tool for tonal ambiguity, the gapped fifths cycle harmonic progression skilfully adds a degree of mystery and excitement to an otherwise banal tonal fabric.

Kuduro as Traditional Dance

Thus far, this analysis has focused on the various technical aspects of 'Danza Kuduro''s musical construction; however, it is also necessary to consider the impact of the cultural and social baggage embedded in traditional performances of the Kuduro dance. The Kuduro is a traditional Angolan dance form that shares roots with traditional Angolan dance rhythms such as semba and kizomba, Western electronic dance music and Afro-Caribbean calypso and soca rhythms. In Portuguese, the word 'Kuduro' literally means 'stiff bottom', and the Angolan dance style directly resembles this lyrical meaning by dancers sticking out their rears and shaking their legs vigorously. Body movement in Angolan Kuduro is extremely distorted and often depicts caricatures of disabled persons, amputees and other victims of trauma (Siegert, 2009, pp. 21–4).[16] Kuduro's roots can be traced to the early 1980s, though the genre only took solid shape in the 1990s, coinciding with changes in Angola's political, social and economic climate.[17]

The corresponding lyrics typical of the Angolan Kuduro include discussions of sex, violence and political criticism, and raise a polemic similar to other protest genres likes hip-hop. Similar to its American hip-hop counterparts, performers of Angolan Kuduro sought a legitimate vehicle for self-expression within contemporary Angolan society.[18] However, as is the fate of many Non-western musical forms adapted for global commercial appeal, Don Omar and Lucenzo utilised the name and musical elements of traditional Angolan Kuduro

[16] One YouTube video that depicts the disabled caricature of the dance has nearly 7 million hits as of 4 June 2012 (see http://www.youtube.com/watch?v=dfA7N2SISCM).

[17] According to scholar Marissa Moorman (2008, p. 193) 'the struggles of daily life have crept back into the instrumentation and lyrics of new musical styles. We can hear the results of economic constraints as keyboards and mixing tables have replaced bands outfitted with instruments. One style that has developed in the last ten to fifteen years and has enlivened street corners, backyards, and discos throughout the country is known simply as *kuduro* (hard ass). At their best, *kuduro* lyrics hark back to those of an earlier period, representing the quotidian struggles of the urban poor … In other words, music in Angola is not immune to the difficult economic and social conditions, but by presenting them in new and different terms, music allows people to engage these conditions critically and mockingly and to celebrate their own survival'.

[18] For a discussion of the role of kuduro in popular culture of Luanda, see also Siegert (2009).

while simultaneously stripping the social and political aspects that constitute the backbone of this musical style. Consequently, the contemporary popularity of Lucenzo and Don Omar's 'Danza Kuduro' has generated strong reactions from Angolans, many of them negative. A quick search in www.youtube.com shows numerous videos of Angolan dancers and musicians showing what they term the 'real' Kuduro, while denouncing Danza Kuduro and challenging its authenticity.[19]

The appropriation of musical styles from the peripheries of the globe and their subsequent modification and launching by multinational music labels has been common practice in the industry for the past half century,[20] with the 'Lambada' as a recent representative example of this process. Issues of authenticity are typical for many ethno-urban music styles (Flamenco, Fado, Rebetiko, Rai, Samba, etc.) which are inherently expressions of intercultural communication.[21] Yet, in an interesting turn of fate, the very elements of 'Danza Kuduro' that so affectively appeal to cultures throughout the globe are, when presented to Angolans, interpreted as false and inauthentic. Ana Maria Ochoa (2002) calls this process 'disguised structures of power' and it presents, in 'Danza Kuduro', an appropriation of the dance and musical style, showing once again the song's potent brand of cultural realism.[22] And yet, 'Danza Kuduro''s perceived authenticity (or inauthenticity) does not reflect directly on the aesthetic value of the song. As Cuban musicologist Leonardo Acosta states, 'Music is in a certain way neutral, just like science and technique, although it is at the same time an ideological fact as it is determined or influenced by a social context with its set of values' (Acosta, 1982, pp. 41–2).

Conclusion

More often than not, it is context that plays a key role in a musician's attitudes and intentions when creating a song, and it frequently determines the use and treatment of sound material and musical form. As we have seen throughout this analysis of 'Danza Kuduro', a wide array of musical elements was employed towards one singular objective: to create a song that reaches the largest possible audience. As

---

[19] For 'real' Kuduro examples see http://www.youtube.com/watch?v=8EKIJsM3HlY and http://www.youtube.com/watch?v=yrb5zxP89Vw [Accessed 12 May 2012].

[20] See also Gebesmair (2002).

[21] For more information about this case, see Aharonian (2005). For more information regarding issues of authenticity in ethno-urban music styles, see Steingress (2006).

[22] According to Ana Maria Ochoa (2002) 'at present, cultural politics are frequently defined precisely from different versions of these notions of authenticity: which groups or types of cultural work are supported by the State and why; what types of market strategies are used both by independent music labels or multinational ones; how are spaces of participation structured. And here are the old and the new ways of feeling and making the world: old needs of acknowledgment are anchored in new market strategies, or, on the contrary, old structures of power are disguised in fashion words: multiculturalism, or regionalism'.

such, all of the aforementioned elements analysed over the course of this study are subordinate to the end goal of inclusiveness. At first listening, this author group was under the impression that 'Danza Kuduro' was yet another Latin American dance tune sporting a danceable beat, clear tonal centre and exotic-sounding instrumentation. However, through repeated listening and an exhaustive analysis, our close reading suggests that 'Danza Kuduro' is an expertly crafted work of dance music that displays a knack for balancing familiarity with exoticness on seemingly every level. This contemporary instructional dance tune captures the success, if not formula, of similar dance song phenomenon the likes of the 'Lambada' or 'Macarena', and succeeds in capturing the attention of dancers in Europe, Latin America and the globe.

References

Acosta, L., 1982. *Música y Descolonización*. La Habana: Editorial Arte y Literatura.

Biamonte, N., 2010. Triadic Modal and Pentatonic Patterns in Rock Music. *Music Theory Spectrum*, 32(2), pp. 95–110, [online] Available at: http://mcgill.academia.edu/NicoleBiamonte/Papers/1484938/Triadic_Modal_and_Pentatonic_Patterns_in_Rock_Music [Accessed 4 June 2012].

Burns, G., 1987. A Typology of 'Hooks' in Popular Records. *Popular Music*, 6(1), pp. 1–20.

Butler, M.J., 2001. Turning the Beat Around: Reinterpretation, Metrical Dissonance, and Asymmetry in Electronic Dance Music, *Music Theory Online*, 7(6) (December), [online] Available at: http://www.mtosmt.org/issues/mto.01.7.6/mto.01.7.6.butler.html [Accessed 4 June 2012].

Capuzzo, G., 2009. Sectional Tonality and Sectional Centricity in Rock Music. *Music Theory Spectrum*, 31(1), pp. 157–74.

Everett, W., 2004. Making Sense of Rock's Tonal Systems, *Music Theory Online*, 10(4) (December), [online] Available at: http://www.mtosmt.org/issues/mto.04.10.4/mto.04.10.4.w_everett.html [Accessed 4 June 2012].

Feld, S., Fox, A.A., Porcello, T. and Samuels, D., 2004. Vocal Anthropology: From the Music of Language to the Language of Song. In: A. Duranti (ed.), *A Companion to Linguistic Anthropology*. Oxford: Blackwell, pp. 321–45.

Floyd, S.A., Jr., 2002. Ring Shout! Literary Studies, Historical Studies, and Black Music Inquiry. *Black Music Research Journal*, 22, pp. 49–70.

Frith, S., 1998. *Performing Rites: On the Value of Popular Music*. Cambridge, MA: Harvard University Press.

Gebesmair, A., 2002. Hybrids in the Global Economy of Music. How the Major Labels Define the Latin Music Market. In: G. Steingress (ed.), *Songs of the Minotaur: Hybridity and Popular Music in the Era of Globalization: A Comparative Analysis of Rembetiko, Tango, Rai, Flamenco, Sardona and English Urban Folk*. Münster: Lit, pp. 1–19.

Gilbert, J. and Pearson, E., 1999. *Discographies: Dance Music, Culture and the Politics of Sound*. London: Routledge.

Kirshenblatt-Gimblett, B., 1995. Theorizing Heritage. *Ethnomusicology*, 39(3) (Autumn), pp. 367–80.

Lipsett-Rivera, S., 2007. History, Latin America. In: M. Flood, J. Kegan Gardiner, B. Pease and K. Pringle (eds), *International Encyclopedia of Men and Masculinities*. Abingdon: Routledge, pp. 284–7.

Maróthy, J., 1974. *Music and the Bourgeois, Music and the Proletarian*. Budapest: Akadémiai Kiadó.

Marshall, W., 2005. We Use so Many Snares. *Wayne & Wax*, [blog] 4 August 2005, [online] Available at: http://wayneandwax.blogspot.com/2005/08/we-use-so-many-snares.html [Accessed 29 May 2013].

Marshall, W., 2008. Dem Bow, Dembow, Dembo: Translation and Transnation in Reggaeton. *Lied und populäre Kultur/Song and Popular Culture. Jahrbuch des Deutschen Volksliedarchivs*, 53 [Sonderband: Populäres Lied in Lateinamerika/ Special Issue: Popular Song in Latin America], pp. 131–51.

Middleton, R., 1990. *Studying Popular Music*. Milton Keynes: Open University Press.

Middleton, R., 1993. Popular Music Analysis and Musicology: Bridging the Gap. *Popular Music*, 12(2) (May), pp. 177–90.

Monaco, B. and Riordan, J., 1980. *The Platinum Rainbow: How to Succeed in the Music Business without Selling Your Soul*. Sherman Oaks, CA: Swordsman Press.

Moore, A.F., 2012. *Song Means: Analysing and Interpreting Recorded Popular Song*. Farnham: Ashgate.

Moorman, M.J., 2008. *Intonations: A Social History of Music and Nation in Luanda, Angola, from 1945 to Recent Times*. Athens, OH: Ohio University Press.

O'Brien Chang, K. and Chen, W., 1998. *Reggae Routes: The Story of Jamaican Music*. Philadelphia, PA: Temple University Press.

Ochoa, A.M., 2002. El desplazamiento de los discursos de autenticidad: Una mirada desde la música, *TRANS – Revista Transcultural de Música*, 6, [online] Available at: http://www.sibetrans.com/trans/a231/el-desplazamiento-de-los-discursos-de-autenticidad-una-mirada-desde-la-musica [Accessed 4 June 2012].

Osborn, B., 2013. Subverting the Verse/Chorus Paradigm: Terminally Climactic Forms in Recent Rock Music. *Music Theory Spectrum*, 35(1) (Spring), pp. 23–47.

Said, E., 1987. *Orientalism*. New York: Random House.

Siegert, N., 2009. Kuduru – Musikmachen ohne Führerschein, *Bayreuth African Studies Working Papers*, 7, [online] Available at: http://opus.ub.uni-bayreuth.de/volltexte/2009/567/pdf/Dokument_Siegert.pdf [Accessed 4 June 2012].

Starr, L. and Waterman, C., 2007. *American Popular Music: From Minstrelsy to Mp3*. New York: Oxford University Press.

Steingress, G., 2006. *Über Flamenco und Flamenco-Kunde. Ausgewählte Schriften 1988–1998*. Münster: Lit.

Summach, J., 2011. The Structure, Function, and Genesis of the Prechorus, *Music Theory Online*, 17(3) (October), [online] Available at: http://www.mtosmt.org/issues/mto.11.17.3/mto.11.17.3.summach.html [Accessed 4 June 2012].

Discography

Daddy Yankee, 2005. 'Gasolina'. Machete Music, 9883426.

Kaoma, 1989. 'Lambada'. CBS, 655011 2.

Las Ketchup, 2002. 'The Ketchup Song (Aserejé)'. *Las Hijas Del Tomate*. Columbia-Sony, 251339.

Lucenzo feat. Big Ali, 2010. 'Vem Dançar Kuduro'. Catchy Tunes, [no number given].

Lucenzo feat. Don Omar, 2011. 'Danza Kuduro'. Yanis, 0060252777154 0.

Nando Boom, 1991. 'Ellos Benia'. *Reggae Espanol*. Shelly's Records, SRCD 07.

Chapter 13
Analytical Approaches to Björk's 'Crystalline': A Convergence of Nature and Technology

Phil Allcock, Natalia Bieletto, Maxime Cottin,
Katharine Nelligan and Yvonne Thieré

Introduction

During the five days of the summer school three females and two males from different cultural backgrounds and scholastic traditions listened attentively to Björk's 'Crystalline' for the purpose of analysis. This song had been released only weeks before, so this was our first listening experience of the song. Thus, the music had not yet been connected to our everyday lives, nor did we have the opportunity to interpret it and/or to ascribe meaning to it in a social setting outside the one provided by the summer school. However, it was impossible to disassociate the listening experience from Björk's firmly established musical persona with which the group were already familiar and which unavoidably filtered our perceptions of the song. Rather than conducting a mere formal analysis of the music, this led us to examine the emotional affects of the song and to study Björk's performance.

Our first attempts to analyse the song consisted of listening to the piece and discussing any immediate responses we had to the music. This was our attempt at applying an analytical method that was not informed by the discourse surrounding the song and the artist. It is important to note, however, that although our responses may have appeared extemporaneously conceived, our interpretations of the music were undoubtedly informed by discourse; first, many of us were already familiar with Björk and her musical style, and secondly, our individual interpretations of the music were indeed informed by our differing scholarly backgrounds and research interests. Next we attempted to organise our thoughts according to structural, timbral and poetic analysis. Finally, we compared our impressions with the discourse surrounding Björk and her current album *Biophilia*, and attempted to find meanings that go beyond the actual sounds.

One of the biggest challenges of this co-written chapter has been the necessity to agree on an epistemological interest that allows for and respects different musicological allegiances and analytical approaches. Such a discussion requires a lot of openness, respect and, not least, empathy for the arguments and interpretations of others. In a group situation, it is important not to criticise unnecessarily the views and objections of the others, and at the same time not to simply agree in order to take what may appear as 'the easiest way out'. Our group decided to put aside our epistemological differences and focus on the experienced commonalities within our joint work in Osnabrück.

The initial discussions of the song focused on its unusual gathering of instruments and sounds, which caused diverse impressions surrounding nature and technology and their relation to each other. On the one hand, we heard sounds that we associated with something natural in terms of its timbral qualities and acoustic sound production. With this in mind, we discussed Björk's individual and unique vocal timbre and singing style, as well as the brazen, continuous ostinato pattern played by a gameleste (this pattern is discussed in detail in the subsequent section of this chapter). In the end, our impressions of nature were strengthened by the lyrics. We only remembered single words and phrases such as 'earth', 'nebula' or 'spread out like my fingers', the eponymous 'crystals' and of course the repeated, memorable title 'crystalline' which appears frequently in the chorus sections. We didn't understand every word, but nature was clearly a central lyrical theme.

Apart from these references to nature we perceived the programmed beats as reflective of 'technology'. Indeed it is clear that these sounds were produced electronically, and consequently they contrast with the aforementioned connotations of nature. The group's reflections on the relationship between the two spheres – nature and technology – mostly took its course from discussions of the striking shift of proportions at the end of the song. This interpretive process showed interesting differences within our group; the interpretations ranged from a serious struggle between man and machine to an assumed coexisting of the three main parameters: the gameleste, Björk's voice and the electronic sounds that finally converged in this final climactic section. While we did not necessarily agree upon the same interpretation of this ending, we could agree on the overall finding that nature and technology are presented as somehow related and interconnected concepts.

In the following, we would like to focus on some salient moments we identified as significant and memorable concerning our first impressions of the concepts 'nature/technology', namely the gameleste motif, pitch organisation, song structure, Björk's vocal performance, and recording techniques.[1] By doing this, we will attempt a simultaneous description of important features, their interactions with metaphoric content in the lyrics as well as with accompanying sonic events, in the hopes of offering a plausible interpretation of the affects this song produced

[1] The reader may identify the diversity of our various allegiances within the sections as we decided mainly to write them separately. Furthermore, we intentionally did not adjust them towards structural and methodological conformity. Owing to the fact that each section is yet built around the central nature/technology topic, we try to maintain and emphasise several possibilities of approaching this facet of the song. However, we do not want to lose all controversial subjects of our group discussions. Thus, important disparities will be mentioned within the text.

in us. We hope to demonstrate how, as individual human beings, we have various understandings of the creative and cultural practice of music making.[2]

The Gameleste Motif

One of the distinctive features of 'Crystalline' is the opening melodic motif that can be heard throughout the song.[3] In particular, the timbral quality of this sound whose source is not evident from the start, had us wondering what instrument we were hearing. Considering its metallic quality, our first impressions of the sound suggested to us a glockenspiel, toy piano, celesta or even a gamelan ensemble, yet there was something utterly precise, not to say mechanical, in its repetition and unchanging articulation. This set the basis of a dichotomy between notions of nature and technology through which we attempted an extra-musical interpretation of this song. After brief Internet browsing, we learned that this very timbre was produced by a custom-made instrument; a hybrid between gamelan and celesta that Björk herself named 'gameleste'. Her first idea had been to have a real gamelan orchestra played by mechanised mallets, but this was logistically too demanding (Björk, 2011).[4] In any case, there was something in this ever-present motif that seemed to be conditioning our perception of the whole song.

Most saliently, when voicing our first impressions, we discussed the atmospheric and almost hypnotic quality of the entire work. Such an atmospheric quality could be related to the lack of musical teleology of this piece, which is to say the effect of not having a goal-directed structure. The persistence of the

---

[2] After some Internet research in Osnabrück, we found out that 'Crystalline' is the lead single from Björk's (at that time upcoming) album *Biophilia* which contains a number of innovative features that are akin to the mechanisms of digital distribution in today's music industry (for example tablet apps being released alongside traditional products such as CD albums). Furthermore, we found out that *Biophilia* tries to mark the coming together of music, nature and technology which could obviously be related to our first discussions. Although it cannot be denied that this information has influenced our subsequent dealing with the song – conscious or unconscious – the basis for our analysis arose from impressions that have not yet been influenced by this paratextual information. Thus, we do not tend to 'prove' those intentions proclaimed by Björk.

[3] The gameleste pattern only stops twice within the whole song: at the beginning for about half of the second verse (1:17–1:38) and during verse 3 (2:55–3:02).

[4] Björk then settled on the much more convenient idea of the gameleste: 'We tried a robotic gamelan, which basically is a normal gamelan, but with robotic hammers. You have it in a big room and you could draw a circle or whatever and then the gamelan would play the circle. But it just didn't … I think it was amazing, the robotic gamelan, but it just wasn't right for this project. I'm such an old rock and roll dog, and I'm just so used to touring, that I kept thinking: "How are you going to put that on stage?"'(Björk, 2011). The making of this gameleste is documented in a short video, available on www.youtube.com/watch?v=J0uXL1E5qn8 [Accessed 30 July 2012].

gameleste motif with its reiteration of the metallic tactus could be interpreted as the sonic principle governing the entire song. It creates the perceptual effect of having no processual change and is the nonlinear element of the piece. This motif thus works as the stimulus leading listeners to 'entrain' a subconscious rhythm, to subconsciously entrain the periodicity within the pattern, thus experiencing the sensation of a stagnant temporality. According to Kramer (1988, p. 21), such reaction in turn favours the experiencing of musical events from a contemplative rather than an interpretive perspective. This would hypothetically condition the perception of events as they happen, rather than linking them to a greater and self-contained, musical narrative. Ralf von Appen (2011) has termed this perceptual modality as a mere 'sensual attraction' to music. Such 'sensual attraction', we infer, would in turn engage the senses and thus potentially enhance the listener's perceptual awareness on a moment-to-moment basis. In other words, it is likely that the sonic context of repetition and nonlinearity within this song will favour the aesthetic perception of sonic elements over an interpretive perception of sections or other overarching structures.

Pitch Organisation

In 'Crystalline', we are dealing with a paradigm different from those that are most often found in popular music[5] as it does not exhibit the harmonic and voice-leading constraints of classical tonality. In fact, it would be very hard to insist that the song is based on any harmonic relations at all for it does not use any chord progression. The song exhibits a horizontal layout rather than a vertical one. 'Crystalline' appears to lack a strong settlement and affirmation of one pitch as a clear and undeniable tonal centre; nevertheless, a closer examination of the underlying gameleste pattern, which can be heard throughout the entire song, is based on a lydian mode in E (this is discussed in more detail below). To complicate this further, the score included in the 'Crystalline' app[6] contains a key signature of two flats which suggests either B♭ major or G minor. Nevertheless, the harmony of the song does not indicate the use of a common major/minor system. It is possible that the key signature has been included for the sake of convenience and for the purpose of the written score. It gives us a hint to delimit the use of the heptatonic scale containing the pitch-classes E♭ and B♭. We shall at first not refer to this pitch-class collection in terms of an ordered scale (that is with a fixed distribution of the tones and semi-tones, that would reveal one modal interpretation) but as an

[5] Regarding the different paradigms one might come across in popular music, see Everett (2004).

[6] The app contains the song itself, the lyrics, a karaoke version with a score running simultaneously and a 3D game where the player's behaviour influences the structure of the song. Additionally, the app includes an essay by musicologist Nicola Dibben which offers an introduction to, and summary of, Björk's ideas behind the song.

unordered collection, without any tonal centre distinction. We thus identified this segment as $C5_3$(h), according to the terminology of interval cycles established by George Perle (1985) (see Example 13.1).

Example 13.1 Unordered pitch-class collection used in 'Crystalline'

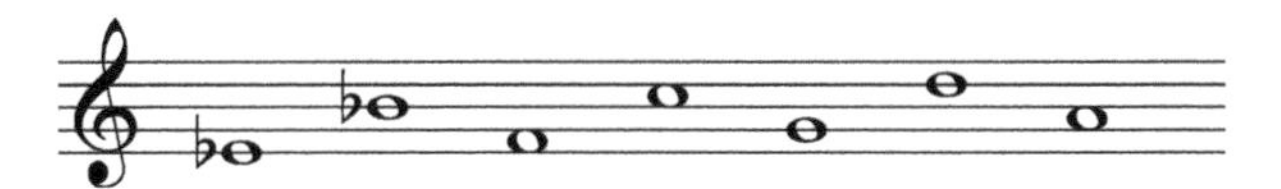

The entire song exclusively consists of the aforementioned pitch-class collection and fails to affirm one clear tonal centre. It therefore gives the listener the feeling of an elusive key that is not grounded by a strong assertion toward one pitch.[7] This does not mean, however, that the musical structures contained in the song are not hierarchically organised. One can easily interpret some structures or melodic patterns as emphasising different modal readings of $C5_3$(h).

Consider the way the gameleste pattern of the first verse (see Example 13.2) is notated. This demonstrates how it can be understood as different melodic lines blending together in order to build the whole pattern. This compositional technique owes a lot to Indonesian gamelan music, which was in all probability one of Björk's influences for this track.[8] Most of gamelan music uses interlocking melodic lines that merge together to produce the overall structure. Therefore, each line taken separately would not have any *raison d'être*. In this aspect the counterpoint heard in the gameleste part of 'Crystalline' is closer to the Indonesian tradition than to Western counterpoint. In the latter, each voice has an identifiable theme that possesses enough consistency to stand alone, whereas the former has atomised melodic motifs that are unsustainable when heard individually. All gameleste patterns heard in the song exemplify this compositional process. The reference to gamelan is thus not only enunciated by the gameleste's 'bronze' sonority, but also

[7] Note that Omar Souleyman's remix 'Crystalline (Omar Souleyman Version)' introduces a drone on G. The track therefore lacks the ethereal mood the original single version has because the tonal ambiguity of the gameleste pattern and the vocal melody is lost. Every melodic or harmonic event is now connected to this G pedal tone.

[8] See footnote 4. The capabilities of gamelan music are nothing new to Björk, as she has already worked with a gamelan orchestra (the Southbank Gamelan Players) at her MTV Unplugged concert in 1994 (see Murphy and Thomas, 2001). Here, the new acoustic arrangement of 'One Day' represents an interesting possibility to remove all electronic sounds that are characteristic and existential for the song's album version on Debut (1993) and replaces it with equally eclectic sounds that are produced by a gamelan orchestra, tuba and tablet.

by the inner melodic layout, and, more broadly, by the constant repetition of the patterns included within a Western pop standard verse/chorus form.

Regarding the quality of sound production, the listener faces a bipolar sound world in which the sharp and almost non-resonant gameleste sonorities, comparable to the saron of Javanese gamelan orchestras, find their counterpart in the highly produced electronic effects and the resonant sub-bass. As discussed in the introduction, this is an instantiation of the way in which the sonic materiality of 'Crystalline' evokes the coexistence of both nature and technology. As contrasting as these two sonorities may seem, they nevertheless somehow work together. One is likely to interpret the sub-bass punctuation (first entrance at 1:23) as assuming the role of a gong that is traditionally played in a gamelan orchestra. This indicates the beginning of the cycle (in the case of 'Crystalline' the sub-bass indicates the first beat of the 17-beat pattern).[9]

Example 13.2 'Crystalline', gameleste pattern of verse 1 (0:00–0:14)[10]

Once again, there is no strong evidence of a particular emphasis on one note, or to be more accurate, the emphasis on several notes obscures the listener's grasp of a clear tonal centre. However, two clues can lead us to the supposed 'tonic'; first, the ascending tritone E♭ – A that runs through the voices 3 and 4 (Example 13.2, from the bottom) is heard right from the beginning of the pattern, and secondly, the short 'cadential figure' D – B♭ – E♭ in the lower voice that establishes the fifth

[9] In order to grasp the full sonic effect of the sub-bass, it is necessary to listen to the record on a proper hi-fi system. But somehow the marketing strategy undertaken by Björk, that is to release the single first under the iPad and iPhone application format, seems at odds with the high sound quality of the recording.

[10] All musical transcriptions are ours, except for examples 13.3 and 13.4a, which were reproduced from the written score published in the 'Crystalline' app.

E♭ – B♭ as the structural element of the pattern. Consequently, it is plausible to hear the pattern as based upon a lydian mode on E♭; one of the seven modal readings of $C5_3$(h). This reading is more pronounced in the third verse as the bass line, with the falling fifth B♭ – E♭ underlines, along with the gameleste, the E♭ priority (at 2:40).

Example 13.3 'Crystalline', vocal melody, first line[11]

The vocal part, however, is more ambiguous than the gameleste pattern. The first line, sung over the words 'underneath our feet' (see Example 13.3), uses the pitch-classes F – G – A – B♭. It is difficult to identify the mode in this case because any of these pitch-classes can assume the role of a tonic. Even though F is the note on which the short vocal melody ends, there is no evidence to suggest with reasonable certainty that this note is the tonic on which the mode is built, and this would yield in the lower tetrachord of an F mixolydian mode, if we stay within the boundaries of $C5_3$(h). But taken in context with the gameleste pattern, one could interpret the vocal line as being in E♭ lydian, the A now forming, with the E♭ polarity of the instrumental part, the characteristic lydian interval of the raised fourth. There is, however, no strong assertion that can be made to settle for a definitive interpretation of the diatonic segment $C5_5$(h). It illustrates what we might call, following Constantin Brailoiu (1973), 'the ambiguity of the tonic' that characterises some pentatonic folk music, but which can also be observed in a heptatonic organisation.

Example 13.4a 'Crystalline', chorus, vocal melody (first appearance at 0:44)[12]

[11] This example is reproduced from the score published in the 'Crystalline' app. The copyright belongs to Björk, who has kindly given us permission to use it for this chapter.

[12] This example is also reproduced from the score published in the 'Crystalline' app, see footnote 11.

Example 13.4b 'Crystalline', chorus, bass line (first appearance at 1:07)

The chorus illustrates the same paradigm. By examining Example 13.4a, it is clear that different interpretations can emerge. The voice leading in this section suggests G as the tonal centre, but the pitch G never really asserts itself as a strong tonal basis for the chorus, and neither does the E♭ that immediately follows. Rather, the whole passage tends to illustrate what Björk is singing, that is, the 'internal nebula', a nebula of pitches that fail to settle the listener on solid grounds.

A second interpretation of the sonic organisation of the chorus, however, would consider the vocal line as focusing on C rather than G. The $C5_3$(h) collection is now reinterpreted in C dorian where the repetition of the pitch G calls for a resolution to C by an ascent. Still, the latter is not heard as a strong tonic, since when the vocal line reaches that pitch, it immediately falls stepwise to G so the short pattern of two bars can be repeated. Within modal practice, one would be inclined to hear a Gregorian influence as the repetition and the focus on G can be construed as the recitation tone, which is devoted to the fifth scale degree in the authentic version of the dorian mode. Much of the melodic inflections heard in 'Crystalline' reveal this Gregorian flavour.

The reader would probably be circumspect toward such a reading of the melodic content of 'Crystalline' in which the different musical elements (timbre, texture, rhythm, et cetera) seem to be more anchored within the modern popular music vocabulary than the ancient ecclesiastical vocal tradition. But one should consider Björk's stance toward the musical tradition of her homeland, Iceland. A strong national commitment arose once the country gained independence after centuries of Danish rule. Björk does not make an exception:

> My theory is that when Iceland got independent in 1944, it still took two generations to develop a real confidence. My parents were born in the late 1940s. But when my generation came along we finally started to ask ourselves what it meant to be Icelandic and how to feel proud of it instead of feeling guilty all the time, like animal creatures colonised by Denmark for 600 years. (Björk, cited in Dibben, 2009, p. 24)

The beginning of Christianity in Iceland goes back to circa 1000 AD, and with it came the tradition of hymn singing, on which Icelandic idiosyncrasies, such as parallel movements in fourths, fifths or octaves and the use of the lydian mode, have been affixed – these specificities stayed the same over a long period of time, merely until the nineteenth century (see Hopkins and Sigurbjörnsson, n.d.). Dibben identifies some of these musical elements within Björk's music:

> [T]here is some similarity to Icelandic folk traditions in the voicing of instrumental parts in her arrangements, and her melodic and modal style. For

> example, the empty, monastic-like sound of the strings in the introduction to "Jóga", and parts of "Hunter" from *Homogenic* is the result of two-part parallel movement in fifths … and the Lydian mode is one of the most frequent to feature in her music. (Dibben, 2009, p. 37)

Traditional Icelandic folk music is used synecdochically to convey her belonging to a culture and her vision of what it means to be an Icelandic singer in contemporary popular music. 'Crystalline' partly conveys this cultural affiliation via the partial use of the lydian mode and modal vocal melodies that owe much more, as we have seen, to folklore traditions than Western common-practice harmony and voice leading. Of course these cultural idiosyncrasies are merged with other idioms, like electronic music or gamelan, in order to achieve a coherent musical object that responds to Björk's artistic volition.

Form

Guided by our common formation as music analysts, we identified chorus sections, and we discussed the surprising and intensive coda-like drum and bass part at the end of the piece. But we were unsure how to classify and even remember details of the unusual sections in between. Although the occurrence of lyrics sung by Björk among distinctively recognised choruses indicated verse-like characteristics, these sections were unconventional and rather impalpable. Consequently, the conglomeration of such different parts generates a specific functional value of form within 'Crystalline'. In this section of the chapter, we will show that the song's formal conception is closely linked to changing interaction of the nature- and technology-connoted parameters and has thus been influential to our interpretation of the song.

Table 13.1 'Crystalline', form sections

Time	Section	Bars
0:00–0:44	Verse 1	$8 \times \frac{17}{8}$
0:45–1:16	Chorus 1	$8 \times \frac{4}{4} + 4 \times$
1:17–2:07	Verse 2	$\frac{4}{4}$ (*instrumental*)
2:08–2:39	Chorus 2	$8 \times \frac{17}{8} + 1 \times \frac{15}{8}$
2:40–3:24	Verse 3	$8 \times \frac{4}{4} + 4 \times$
3:25–3:45	Chorus 3	$\frac{4}{4}$ (*instrumental*)
3:46–4:06	Chorus 4	$8 \times \frac{17}{8}$
4:07–4:17	Chorus 5	$8 \times \frac{4}{4}$
4:18–4:59	Terminal Climax	$8 \times \frac{4}{4}$
5:00–5:06	Outro	$4 \times \frac{4}{4}$ (*instrumental*)
		$16 \times \frac{4}{4}$
		$1 \times \frac{4}{4}$

Verses

In his deliberations on verses, Richard Middleton states: '"Verse" is a term describing a complete unit (generally a stanza) in the lyrics, and the music used to set several such units. The same music is used for each verse, though perhaps with some variation' (Middleton, 2003 p. 519). Regarding the verses of 'Crystalline', one can definitely perceive this unit within the lyrics. While there are no rhyming lyrics and there is only scant evidence of a coherent narrative, most of the lines are connected, or can easily be referred to former or subsequent lines, especially by completing a sentence through yet missing, respectively added clauses (for example, 'underneath our feet/crystals grow like plants').

When we first heard the song, we (and especially the non-native-English-speakers among us) were not aware of these coherences. The fact that we initially could not classify these verses can be explained by the construction of the musical material, which seemed to lack the accustomed unity of such sections. In spite of this, the verses reflect the nearly continuously played gameleste pattern, Björk's voice (including background vocals in verse 1), several electronic sounds (appearing as now and then flashing, unpredictable, subtle, soft and rather atmospheric sounds), a strikingly active bass drum in verse 2 and 3 as well as a rarely played sub-bass. A strong means of differentiation is provided in dealing with rhythmic confusion. We noticed the unconventional use of a $\frac{17}{8}$ metre that is barely recognisable by the human ear, but rather is made perceptible through computer-assisted analysis.[13] There are eight bars of $\frac{17}{8}$ in the first and third verse, and eight bars of $\frac{17}{8}$ plus one bar of $\frac{15}{8}$ in the second verse. Even though in verse 2 the first beat of the bar is emphasised by the sub-bass (in addition to a bass kick drum), we did not initially identify the $\frac{17}{8}$ time. First, we did not expect this metre as it is extremely unconventional in popular contexts, and secondly, the drum pattern includes obvious backbeat passages which guide the listener's attention in the direction of a common $\frac{4}{4}$ time. At these points, when the listener gets the satisfying feeling of finally having 'found' the 'one' and therefore finding rhythmic orientation, this is quickly subverted by one or the other alleged superfluous hit (still thinking in a $\frac{4}{4}$ time) which consequently reverts one back to a sense of rhythmic uncertainty (see Example 13.5).

Example 13.5 'Crystalline', $\frac{17}{8}$ drum pattern at 1:31

[13] Thanks for the kind hint go to Dietmar Elflein.

Another characteristic of the verses is the vocal melody which is also responsible for this rhythmic confusion. Sometimes, when the melody emphasises particular beginnings or individual words or syllables in a phrase and these are also emphasised by the gameleste or bass drum hit, one is encouraged to hear these emphases as beats (for example the distinctively emphasised vowels of 'Crystals grow like pla ...' in verse 1 which can easily be heard as crotchet metre 1, 2, 3, 4 within a 4/4 time; especially as this is sung on one steady pitch). Otherwise, in 'Crystalline', Björk is rather often dealing with rhythmically loose entries and is using note values that fall off the beat which works in contrast to the rigid quaver pattern of the gameleste. Thus, she somehow uncouples the melody from all other sonic events to break the mould for an instant, which is why those melodies can hardly be remembered. Though they definitely exhibit relations to each other – verse two and three in particular – we did not perceive these melodies as evidently familiar when we first heard them.

To us, the main function of the verses is therefore to support the creation of a distinctive atmosphere. This is achieved by avoiding functional harmony, through the part use of cryptic and metaphoric lyrics and through repeatedly modified vocal lines. Furthermore, there is also the conflation of quite unique sounds, such as the gameleste and Björk's voice, and the overall uncertainty of the metre and therefore rhythmic disorientation. Finally, the verses are constructed with the aid of varying electronic sounds and their unpredictable, ever-changing appearances. Consequently, a feeling of suspense is evoked and sustained throughout each instantiation of the verse, and a listener might be tempted (especially during verse 1) to pay less attention to more prevalent sounds (Björk's voice and the gameleste) and to explore the peculiar sonic space.

Finally, it is clear that, within these sections, all the initially nature-connoted parameters (Björk's voice including the lyrics, and the gameleste) are relatively dominant and constant. The technology-connoted electronic (and) drum sounds develop slowly, becoming more prominent with each instantiation of the verse. Hence, the latter sounds undergo the change from more outside, independent parameters to more and more constituent ones for the verses.

Choruses

From our first impressions of the song, it is clear that the chorus of 'Crystalline' follows a standardised pop/rock format; for instance, repeated melodic and harmonic structures, repeated lyrics of which include the song's title and a simple and catchy melody (Middleton, 2003, p. 508; Appen and Frei-Hauenschild, 2012, p. 59–60). The chorus of 'Crystalline' consists of 12 bars based on a 4/4 metre, 8 of these include Björk's vocals and 4 are instrumental only. The gameleste continues to play (but is re-figured in a 4/4 rather than a 17/8 metre), there are four identical melodies in the vocals, always starting with the word 'Crystalline', and the choruses are finally grounded through bass notes played by the gameleste and by the sub-bass. In addition, there is a sturdy bass drum and various electronic sounds and timbres.

The chorus's density builds through the addition of sonic events and textures, for instance the addition of a clear and active bass drum and the use of noise-like electronic sounds that are much more present, striking and definite than those heard in the verse sections. Consequently, these programmed sounds have a clear structural function and are thus presented as integral components of the chorus.

The memorable character of the four identical vocal melodies is attested by their structural simplicity; a repetition of several notes of the same pitch followed by a small ascending and again descending melodic contour (see Example 13.4a). The lyrics in the chorus are related to those in the verse, and this is a typical characteristic of a chorus structure. The four phrases describe the slow but successful overcoming of a restrictive situation. This imagery can be seen as the essence of the crystal's process of growing (and glowing) in verse 1, the achievement of love in verse 2 and finally the core process of any crystallising process: the phase when things transform reaching a whole new level. This can be taken on a personal level, or it can be related to people or to life more broadly; the lyrics enable several readings.

On the whole, the choruses occur with sonic and structural variations. While the first chorus still develops with the help of electronic sounds added from the fourth bar on, and evolves with the supervening sub-bass in the last four instrumental bars, the second chorus contains both from the beginning. In addition, the third chorus sounds more like the first, and the fourth more like the second, whereas these last consecutive sounding choruses each exist of only the eight-bar section containing Björk's vocals. This increasing intensity through repeated choruses seems like the common turning at the end of a rock or pop song to mark its climax and thereby signal the imminent ending. Furthermore, this hint is supported through the additional background vocals in the fourth chorus. The double chorus is followed by four instrumental bars (Chorus 5) that seem to be a 'light version' of the chorus's familiar instrumental section. Even though the important vocal part is missing, these bars are still recognisable as chorus-related. Through the solely playing of the gameleste in Chorus 5 – familiar from the beginning –, this section seems to end the song. Because of this finalising gesture the listener is even more startled by the following terminal climax.

Overall, the chorus section functions to provide 'Crystalline" with a cohesive consistency that is as striking as it is important. In the case of 'Crystalline", this cohesion is even more important than in many other songs with a verse/chorus-based form, because the idiosyncratic verses lack this very consistency. Certainly the chorus remedies the 'lost' feeling evoked by the previous verse (respectively *uni*verse, indeed some of us were even imagining an outer space setting here) and with this 'lost' feeling, one is proverbially starving for such a chorus. Here, the chorus provides what the verses lack: foundation, orientation and familiarity. In fact, impressions such as these are not least triggered by the close interconnection of all sounds (especially on the rhythmic level), independently of any nature or technology connotation. For this reason, we argue that the positive attributions to the choruses as mentioned above are likewise applicable to the perceived relation of nature and technology within these sections.

Terminal Climax and Outro

One thing that is even more memorable than the choruses is the song's ending with an unimagined turn, after the minimised Chorus 5, towards 42 seconds of a powerful drum and bass section which is followed by a brief one-bar outro. The drum and bass section presents new extents of sonic and rhythmic density in 'Crystalline'. This is achieved through additional electronic (and) drum sounds to create a recognisable drum and bass sound (keeping the $\frac{4}{4}$ time from the choruses). Additionally, there is a shift to double time and an increase in dynamics. At the same time a complete new vocal part is established. This one consists of two (lyrically and melodically) related lines that appear four times in total.

The lines 'It's the sparkle you become/When you conquer anxiety' can easily be connected to the previous lyrics. One can (then) understand them as the resumption of the chorus lines: the conquest of claustrophobia now becomes the conquest of (any) anxiety. This is presented even more positively as it implies becoming a sparkle once you accomplish this conquest. The fact that the first-person perspective from the chorus changes to an external perspective here, generalises the said process. Thus, this 'promise' is offered to be possibly experiences by every listening 'you'. In this (lyrical) context, it is not surprising to hear such a climactic part as it can easily be interpreted as the explosive moment when anxiety vanishes, while the one-bar outro could mark the following sparkle in the form of a becalmed surrounding.

This was not, however, our initial interpretation; indeed coming to this conclusion required acute attention to the detail of the lyrics which, for the first time in the song, were not foregrounded above the rest of the music. Similarly, the gameleste pattern is hardly audible despite its continued repetition in this section as it is suffocated by other sonic events. Through this overall shift of proportions an audible paradox is established. Considering all of these sonic events and referring to Bradley Osborn (2010, p. 79), we term this section 'terminal climax'.

The terminal climax raised a number of interesting and essential ideas for us in Osnabrück. The presented interaction of primarily nature-connoted parameters, and all of the obviously electronically produced sonorities and technology-connoted sounds in the terminal climax, greatly impacted on our reflections and interpretations of this section. Some of us interpreted it as an obvious struggle or battle between nature and technology (because of several 'machine-gun-like' sounds) while others, in contrast, had the impression of a non-conflicting coexistence of the two, not least as Björk is well known for being attracted to electronic popular music. In addition, we had different ideas about the brief outro and asked ourselves what this solo gameleste could possibly stand for in this context and raising questions such, as is this gameleste representing the only survivor of the preceding struggle? Later on, we learned that the gameleste sounds are produced acoustically – as we assumed, and why we perceived it as nature-connoted – but that the impulse for every stroke of the gameleste is in fact triggered by a programmed computer. Consequently, the gameleste suddenly appeared as a hybrid instrument concerning our nature/technology attribution, so we could hence interpret this outro as the sturdy symbiosis of man and machine.

The latter deliberations have shown that the song's terminal climax, and even the one-bar outro, evoked diverse interpretations which are highly dependent on further contextual and paratextual knowledge (which is also true for the rest of the song): do we understand or even (want to) listen to the lyrics? What do we know about Björk's special construction of the gameleste? How familiar are we with electronic popular music and thus perceive the song's terminal climax as a pleasure or a danger? Are we familiar with further music by Björk? And so on.

This analysis of the song's formal construction attempted to highlight the way in which particular sections, and therefore the utilisation of possible functional effects, can have a strong influence on the overall impression and interpretation of a song. Regarding the nature/technology dichotomy in 'Crystalline', the song's verses and choruses, the terminal climax and even the brief outro present highly different occurrences of and varied interactions between the corresponding parameters. In the end, the impression of a repeatedly changing interaction of nature and technology as we experienced it in Björk's 'Crystalline' has surely not only but definitely been created through formal composition.

Vocal Performance

Regardless of the individual emotions 'Crystalline' triggered among the different members of the team, we all agreed that a great deal of the emotional content of this song can be attributed to Björk's vocal performance, and its interactions with other sonic events. Similarly, we perceived something both haunting and uncanny about Björk's vocal delivery. Most apparent in our first listening was the somehow blurred character of the lyrics that made us wonder whether this song was entirely sung in English or if there were other languages involved. This impression was true for both the two native English speakers in the team as well as the three non-native speakers. The fact that Björk sings 'Crystalline' in English (not her native language) generated some interesting ways in which to consider this song, such as treating the lyrics as sounds rather than words – a quite usual process among non-native-English-speaking listeners. Indeed, this appears to be something that Björk too takes into account during her performance. The ambiguity of her vocal delivery became our departing point for speculating on the reasons behind such lack of clarity and on possible meanings associated with it.

When unravelling the poetic content we became aware that the lyrics do not intend to establish a narrative, but that the semantic content is rather evocative and therefore suited to the atmospheric quality of the sound events. The status granted to structural listening by traditional music analysis has received strong criticism (see Subotnik, 1988). Such critiques have opened the ground to alternative analysis that associate moment-to-moment listening with a contemporary listener's postmodern condition and, therefore, to a derived 'postmodern ways of hearing' (see Dell'Antonio, 2004). Timbre has then become a central element in identifying music's meaning and thus has been positioned as highly relevant for the purpose of musical analysis. Further reflections on the relevance of musical timbre have then cautioned music analysts on the risks of conceiving timbre as a strictly acoustic phenomenon, thus dissociating it from the socialised perceptions and isolating it from resulting connotations attributed to it by a given listener, or group of listeners. By contrast, musicologists such as Philip Tagg (2011, Chapter 10) or Nina Eidsheim (2009) have argued that phenomenological implications in the perception of timbre would reveal the social representations evoked by specific listeners.

A reiterative pattern frequently voiced throughout the song is presented in the chorus motif that contains the word 'crystalline'. This pattern would likely trigger evocations of, for example, brightness, transparency, glass, purity, etc., all depending on the connotations that crystals have for each perceptual subject. Predisposition to perceive the stimuli that follow and to interpret timbre within the semantic frame provided by the word 'crystalline' may then also shape the perception of aspects such as metre, performance aspects, voice quality, and so on. At this point, there are no reasons to believe that the word 'crystalline' would necessarily evoke images related to nature and/or technology, though there may be cases where this happens. However, familiarity with Björk's musical persona may have led to recognition of her vocal timbre after she voiced the word, regardless of its meaning. Subsequently, this identification may have triggered evocations of Björk's history of technological manipulation of sound, which, in turn, may have set the conditions to seek, or discard, artificiality/naturalness in the first sounds of this song.

The frequently repeated word 'crystalline' is sung with a staccato articulation and interrupted by quaver silences, notably endowing the melody with a sharp, 'spiky' rather than a mellifluous character. The motif may therefore act as a signifier connoting some attributes associated with crystals, such as sharpness and pointedness. Although the sense of immobility is reinforced by the reiteration of G, the rising motif sequence (minor third and then minor second) and the subsequent descending motif are paired with a change in the sound's colour. As the word 'nebula' is sung, the tone colour becomes fuller, and one can imagine the singer opening her chest (filling her chest with air so that a louder vocal sound is produced) thus releasing a richer, louder timbre most characteristically associated with Björk.[14]

---

[14] This would be a case of the 'vocal choreography' that, following to Eidsheim's claim, the perceiver would evoke as a resulting visual representation triggered by sound stimuli. The perception of timbre is thus mediated by such visual images (see Eidsheim,

Similar instances of musical metaphors and word painting can be found in the song. As Björk sings 'we mimic the openness' (1:17), the gameleste motif recedes while a low gong-like, echoing sound metaphorically opens the sonic space, thus creating the impression of a greater physical space. Likewise, as the sentence 'equalise the flow' is voiced (1:38), the gameleste motif is resumed as if recovering a lost, or suspended, sonic stream. As previously mentioned, the unfolding of this sonic imagery as a continuous flow of events rather than as a sequence of sonic causes and effects favours a contemplative mood than an interpretive one.[15]

The Mechanics of Voice Production

Closer attention to the lyrics revealed not only that the song was indeed entirely sung in English but, more intriguingly, that Björk's performance entails a distorted, or modified, version of authorised regional variants of English, which contributes to the unusual character of some words. Of this recorded performance, it could be metaphorically said that Björk 'rests' on the resounding sounds of consonants, thus making the words seem 'strange' to the ear and consequently directing greater perceptual attention to them. This strangeness seemed to us quite contrasting to most popular music songs where the *meaning* of the words (and therefore, the story) is usually more important than the *sound* of the words. Table 13.2 lists some instances of the distortions generated from the elongation of consonant sounds and which account for this alleged strangeness.

Table 13.2 'Crystalline', original lyrics and our spelling of the sounding words as recorded by Björk

generosity	Gener/ɔ/s/eə/eity
hearts	H/e//rrr/t/tʃ/
quartz	Qua/rrr/t/tʃ/
octagone	O/kkk/tagon
polygone	Poly/ggg/on
chisel	Chi/tʃtʃ/el
equalise	Equali/tʃ/

2009). The openness of Björk's chest could then in turn be associated with the verse 'we mimic the openness' in the lyrics.

15 This is not to imply that no interpretation occurs in a predominantly contemplative mode of listening, but rather that the song would have a greater potential to be experienced in what Peirce calls the first moment (presentness), and that interpretive motion to the second moment, or the struggle for interpretation, would either be delayed, suspended or – in spite of its inevitability – not so relevant for the overarching experience of the song (see Dougherty, 1994).

Nearly all of Björk's songs in English prove that she is definitely able to pronounce an English non-rhotic 'r' as it appears in 'hearts' and 'quartz'. Allegedly, the persistent emphasis on consonant sounds, which are also cacophonic due to immediate reiteration, seems to be a deliberate choice suggesting Björk's self-indulgence in the pleasure of enunciation. Her choice of voicing may therefore communicate matters that go beyond mere linguistic idiosyncrasies to the realm of poietic intentionality that is, perhaps, connected to the desire to create a given sensorial effect, or using von Appen's terms, a 'sensual attraction' to music. The claim for the existence of a deliberate intention to direct the listener's attention to an enhanced sensorial experience is reinforced by instances of synesthetic imagery in the lyrics such as in the verses 'listen how they grow', 'listen how they glow' or 'sonic branches'.

The idiosyncrasies of her pronunciation thus suggest the presence of singing pleasures that go beyond the sonic realm and into the corporeality of performance thus connecting musical and cultural meanings to Björk's musical persona. Contesting the naturalisation of race-based interpretations of vocal performances, Eidsheim (2009) has argued that, regardless of the singer's phenotypical constitution, vocal timbre results from active choices on the performer's part:

> By considering timbre instead as the sound that results from the *vocal body – the vocal apparatus as it is fashioned through repetition of particular sounds, rather than the inner structure of an essential phenotype* – we may come to the realisation that timbre is actively *shaped*, rather than passively projected. In essence, each part of the body that participates in the creation of vocal sounds (vocal tract, torso, tongue, mouth cavities and so on) has been actively fashioned. I term both this active sculpting of the vocal apparatus, and the shaping that takes place on the fly, *the performativity of timbre* – the sonic event is merely a confirmation that an inner choreography has taken place. (Eidsheim, 2009, original emphasis)

Eidsheim's argument on the choreography of vocal performance proves particularly suitable for Björk's case, as the Icelandic singer's musical persona has been shaped by a foundational opposition: the relative naturalness of her vocal timbre, and the artificiality and theatricality of her performances. The distinction between *performative* – as those elements that within a given performance endow sound with its inherent qualities (for example, micro-intonation, timbre, micro-rhythms) – and *performatic* – those elements linked to the theatricality utilised in said performance (gestuality, uses of the body, et cetera) – may assist the interpretation of this opposition.[16]

[16] After long debate in the conference of the SIBE (Society of Ethnomusicology) in 2008, Alejandro Madrid reports that participants agreed on the need to distinguish between the two categories – performative and performatic – as descriptive of different performance traits (see Madrid, 2009).

Björk's stage persona has drawn on previous performing traditions such as that of glam rock, punk, opera and cabaret, all of which are characterised by the flamboyancy of stage characters impersonated by musicians. Elaborated – and even farcical – costumes, eccentric makeup and outlandish wigs, have been frequently utilised in both Björk's live performances as well as in her video clips.

Following Eidsheim's claim that embodied performance is vocal choreography and that perception of timbre is the result of socialised processes of signification, it could be concluded that the perception of emphasis in the consonant sounds, ensues from both, deliberate choices concerning *performative* elements and our expectations about these sounds. These conduced us to perceive the lyrics as bizarre with respect to more conventional versions of English singing. In turn, our interpretation of the song would have been reinforced by a combination of *performatic* aspects – namely the theatricality of her public persona – and our conditioned and socialised pre-existing knowledge – such as our familiarity with Björk's history as a non-native speaker, our own (varied) competences in English and our appreciation of Björk as a somehow eccentric performer. Although we deliberately avoided considering much of these extra-musical elements when analysing 'Crystalline', it seems plausible that this knowledge underlined our perception and thus shaped our interpretation of the sounds we heard. Hence the validity of the question concerning to what extent the well-known artificiality of her performing persona may have affected our perception of her vocal performance as well. The difficulties we faced in positioning ourselves within Björk's performance could make a case for the previously mentioned postmodern ways of hearing, particularly in that they are over-informed and pluri-located, both temporally and spatially. Our perception of timbre therefore entailed an irresolvable ambiguity between hearing 'naturalness', 'artificiality' or both simultaneously.

Recording Techniques

The recording of a voice is conceived paradoxically as both natural and artificial; certainly what we hear as a 'natural' sounding voice has often been heavily processed with effects such as compression, reverb, equalisation or delay. It is also important to note that no matter how 'natural' a recorded voice sounds, it is unavoidably mediated through recording techniques and artistry. This aside, the themes of nature and technology, as identified through an analysis of 'Crystalline', can be demonstrated through an analysis of the recording techniques used to capture both Björk's lead and backing vocals.

Björk's lead vocal has been recorded within close proximity to the microphone, and this recording technique certainly contributes to producing a 'natural' sound. Close-mic recording ensures that a vocal delivery is captured in a realistic manner (despite the artificial medium of the recording studio) as the listener can hear in detail the various nuances and timbres of the voice. For example, Björk's delivery rarely utilises one vocal tone; rather, she moves between nasal, clear and raspy tones, and the close-mic recording of her voice ensures that these timbres are clearly audible in the recording. Close-mic recording also ensures that the higher frequencies of the sound source are not attenuated during the recording process, and this creates the illusion that the singer is 'close' to the listener. This perceived 'closeness' allows us to connect on an intimate and personal level with Björk; in other words, we feel as though she is singing or speaking directly to us. The intimacy evoked by the 'closeness' of the voice in turn masks the artificiality of the recording and studio medium.

The lead vocal has also been placed 'forward' in the mix enabling the voice to be clearly heard above the accompanying instruments and sound layers. These instruments and sound textures do not sound natural; their timbres suggest that they are digitally conceived. The juxtaposition of Björk's voice with these electronic timbres further highlights the naturalness of the lead vocal by providing a contrast between the mechanically driven accompaniment and the naturally produced voice. Furthermore, we can clearly hear the human qualities in Björk's lead vocal: the conveying of words, the breathing of air and the controlling of pitch are all elements that are considered characteristic of the natural human voice.

While the lead vocal certainly sounds 'natural' by the way it has been captured in the recording studio, there is, nonetheless, an ethereal sound to Björk's voice. While each lyric in the verse is carefully and clearly enunciated, and the voice sounds close and forward in the mix, something of Björk's voice lags behind the main vocal. This sound has been created by applying reverb or pre-delay to Björk's lead vocal leaving a tail or remnant of her voice hovering underneath and behind the lead vocal. Here, the ethereal sonority of the vocal can be aptly described as representing technological intervention.

The recording techniques used to capture the backing vocals similarly produce an 'unnatural' sonority. For example, as the first verse begins, a reversed vocal line is used to anticipate the first lyric of the lead vocal 'underneath our feet'. The reversed vocal line is used as a sound effect that provides a texture rather than conveying a given melody or lyric. The process of reversing the audio obscures the human qualities and characteristics of the voice and the outcome sounds more like an electronic timbre that has been created by a computer rather than a human voice. This we understand as a representation of technology.

However, this is not the case for all the backing vocals in 'Crystalline'. The backing vocals in the first verse (conveying the lyrics 'listen how they grow') have been heavily processed with phasing, reverb and panning. Unlike the reversing effect, these do not completely obscure the human qualities of the vocal recording – the vocal lines are still identifiable as Björk's voice – nonetheless, the resultant effect still sounds more technologically altered rather than natural.[17] The application of phasing and reverb attenuates the higher frequencies in the

[17] Note that this technologically altered sound was completely removed by Björk in the album version of 'Crystalline' in favour of a more natural and dry sonority. See footnote 18 for a closer look at the changes that occur in the album version.

sonority of the voice, and this makes the backing vocals sound somewhat 'distant'. Consequently the vocal nuances are less audible, or not as clearly portrayed. The phasing process (where two identical audio signals are mixed together but with one slightly delayed behind the other) also creates the illusion that there is more than one voice, and this conceals the nuance and detail of Björk's voice, while the panning process creates a sweeping effect across the stereo spread. The culmination of these mixing techniques creates a rather 'unnatural' sound, particularly when compared to the 'naturalness' of the lead vocal.

But the meeting of nature and technology is not only evident in the vocals of 'Crystalline'. It is important to also consider what sounds, textures and timbres cradle the voice and how these contribute to the way we consume and understand this song. Besides the voice, there are no other acoustic-styled instruments used in the recording. This means that computer-generated sounds, and thus technological devices, feature as a primary way of producing the instrumentation that accompanies the voice. These electronic timbres build slowly throughout the song, becoming more prominent in each chorus and reaching a climax in the final section. Listening to the piece, one gets the sense of an industrial or mechanical environment, an ambience which is not organic or natural sounding, but rather electronic, computer-generated or other-worldly.

In the verses and choruses of 'Crystalline', these electronic sounds, while certainly a prominent feature of the music, operate more as an accompaniment to the voice. However, by the terminal climax section computer-generated beats become the primary focus of the song. In this section, electronic timbres, particularly the electronic drumming, no longer merely accompany the lead vocal; rather, they take a primary role and are positioned forward in the mix. The lead vocal is still audible, but can no longer be described as solely the focal point. Here the rhythm section and lead vocal are battling for the primary position and some members of the group interpreted this as a battle between the themes of nature and technology: the lead vocal indicative of nature while the rhythm section, which is clearly computer-generated and most likely sample based, a marker of technology. The intensity of the drumming and the machine gun-like sonorities initially drown out the voice, and some members of the group viewed this as nature's demise as a result of technology. However, despite the intensity and powerful sonority of the electronic drums, the voice can still be heard. Björk's voice prevails refusing to be consumed by the hard-core rhythms. This, by contrast, was understood by some of the authors as nature's sustainability in a modern and highly technological world. Other members of the group interpreted this as the coexistence of both nature and technology.[18]

[18] The definite version of 'Crystalline' was released in the *Biophilia* album some weeks after our work in Osnabrück. Several things differ from the single version: the overall sound of the track seems more compressed and more dry; the volume of the background vocals was raised, which makes them much more present in the foreground (almost equal to the lead vocal) and they sound very dry. Björk included another break of the gameleste pattern

Conclusion

It has been our aim to document our approach to analysing and understanding 'Crystalline'. This chapter focuses on the process of analysis, from our initial hearing of the song, to the point where we have attempted to articulate our perceptions of what seemed to us as the salient features of the music. The process of analysis began from a blank canvas – certainly no member of the group had heard 'Crystalline' before attempting to analyse the music – and this is an important aspect of the procedure that would have certainly had implications for our interpretations of the song. Admittedly, Björk's persona significantly contributes to our understanding of 'Crystalline'. In addition, despite being in a 'controlled' environment (such as a summer school) we felt our interpretations were conceived in a manner that drew from our individual and divergent scholarly backgrounds.

Focusing on pitch, form, vocal delivery, timbre and recording techniques, we found our interpretations of the music often discussed these aspects in terms of nature and technology: two themes that we decided would form the basis of our analysis. As we demonstrated in this chapter, technology and nature both play important roles in the production and composition of 'Crystalline'. Perhaps the release of mobile apps for this song, and the album to which it belongs, are merely passing technological crazes, harnessing the power of new technology. But even so, the way in which humans must interact with technology in order to engage with the current sociological climate is the larger comment here.

Creative arts practices, and particularly music, offer practitioners and consumers a medium for self-expression, whether through the composition of music or the process of analysis. Music in particular can be viewed as a medium that engages one's emotions or informs one's relationship with surrounding environments. In this way, 'Crystalline' is a fine example of what makes us human. Perhaps this is the final layer of the dichotomy between nature and technology which is evident in 'Crystalline'; this dichotomy depends upon a human listener for it to work.

---

before chorus 3; but the major changes are for the end of the track, the drum and bass part. It is now introduced by a four-bar electronic snare drum roll which completely takes away the effect of surprise it previously had. This roll, played with a crescendo, warns the listener that something huge is going to happen, whereas in the single version, the apocalyptic drum part would just punch you right in the face without even preparing you for it. Besides, the whole drum part was slightly re-programmed and it now closes the track all by itself (the gameleste pattern and the vocals have been removed). We suggested an interpretation of that last section as a possible 'battle' between nature, embodied by the gameleste and Björk's voice, and the highly technological drum sound. A new perspective is now brought to us for there is no fight, no battle any more. The reasons for this change remain unavailable to us so far; it obviously suited Björk's vision of the song more accurately than before, and it is perhaps more consistent regarding the other tracks that comprised *Biophilia*.

References

Appen, R. v., 2011. Three Attractions of Music – Three Challenges for Analysis. Lecture presented at the ASPM International summer school 'Methods of Popular Music Analysis', 12 September 2011, University of Osnabrück (Germany), unpublished.

Appen, R. v. and Frei-Hauenschild, M., 2012. AABA, Refrain, Chorus, Bridge, PreChorus – Songformen und ihre historische Entwicklung. In: D. Helms and T. Phleps (eds), *Black Box Pop. Analysen populärer Musik*. Bielefeld: Transcript, pp. 57–124, English version available at: http://www.gfpm-samples.de/Samples13/appenfrei.pdf.

Björk, 2011. Stereogum Q&A: Björk Talks 'Biophilia' [interview], *Stereogum*, [online] Available at: http://stereogum.com/744502/stereogum-qa-bjork-talks-biophilia/top-stories/lead-story/ [Accessed November 2011].

Brailoiu, C., 1973. Sur une mélodie russe. In: G. Rouget (ed.), *Problèmes d'Ethnomusicologie*. Genève: Minkoff Reprint, pp. 343–403.

Dell'Antonio, A. (ed.), 2004. *Beyond Structural Listening? Postmodern Modes of Hearing*. Berkeley, CA: University of California Press.

Dibben, N., 2009. *Björk*. Bloomington, IN: Indiana University Press.

Dougherty, W.P., 1994. The Quest for Interpretants: Towards a Peircean Paradigm for Musical Semiotics. *Semiotica*, 99(1/2), pp. 163–84.

Eidsheim, N., 2009. Synthesizing Race: Towards an Analysis of the Performativity of Vocal Timbre, *TRANS – Revista Transcultural de Música*, 13, [online] Available at: http://www.sibetrans.com/trans/a57/synthesizing-race-towards-an-analysis-of-the-performativity-of-vocal-timbre [Accessed 4 January 2012].

Everett, W., 2004. Making Sense of Rock's Tonal Systems, *Music Theory Online*, 10(4), [online] Available at: http://www.mtosmt.org/issues/mto.04.10.4/mto.04.10.4.w_everett.html#AUTHORNOTE1 [Accessed 15 January 2012].

Hopkins, P. and Sigurbjörnsson, T., n.d. Iceland, *Grove Music Online*, [online] Available at: http://www.oxfordmusiconline.com/subscriber/article/grove/music/ [Accessed November 2011].

Kramer, J.D., 1988. *The Time of Music: New Meanings, New Temporalities, New Listening Strategies*. New York: Schirmer Books.

Madrid, A.L., 2009. ¿Por qué música y estudios de performance? ¿Por qué ahora?: Una introducción al dossier, *TRANS – Revista Transcultural de Música*, 13, [online] Available at: http://www.sibetrans.com/trans/trans13/art01esp.htm [Accessed 13 January 2012].

Middleton, R., 2003. Form. In: J. Shepherd, D. Horn, D. Laing, P. Oliver and P. Wicke (eds), *Continuum Encyclopedia of Popular Music of the World*. London: Continuum, pp. 503–20.

Osborn, B., 2010. Beyond Verse and Chorus: Experimental Formal Structures in Post-Millennial Rock Music. PhD, University of Washington, [online] Available at: https://digital.lib.washington.edu/researchworks/bitstream/handle/1773/15910/

Brad%20Osborn%e2%80%94Beyond%20Verse%20and%20Chorus.pdf?sequence=3 [Accessed 19 December 2011].
Perle, G., 1985. *The Opera of Alban Berg, Vol. 2: Lulu*. Berkeley, CA: University of California Press.
Subotnik, R.R., 1988. Toward a Deconstruction of Structural Listening: A Critique of Schoenberg, Adorno, and Stravinsky. In: E. Narmour and R. Solie (eds), *Explorations in Music, the Arts and Ideas*. New York: Pendragon, pp. 87–122.
Tagg, P., 2011. *Music's Meaning* [provisional version], [online] Available at: http://tagg.org/bookxtrax/NonMuso/NonMuso.pdf [Accessed 8 December 2011].

Filmography

Murphy, J. and Thomas, R., 2001. *MTV Unplugged & Live* [DVD]. Björk Overseas/One Little Indian.

Discography

Björk, 1993. 'One Day'. *Debut*. One Little Indian, TPLP 31 CD.
Björk, 2011. 'Crystalline'. One Little Indian, iTunes Download.
Björk, 2011. 'Crystalline'. *Biophilia* [Deluxe Edition]. Polydor, 2780179.
Björk, 2011. 'Crystalline (Omar Souleyman Version)'. Wellheart/One Little Indian, iTunes Download.

Index

Authors

Acosta, L. 248
Adorno, T.W. 79, 138
Agawu, K. 190
Appen, R. v. 3, 24, 46, 160, 256, 263, 269
Averill, G. 205
Bakhtin, M.M. 55, 97, 116, 119
Barber-Kersovan, A. 100
Bengtsson, I. 54
Biamonte, N. 246
Blaukopf, K., 137
Bourdieu, P. 134f.
Brailoiu, C. 259
Burns, G. 241f.
Burns, R.G.H. 100f., 110
Burstein, L.P. 183
Butler, M.J. 56, 117, 133–5, 137f., 144, 240
Byrne, D. 48
Bühler, K. 74f.
Capuzzo, G. 246
Cascone, K. 137
Chace, Z. 50
Chen, W. 236
Chernoff, J.M. 54
Chester, A. 161
Chor, I. 64
Christgau, R. 10
Clarida, B. 74, 78, 205
Clarke, E.F. 56, 65, 115–7
Damasio, A. 115
Danielsen, A. 3, 57, 59, 62f., 67f., 134, 137, 143, 197, 202, 224f.
Deleuze, G. 55
Dell'Antonio, A. 267
Desain, P. 56, 65
Deutsch, D. 117
Dibben, N. 256, 260f.
Dockwray, R. 191
Doehring, A. 3, 138, 148, 167, 242
Dougherty, W.P. 268
Doyle, P. 120
Doyle, T. 227
Echard, W. 191
Eggebrecht, H.H. 140
Eidsheim, N. 267, 269f.
Elflein, D. 105, 262
Everett, W. 3, 9, 17f., 21–3, 25, 197, 199, 207, 217, 226, 246, 256
Fauconnier, G. 161
Feld, S. 235
Feldman, J.A. 115
Ferreira, P.P. 137
Fikentscher, K. 135
Fink, R. 67
Floyd, S.A., Jr. 198, 236
Frei-Hauenschild, M. 263
Friberg, A. 57
Frith, S. 81, 198, 208, 236
Gabrielsson A. 54
Galenza, R. 98
Gates Jr., H.L. 197f., 201, 205, 208
Gebesmair, A. 248
Gerryts, R. 192
Gibson, J.J. 55, 115, 121
Gilbert, J. 236f.
Gracyk, T. 207
Griffiths, D. 162
Grossberg, L. 100
Hall, E.T. 122
Harrison, D. 207
Havemeister, H. 98
Hawkins, S. 137
Helms, D. 3, 75f., 84
Herrmann, T. 133
Hitzler, R. 137
Hoffmann, F.W. 207
Honing, H. 56, 65
Hopkins, P. 260

Horschig, M. 98
Ingenhoff, S. 150
Iyer, V. 56
Jakobson, R. 74–6, 81f., 90–92, 95
Johansson, M. 68
Johnson, M. 115, 176, 191–3
Jones, S. 148
Kaufman, G. 119
Keil, C. 56, 68
Kellman, A. 133
Kennett, C. 140
Kettlewell, D. 176
Kirshenblatt-Gimblett, B. 239
Klotschkow, P. 19
Klotz, S. 137
Kramer, J.D. 256
Krims, A. 135
Kvifte, T. 56
Lacasse, S. 66
Lakoff, G. 115, 176, 191f.
Langlois, T. 135
Large, E. 76
Latour, B. 97
Lilja, E. 200, 206
Lipsett-Rivera, S. 236
Long, L.M. 176
Madrid, A.L. 269
Marshall, W. 233, 237, 239
Maróthy, J. 236
Mathieu, W.A. 205f.
McLeod, K. 134
Merwe, P. v. d. 200
Meyer, E. 137
Middleton, R. 236, 262f.
Monaco, B. 241
Monson, I. 116, 198, 191, 197, 214, 236
Moore, A.F. 1, 3, 48, 93f., 104, 110, 116, 120, 134f., 139, 151, 163
Moore, R.F. 127f.
Moorefield, V. 227f.
Moorman, M.J. 247
Moylan, W. 120
Mühlmann, W.-R. 99f.
Müller, L. 110
Neal, J. 217
Nketia, J.H.K. 54f., 62
Nozaradan, S. 56
Ochoa, A.M. 248
Osborn, B. 179, 246, 265
O'Brien Chang, K. 236
Pearson, E. 236f.
Perle, G. 257
Pfadenhauer, M. 137
Phleps, T. 3, 137
Poland, T. 149
Poschardt, U. 137
Rapp, T. 135
Rauhut, M. 110
Reynolds, S. 135
Ricoeur, P. 55
Riedemann, F. 50
Riordan, J. 241
Ripani, R. 181
Rossing, T.D. 127f.
Ryce, A. 139, 150f.
Rösing, H. 137
Said, E. 232
Salzer, F. 217
Saslaw, J. 191
Saussure, F. de. 55
Schmidt, P. 191
Schulz von Thun, F. 82
Shapiro, P. 148
Siegert, N. 247
Sigurbjörnsson, T. 260
Smalley, D. 116
Snyder, J. 56
Spitzer, M. 191
Starr, L. 237
Steingo, G. 137
Steingress, G. 248
Straw, W. 139
Subotnik, R.R. 267
Summach, J. 242
Sundström, A. 57
Tagg, P. 74, 78, 81, 134f., 137, 146, 161, 165, 205, 267
Tallmadge, W. 206
Tangari, J. 10
Thornton, S. 135
Thorsén, S.M. 54
Théberge, P. 227
Tingen, P. 119, 123
Tomlinson, G. 198
Tortorello, M. 20
Turner, M. 161

Veal, M.E. 145
Volkwein, B. 137
Waadeland, C.H. 57
Walser, R. 148, 201
Warner, T. 125
Waterman, C. 237
Wheeler, P.A. 127f.
Wicke, P. 98f., 110, 134, 148
Zagorski-Thomas, S. 3, 115, 119f., 123, 197f., 200, 239f.
Zarlino, G. 205
Zbikowski, L. 191
Zeiner-Henriksen, H.T. 63, 138, 143

Songs

'15 Minutes' (The Strokes) 23
'A Day In The Life' (The Beatles) 217
'Amerika' (Rammstein) 111
'Angel's Doorway' (Suzanne Vega) 24
'Baby It's Cold Outside' (Frank Loesser) 93
'Bad Influence' (Pink) 48
'Bernadette' (Four Tops) 198
'Big Me' (Foo Fighters) 23
'Bohemian Rhapsody' (Queen) 166
'Boom Boom Pow' (Black Eyed Peas) 44
'California Gurls' (Katy Perry) 49
'Call the Law' (OutKast feat. Janelle Monáe) 209
'Can't Help Falling In Love' (Elvis Presley) 22
'Carrying Cathy' (Ben Folds) 18
'Cold Sweat' (James Brown) 199
'Creep' (Radiohead) 23
'Crosstown Traffic' (The Jimi Hendrix Experience) 200
'Crystalline (Omar Souleyman Version)' (Björk; Omar Souleyman) 257
'Crystalline' [album version] (Björk) 271
'Crystalline' [single version] (Björk) 253–75
'Danza Kuduro' (Lucenzo feat. Don Omar) 2, 18, 48, 231–51
'Don't Wanna Go Home' (Jason Derulo) 48
'Don't You Worry Child' (Swedish House Mafia) 151
'Dreaming Of You' (The Coral) 162
'Dynamite' (Taio Cruz) 48f.
'E.T.' (Katy Perry) 49
'Ellos Benia' (Nando Boom) 237
'Evening Sun' (The Strokes) 23f.
'Fire And Rain' (James Taylor) 226
'Firework' (Katy Perry) 49
'Four-Chords' (The Axis of Awesome) 18
'Foxy Lady' (The Jimi Hendrix Experience) 200
'Gasolina' (Daddy Yankee) 237
'Geburt einer Nation' (Laibach) 101
'Get The Party Started' (Pink) 48
'Getting Better' (The Beatles) 16
'Get Up (I Feel Like Being A) Sex Machine' (James Brown) 199
'Good Morning Schoolgirl' (Junior Wells) 181
'Good Vibrations' (The Beach Boys) 228
'Hangover' (Taio Cruz) 48f.
'Heart Of Gold' (Neil Young) 45
'Helplessness Blues' (The Fleet Foxes) 3, 25, 213–29
'Hey Jude' (The Beatles) 42
'How To Disappear Completely' (Radiohead) 22
'I Am A Rock' (Simon and Garfunkel) 227
'Ich tu Dir weh' (Rammstein) 104
'I Don't Want To Let You Go' (Weezer) 17
'If I Should Fall Behind' (Bruce Springsteen) 10f., 13f., 18, 25
'I Gotta Feeling' (Black Eyed Peas) 48
'I Kissed A Girl' (Katy Perry) 44
'In Bloom' (Nirvana) 21
'Ironic' (Alanis Morissette) 121
'I Should Have Known Better' (The Beatles) 23
'I Want To Hold Your Hand' (The Beatles) 17
'I Will Follow You Into The Dark' (Death Cab for Cutie) 9–28
'Just Dance' (Lady Gaga) 48
'Knives Out' (Radiohead) 23
'Knockin' On Heaven's Door' (Guns N' Roses) 42
'Lambada' (Kaoma) 231, 234, 248f.
'Last Friday Night (T.G.I.F.)' (Katy Perry) 48f.

'Let's Start A Band' (Amy Macdonald) 167
'Live Is Life' (Opus) 100f.
'LoveGame' (Lady Gaga) 91
'Ma Baker' (Boney M) 81f., 92
'Macarena' (Los del Río) 231, 234, 249
'Maybach Music 2' (Rick Ro$$ feat. Kanye West, T-Pain and Lil' Wayne) 146
'Mein Teil' (Rammstein) 100
'Mercy' (Duffy) 200
'My Best Friend' (Weezer) 19
'Nasty Girl' (Destiny's Child) 53–71
'Neighborhood #1 (Tunnels)' (Arcade Fire) 23
'New For U' (Andrés) 133–55
'Next Year' (Foo Fighters) 23
'Nice Dream' (Radiohead) 18
'Nude' (Radiohead) 23
'One Day' (Björk) 257
'One O'Clock Jump' (Count Basie) 200
'One Vision' (Queen) 100f.
'Papa's Got A Brand New Bag' (James Brown) 199
'Part Of Me' (Katy Perry) 49
'Party Rock Anthem' (L.M.F.A.O.) 48
'Poison Prince' (Amy Macdonald) 162
'Poison' (Alice Cooper) 162
'Poker Face' (Lady Gaga) 73–96
'Pretty Pink Ribbon' (Cake) 17
'Proud Mary' (Ike and Tina Turner) 199, 217
'Purple Haze' (The Jimi Hendrix Experience) 200
'Push It' (Salt-N-Pepa) 58
'Pussy' (Rammstein) 97–113
'Rammlied' (Rammstein) 101
'Right Round' (FloRida feat. Ke$ha) 45
'Rock Around The Clock' (Bill Haley) 29
'Sex On Fire' (Kings of Leon) 115–32
'She Loves You' (The Beatles) 162
'Sister Jack' (Spoon) 17
'Soul Meets Body' (Death Cab for Cutie) 14, 20
'Spinning Wheel' (Blood, Sweat & Tears) 201
'St. Peter's Cathedral' (Death Cab for Cutie) 22
'Strawberry Fields Forever' (The Beatles) 17
'Stripped' (Depeche Mode) 99
'Summertime Blues' (Eddie Cochran) 188–90
'Super Bad' (James Brown) 198
'Take The A Train' (Duke Ellington) 200
'Taxman' (The Beatles) 201
'Tears In Heaven' (Eric Clapton) 25
'Teenage Dream' (Katy Perry) 49
'The Ascent Of Stan' (Ben Folds) 22
'The Darker Days Of Me & Him' (PJ Harvey) 176
'The Hustle' (Van McCoy and the Soul City Symphony) 234
'The Ketchup Song (Aserejé)' (Las Ketchup) 234
'The Luckiest' (Ben Folds) 18
'The Sounds of Silence' (Simon and Garfunkel) 227
'The Twist' (Chubby Checker) 234
'The Words That Maketh Murder' (PJ Harvey) 9, 117, 175–95
'Thing Called Love' (John Hiatt) 57
'Things We Said Today' (The Beatles) 24
'This Is The Life' (Amy Macdonald) 157–71
'Thriller' (Michael Jackson) 166
'Tightrope' (Janelle Monáe) 197–212
'Tik Tok' (Ke$ha) 29–51
'Time Is The Teacher' (Dexter Wansel) 146f.
'Ukulele Lady' (Vaughn DeLeath) 207
'United We Stand' (Brotherhood of Man) 93
'Vem Dançar Kuduro' (Lucenzo feat. Big Ali) 231, 233
'Video Killed The Radio Star' (The Buggles) 94
'Wait' (The Beatles) 18
'Wake Up' (Arcade Fire) 22
'We Shall Overcome' 93
'Wiener Blut' (Rammstein) 109
'Yesterday' (The Beatles) 16
'You Can't Do That' (The Beatles) 23
'Zak And Sara' (Ben Folds) 24

Musicians

ABBA 30
Adele 200
Andrés 133–55
Apokalyptischen Reiter, Die 100
Arcade Fire 17, 22f.
Axis of Awesome, The 18
Baez, Joan 216
Baker, Ginger 200
Bassi, Maurizio 58
Beach Boys, The 29, 228
Beatles, The 2, 13, 16–18, 24, 162, 200
Beyoncé 58
Big Ali 231
Big Boi 198f., 208f.
Björk 2, 253–75
Black Eyed Peas 48
Blanco, Benny (Benjamin Levin) 34, 44f., 49
Blood, Sweat & Tears 201
Boney M 81f., 92, 95
Bonzo Dog Doo Dah Band, The 13
Brotherhood of Man 93
Brown, James 62, 67, 198f., 201
Buggles, The 94
Byrds, The 214, 216
Cake 17
Clapton, Eric 25f.
Clarkson, Kelly 45
Clinton, George 201
Cochran, Eddie 188–90, 193f.
Collins, Bootsy 198
Cooder, Ry 57
Cooper, Alice 162
Coral, The 162
Count Basie 200
Cruz, Taio 48f.
Daddy Yankee 237
Death Cab for Cutie 2, 9–26, 46
DeLeath, Vaughn 207
Dent, Anthony 58
Depeche Mode 99–101, 104
Derulo, Jason 48
Destiny's Child 2, 53–69
Don Omar 48, 231–51
Dr. Luke (Lukasz Gottwald) 29–50
Duffy 200
Dylan, Bob 44, 214, 216
Ellington, Duke 200
E Street Band 10
Feeling B 98f.
Firma, Die 98f.
Fleet Foxes, The 2f., 25, 46, 213–29
FloRida 32, 45
Folds, Ben 18, 22, 24
Followill, Caleb 117, 120, 122, 125, 127f.
Followill, Jared 117, 120, 123
Followill, Matthew 117f., 120, 122, 124f.
Followill, Nathan 117, 120
Foo Fighters 23
Four Tops 198
Funkadelic 201
Gibbard, Ben 13f., 16–26
Guetta, David 32
Guy, Buddy 181
Hackett, Naimy 58
Harvey, Mick 175f.
Hiatt, John 57, 59
Inchtabokatables, The 99
Jamerson, James 198
Jimi Hendrix Experience, The 200
Ke$ha 2, 29–51
Keltner, Jim 57
King, Jacquire 118, 123–5, 130
Kings Of Leon 2, 115–32
Kruspe, Richard 99, 108
L.M.F.A.O. 48
Lady Gaga 2, 48, 73–96
Laibach 99–101
Landers, Paul 98
Las Ketchup 234
Lavigne, Avril 31
Lennon, John 16, 217
Lil' Wayne 146
Lindemann, Till 99–103, 107f., 110
Loesser, Frank 93
Lorenz, Christoph 98, 100, 102
Lucenzo 231–51
Lydon, John 111
Macdonald, Amy 2, 157–71
Madonna 30, 102
McCartney, Paul 16, 217
Ministry 101, 109
Mitchell, Mitch 200
Monáe, Janelle 2, 197–212

Morissette, Alanis 121
Myers, Jack 181
Nando Boom 237
Nirvana 21
Opus 93, 100
OutKast 198, 209
P. Diddy 43f., 50
Parish, John 175f.
Parliament 57, 67, 201
Pecknold, Robin 214, 217, 223, 225
Perry, Katy 29f., 41, 45, 48f.
Petraglia, Angelo 123
Pink 31, 48
PJ Harvey 2, 9, 46, 117, 175–95
Presley, Elvis 22
Queen 100
Radiohead 18, 22f.
Rammstein 2, 97–113
Red Hot Chili Peppers, The 23
RedOne 85, 91
Rick Ro$$ 146
Riedel, Oliver 98f.
Roach, Max 200
Salt-N-Pepa 58
Schneider, Christoph 98
Sex Pistols 111
Simon, Paul 9
Simon and Garfunkel 42, 227
Souleyman, Omar 257
Spector, Phil 228
Spoon 17
Springsteen, Bruce 10f., 13–16, 18, 25f.
Steely Dan 9
Strokes, The 23f.
Sun Ra 201
Swedish House Mafia 151
Swift, Taylor 43, 47
T-Pain 146
Taylor, James 226
Turner, Ike and Tina 199, 217
Van Morrison 214
Vega, Suzanne 24
Wansel, Dexter 146, 148
Warren, Bill 181
Weezer 17, 19
Wells, Junior 181
West, Kanye 146
Williams, Tony 200
Wilson, Brian 214, 228
Winehouse, Amy 200
Young, Neil 214